2015

the best campsites
in Netherlands
Belgium & Luxembourg

over 340 independent reviews

Compiled by: Alan Rogers Travel Ltd

Designed by: Vine Design Ltd

Additional photography: T Lambelin, www.lambelin.com
Maps created by Customised Mapping (01769 540044)
contain background data provided by GisDATA Ltd

Maps are © Alan Rogers Travel Ltd and GisDATA Ltd 2015

© Alan Rogers Travel Ltd 2015

Published by: Alan Rogers Travel Ltd,
Spelmonden Old Oast, Goudhurst, Kent TN17 1HE
www.alanrogers.com Tel: 01580 214000

British Library Cataloguing-in-Publication Data:
A catalogue record for this book is available
from the British Library.

ISBN 978-1-909057-70-8

Printed in Great Britain by Stephens & George Print Group

Contents

Alan Rogers - in search of 'the best'

Alan Rogers Guides were first published over 40 years ago. Since Alan Rogers published the first campsite guide that bore his name, the range has expanded and now covers 27 countries in six separate guides. No fewer than 20 of the campsites selected by Alan for the first guide are still featured in our 2015 editions.

The Low Countries have seen a real rise in tourism in recent years (and it's not just those in search of tulips, cheese, lace or diamonds!). This guide contains impartially written reports on over 340 campsites, including many of the very finest, each being individually inspected and selected. We aim to provide you with a selection of the best, rather than information on all – in short, a more selective, qualitative approach. New, improved maps and indexes are also included, designed to help you find the choice of campsite that's right for you.

Finally, in 2013 we launched the new Alan Rogers Travel Card. Free to readers, it offers exclusive online extras, money saving deals and offers on many campsites. Find out more on page 12.

We hope you enjoy some happy and safe travels – and some pleasurable 'armchair touring' in the meantime!

" …the campsites included in this book
have been chosen entirely on merit,
and no payment of any sort is made
by them for their inclusion."

Alan Rogers, 1968

How do we find the best?

The criteria we use when inspecting and selecting campsites are numerous, but the most important by far is the question of good quality. People want different things from their choice of site so we try to include a range of campsite 'styles' to cater for a wide variety of preferences: from those seeking a small peaceful campsite in the heart of the countryside, to visitors looking for an 'all singing, all dancing' site in a popular seaside resort. Those with more specific interests, such as sporting facilities, cultural events or historical attractions, are also catered for.

The size of the site, whether it's part of a chain or privately owned, makes no difference in terms of it being required to meet our exacting standards in respect of its quality and it being 'fit for purpose'. In other words, irrespective of the size of the site, or the number of facilities it offers, we consider and evaluate the welcome, the pitches, the sanitary facilities, the cleanliness, the general maintenance and even the location.

Expert opinions

We rely on our dedicated team of Site Assessors, all of whom are experienced campers, caravanners or motorcaravanners, to visit and recommend campsites. Each year they travel some 100,000 miles around Europe inspecting new campsites for the guide and re-inspecting the existing ones. Our thanks are due to them for their enthusiastic efforts, their diligence and integrity.

We also appreciate the feedback we receive from many of our readers and we always make a point of following up complaints, suggestions or recommendations for possible new campsites. Of course we get a few grumbles too – but it really is a few, and those we do receive usually relate to overcrowding or to poor maintenance during the peak school holiday period. Please bear in mind that, although we are interested to hear about any complaints, we have no contractual relationship with the campsites featured in our guides and are therefore not in a position to intervene in any dispute between a reader and a campsite.

Independent and honest

Whilst the content and scope of the Alan Rogers guides have expanded considerably since the early editions, our selection of campsites still employs exactly the same philosophy and criteria as defined by Alan Rogers in 1968.

'telling it how it is'

Firstly, and most importantly, our selection is based entirely on our own rigorous and independent inspection and selection process. Campsites cannot buy their way into our guides – indeed the extensive Site Report which is written by us, not by the site owner, is provided free of charge so we are free to say what we think and to provide an honest, 'warts and all' description. This is written in plain English and without the use of confusing icons or symbols.

Looking for the best

Highly respected by site owners and readers alike, there is no better guide when it comes to forming an independent view of a campsite's quality. When you need to be confident in your choice of campsite, you need the Alan Rogers Guide.

- Sites only included on merit

- Sites cannot pay to be included

- Independently inspected, rigorously assessed

- Impartial reviews

- Over 40 years of expertise

Written in plain English, our guides are exceptionally easy to use, but a few words of explanation regarding the layout and content may be helpful. This guide is divided firstly by country, subsequently (in the case of the two larger countries) by region. For a particular area the town index at the back provides more direct access.

Index town
Site name
Postal address (including region) T: telephone number. E: email address
alanrogers.com web address (including Alan Rogers reference number)

A description of the site in which we try to give an idea of its general features – its size, its situation, its strengths and its weaknesses. This section should provide a picture of the site itself with reference to the facilities that are provided and if they impact on its appearance or character. We include details on pitch numbers, electricity (with amperage), hardstandings etc. in this section as pitch design, planning and terracing affects the site's overall appearance. Similarly we include reference to pitches used for caravan holiday homes, chalets, and the like. Importantly at the end of this column we indicate if there are any restrictions, e.g. no tents, no children, naturist sites.

Facilities	Directions
Lists more specific information on the site's facilities and amenities and, where available, the dates when these facilities are open (if not for the whole season). Off site: here we give distances to various local amenities, for example, local shops, the nearest beach, plus our featured activities (bicycle hire, fishing, horse riding, boat launching). Where we have space we list suggestions for activities and local tourist attractions.	Separated from the main text in order that they may be read and assimilated more easily by a navigator en-route. Bear in mind that road improvement schemes can result in road numbers being altered.
	GPS: references are provided in decimal format. All latitudes are North. Longitudes are East unless preceeded by a minus sign e.g. 48.71695 is North, 0.31254 is East and -0.31254 is West.
Open: Site opening dates.	**Charges 2015** (or a general guide)

Maps, campsite listings and indexes

In our 2015 guide series we have changed the way in which we list our campsites and also the way in which we help you locate the sites within each region.

We now include a map immediately after our introduction to each region. These maps show the towns near which one or more of our featured campsites are located.

Within each country section of the guide, we list these towns and the site(s) in that vicinity in alphabetical order.

You will certainly need more detailed maps for navigation, for example the Michelin atlas. We provide GPS coordinates for each site to assist you. Our two indexes will also help you to find a site by region and site name, or by the town where the site is situated.

Understanding the entries

Facilities

Toilet blocks

Unless we comment otherwise, toilet blocks will be equipped with WCs, washbasins with hot and cold water and hot showers with dividers or curtains, and will have all necessary shelves, hooks, plugs and mirrors. We also assume that there will be an identified chemical toilet disposal point, and that the campsite will provide water and waste water drainage points and bin areas. If not the case, we comment. We do mention certain features that some readers find important: washbasins in cubicles, facilities for babies, facilities for those with disabilities and motorcaravan service points. Readers with disabilities are advised to contact the site of their choice to ensure that facilities are appropriate to their needs.

Shop

Basic or fully supplied, and opening dates.

Bars, restaurants, takeaway facilities and entertainment

We try hard to supply opening and closing dates (if other than the campsite opening dates) and to identify if there are discos or other entertainment.

Children's play areas

Fenced and with safety surface (e.g. sand, bark or pea-gravel).

Swimming pools

If particularly special, we cover in detail in our main campsite description but reference is always included under our Facilities listings. We will also indicate the existence of water slides, sunbathing areas and other features. Opening dates, charges and levels of supervision are provided where we have been notified. There is a regulation whereby Bermuda shorts may not be worn in swimming pools (for health and hygiene reasons). It is worth ensuring that you do take 'proper' swimming trunks with you.

Leisure facilities

For example, playing fields, bicycle hire, organised activities and entertainment.

Dogs

If dogs are not accepted or restrictions apply, we state it here. Check the quick reference list at the back of the guide.

Off site

This briefly covers leisure facilities, tourist attractions, restaurants etc. nearby.

Charges

These are the latest provided to us by the sites. In those cases where 2015 prices have not been provided to us by the sites, we try to give a general guide.

Reservations

Necessary for high season (roughly mid-July to mid-August) in popular holiday areas (i.e. beach resorts). You can reserve many sites via our own Alan Rogers Travel Service or through other tour operators. Or be wholly independent and contact the campsite(s) of your choice direct, using the phone or e-mail numbers shown in the site reports, but please bear in mind that many sites are closed all winter.

Telephone Numbers

The numbers given assume you are actually IN the country concerned.

If you are phoning from the UK remember that the first '0' is usually disregarded and replaced by the appropriate country code. For the latest details you should refer to an up-to-date telephone directory.

Opening dates

These are advised to us during the early autumn of the previous year – sites can, and sometimes do, alter these dates before the start of the following season, often for good reasons. If you intend to visit shortly after a published opening date, or shortly before the closing date, it is wise to check that it will actually be open at the time required. Similarly some sites operate a restricted service during the low season, only opening some of their facilities (e.g. swimming pools) during the main season; where we know about this, and have the relevant dates, we indicate it – again if you are at all doubtful it is wise to check.

Sometimes, campsite amenities may be dependent on there being enough customers on site to justify their opening and, for this reason, actual opening dates may vary from those indicated.

Some campsite owners are very relaxed when it comes to opening and closing dates. They may not be fully ready by their stated opening dates – grass and hedges may not all be cut or perhaps only limited sanitary facilities open. At the end of the season they also tend to close down some facilities and generally wind down prior to the closing date. Bear this in mind if you are travelling early or late in the season – it is worth phoning ahead.

The Camping Cheque low season touring system goes some way to addressing this in that many participating campsites will have all key facilities open and running by the opening date and these will remain fully operational until the closing date.

Taking a tent?

In recent years, sales of tents have increased dramatically. With very few exceptions, the campsites listed in this guide have pitches suitable for tents, caravans and motorcaravans. Tents, of course, come in a dazzling range of shapes and sizes. Modern family tents with separate sleeping pods are increasingly popular and these invariably require large pitches with electrical connections. Smaller lightweight tents, ideal for cyclists and hikers, are also visible on many sites and naturally require correspondingly smaller pitches. Many (but not all) sites have special tent areas with prices adjusted accordingly. If in any doubt, we recommend contacting the site of your choice beforehand.

Our Accommodation section

182 Over recent years, more and more campsites have added high quality mobile home and chalet accommodation. In response to feedback from many of our readers, and to reflect this evolution in campsites, we have now decided to include a separate section on mobile homes and chalets. If a site offers this accommodation, it is indicated above the site report with a page reference where full details are given. We have listed three sites offering some of the best accommodation available and have included full details of one or two accommodation types at these sites.

Please note however that many other campsites listed in this guide may also have a selection of accommodation for rent.

You're on your way!

Whether you're an 'old hand' in terms of camping and caravanning or are contemplating your first trip, a regular reader of our Guides or a new 'convert', we wish you well in your travels and hope we have been able to help in some way.

We are, of course, also out and about ourselves, visiting sites, talking to owners and readers, and generally checking on standards and new developments.

We wish all our readers thoroughly enjoyable Camping and Caravanning in 2015 – favoured by good weather of course! The Alan Rogers Team

NETHERLANDS

BELGIUM

LUXEMBOURG

The Alan Rogers Awards

The Alan Rogers Campsite Awards were launched in 2004 and have proved a great success.

Our awards have a broad scope and before committing to our winners, we carefully consider more than 2,000 campsites featured in our guides, taking into account comments from our site assessors, our head office team and, of course, our readers.

Our award winners come from the four corners of Europe, from Spain to Croatia, and this year we are making awards to campsites in 12 different countries.

Needless to say, it's an extremely difficult task to choose our eventual winners, but we believe that we have identified a number of campsites with truly outstanding characteristics.

In each case, we have selected an outright winner, along with two highly commended runners-up. Listed below are full details of each of our award categories and our winners for 2014.

Alan Rogers Progress Award 2014

This award reflects the hard work and commitment undertaken by particular site owners to improve and upgrade their site.

Winner	
IT60450	Camping Marina di Venezia *Italy*

Runners-up	
NL6160	Camping Landclub Ruinen *Netherlands*
BE0760	Goolderheide Vakantiepark *Belgium*

Alan Rogers Welcome Award 2014

This award takes account of sites offering a particularly friendly welcome and maintaining a friendly ambience throughout readers' holidays.

Winner	
FR24090	Domaine de Soleil Plage *France*

Runners-up	
BE0670	Camping Parc la Clusure *Belgium*
ES90290	Kawan Village El Astral *Spain*

Our warmest congratulations to all our award winners and our commiserations to all those not having won an award on this occasion.

The Alan Rogers Team

Alan Rogers Active Holiday Award 2014

This award reflects sites in outstanding locations which are ideally suited for active holidays, notably walking or cycling, but which could extend to include such activities as winter sports or watersports.

Winner

FR83170	Camping Domaine de la Bergerie *France*

Runners-up

AU0100	Camping Seeblick Toni *Austria*
DK2010	Hvidbjerg Strand *Denmark*

Alan Rogers Innovation Award 2014

Our Innovation Award acknowledges campsites with creative and original concepts, possibly with features which are unique, and cannot therefore be found elsewhere. We have identified innovation both in campsite amenities and also in rentable accommodation.

Winner

ES82000	Camping Cala Llevadó *Spain*

Runners-up

FR24010	Kawan Village Château le Verdoyer *France*
DE28990	Camping Stover Strand International *Germany*

Alan Rogers Small Campsite Award 2014

This award acknowledges excellent small campsites (less than 75 pitches) which offer a friendly welcome and top quality amenities throughout the season to their guests.

Winner

UK0745	Riverside Caravan and Camping Park *England*

Runners-up

NL5715	Camping WeidumerHout *Netherlands*
DE36420	Lech Camping *Germany*

Alan Rogers Seaside Award 2014

This award is made for sites which we feel are outstandingly suitable for a really excellent seaside holiday.

Winner

CR6782	Zaton Holiday Resort *Croatia*

Runners-up

ES84830	Camping Tamarit Park Resort *Spain*
FR29180	Camping les Embruns *France*

Alan Rogers Country Award 2014

This award contrasts with our former award and acknowledges sites which are attractively located in delightful, rural locations.

Winner

IT62030	Caravan Park Sexten *Italy*

Runners-up

FR74140	Camping Les Dômes de Miage *France*
DE32540	Camping Harfenmühle *Germany*

Alan Rogers Family Site Award 2014

Many sites claim to be child friendly but this award acknowledges the sites we feel to be the very best in this respect.

Winner

IT60200	Camping Union Lido Vacanze *Italy*

Runners-up

CH9890	Camping Campofelice *Switzerland*
NL6480	Camping De Molenhof *Netherlands*

Alan Rogers Readers' Award 2014

We believe our Readers' Award to be the most important. We simply invite our readers (by means of an on-line poll at www.alanrogers.com) to nominate the site they enjoyed most.

The outright winner for 2014 is:

Winner

FR24060	Camping le Paradis *France*

Alan Rogers Special Awards 2014

A Special Award is made to campsites which have suffered a significant setback, but have coped admirably in difficult circumstances.

For 2014, we wish to acknowledge a top quality Slovenian campsite, which suffered extensive storm damage but, thanks to a very great deal of hard work, soon reverted to its normal high standard.

SV4210	Camping Šobec *Slovenia*

The Alan Rogers Travel Card

At Alan Rogers we have a network of thousands of quality inspected and selected campsites. We also have partnerships with numerous organisations, including ferry operators and tourist attractions, all of whom can bring you benefits and save you money.

Our **FREE** Travel Card binds all this together at

alanrogers.com/travelcard

So register today...and start saving.

alan rogers

Benefits that add up

- Offers and benefits on many Alan Rogers campsites across Europe

- Save up to 60% in low season on over 600 campsites

- Free cardholders' magazine

- Big savings on rented accommodation and hotels at 400 locations

HOLIDAY CHEQUE

- Discounted ferries

- Savings on Alan Rogers guides

- Vote for your favourite campsite in the Alan Rogers Awards

Register today...
and start saving

Carry the Alan Rogers Travel Card on your travels through Europe and save money all the way.

You'll enjoy exclusive deals with ferry operators, continental partners, tourist attractions and more. Even hotels, apartments, mobile homes and other campsite accommodation.

We've teamed up with Camping Cheque, the leading low season discount scheme, to offer you the widest choice of quality campsites at unbelievable prices. Simply load your card with Cheques before you travel.

Step 1
Register at **www.alanrogers.com/travelcard**

Step 2
You'll receive your activated card, along with a Welcome email containing useful links and information.

Step 3
Start using your card to save money or to redeem benefits during your holiday.

alanrogers.com/travelcard

Getting the most from
off peak touring

£14.95
night
outfit +
2 people

There are many reasons to avoid high season, if you can. Queues are shorter, there's less traffic, a calmer atmosphere and prices are cheaper. And it's usually still nice and sunny!

And when you use Camping Cheques you'll find great quality facilities that are actually open and a welcoming conviviality.

Did you know?

Camping Cheques can be used right into mid-July and from late August on many sites. Over 90 campsites in France alone accept Camping Cheques from 20th August.

Save up to 60% with Camping Cheques

Camping Cheque is a fixed price scheme allowing you to go as you please, staying on over 600 campsites across Europe, always paying the same rate and saving you up to 60% on regular pitch fees. One Cheque gives you one night for 2 people + unit on a standard pitch, with electricity. It's as simple as that.

Special offers mean you can stay extra nights free (eg 7 nights for 6 Cheques) or even a month free for a month paid! Especially popular in Spain during the winter, these longer-term offers can effectively halve the nightly rate. See Site Directory for details.

Check out our amazing Ferry Deals!

Why should I use Camping Cheques?

- It's a proven system, recognised by all 600+ participating campsites
  - so no nasty surprises.

- It's flexible, allowing you to travel between campsites, and also countries, on a whim - so no need to pre-book. (It's low season, so campsites are rarely full, though advance bookings can be made).

- Stay as long as you like, where you like - so you travel in complete freedom.

- Camping Cheques are valid at least 2 years - so no pressure to use them up. (If you have a couple left over after your trip, simply keep them for the following year, or use them up in the UK).

Tell me more... (but keep it brief!)

Camping Cheques was started in 1999 and has since grown in popularity each year (nearly 2 million were used last year). That should speak for itself. There are 'copycat' schemes, but none has the same range of quality campsites that save you up to 60%.

Ask for your **FREE** continental road map, which explains how Camping Cheque works

01580 214002

Order your 2015
Directory
alanrogers.com/directory

CAPITAL: BRUSSELS

Tourist Office

Belgian Tourist Office Brussels & Wallonia,
217 Marsh Wall, London E14 9FJ
Tel: 020 7537 1132 Fax: 020 7531 0393
Email: info@belgiumtheplaceto.be
Internet: www.belgiumtheplaceto.be

Tourism Flanders-Brussels, Flanders House,
1a Cavendish Square, London W1G 0LD
Tel: 020 7307 7738
Email: info@visitflanders.co.uk

A small country divided into three regions,
Flanders in the north, Wallonia in the south
and Brussels, the capital. Belgium is rich in
scenic countryside, culture and history, notably
the great forest of Ardennes, the historic cities
of Bruges and Ghent and the western coastline
with its sandy beaches.

Brussels is at the very heart of Europe and
doubles as the capital of the European Union.
A multi-cultural and multi-lingual city full of
remarkable monuments, interesting museums
and highly acclaimed restaurants. In the French-
speaking region of Wallonia lies the mountainous
Ardennes, an area famous for its forests, lakes,
streams and grottoes, making it a popular holiday
destination, especially for those who like nature
and walking. The safe, sandy beaches on the
west coast run for more than sixty kilometres.
Here lies Ostend, a popular seaside resort with
an eight kilometre long beach and a promenade
coupled with a bustling harbour and shops.
Bruges is Europe's best preserved medieval
city and is certainly one of the most attractive,
whether you want to relax on a boat trip along
the canals, explore the narrow streets or visit
one of the many churches and art museums.

Population

11 million

Climate

Temperate climate similar to Britain.

Language

There are three official languages. French
is spoken in the south, Flemish in the north,
and German is the predominant language in
the eastern provinces.

Telephone

The country code is 00 32.

Money

Currency: The Euro
Banks: Mon-Fri 09.00-15.30.
Some banks open Sat 09.00-12.00.

Shops

Mon-Sat 09.00-17.30/18.00 – later on
Thurs/Fri; closed Sundays.

Public Holidays

New Year's Day; Easter Mon; Labour Day;
Ascension; Whit Monday; Flemish Day
11 July; National Day 21 July; Assumption
15 Aug; French Day 27 Sept; All Saints
1, 2 Nov; Armistice Day 11 Nov; King's
Birthday 15 Nov; Christmas 25, 26 Dec.

Motoring

For cars with a caravan or trailer, motorways
are toll free except for the Liefenshoek
Tunnel in Antwerp. Maximum permitted
overall length of vehicle/trailer or caravan
combination is 18 m. Blue Zone parking
areas exist in Brussels, Ostend, Bruges,
Liège, Antwerp and Gent. Parking discs can
be obtained from police stations, garages,
and some shops.

CAPITAL: ANTWERP

This province offers the lively city of Antwerp and the rural landscapes of the Kempen. It is a wonderful region of contrasts where people embrace the pleasures of life, whether in the bustling city streets or the idyllic countryside.

Antwerp has a holiday to suit every taste and budget, whether you love the bright lights of the city or the tranquillity of the forest, enjoyment is the order of the day. Why not relax on the terrace and savour a traditional Trappist beer, or treat yourself to a delicious gourmet weekend? The city of Antwerp is a fascinating mixture of the ancient and modern, famous for its welcoming atmosphere. Highlights include the 14th-century cathedral, the largest Gothic building in the Low Countries; the Central Station, said to be among the most beautiful in the world; the city zoo; and the home of Rubens, the most famous Baroque painter north of the Alps.

Venturing beyond the city, you might glimpse a deer in Kalmthout Heath – the children will love exploring the magical, fragrant pine forest. The charming cobblestone streets of Lier and Turnhout are waiting to be discovered, and Mechelen is a captivating city with an historic past. For the active holidaymaker, the Antwerp Kempen cycle network offers 2,000 kilometres of paths and roadways, and the view from St. Rumbold's Tower is well worth the climb. No trip would be complete without a visit to the Het Anker brewery, which reopened in September 2010.

Places of interest

Antwerp: a bustling city of culture and entertainment, where everyone feels at home.

Mechelen: historical city centre with late medieval St. Rumbold's tower.

Lier: charming small city known for its beers.

Turnhout: lively city near the Dutch border, within a beautiful nature reserve.

Gestel: originally the smallest community of the province, situated on the River de Grote Nete.

Attractions

Technopolis: Mechelen's science and technology centre with over 280 interactive exhibits.

Diamond district of Antwerp: look out for the 'Antwerp Cut', synonymous with quality and brilliance.

Ruben's House Museum: Rubens lived in this Antwerp house for most of his life. Now a museum, this is where most of his paintings (around 25,000) were created by him and his students.

Abbeys: in Malle, Mol, Oud-Turnhout and Westerlo, open to visitors and offering their own quality products.

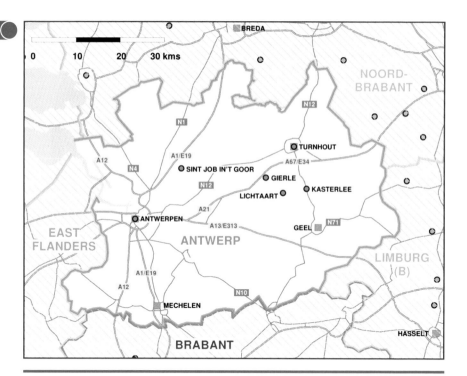

Antwerpen
Camping de Molen

Jachthavenweg, B-2050 Antwerpen (Antwerp) T: 032 198 179. E: info@camping-de-molen.be

alanrogers.com/BE0750

This is a convenient, former municipal site located on the bank of the River Schelde opposite the city centre. It is possible to walk into the heart of this ancient and interesting city (the tunnel is 2 km. from the campsite, and is about 500 m. long), although cycling may be a better option. The site is fairly level with tarmac roads, and has 70 pitches, 65 for touring units, all with access to 10A electricity hook-ups. You will need the adapter cable (deposit payable) as the electric hook-ups are not like any you have seen before, and some long leads may be necessary.

Facilities	Directions
New toilet facilities, clean when visited, could be hard pressed at times, especially when everyone returns from a hard day of sightseeing. Basic facilities for disabled campers. WiFi over site (first 30 minutes free). Overall the facilities are quite acceptable given the very modest campsite fees. Twin-axle caravans are not admitted. Off site: Shops, hot food, bar and outdoor pool nearby.	From north follow ring road around Antwerp through Kennedy tunnel and keep right to Linkeroever. Turn right at Esso petrol station, then left at first lights. Turn left at St Annastrandens tunnel on Thonetlaan. Site is on right after 2 km. GPS: 51.22100, 4.37967

Open: All year.

Charges guide

Per unit incl. 2 persons and electricity	€ 22.00 - € 35.00

Kasterlee
Camping Houtum

Houtum 39, B-2460 Kasterlee (Antwerp) T: 014 859 216. E: info@campinghoutum.be

alanrogers.com/BE0647

This quietly situated, family owned campsite can be found on the outskirts of Kasterlee, famous for its gastronomic restaurants. There are 175 pitches, 60 for touring, all with 10A electric hook-ups, water and drainage. These pitches will be relocated to a new area of the site with upgraded facilities. On-site amenities include an excellent children's play area and a popular bar and restaurant.

Facilities	Directions
New toilet block (2013) with facilities for families and disabled visitors. Launderette. Motorcaravan services. Bar. Restaurant and takeaway (open daily July/Aug, then Wed. and weekends). TV room. Playground. Boules pitch. Free WiFi over part of site. Off site: Golf 200 m. Fishing 500 m.	From E34, take exit 24 towards Kasterlee. The site is signed 500 m. past the village centre, near the windmill. GPS: 51.229801, 4.979854

Open: All year.

Charges guide

Per unit incl. 2 persons and electricity	€ 18.50
extra person	€ 4.00

For latest campsite news, availability and prices visit

alanrogers.com

Gierle

Camping De Lilse Bergen

Strandweg 6, Gierle, B-2275 Lille (Antwerp) T: 014 557 901. E: info@lilsebergen.be
alanrogers.com/BE0655

This attractive, quietly located holiday site has 513 shady pitches, of which 238 (all with 10A Europlug electricity) are for touring units. Set on sandy soil among pine trees and rhododendrons and set around a large lake, the site has a Mediterranean feel. It is well fenced, with a night guard and comprehensive, well labelled, fire-fighting equipment. Cars are parked away from units. The site is really child friendly with each access road labelled with a different animal symbol to enable children to find their own unit easily. An entertainment programme is organised in high season. The lake has marked swimming and diving areas (for adults), a sandy beach, an area for watersports, plus a separate children's pool complex (depth 50 cm) with a most imaginative playground. There are lifeguards and the water meets Blue Flag standards. A building by the lake houses changing rooms, extra toilets, showers and a baby room. There are picnic areas and lakeside and woodland walks.

Facilities

One of the six heated toilet blocks has been fully refitted to a good standard. Some washbasins in cubicles and good hot showers (on payment). Well equipped baby rooms. Facilities for disabled campers. Laundry. Barrier keys can be charged up with units for operating showers, washing machine etc. Motorcaravan services. First aid post. Restaurant (weekends only in winter), takeaway and well stocked shop (Easter-15/9; weekends only). Tennis. Minigolf. Boules. Climbing wall. Playground, trampolines and skateboard ramp. Pedalo, kayak and bicycle hire. Children's electric cars and pedal kart tracks (charged). Free WiFi over site.

Open: All year.

Directions

From E34 Antwerp-Eindhoven take exit 22. On the roundabout take the exit for De Lilse Bergen and follow forest road to site entrance. GPS: 51.28908, 4.85508

Charges guide

Per unit incl. 4 persons and electricity	€ 20.00 - € 26.50
dog	€ 4.50

Supercool camping!
• Modern camping spaces for tents, caravans and motor homes
• Vast swimming pond with sandy beaches, giant playground, miniature golf, go-cart race track, minicars, biking,...
• Rent your own hiking cabin, teepee, caravan or fully furnished family tent!
Strandweg 6 • 2275 Lille-Gierle, Belgium
Tel. 00-32-14 55 79 01 • www.lilsebergen.be

Lichtaart

Camping Floréal Kempen

Herentalsesteenweg 64, B-2460 Lichtaart (Antwerp) T: 014 556 120. E: kempen@florealgroup.be
alanrogers.com/BE0665

This is an attractive woodland site and a member of the Floréal group. It is located close to the well known Purperen Heide, a superb nature reserve with 15 scenic footpaths leading through it. There are 228 pitches, of which only 32 are reserved for touring units. These are of a good size (100 sq.m. or more), all with 16A electricity and most with their own water supply. Two simple cabins are available for hikers, as well as fully equipped mobile homes. There are some good leisure facilities, including tennis and a multisports pitch, as well as a popular bar and restaurant.

Facilities

Three modern, heated toilet blocks are well equipped with some washbasins in cabins and facilities for disabled visitors. Hairdryer. Laundry facilities. Motorcaravan services. Washing machine. Bar. Restaurant. TV room. Tennis. Play area. Multisports terrain. Pétanque. Bicycle hire. Mobile homes for rent (one adapted for disabled users). Free WiFi over site. Off site: cycling tracks. Golf.

Open: All year.

Directions

Approaching from Antwerp, head east on A21/E34 motorway as far as exit 24 (Turnhout). Leave here and head south on N19 to Kasterlee, and then west on N123 to Lichtaart. Follow signs to the site. GPS: 51.21136, 4.90298

Charges guide

Per unit incl. 2 persons	€ 13.95 - € 19.90
extra person	€ 4.70

FREE Alan Rogers Travel Card
Extra benefits and savings - see page 12

Turnhout
Camping Baalse Hei

Roodhuisstraat 10, B-2300 Turnhout (Antwerp) T: 014 448 470. E: info@baalsehei.be

alanrogers.com/BE0660

The Campine is an area covering three quarters of the Province of Antwerp, noted for its nature reserves, pine forests, meadows and streams and is ideal for walking and cycling, while Turnhout itself is an interesting old town. Baalse Hei, a long established, friendly site, has 469 pitches including a separate touring area of 71 large grass pitches (all with 16A electricity, TV connections and shared water point), thoughtfully developed with trees and bushes. Cars are parked away from, but near the pitches. Large motorcaravans can be accommodated (phone first to check availability). There is also accommodation to rent. It is 100 m. from the edge of the field to the modern, heated, sanitary building. There is a small lake for swimming with a beach, a boating lake and a large fishing lake (on payment). Entertainment and activities are organised in July and August. Follow the walking trails in the woods (and you will undoubtedly come across some of the many red squirrels) and the nature reserves, or take the pleasant 1.5 km. riverside walk to the next village.

Facilities

Three toilet blocks provide hot showers on payment (€ 0.50), some washbasins in cabins and facilities for disabled visitors. Dishwashing (hot water € 0.20). Launderette. Motorcaravan services. Shop (1/4-30/9). Café/restaurant (daily 1/4-30/9, w/ends only other times, closed 16/11-25/1). Breakfast served in high season. Club/TV room. Lake swimming. Fishing. Tennis. Boules. Volleyball. Basketball. Adventure play area. Bicycle hire. English is spoken. Overnight pitches for vehicles under 3.5t. Reception open for limited hours (14.00-17.00) in low season. WiFi throughout (free). Off site: Riding 1.5 km.

Open: 16 January - 15 December.

Directions

Site is northeast of Turnhout off the N119. Approaching from Antwerp on E34/A12 take Turnhout ring road to the end (not a complete ring) and turn right. There is a small site sign to right in 1.5 km. then a country lane.
GPS: 51.35757, 4.95896

Charges guide

Per unit incl. 2 persons	
and electricity	€ 19.00 - € 25.00
dog	€ 1.50

Sint-Job-in't-Goor
Camping Floreal Het Veen

Eekhoornlaan 1, B-2960 Sint-Job-in't-Goor (Antwerp) T: 036 361 327. E: het.veen@florealgroup.be

alanrogers.com/BE0650

Floreal Het Veen can be found 20 km. north of Antwerp in a woodland area, and with many sports facilities. There are 305 marked pitches (65 for touring units) on level grass, most with some shade and 10A electricity (long leads in some places) and also five hardstandings. Amenities include an indoor sports hall (hourly charge), while tennis courts, football, basketball and softball are outside. Good cycling and walking opportunities exist in the area. English is spoken.

Facilities

Four spacious toilet blocks include a few washbasins in cubicles (only two are close to touring pitches). Facilities for disabled visitors. Laundry facilities. Motorcaravan services. Shop. Restaurant, bar, café and takeaway (daily July/Aug. weekends only at other times). Tennis. Badminton. Boules. Playgrounds. Children's entertainment in season. Fishing. Canoeing. Bicycle hire. WiFi (free). Wooden chalets for rent. Off site: Riding and golf 8 km.

Open: All year.

Directions

Sint-Job-in't-Goor is northeast of Antwerp. From A1 (E19) exit 4, turn southeast towards Sint-Job-in't-Goor, straight on at traffic lights and, immediately after canal bridge, turn left at campsite sign. Continue straight on for 1.5 km. to site.
GPS: 51.30513, 4.58622

Charges guide

Per unit incl. 2 persons	
and electricity	€ 17.45 - € 23.40

For latest campsite news, availability and prices visit

alanrogers.com

CAPITALS: LEUVEN, NIJVEL AND BRUSSELS

The region of Brabant and Brussels is today formed by three provinces. Flemish Brabant and Wallonian Brabant were split along the language border in 1995, and Brussels became an administrative unit on its own.

The ancient university city of Leuven is ideal to wander through and admire the beautiful town hall, the many terraces, the Grand Convent, the Museum of M and much more. Nature is never far away – De Groene Gordel (the green belt) encircles Brussels, and in the shadow of the metropolis are dozens of beautiful parks and gardens. East of Leuven is the rural region of Het Hageland which features six charming small towns.

In French-speaking Brabant (Brabant Wallon) the best known city is Waterloo; here and in the surrounding villages are echoes of the atmosphere of the great battle of 1815. There are 500 kilometres of footpaths passing through a landscape with diverse fauna and flora. High-tech meets nature south of Brussels in the 'Ardennes brabançonnes', a region of dynamic towns (Louvain-la-Neuve, Wavre), with rich heritage and a wealth of tourist attractions, from castles and museums to rural scenery.

Brussels, the capital city of Belgium and home to the EU, offers everything you would expect from a major European city. The stunningly rich architecture of the 16th-century houses at the Great Market, in the very heart of the city, is a magnet for visitors.

Places of interest

Leuven: town hall and Great Market, new M-Museum, many cafés and restaurants.

Brussels: Great Market, Royal Museum of Fine Arts of Belgium, themed walks, cafés and restaurants.

Villers-la-Ville: impressive monastery ruins hidden in a forest.

Napoleon's last headquarters: Belgium's only Napoléon Museum with battle memorabilia and items relating to the emperor.

Attractions

The Magic Spell: themed adventure game for the whole family combining entertainment, skill and team building in a Middle Ages setting.

The Waterloo Battlefield: carefully preserved site of the famous conflict of 1815.

Horst Castle: beautiful moated castle in the green valley of the Wingebeek, among the Hageland hills.

National Botanic Garden of Belgium: one of the largest botanic gardens in the world, set in historical castle grounds.

't Wit Gebrouw: visitor centre where you can learn the secrets of, and sample, the famous Hoegaarden white beer.

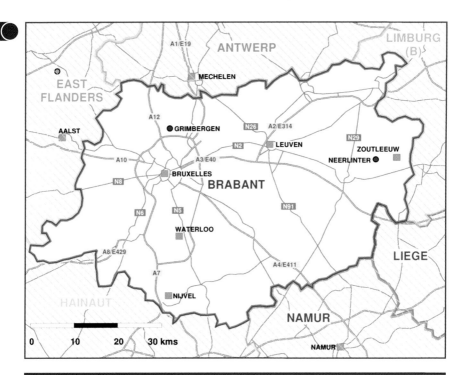

Grimbergen
Camping Grimbergen

Veldkantstraat 64, B-1850 Grimbergen (Brabant) T: 022 709 597. E: camping.grimbergen@telenet.be

alanrogers.com/BE0630

A popular little site with a friendly atmosphere, Camping Grimbergen has 90 pitches on fairly level grass, of which around 50 have 10A electricity. The site is not really suitable for large units, although some hardstandings for motorcaravans have been added. The municipal sports facilities are adjacent and the site is well placed for visiting Brussels. The bus station is by the traffic lights at the junction of N202 and N211 and buses run into the city centre every hour, 200 m. from the site, excluding Sunday mornings.

Facilities

Immaculate new sanitary facilities are heated in colder months. Separate facilities for disabled visitors. Motorcaravan services. Shop (with milk and bread) and bar (July/Aug). Off site: Restaurant 100 m. Fishing 2 km. Riding 5 km.

Open: 1 April - 25 October.

Directions

From Brussels ring road exit 7 (N202) to Grimbergen. After 2.5 km, turn right at lights on N211 towards Vilvoorde, then left at second set of lights (slight oblique turn) to site. GPS: 50.93486, 4.38257

Charges guide

Per unit incl. 2 persons and electricity	€ 23.00

Neerlinter
Mini-Camping Leeuwerikenveld

Ransbergstraat 26, B-3350 Neerlinter (Brabant) T: 011 784 040. E: info@mini-camping-leeuwerikenveld.be

alanrogers.com/BE0624

Het Leeuwerikenveld, located between Brussels and Liege, is a quiet, very well kept site where you are made welcome by friendly, family owners. The flat grass and hardstanding pitches in one area all have 10A electricity with water nearby. Another area is for tents and is kept car free. The fields are surrounded by tall beech hedging, giving shelter from any wind. There is a paved area for overnight motorcaravans and three paddocks for up to nine horses. The small, quiet campsite caters for a wide range of clients including hikers, cyclists and cars pulling horse boxes for riding in the area.

Facilities

Heated toilet blocks with showers and washbasins. Laundry facilities. Motorcaravan services. Breakfast, sandwiches, soups and lunches to order. Bicycle hire. WiFi over part of site. Off site: Many marked walks, cycle tracks and horse trails. Tienen 9 km. Leuven 27 km.

Open: 1 April - 30 September.

Directions

From A3 exit 25 take N29 (north). At first roundabout take second exit (Diest). Turn right to Oplinter and at next roundabout first exit towards Linter. Pass sign for Neirlinter, site is on left. GPS: 50.84332, 5.02819

Charges guide

Per unit incl. 2 persons	€ 17.50 - € 20.00

For latest campsite news, availability and prices visit

alanrogers.com

CAPITAL: GENT

East Flanders is a land of rolling hills and vast dykes, winding rivers and straight canals; its vibrant towns and charming villages are home to a rich tapestry of arts and culture, with unspoiled nature on their doorstep.

The vibrant city of Gent combines an impressive past with a lively present. Its beautiful historic centre boasts a wealth of culture, with over 900 listed buildings, several museums and a host of visitor attractions including the magnificent Citadel Park. There are also some picturesque villages waiting to be discovered just a short boat ride down the river. In the region of Scheldeland, three major watercourses converge to offer over 200 kilometres of navigable waterways with numerous landing stages and marinas – there are several boat companies and trips can be arranged. There are also many opportunities for bicycle rides and walks, both ideal for exploring the many monuments in the area, from protected chapels and Maria caves in the countryside to towering castles, strongholds and cathedrals.

The landscape is dotted with wind- and watermills; many are still working and produce their own grain, others have been converted to cosy pubs and restaurants. The beautiful rolling countryside of the Flemish-Ardennes is the home to the classic road cycling race, the Tour de Flandres, and a network of 830 kilometres of recreational cycle paths allows you to feel like a professional while taking in the captivating landscapes at your own, more leisurely pace.

Places of interest

St Bavo's Cathedral, Gent: the Van Eyck brothers' unique altarpiece, The Adoration of The Mystic Lamb, painted in 1432 and renovated in 2010.

Castle of the Counts, Gent: the 'Gravensteen', an imposing stronghold in the heart of the city .

Aalst: popular, regional museum featuring historical and contemporary exhibitions.

Ninove: Abbey church and archaeological site.

Roger Raveel Museum, Zulte: a collection of 300 paintings, 2,500 drawings and graphic works by one of the most important Belgian artists of the post-World War Two period.

Attractions

Fort Liefkenshoek: 16th-century military fort, built to protect the city and port of Antwerp against advancing Spanish troops.

The Mercator Museum, Sint-Niklaas: home to maps and globes by the famous cartographer Gerardus Mercator, alongside exhibits related to modern cartography.

Dendermonde-Puurs Steam Railway: 14 kilometres of standard gauge track, running Sundays and holidays from June to September.

Recreation Park De Ster, Sint Niklaas: 100 acres of parkland featuring minigolf, trampolines, go-karts, trains, boats, tennis, football, a running track and much more.

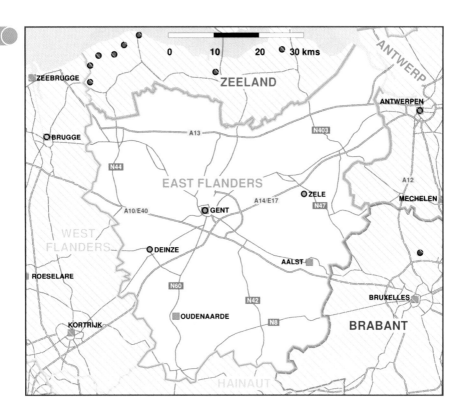

Deinze
Camping Groeneveld

Groenevelddreef 14, Bachte-Maria-Leerne, B-9800 Deinze (East Flanders) T: 093 801 014.
E: info@campinggroeneveld.be **alanrogers.com/BE0600**

Quiet and clean is how Marc Gysemberg describes his campsite. Groeneveld is a traditional site in a small village within easy reach of Gent. It has a friendly atmosphere and is also open over a long season. Although this site has 98 pitches, there are a fair number of seasonal units, leaving around 50 large touring pitches with 10A electricity. Hedges and borders divide the grassy area, access roads are gravel and there is an area for tents. Family entertainment and activities organised in high season include musical evenings, barbecues and pétanque matches. The village of Bachte-Maria-Leerne has a butcher, general store, café and bar, chemist, two restaurants, baker, plus a newsagent, tabac and ATM. The site has produced a location map of these for guests. The city of Gent is just 15 km. north of the site and 5 km. to the south is the pleasant town of Deinze.

Facilities

Two fully updated toilet blocks provide British style WCs, washbasins and free hot showers. Motorcaravan services. Washing machine. Freezer (free). Traditional Flemish style bar (July/Aug; Thu-Sun low season) with comprehensive range of speciality and local beers. Small coarse fishing lake. Floodlit pétanque court. Adventure play area. TV room. Pool. Internet (at reception) and WiFi (€ 1.50 per stay). Bicycles on loan from reception (free). Max. 2 dogs. Off site: Shops and restaurants nearby. Golf 3 km. Swimming pool and free kayaking 1 km.

Open: 1 April - 30 September.

Directions

From A10 (E40) exit 13, turn south on N466. After 3 km. continue straight on at roundabout and site is on left on entering village (opposite large factory). Note: yellow signs are very small.
GPS: 51.00509, 3.57229

Charges guide

Per unit incl. 2 persons	
and electricity	€ 21.00 - € 25.00
extra person	€ 3.00 - € 4.00
child (0-13 yrs)	€ 2.00 - € 3.00

No credit cards.

For latest campsite news, availability and prices visit
alanrogers.com

Gent

Camping Blaarmeersen

Zuiderlaan 12, B-9000 Gent (East Flanders) T: 092 668 160. E: camping.blaarmeersen@gent.be
alanrogers.com/BE0610

Blaarmeersen is a comfortable, well managed municipal site in the west of the city. It adjoins a sports complex and a fair sized lake which together provide facilities for a variety of watersports, tennis, squash, minigolf, football, athletics track, roller skating and a playground. There are 238 pitches for touring units, these are flat, grassy, individually separated by hedges and mostly arranged in circular groups, all with electricity. There are 43 hardstandings for motorcaravans, plus a separate area for tents with barbecue facilities. There is noise from the nearby city ring road. There is a good network of paths and cycle routes around the city.

Facilities

Five sanitary units of a decent standard vary in size. Showers and toilets for disabled visitors. Laundry. Motorcaravan services. Shop, café/bar (both daily March-Oct). Takeaway. Sports facilities. Playground. Fishing. Bicycle hire. Lake swimming. Communal barbecue. WiFi by restaurant, whole site planned for 2014. Off site: Riding and golf 10 km.

Open: 1 March - 31 October.

Directions

From E40 take exit 13 (Gent-West) and follow dual carriageway for 5 km. Cross second bridge and look for Blaarmeersen sign, turning sharp right and following signs to leisure complex. In city avoid overpasses – most signs are on the lower levels. GPS: 51.04722, 3.68333

Charges guide

Per unit incl. 2 persons and electricity (plus meter)	€ 15.00 - € 18.25
extra person	€ 4.50 - € 5.50
child (5-12 yrs)	€ 1.75 - € 2.50

Zele

Camping Groenpark

Gentsesteenweg 337, B-9240 Zele (East Flanders) T: 093 679 071. E: groenpark@scarlet.be
alanrogers.com/BE0615

Camping Groenpark is a popular wooded campsite in the heart of the Scheldt region of eastern Flanders. Between Antwerp and Ghent, it is only ten minutes walk from a lake and close to the Donkmeer, the second largest lake in Flanders. There are 78 pitches, of which 55 good sized, level, grass pitches are for touring and access is good for large units. The pitches are naturally laid out in glades between the trees, some shady, some sunny and all have 16A electricity. There is an area especially for motorcaravans and a large, quiet open camping meadow. The site has large shower rooms, popular with families and a giant central barbecue area. There is no on-site entertainment, but this is an ideal area for cycling and walking, with many picturesque villages close by. You can relax on site around the central barbecue point or stroll to the nearby bars and restaurants. The small village of Donk, only 500 m, has a weekly market and restaurants and outdoor cafés where, in the summer, you can taste the delicious eel. The site is around two hours from Dunkirk and Calais making it an ideal stopover between France, Belgium and Holland. It is also only 25 minutes away by car from the beautiful, historic city of Ghent.

Facilities

One large, modern toilet block at entrance and a smaller block on site with cabins containing toilet, shower and washbasin. Family shower room. Washing machine and dryer. Motorcaravan services. No shop, bar or meals but the town is only 500 m. TV room. Play area. WiFi on part of site (charged). Off site: Supermarket, restaurants and leisure facilities with easy walking distance. Bicycle hire 2 km. Ghent 15 km. Brussels 35 km. Antwerp 40 km. All can be reached by public transport.

Open: 1 March - 3 November.

Directions

Leave E17 motorway exit 12 (Lokeren) onto N47 southeast for 4.7 km. then N445 west towards Ghent for 5.7 km. Site is on left just beyond the Zele exit sign. GPS: 51.05367, 3.97982

Charges guide

Per unit incl. 2 persons and electricity	€ 25.00
extra person	€ 3.00
dog	free

CAPITAL: MONS

Hainaut province is a region full of surprises and hidden treasures, with a diverse range of attractions to suit all visitors – gourmands, lovers of art and culture, sports enthusiasts and nature lovers.

Hainaut, formerly a thriving industrial province, is now one of the foremost agricultural regions of Wallonia. Tournaisis, Pays des Collines, Pays de Ath, Val de Sambre et Thudinie, Botte de Hainaut and the Hauts Pays typify the verdant, rural landscape while retaining their individual characters. The province is blessed with three nature parks and the lakes of the Eau d'Heure.

Apart from Charleroi, the main provincial towns have retained an atmosphere of rural charm. This is thanks to the heritage policies applied in many towns like Mons, Tournai and Enghiens, whose bustling day-to-day existence comfortably embraces the art of living. The more remarkable destinations include Tuin, located on a rock, and Chimay, which has a gem of a castle. Hainaut has 264 kilometres of navigable lakes, and is home to the Park of Canals and Castles between La Louvière, Ronquières and Seneffe.

Places of interest

Mouscron: discover the architectural heritage of Mouscron with a guided tour.

Comines: former capital of the textile industry. Go back in time in the living museum of ribbon manufacture.

Mons: prestigious art collections are housed in the city's museums, including the Museum of Fine Arts and the Museum of Decorative Arts.

Charleroi: an amazing town with a rich cultural heritage – Art Deco town hall, museums, parks, Art Nouveau façades.

Tournaisis: two natural parks, the Pays des Collines and the Plains of the Schelde, with heritage buildings and tours featuring local products.

Attractions

Mont-sur-Marchienne: admire the original pictures in the Museum of Photography.

Abbey of Aulne: impressive Cistercian ruins and the Brewery of Val de Sambre which markets the Abbaye d'Aulne branded beers.

Chimay: discover the steep streets and castle within the ramparts, seat of the Princes housing a marvellous Italianate theatre.

Le Bois du Cazier: old mine in the Marcinelle district and site of a great disaster in August 1956. Exhibits relate to the disaster and mining in the region.

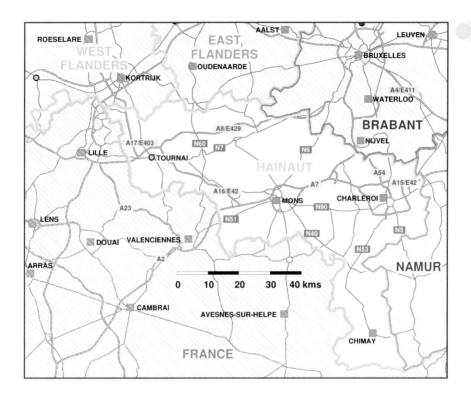

Tournai

Camping de l'Orient

8 rue Jean Baptiste Moens, B-7500 Tournai (Doornik) (Hainaut) T: 069 222 635. E: tourisme@tournai.be
alanrogers.com/BE0540

L'Orient is an attractive, good quality municipal site in a quiet, green location close to the historic town of Tournai and convenient for the E42. It is immaculately kept by its manager. The 51 level, grassy, individual pitches (all for touring units) are separated by laurel hedges and have shade in some parts and 16A electricity. Adjoining the site is an attractive restaurant and bar with a superb terrace overlooking the lake where campers can fish and hire pedaloes. There is also a new, high quality pool complex with cafeteria, indoor pool with spectator seating and outdoor pool with water slides. Tournai has the oldest belfry in Europe and you can also see the cathedral and museums dedicated to decorative arts, folklore, tapestry and military history. There is a good network of cycle ways and footpaths around the town.

Facilities

Two modern sanitary units are of high quality, spotlessly clean and heated in cool weather. They include some washbasins in cubicles and roomy showers on payment. Washing machine and dryer. Facilities for disabled campers (but no ramped access). Basic provisions available from reception (bread can be ordered). Off site: Restaurant/bar adjoining site. Swimming pool (50% discount for campers) and waterslide complex. Lake with picnic and barbecue areas, lakeside walks, fishing, pedalo hire and playground.

Open: All year.

Directions

From E42 exit 32 take N7 towards Tournai centre. Turn left at first traffic lights (site signed), left at small roundabout and site entrance is immediately on the left. GPS: 50.599883, 3.413767

Charges guide

Per unit incl. 2 persons and electricity	€ 15.00

CAPITAL: LIÈGE

The province of Liège is characterised by green hills, the dams that create the many water reservoirs and the small villages with their distinctive Belgian houses and imposing castles.

The Valley of the Meuse is a vast area of natural landscape moulded by the path of the Meuse river and featuring a number of top attractions, including the mine at Blegny. The green pastures of Herve, a Walloon municipality, are criss-crossed by slowly eroding hedges, originally planted to protect the grazing animals in harsh weather. There are many orchards, so it is not surprising that alongside Herve cheese, sparkling cider and pear and apple syrups are regional specialities.

The Valley of the Vesdre was once an important source of income with its profitable wool industry located at Eupen and Verviers. Today the Vesdre is known for water, as it supplies the entire city of Liège. The East Cantons form a unique part of Belgium, being German speaking and almost entirely occupied by the nature reserve of the High Fens, a wilderness of moorland and forest. Spa is a health and wellbeing resort, home to the Belgian Grand Prix, and the perfect location to enjoy a varied holiday. Nearby there are zoos in Theux and Aywaille, castle ruins, museums in Stavelot, caves in Remouchamps and waterfalls in Coo.

Places of interest

Eupen: St Niklaas Church and some ancient houses, Chocolaterie Jacques with visitor centre, the Vesdre barrier with viewpoint and restaurant.

Verviers: Maison de l'Eau (House of Water); Maison de la Laine (House of Wool) tracing the fortunes of the local wool industry.

Stavelot Abbey: renovated and restored abbey housing three museums; the Museum of the Principality of Stavelot-Malmédy, the Spa-Francorchamps Racetrack Museum and the Guillaume Apollinaire Museum.

Liège: cathedral, interactive Archeoforum, citadel, museums, cafés and restaurants.

Attractions

Blegny-Mine: museum with exhibits and history up to its closure in 1980. The descent into the mine is a fascinating experience.

Herve: Espace des Saveurs, a multimedia show and ideal introduction to the Herve region with its groves, castles, hills and villages.

Limbourg: deservedly one of the most beautiful villages of Wallonia, located on a rock and spanning two centuries as an independent duchy.

Caves of Remouchamps: features a 600 m. long subterranean boat trip to comfortably enjoy the wonders of nature.

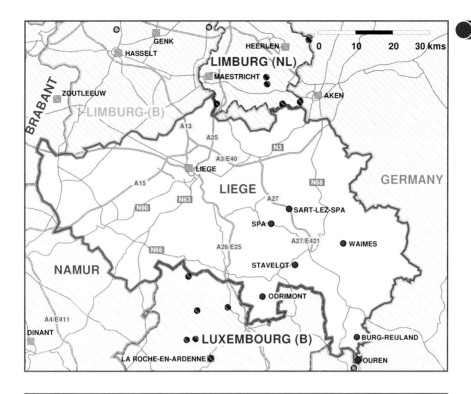

Burg-Reuland
Camping Hohenbusch

Grüfflingen 44A, B-4791 Burg-Reuland (Liège) T: 080 227 523. E: info@hohenbusch.be

alanrogers.com/BE0708

Camping Hohenbusch is located in the Our valley on the edge of the Ardennes and 30 km. from the Grand Prix circuit at Spa-Francorchamps. This is a well equipped site with a swimming pool, restaurant and even a children's petting zoo. There are 195 pitches which are grassy and of a good size, all with 5A (Europlug) electricity, water and drainage, with a number of smaller pitches available for hikers. Hohenbusch also boasts a number of luxury pitches which are 150 sq.m. and equipped with satellite TV connections. A number of mobile homes are available for rent, as well as rooms in the main building. This is, of course, a great region for walking and cycling, and the long distance GR5 path passes close to the site. The Circuit de Ravel is a recently established network of routes suitable for walkers and cyclists, with one route passing through the site.

Facilities

Excellent sanitary facilities with family shower rooms. Laundry facilities. Small shop. Bar. Snack bar and takeaway. All open all season. Swimming pool (heated 14/5-1/9). Paddling pool. Play area. Petting zoo. Bicycle hire. Entertainment and activities in peak season. Mobile homes and rooms for rent. WiFi throughout (charged). Off site: Shops and restaurants in St Vith, the nearest town, 5 km. Tennis. Cycle and walking trails. Riding 5 km. Fishing 10 km. Grand Prix circuit 30 km.

Open: 1 April - 1 November.

Directions

From Liège, head east on the A3(E42) and then south on the A27 to pass Spa and Malmedy. Leave this motorway at exit 15 and join the N62 following signs to Grüfflingen. The site is well signed from here. GPS: 50.241249, 6.092949

Charges guide

Per unit incl. 2 persons and electricity	€ 17.00 - € 48.00
extra person	€ 3.50 - € 5.00
child (4-11 yrs)	€ 1.50 - € 3.00
dog	€ 1.00 - € 2.50

FREE Alan Rogers Travel Card
Extra benefits and savings - see page 12

Odrimont
Camping Gossaimont

Gossaimont 1, B-4990 Odrimont (Liège) T: 080 31 98 22. E: camping.gossaimont@florealgroup.be

alanrogers.com/BE0701

Located in beautiful countryside on the southern slope of one of the Belgian Ardennes' highest hills, this relaxing site of 295 pitches has direct access to the forest for hikers and cyclists. Under the new ownership of the Floreal group, there is a warm welcome from the managers. The 133 spacious touring pitches are set alongside mature trees, and all have 10A electricity. Mobile homes and tents can be rented from April to October. An indoor games room, a cosy café, and outdoor playgrounds for young children are provided. The campsite is open over the winter season, when sledging and snowman building are popular. There is a ski slope just 4 km. away and its café has a welcoming log fire.

Facilities

Three heated toilet blocks are well spaced around the site. Facilities for disabled visitors in two blocks. Laundry. Shop, bar and café (all year). Play areas. Games room. Pétanque. Accommodation for rent. WiFi (charged). Off site: Walking and mountain biking. Fishing and riding 2 km. Bicycle hire 5 km. Local market towns. Swimming pool. Waterfalls and caves.

Open: All year
(rental accommodation 1 April - 15 October).

Directions

From A26 autoroute take exit 49 and follow N651 northeast towards Lierneux. Turn right on N645 then left on local road for Odrimont. Follow signs to site. GPS: 50.32103, 5.81857

Charges guide

Per unit incl. 2 persons	
and electricity	€ 17.05 - € 23.05
extra person	€ 3.60
child (3-11 yrs)	€ 2.60

Ouren
Camping International

Ouren 14, B-4790 Ouren (Liège) T: 080 329 291. E: info@camping-international.be

alanrogers.com/BE0688

This attractive, rural site is located in a wooded valley alongside the River Our in the Belgian Ardennes. Jointly owned by the Kappert and the Van der Linden families, it offers complete peace and quiet and some excellent walking and cycling opportunities in the local area. A variety of more strenuous activities such as zip wire and abseiling are also possible. Children will enjoy the playground and can paddle safely in the river. There are 170 pitches in total, 120 for tourers, 50 of these with 6/10A electricity. There are five cabins and two tents for rent.

Facilities

One sanitary block is clean and well maintained with hot showers. Washing machine. Shop sells basics. Fresh bread daily. Bar/snack bar. Play area. Sports field. Boules. Free fishing (licence required; available at post office). Off site: Bicycle hire 1 km. Riding and golf 10 km.

Open: 31 March - 30 October.

Directions

From E42 exit 15 follow E421 south, taking left turn for Lieler. Follow signs to Ouren and site is in the village. GPS: 50.141971, 6.142125

Charges guide

Per unit incl. 2 persons and electricity	€ 23.50
extra person	€ 4.50
child (4-13 yrs)	€ 2.50
dog (max. 2)	€ 2.50

Sart-lez-Spa
Camping Spa d'Or

Stockay 17, B-4845 Sart-lez-Spa (Liège) T: 087 474 400. E: info@campingspador.be

alanrogers.com/BE0700

Camping Spa d'Or is set in a beautiful area of woodlands and picturesque villages, 4 km. from the town of Spa (Pearl of the Ardennes). The site is on the banks of a small river and is an ideal starting point for walks and bicycle trips through the forests. With 310 pitches in total, 240 are for touring, and all have 10A electricity (40 places are reserved for tents). The touring pitches have an open aspect, most are slightly sloping and all have 10A electricity connections.

Facilities

One new large, bright and cheerful sanitary block and one new smaller, prefabricated block, both with all the usual facilities. Room for visitors with disabilities. Laundry. Shop. Bar, restaurant (weekends only in low season) and takeaway. Outdoor heated swimming pool (1/5-15/9). Play area with good equipment. TV in bar. Goal posts and two boules courts. Entertainment during July/Aug. Mountain bike hire. Maps for mountain biking and walking on sale at reception. WiFi over site (charged). Off site: Fishing 2 km. Golf and riding 5 km. Spa 4 km.

Open: 1 April - 7 November.

Directions

From E42 take exit 9 and follow the signs to Spa d'Or. GPS: 50.50758, 5.91952

Charges guide

Per unit incl. 2 persons	
and electricity	€ 20.00 - € 31.50
extra person	€ 4.25 - € 5.50
dog	€ 4.00 - € 5.00
Camping Cheques accepted.	

For latest campsite news, availability and prices visit

alanrogers.com

Spa

Camping Parc des Sources

Rue de la Sauvenière 141, B-4900 Spa (Liège) T: 087 772 311. E: info@campingspa.be

alanrogers.com/BE0683

Parc des Sources is a small, quietly situated site, close to the town of Spa (Pearl of the Ardennes). It is on the outskirts of a large nature reserve and close to the starting point of the famous Promenade des Artistes and many other interesting walks. There are 155 grassy pitches (60-70 sq.m), of which 110 are for touring; 70 of these have electricity (6A) and there are 13 hardstandings. The site does not have a wide range of amenities, but there is a small shop and a bar, restaurant and takeaway available daily in high season. The nearby resort town of Spa has shops, bars and restaurants, parks and museums, as well as the Thermes de Spa, where a wide range of treatments are offered. Parc des Sources is conveniently situated for the Francorchamps racing circuit.

Facilities

One heated toilet block is clean and well maintained, with hot showers (on payment), open style washbasins and baby changing facilities. Facilities for disabled visitors (key access). Washing machine. Motorcaravan services. Small shop, bar, restaurant and takeaway (open daily July/Aug). Fresh bread to order (July/Aug). Outdoor swimming pool (July/Aug). Playground (under 5s). Bicycle hire. Torches useful. Free WiFi throughout. Off site: Shops 1 km.

Open: 1 April - 31 October.

Directions

From E42, take exit 11 and site is 1.5 km. from Spa on the N62 towards Malmedy.
GPS: 50.485284, 5.883828

Charges guide

Per unit incl. 2 persons and electricity	€ 22.00 - € 28.00
extra person	€ 3.00 - € 4.50
child (4-15 yrs)	€ 2.50 - € 4.00

Stavelot

Camping l'Eau Rouge

Cheneux 25, B-4970 Stavelot (Liège) T: 080 863 075. E: fb220447@skynet.be

alanrogers.com/BE0740

A popular, lively and attractively situated site, l'Eau Rouge is in a sheltered valley close to Spa and the Grand Prix circuit. There are 140 grassy pitches of 110 sq.m. on sloping ground either side of a central road (speed bumps) – 120 for touring units, 80 with 10A electricity (70 with water and waste water), the remainder for static units. The main building houses the busy reception, shop, bar and the main sanitary facilities. There are plenty of sporting activities in the area including skiing and luge in winter. The site is close to the motor race circuit at Spa-Francorchamps and is within walking distance for the fit. The site's Dutch owners have completed a five-year programme upgrading the infrastructure and have other ideas in the pipeline.

Facilities

A brand new environmentally friendly toilet block has showers (on payment), private cubicles, and facilities for babies and children. Motorcaravan services. Washing machine. Shop. Baker calls daily at 08.30 (in season). Takeaway (in summer). Bar. Boules. Archery (free lessons in high season). Playground. Entertainment in season. WiFi over part of site (charged). Max. 2 dogs.

Open: All year.

Directions

Site is 1 km. east of Stavelot on road to race circuit. Leave E42 exit 11 Malmédy, at roundabout, follow signs for Stavelot. At end of road at T-junction turn right, then first right. Do not follow sat nav.
GPS: 50.41203, 5.95317

Charges guide

| Per unit incl. 2 persons and electricity | € 19.00 |
| extra person | € 3.50 |

Waimes

Camping Anderegg

Bruyères 4, B-4950 Waimes (Liège) T: 080 679393. E: campinganderegg@skynet.be

alanrogers.com/BE0632

Camping Anderegg is an attractive, family owned site in village of Bruyeres in the Belgian Ardennes, close to the picturesque towns of Malmedy and Waimes. The 45 grassy touring pitches are well laid out, separated by low hedges, and have 6A electricity. Some are shaded by trees, others more open. A shallow, unfenced stream runs through the site, where children can play under supervision. There are miles of cycle routes in the area including the Ravel Routes, extending 150 km. along the former railway line. Road, mountain and electric bikes can be hired locally. This lovely, rural site is ideal for families.

Facilities

The modern, heated sanitary building is clean and has showers (coin operated), washbasins in cubicles and baby facilities. It may be a distance from some pitches. Small shop for basics (bread to order July/Aug). Snack bar with terrace. Takeaway. Adventure play area. Smaller play area for younger children. Badminton court. WiFi (charged).

Open: All year.

Directions

From Waimes take N676 towards Robertville. Site is well signed on the left. GPS: 50.43916, 6.11793

Charges guide

Per unit incl. 2 persons and electricity	€ 19.25
extra person	€ 4.50
child (2-12 yrs)	€ 2.50

FREE Alan Rogers Travel Card
Extra benefits and savings - see page 12

CAPITAL: HASSELT

Hiking, biking, horse riding...there is a surprise around every corner of Belgian Limburg. Its rich cultural heritage dominates the region, each with its own landscape and character.

In Haspengouw you can picnic beside the orchards, cycle through countryside dotted with fairytale castles, and enjoy the delicious regional cuisine. Borgloon is an attractive town, ideal for an afternoon stroll, and the 17th-century abbey tower of St Truiden offers a splendid view of this fertile region. The Voerstreek is a lush walker's paradise with six picturesque villages. The undulating hills, hollows and varied topography are a feast for the eyes, and it is an ideal base for cultural excursions with Liège, Aachen and Maastricht all being close by.

The Limburg Kempen comprises the sands of the Lommel Sahara, vast pine forests, babbling brooks, lakes and waterways. An area with a rich industrial heritage, it is also famed for its beer and cheese. The Meuse runs like a glittering blue thread through The Maasland, connecting Belgian and Dutch Limburg. Hop on one of the small ferries and observe the contrasting styles on either bank as you sail through the enchanting, waterside villages with their floral displays.

Places of interest

Hasselt: shopping streets, market places, historical buildings and striking, modern architecture; National Genever Museum and fashion museum.

Maaseik: cultural pearl of the Maasland, renaissance architecture, birthplace of the Van Eyck brothers, Museactron – three museums under one roof.

Tongeren: Roman and Middle Ages history; Benelux's largest antiques and brocante market (Sundays).

Borgloon: a charming town combining 13 former communities, with orchards, castles, cloisters and churches; good hiking country.

Attractions

Cosmodrome, Genk: gigantic dome with full dome projection system showing astronomical projections, nature and cultural films.

Bokrijk: step back in time in the Open Air Museum, with more than 100 historic buildings rebuilt in their original condition.

De Blauwe Kei (Lommel): idyllic village near the historic 'blue boulder' lock and canals, with cosy pub terraces.

The markets of St Truiden: landmark market square with its many cafés, monuments, events and a range of different markets.

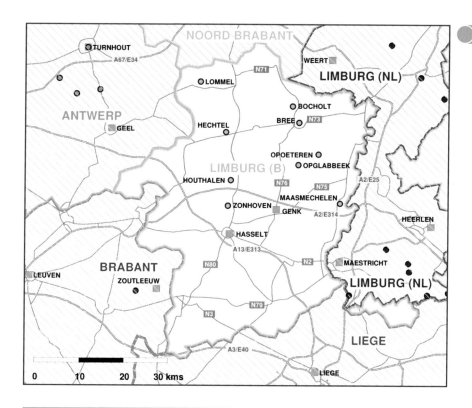

Bree

Camping De Kempenheuvel

Heuvelstraat 8, B-3960 Bree (Limburg) T: 089 462135. E: de.kempenheuvel@telenet.be

alanrogers.com/BE0781

Kempenheuvel is located around 2 km. from the bustling Limburg town of Bree (with an excellent Friday morning market). This is a friendly, family site with a heated outdoor swimming pool and a children's pool. It is a popular choice with anglers, thanks to a large well stocked carp pond. Other amenities include a tennis court and a boules pitch. Cycling is popular and Kempenheuvel is linked to the Limburg cycling route network. Pitches are of a good size and are supplied with 6A electricity. Many activities are on offer in peak season, including darts tournaments and line dancing. Bree has a good range of facilities including a large indoor pool and an interesting motor museum.

Facilities

Two toilet blocks, both with good, clean facilities including free, preset showers and facilities for babies. The older one has facilities for disabled visitors, the new prefabricated unit is on the touring field. Bar/restaurant. Takeaway. Outdoor heated swimming pool and paddling pool (May-Sept). Tennis. Play area. Fishing lake. Activity and entertainment programme. WiFi over site (charged). Mobile homes for rent. Off site: Shops and restaurants in Bree, 2 km. Bicycle hire 2 km. Hasselt 30 km. Cycle tracks through the Limburg countryside.

Open: 1 March - 31 October.

Directions

Approaching from the north use E314 as far as Genk. Then take northbound N76 to Bree, bypassing Meeuwen. The site can be found (on left) before reaching the town centre. GPS: 51.137261, 5.568301

Charges guide

Per unit incl. 2 persons	
and electricity	€ 20.00 - € 22.50
extra person	€ 3.00
dog	€ 3.00

FREE Alan Rogers Travel Card
Extra benefits and savings - see page 12

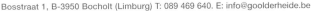

Bocholt

Goolderheide Vakantiepark

Bosstraat 1, B-3950 Bocholt (Limburg) T: 089 469 640. E: info@goolderheide.be

alanrogers.com/BE0760

A large family holiday site with 900 individual pitches, Goolderheide has been owned and operated by the same family for many years and has an excellent pool complex and playgrounds. There are many seasonal and rental units, plus around 300 touring pitches with 4/6A electricity, all in a forest setting. The pitches are of variable size and access roads are quite narrow. The outdoor pool complex has two large pools (one of Olympic size), a slide and a paddling pool. There is also a fishing lake, and a lake with a small sandy beach. An enormous area is devoted to a comprehensive play area with a vast range of equipment. During the main season there is also a weekly supervised assault course with aerial ropeways etc, a soundproofed over-16s disco, plus a younger kids' disco and an extensive programme of varied activities to keep the family occupied. There are no extra charges for most of these activities.

Facilities

Four sanitary buildings provide an ample supply of WCs and washbasins in cabins, but rather fewer preset showers. Baby areas. Two en-suite units for disabled visitors (key access). Laundry facilities. Shop, bar and takeaway (daily in July/Aug, w/ends and public holidays in low season). Takeaway. Swimming pools. Tennis. Fishing. Boules. Minigolf. Play area and assault course. Children's discos. Programme of activities (July/Aug). Off site: Bicycle hire 1 km.

Open: 1 April - 30 September.

Directions

From A13 (E313, Antwerp-Liege) take exit 25 and N141 to Leopoldsburg, then N73 through Peer, to outskirts of Bree (35 km). Take N76 north for 3 km, turn left at large roundabout into Bocholt, and towards Kaulille. Site road is on left towards edge of town. GPS: 51.17343, 5.53902

Charges guide

Per unit incl. 2 persons and electricity	€ 30.00
extra person	€ 5.00
dog	€ 5.00

No credit cards.

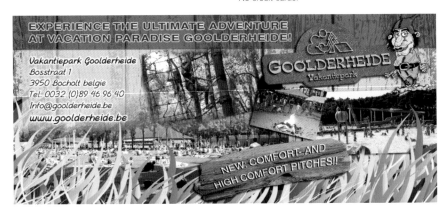

Hechtel

Vakantiecentrum De Lage Kempen

Kiefhoekstraat 19, B-3941 Hechtel-Eksel (Limburg) T: 011 402 243. E: info@lagekempen.be

alanrogers.com/BE0796

This is a small, good quality site of which the owners are rightly proud. There are 100 pitches with 70 for touring units. The pitches are large, all with 6/10A electricity, and are laid out in rows. A pleasant swimming pool complex has three heated pools, two for children and one with a large slide, and they are supervised in high season. A new bar and restaurant building opened in July 2012 and a shop is open in high season. Entertainment is provided daily in high season. This is a friendly and welcoming site with a good atmosphere. The owners have found the right balance of entertainment and time for relaxation.

Facilities

Single, high quality toilet block providing very good facilities including free hot showers, washbasins in cabins and good facilities for babies and disabled visitors. Laundry facilities. Motorcaravan services. Small shop with fresh bread (high season). Bar/restaurant and takeaway (all 15/5-1/9). Outdoor heated pool complex (May-Sept). Large adventure playground. Magical minigolf. Bicycle hire. WiFi over most of site (charged). Max. 1 dog.

Open: Easter - 30 October.

Directions

From the E314/A2 motorway take exit for Houthalen and follow signs to Hechtel. Shortly after passing through Hechtel, on Kiefhoekstraat, site is 3.5 km. on the right. GPS: 51.16092, 5.31433

Charges guide

Per unit incl. 2 persons and electricity	€ 24.00
extra person	€ 4.00
child (0-2 yrs)	free
dog (max. 1)	€ 2.00

For latest campsite news, availability and prices visit

alanrogers.com

Houthalen
Camping De Binnenvaart

Binnenvaartstraat 49, B-3530 Houthalen-Helchteren (Limburg) T: 011 526 720. E: info@debinnenvaart.be
alanrogers.com/BE0793

De Binnenvaart is a well equipped family site north of Hasselt, open all year. This is a very well equipped holiday centre with a good range of leisure amenities including minigolf and a sports field. The site has been developed alongside a small lake, with its own sandy beach, and is surrounded by woodland. Of the 180 pitches, 34 are for touring, all are of a good size and equipped with electricity (16A Europlug). Many pitches here are reserved all year. The site is part of the same group as BE0792 and BE0780, both of which are nearby, and guests are able to use amenities at these sites too. Some unusual activities are on offer at de Binnenvaart, including paintball and Nordic walking. A children's zoo is a popular feature. There are some excellent walking and cycle tracks through the surrounding woods. Nearby Hasselt is the capital of the Belgian province of Limburg. The small city dates back to the 7th century and boasts a fine cathedral (Saint Quentin) as well as an attractive pedestrianised centre.

Facilities
Two sanitary blocks, one being upgraded, have facilities for disabled visitors. Motorcaravan services. Cafeteria and bar. Lake (swimming, fishing and windsurfing) with sandy beach. Tennis. Sports field. Minigolf. Play area. Animal park. Activity and entertainment programme. Free WiFi over site. No charcoal barbecues. Off site: Walking and cycling routes. Riding. Paintball. Hot-air ballooning. Golf 5 km.

Open: All year.

Directions
Leave the A2 motorway at Houthalen - Helchteren exit (number 29) and join northbound N715 to town. The site is clearly signed from here.
GPS: 51.032158, 5.415949

Charges guide
Per unit incl. 2 persons and electricity	€ 26.00
extra person	€ 8.00
child	€ 4.00
dog	€ 4.00

Houthalen
Camping Molenheide

Molenheidestraat 7, B-3530 Houthalen-Helchteren (Limburg) T: 070 222 034. E: info@molenheide.be
alanrogers.com/BE0794

In the centre of a naturally beautiful area, Park Molenheide is predominantly a high class bungalow park. However, it does have 30 large touring pitches which are located in a flat, grassy field with easy access. All the pitches have 6/10A electricity. What sets this site aside from others in the area is its amazing range of activities and high class facilities. All manner of recreational activities are housed indoors with a large tropical-style swimming pool with slides and an excellent Disney themed children's pool, all supervised. There are numerous high quality bars and restaurants, all housed under the same roof. There is also an incredible indoor playground for children (free access once per day for camping guests). The children's playground is of Disney standard with an amazing array of activities ranging from 'climbing the red volcano' to the 'snuggle room'. Adjoining the site is a wildlife and rambling park where red and roe deer are free to roam and stop for the bread offered to them by children. The breathtaking indoor crazy golf course is new and has a mining theme. It is quite unique and is on two levels with amazing attention to detail (this is charged). Other activities include quad biking, squash, bowling, football and many other activities too numerous to mention.

Facilities
One single well equipped, modern toilet block (bring your own paper) with large free controllable showers. Fully equipped en-suite unit for disabled visitors. Excellent bars and restaurants. Outstanding leisure facilities with tropical indoor heated swimming pool, bowling, incredible children's indoor play area, unique indoor crazy golf course. Bicycle hire. Max. 1 dog – allowed on the campsite but not in the facilities. WiFi (charged). Off site: Golf 5 km. Riding 10 km.

Open: All year.

Directions
Follow the E314 motorway towards Aken and take exit 29. Follow the N74 for 8 km. and site well signed on the right. GPS: 51.0791, 5.3955

Charges guide
Per unit incl. up to 4 persons and electricity	€ 16.00 - € 90.00
extra person	€ 19.00
dog	€ 4.00

FREE Alan Rogers Travel Card
Extra benefits and savings - see page 12

Lommel

Oostappen Vakantiepark Blauwe Meer

Kattenbos 169, B-3920 Lommel (Limburg) T: 011 544 523. E: info@blauwemeer.be

alanrogers.com/BE0785

Surrounded by woodland, and with shade from tall pines, this large site has 976 pitches, of which 277 are for touring units. The touring pitches are attractively arranged around a large man-made lake with a fence surrounding it. Each pitch has 10A electricity, water, drainage and television connections. There is a whole range of activities, including a disco and a heated outdoor pool with slide. There are two additional small pools for children. A bar offers takeaway food and a good supermarket is on the site. This is a popular and lively site with an extensive entertainment programme which is varied to suit all age groups.

Facilities

Good clean toilet blocks are located throughout the site. Free hot showers, washbasins in cabins. Facilities for babies and children. Good facilities for disabled visitors. Laundry room. Supermarket, bar and takeaway (all July/Aug; weekends in low season). Heated outdoor swimming pool, two smaller ones for children (May-Aug). Several adventure style playgrounds. Children's zoo. Minigolf. Bicycle hire. WiFi over most of site (charged). Max. 1 dog. Off site: Forest Park adjacent for walking and cycling. Riding 7 and 12 km. Golf 10 km.

Open: Easter - 30 October.

Directions

Lommel is 35 km. north of Hasselt. From the N71 at Lommel, turn south at traffic lights on N746 (signed Leopoldsburg), for 2 km. to Kattenbos, and site entrance is on southern side of village on left. GPS: 51.19407, 5.30322

Charges guide

Per unit incl. up to 4 persons	€ 31.00 - € 33.00

Minimum stays apply (1 week in high season, 3 or 4 nights on public holidays. American RVs, 12 m. max. in high season, larger at other times).

Lommel

Oostappen Vakantiepark Parelstrand

Luikersteenweg 313A, B-3920 Lommel (Limburg) T: 011 649 349. E: info@vakantieparkprinsenmeer.nl

alanrogers.com/BE0798

This large, attractive site is situated alongside the Bocholt-Herentals canal and the Lommel yacht marina. It has 800 pitches of which 250 are for touring units. Each pitch has 10A electricity, water and drainage. The site fronts onto a large lake with a safe beach and there are three smaller lakes within the site, one of which is used for fishing (well stocked but all fish must be returned). The Olympic-size, outdoor pool has a large slide and there is a small pool for children (not supervised). Several good quality play areas are spread throughout the site. This site is ideal for relaxing or enjoying the canal and other water-based activities.

Facilities

All the facilities that one would expect from a large site are available. Free hot showers, some washbasins in cabins. Facilities for babies and children. Good facilities for disabled visitors. Laundry room. Supermarket. Bar. Takeaway. Outdoor swimming pools (July/Aug), one for children. Bicycle hire. Fishing. WiFi (charged).

Open: Easter - 30 October.

Directions

Take the N712 from Lommel and after 3 km. turn left on the N715. After a further 3 km. the site is on the right hand side. It is well signed from Lommel. GPS: 51.2431, 5.3791

Charges guide

Per unit incl. 2 persons and electricity	€ 13.00 - € 25.00

Maasmechelen

Recreatieoord Kikmolen

Kikmolenstraat 3, B-3630 Opgrimbie/Maasmechelen (Limburg) T: 089 770 900. E: info@kikmolen.be

alanrogers.com/BE0784

This is a large and very lively site situated around a large, man-made lake which also serves as the site swimming pool. The site is very much targeted at a family clientele. Large pitches are spread throughout the site, with the 120 for touring separate from the 680 seasonal and rental units. The pitches are on grass and all have 6A electricity and water. Dogs are officially not accepted but when we visited there were many dogs on the site. Two water slides run into the large artificial lake (not fenced and unsuitable for young children).

Facilities

Eight modern blocks are spread throughout the site, and one was rebuilt for 2012. All have good facilities with some washbasins in cabins, and hot water is charged via a prepaid SEP key system. One disabled toilet per block which is unlocked and used by all. Two restaurants and bars. Takeaway. Well stocked shop. Games room. Lake swimming with water slides. Sports field. Lively activity and entertainment programme. Bicycle hire.

Open: 1 April - 31 October.

Directions

From A76 Antwerpen-Koln motorway take exit 33 towards Maasmechelen. Follow N78 from 1 km. and site is well signed on right. GPS: 50.95387, 5.66198

Charges guide

Per unit incl. 2 persons and electricity	€ 17.00 - € 19.00
extra person	€ 5.00 - € 5.50
child (4-15 yrs)	€ 3.00 - € 3.50

For latest campsite news, availability and prices visit

alanrogers.com

Opglabbeek
Family Camping Wilhelm Tell

Hoeverweg 87, B-3660 Opglabbeek (Limburg) T: 089 810 014. E: receptie@wilhelmtell.com
alanrogers.com/BE0780

Wilhelm Tell is a family run site that caters particularly well for children with its indoor and outdoor pools and lots of entertainment throughout the season. There are 128 pitches with 70 available for touring units, some separated, others on open fields and 60 electricity connections (10A). The super bar/restaurant has access for wheelchair users. M. Lode Nulmans has a very special attitude towards his customers and tries to ensure they leave satisfied and want to return. For example, in his restaurant he says 'it serves until you are full'. The Limburg region is a relaxing area with much to do, including shopping or touring the historic towns with a very enjoyable choice of food and drink!

Facilities

Toilet facilities are adequate, but might be under pressure in high season. Facilities around the pool supplement at busy times. Baby room in reception area. Two en-suite units for disabled visitors. Laundry facilities. Motorcaravan services. Fridge hire. Bar/restaurant and snack bar (times vary acc. to season). Outdoor heated pool with slide and wave machine (July/Aug) and indoor pool (all year), both well supervised. Play area. WiFi. No charcoal barbecues. Off site: Riding 1 km. Fishing 6 km. Golf 10 km.

Open: All year.

Directions

From E314 take exit 32 for Maaseik and follow 730 road towards As. From As follow signs to Opglabbeek. In Opglabbeek take first right at roundabout (Weg van Niel) then first left (Kasterstraat) to site. GPS: 51.02852, 5.59813

Charges guide

Per unit incl. 2 persons and electricity	€ 32.00
extra person	€ 8.00
child (0-12)	€ 4.00
dog	€ 4.00

Opoeteren
Camping Zavelbos

Kattebeekstraat 1, B-3680 Opoeteren (Limburg) T: 089 758 146. E: receptie@zavelbos.com
alanrogers.com/BE0792

Camping Zavelbos lies between woodland and moorland in a nature park of 2,000 hectares. It is a lovely spot for nature lovers and those who enjoy peace and quiet. There are many cycling and walking routes to enjoy in this beautiful region, alternatively you can simply relax in the peaceful campsite grounds complete with a large fishpond. There is no swimming pool but guests have free use of the pool complex at Wilhelm Tell Holiday Park (6 km). The 60 touring pitches (100-120 sq.m) all have 16A electricity (Europlug) and water. Bungalows and chalets are available to rent. The site is next to a wooded, hilly area, which has excellent off-road cycle and walking routes. Only five kilometres away is the Hoge Kempen National Park, covering almost 60 square kilometres, and a haven for nature lovers.

Facilities

New sanitary facilities include family bathrooms, baths with jacuzzi and jet stream (key access € 50 deposit). Provision for disabled visitors. Laundry facilities. Dog shower. Motorcaravan services. Bar and snack bar. Tavern. Fishpond. Playground. Boules. Bicycle hire and free recharging of electric bikes. WiFi over site (free). No charcoal barbecues. Off site: Riding 6 km. Golf 10 km. Shops. Cycling and walking routes. National Park Hoge Kempen. Bobbejaanland. Maastricht. Hasselt. Genk.

Open: All year.

Directions

Take the Maaseik exit from the A2 (Eindhoven-Maastricht) motorway and drive via Neerpoeteren to Opoeteren. The site is on the right heading to Opglabbeek. GPS: 51.0583, 5.6288

Charges guide

Per unit incl. 2 persons and electricity	€ 21.00 - € 30.00
extra person	€ 8.00
child (under 12 yrs)	€ 4.00
No credit cards.	

Zonhoven
Camping Holsteenbron

Hengelhoefseweg 9, B-3520 Zonhoven (Limburg) T: 011 817 140. E: camping.holsteenbron@telenet.be

alanrogers.com/BE0786

Situated in the heart of the Park Midden-Limburg, this is a delightful site. There are 91 pitches with 60 for touring units, numbered and arranged in rows that are separated by hedges. All have easy access and 6A electricity. Water is provided by a single supply at the toilet block, but being such a small site, this is not a problem. A pretty lake is at the centre of the site and is well stocked with fish for the exclusive use of the camping guests. The site is situated only 500 m. from the start of a network of cycle tracks that stretches for 1,600 km. throughout the national park. The site is highly recommended.

Facilities

One single well equipped toilet block with large token operated showers. Laundry room. Excellent bar and restaurant with limited but good menu (all season). Playground. Sports field. Fishing. TV in bar. Free WiFi over site. Off site: Riding 3 km.

Open: 1 April - 11 November.

Directions

Site is situated on the N29 Eindhoven-Hasselt road and is well signed from Zonhoven.
GPS: 50.99826, 5.42451

Charges guide

Per unit incl. electricity	€ 19.00 - € 24.00
dog	€ 6.00

Zonhoven
Camping Heidestrand

Zwanenstraat 105, B-3520 Zonhoven (Limburg) T: 011 520 190. E: info@heidestrand.be

alanrogers.com/BE0787

Heidestrand is a large family site of 30 hectares with a broad range of facilities. The site can be found north of Hasselt in the Flemish province of Limburg. There are over 600 seasonal pitches here and around 90 touring pitches, all with electricity and water. The site boasts an excellent outdoor swimming pool with a separate paddling pool, slides, diving tower and diving pool, as well as a large shallow swimming pond with a sandy beach. A separate fishing pond is well stocked with a wide variety of coarse fish.

Facilities

Two toilet blocks have free showers and facilities for disabled visitors, but may be stretched in peak season. Laundry in one block (some distance from touring field). Swimming pool complex. Supermarket. Bar. Restaurant. Snack bar. Disco. Sports fields. Play area. Leisure pavilion for children. Entertainment for children. Dance evenings. Boat hire. Fishing ponds. WiFi in reception (charged). Off site: Motor racing circuit at Zolder. Hasselt. Nature reserve at De Bolderberg. Flemish Mine museum.

Open: Easter - 1 October.

Directions

Zonhoven is located 8 km. north of Hasselt close to the N74. From Zonhoven take N72 towards Beringen. After 2 km, just after the railway, turn left to Wijvestraat. The site is 2.5 km. on the right.
GPS: 50.98668, 5.31342

Charges guide

Per unit incl. 2 persons and electricity	€ 22.30
extra person	€ 3.90
dog	€ 2.85

CAPITAL: ARLON

Belgian Luxembourg is a land of forests, rivers and deep valleys criss-crossed by a network of marked footpaths and cycling routes, a land of medieval castles and ancient hamlets.

The region of the rivers Ours and Aisne in the north is made up of many small villages, the little medieval town of Durbuy and a very interesting cave. Dominated by the ruins of a medieval castle, La Roche-en-Ardenne is an important tourist resort nestling in a meander of the River Ourthe and surrounded by forests. Houffalize, higher up in the Ourthe valley, is an attractive town famous for its colourful floral decorations and known worldwide as the Belgian mountain bike capital. The Land of Bastogne has several small towns and was the site of the Battle of the Bulge in 1944.

Bouillon is not only the historical site from where the First Crusade departed to Jerusalem, but also the starting point for those wishing to explore the magnificent valley, by canoe for instance. The Land of the Anlier Forest is one of the largest and most beautiful forests of the Ardennes. A significant number of villages and hamlets remain, a testament to the area's agricultural history. The Land of the Val de Salm is a treasure trove of architectural and natural sites, signposted walks and mountain bike trails with an abundance of bilberries and raspberries, and a wealth of nature reserves and game parks.

Places of interest

Bastogne: Bastogne historical centre and war museum; historical museum within an old city gate, Saint Peter's church.

Durbuy: charming medieval town where attractions include a unique collection of pruned bushes, a diamond museum and a jam-maker.

The stones of the Liberty Way: one set every kilometre from Omaha beach to the Bastogne Historical Center tracing the route followed by General Patton's 3rd Army. The last three markers can be seen in Bastogne.

Attractions

Herbeumont: ruins of a 13th-century castle perched on a rocky spur dominating the river – one of Wallonia's exceptional sites (free entrance).

Nature Park of the Valley of the Attert: comprises 17 villages and is a paradise for hikers and cyclists. The village of Nobressart is designated one of 'The Most Beautiful Villages of Wallonia'.

Moulin de la Petite Strument, La Roche-en-Ardenne: working 19th-century water mill, a tribute to the miller's work.

Animal Park, Bouillon: 200 animals from the forest, including fallow deer, wild sheep, wild boar, bison, foxes and wolves.

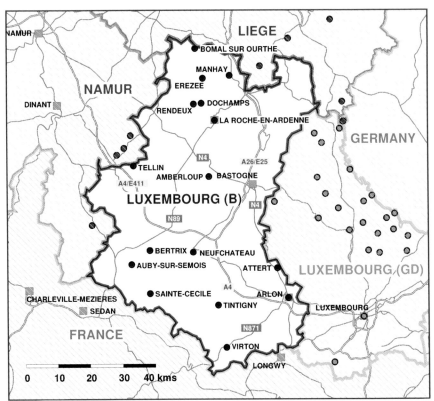

Amberloup
Camping Tonny

Rue des Rainettes 1, B-6680 Sainte-Ode (Luxembourg) T: 061 688 285. E: info@campingtoony.be

alanrogers.com/BE0720

The Dutch owners here are rightly proud of their site. With a friendly atmosphere, it is an attractive, small campsite in a pleasant valley by the River Ourthe. A family site, there are 75 grass touring pitches, with wooden chalet buildings giving a Tirolean feel. The pitches (80-100 sq.m) are separated by small shrubs and fir trees, 4/6A electricity is available. Cars are parked away from the units and there is a separate meadow for tents. Surrounded by natural woodland, Camping Tonny is an ideal base for outdoor activities. In bad weather, the homely bar acts as a meeting place. There is a freestanding fireplace and a shady terrace for relaxing outside.

Facilities

A new sanitary unit (heated in cool weather) includes showers (now free). Baby area and laundry. Freezer for campers' use. TV lounge and library. Sports field. Boules. Games room. Playgrounds. Fishing. Bicycle hire. Cross-country skiing. WiFi (free by reception).

Open: 30 March - 2 November.

Directions

From N4 take exit for Libramont at km. 131 (N826), then to Amberloup (4 km) where site is signed just outside of the southwest town boundary.
GPS: 50.02657, 5.51283

Charges guide

Per unit incl. 2 persons	
and electricity	€ 18.00 - € 26.00
extra person	€ 4.50
child (3-12 yrs)	€ 2.50

For latest campsite news, availability and prices visit
alanrogers.com

Arlon

Camping Officiel Arlon

Route de Bastogne 373, B-6700 Arlon (Luxembourg) T: 063 226582. E: campingofficiel@skynet.be

alanrogers.com/BE0684

An attractive and well maintained, family owned site situated close to Belgium's largest forest. There are 80 grassy touring pitches (100 sq.m) with 6A electricity. The excellent on-site amenities include a clean sanitary block, a bar and restaurant and a pleasant terrace and swimming pool. This is an ideal stopover site when travelling north or south, with good access from the E411. However, the Roman city of Arlon has many interesting sights, and a large flea market is held on the first Sunday of the month from March until October, so you may be tempted to linger. Luxembourg is just 4 km. away for cheaper fuel.

Facilities

One clean, well maintained sanitary block by the entrance has free, controllable, hot showers and some washbasins in cubicles. Facilities for disabled visitors (key access). Dishwashing area and washing machine. Motorcaravan services. Bar/restaurant/takeaway (April-Oct; limited menu). Spring water swimming pool (15/6-31/8). Free WiFi over site. Off site: Shops, bars, restaurants and market (Thurs) in Arlon 2 km. Riding 4 km. Golf and fishing 6 km.

Open: All year.

Directions

From E41 exit at junction 31 towards Arlon. Follow signs for Bastogne. Continue on N82 for 4 km. before merging onto N4. Site is just after the bend, 200 m. on right. GPS: 49.702009, 5.806765

Charges guide

Per unit incl. 2 persons and electricity	€ 20.40
extra person	€ 4.00
child (4-9 yrs)	€ 2.50
dog	€ 2.00
No credit cards.	

Attert

Camping Sud

Voie de la Liberté 75, B-6717 Attert (Luxembourg) T: 063 223 715. E: info@campingsudattert.com

alanrogers.com/BE0680

This is a pleasant, family run site which would make a good base for a short stay and is also well situated for use as an overnight halt. The 86 touring pitches are on level grass, all with 6A electricity. There are 11 drive-through pitches especially for stopovers, plus four hardstandings for motorcaravans and a tent area. The far end of the site is close to the N4 and may suffer from some road noise. On-site facilities include a small, but welcoming restaurant/bar with takeaway facility, a shop for basics, an outdoor swimming pool (12x6 m) with paddling pool and a sports field. The site is very close to the border with Luxembourg and only 40 km. from its capital city.

Facilities

A single building provides modern sanitary facilities including some washbasins in cubicles and baby areas. Showers are free in low season (€ 0.50 July/Aug). No facilities for disabled campers. Small shop (July/Aug). Pleasant bar/restaurant and takeaway (1/4-15/10). TV in bar. Swimming and paddling pools (June-Sept). Small playground. Children's entertainment (4-12 yrs) three afternoons per week during July/Aug. Free WiFi in reception area. Dogs are not accepted. Off site: Attert village has two churches and a museum and the Liberation Route passes the site. Internet café and Roman Museum in Arlon 8 km. Local nature parks. Supermarket, riding 5 km. Golf 8 km. Fishing 10 km. Bicycle hire 12 km.

Open: 1 April - 15 October.

Directions

Attert is 8 km. north of Arlon. From E25/E411 from Luxembourg take exit 31 and follow signs for Bastogne to join N4 north; take Attert exit, continue east for 1 km. to Attert village, site entrance is immediately on your left as you join the main street. GPS: 49.74833, 5.78698

Charges guide

Per unit incl. 2 persons and electricity	€ 20.50
extra person	€ 4.50
child (2-11 yrs)	€ 2.25
No credit cards.	

FREE Alan Rogers Travel Card
Extra benefits and savings - see page 12

Auby-sur-Semois

Camping Maka

Route du Maka 100, B-6880 Auby-sur-Semois (Luxembourg) T: 061 411 148. E: info@campingmaka.be
alanrogers.com/BE0716

Camping Maka is a delightful, rural site on the banks of the River Semois, reputedly Belgium's cleanest river. Fifty touring pitches, with 10A electricity and water, are sited close to the water, allowing everyone access to the river and its banks and there is space for 30 tents. Forty-eight private mobile homes are hidden on two higher terraces. Two fully equipped wooden cabins and two tents are for rent. The river is popular for swimming, fishing and canoeing. Canadian canoes, mountain bikes, barbecues and outdoor cooking equipment are available for hire. Facilities include a bar with a terrace overlooking the water and a shop. Not suitable for large units (over 8 m. long).

Facilities	Directions
A modern, heated toilet block includes facilities for babies and for disabled campers (key access). Pub/café/takeaway with terrace, shop (all season). Play area. Fishing. Games area. Direct river access. Campfire area. Canoe and mountain bike hire. Occasional activities and entertainment. Tents and cabins for rent. WiFi over site (charged). No electric barbecues.	Site is close to village of Auby-sur-Semois, east of Bouillon. From the east on N89, leave at N853 exit and follow signs to Bertrix. Before centre of Bertrix, follow signs to Auby-sur-Semois to the southwest, and then signs to site. GPS: 49.808842, 5.164824

Open: 1 April - 19 September.

Charges guide

Per unit incl. 2 persons and electricity	€ 30.35
extra person	€ 4.95

Bertrix

Ardennen Camping Bertrix

Route de Mortehan, B-6880 Bertrix (Luxembourg) T: 061 412 281. E: info@campingbertrix.be
alanrogers.com/BE0711

Bertrix is located at the heart of the Belgian Ardennes, between the towns of Bastogne and Bouillon and overlooking the hills of the Semois valley. Part of a Dutch chain, the site has 498 terraced pitches of which 303 are for touring, all with 10A electricity, and 43 also have water and drainage. A variety of seasonal caravans are sited among them and there is a friendly feel to the area. Some pitches are available with children's play huts on stilts! A wide range of imaginative activities are organised in the holidays, including some exciting excursions on horseback to the nearby working slate mine.

Facilities	Directions
Five well appointed toilet blocks, one with facilities for disabled visitors. The central one has a large laundry. Motorcaravan services. Shop for basics and bread. Excellent restaurant and bar (closed low season on Tues. and Thurs) has satellite TV and Internet access and a terrace overlooking the large, heated swimming and paddling pools (27/4-16/9, supervised high season). Tennis. Bicycle hire. Children's games room. Woodland adventure trail. Ardennes chalets and holiday homes for rent. WiFi over part of site (charged).	Bertrix is 90 km. south of Namur. Take exit 25 from the E411 motorway and take N89 towards Bertrix. After 6.5 km. join the N884 to Bertrix then follow yellow signs to site south of town. GPS: 49.83861, 5.25122

Open: 28 March - 12 November.

Charges guide

Per unit incl. 2 persons and electricity	€ 20.00 - € 34.00
extra person (over 2 yrs)	€ 4.00 - € 6.00
Camping Cheques accepted.	

Bomal-sur-Ourthe

Camping International

Pré Cawai 3, B-6941 Bomal-sur-Ourthe (Luxembourg) T: 049 8629 079. E: info@campinginternational.be
alanrogers.com/BE0718

Camping International is a small site in the Belgian Ardennes, located on the banks of the River Ourthe. Although in a French-speaking area, it has a very Dutch ambience. The 60 pitches (20 for seasonal caravans) are of a good size and most have (metered) electrical connections. A central area is available for groups. The campsite tavern, which also houses reception, serves a selection of bar meals to eat in or take away. A wide range of activities are on offer in the area, including canoeing on the Ourthe, raft building, abseiling and mountain biking. There is occasional railway noise.

Facilities	Directions
The basic sanitary facilities are adjacent to the tavern and have preset showers, cold water to washbasins (cabins in ladies). No facilities for disabled visitors. Bar. Snack bar. Takeaway. Play area. Bicycle hire. Canoeing. Activity and entertainment programme. Direct river access. Fishing (licence needed). WiFi (charged). Off site: Adventure sports 200 m. Bar and restaurants 200 m. Shops and bicycle hire in Bornal-sur-Ourthe 500 m.	From the E411 Brussels/Luxembourg motorway take exit 18 for Assesse. South on N4 to Sinsin and turn east on N929 and N933 to Le Petit Han. Take N983 to Barvaux-sur-Ourthe and N86 to Bomal. Turn west on N683 to site. GPS: 50.374925, 5.519439

Open: 4 March - 13 November.

Charges guide

Per unit incl. 2 persons and electricity (plus meter)	€ 15.50 - € 19.50
extra person	€ 4.50

42

Dochamps
Panoramacamping Petite Suisse

Al Bounire 27, B-6960 Dochamps (Luxembourg) T: 084 444 030. E: info@petitesuisse.be

alanrogers.com/BE0735

This quiet site is set in the picturesque countryside of the Belgian Ardennes, a region in which rivers flow through valleys bordered by vast forests where horses are still usefully employed. Set on a southerly slope, the site is mostly open and offers wide views of the surrounding countryside. The 193 touring pitches, all with 10A electricity, are either on open sloping ground or in terraced rows with hedges in between, and trees providing some separation. Gravel roads provide access around the site. To the right of the entrance barrier a large wooden building houses reception, a bar and a restaurant.

Facilities

All the facilities that one would expect of a large site are available. Showers are free, washbasins both open and in cabins. Baby room. Laundry room with washing machines and dryers. Shop, restaurant, bar and takeaway (4/4-2/11). Heated outdoor swimming pool (1/5-1/9), paddling pool and slide. Sports field. Tennis. Bicycle hire. Playground and club for children. Entertainment programme during school holidays. Varied activity programme, including archery, canoeing, climbing, abseiling and walking. WiFi (charged). Off site: Fishing 8 km. Riding 10 km. La Roche en Ardennes and Baraque de Fraiture (ski resort) 10 km. Golf 25 km.

Open: All year.

Directions

From E25/A26 autoroute (Liège-Luxembourg) take exit 50 then the N89 southwest towards La Roche. After 8 km. turn right (north) on N841 to Dochamps where site is signed. GPS: 50.23127, 5.62583

Charges guide

Per unit incl. 2 persons and electricity	€ 21.50 - € 37.50
extra person (over 4 yrs)	€ 3.00 - € 6.00
dog (high season max. 1)	€ 2.00 - € 4.00

Camping Cheques accepted.

Erezée
Camping le Val de l'Aisne

Rue du TTA 1 A, B-6997 Erezée (Luxembourg) T: 086 470 067. E: info@levaldelaisne.be

alanrogers.com/BE0725

From a nearby hill, Château de Blier overlooks Camping le Val de l'Aisne, a large site attractively laid out around a 1.5-hectare lake in the Belgian Ardennes. The site has 450 grass pitches with 150 for touring units, on level ground and with 16A electricity. Tarmac roads circle the site providing easy access. Trees provide some shade although the site is fairly open allowing views of the surrounding hills and the château. Activities play a large part on this site, ranging from quiet fishing in the lake to hectic quad bike tours in the surrounding hills. To the left of the entrance a building houses reception and the bar and restaurant. Behind this is a large fenced playground.

Facilities

Three toilet blocks provide showers (paid for by sep key) and mainly open washbasins. Facilities for disabled visitors. Baby room. Washing machines and dryers. Motorcaravan services. Bar/restaurant and snack bar with takeaway. Bread can be ordered in reception. On the lake: fishing, swimming, kayaks (to hire). Quad bike hire and tours arranged. Mountain bike hire. Play area. Entertainment programme (summer). Activities team arrange a range of adventure activities including paintball, canyoning, etc. WiFi (free). Off site: Riding, cycling and walking routes in the Ardennes forest. Golf 5 km. Riding 6 km.

Open: All year.

Directions

From E411/A4 (Brussels-Luxembourg) take exit 18 (Courière, Marche), then southeast on N4 to Marche. At Marche head northeast on N86 to Hotton, crossing river bridge. In Hotton follow signs for Soy and Erezée. Just west of Erezée at roundabout follow signs for La Roche. Site is 900 m. on left. GPS: 50.2815, 5.5505

Charges guide

Per unit incl. 2 persons and car	€ 18.00
extra person (over 3 yrs)	€ 3.00
electricity (10A)	€ 3.00
dog	€ 3.00

No credit cards.
Reductions for longer periods of stay.

FREE Alan Rogers Travel Card
Extra benefits and savings - see page 12

La Roche-en-Ardenne
Camping Floréal La Roche

Route de Houffalize 18, B-6980 La Roche-en-Ardenne (Luxembourg) T: 084 219 467.
E: camping.laroche@florealgroup.be **alanrogers.com/BE0732**

Maintained to very high standards, this site is set in a beautiful wooded valley bordering the Ourthe river. Open all year, the site is located on the outskirts of the attractive small town of La Roche-en-Ardenne, in an area understandably popular with tourists. The site is large with 587 grass pitches (min. 100 sq.m), of which 290 are for touring units. The pitches are on level ground and all have 10/16A electricity and water connections. Amenities on site include a well stocked shop, a bar, a restaurant and takeaway food. In the woods and rivers close by, there are plenty of opportunities for walking, mountain biking, rafting and canoeing. For children there is a large adventure playground and during the summer entertainment is organised. The Ardennes region is rightly proud of its cuisine in which game, taken from the forests that cover the area, is prominent; for those who really enjoy eating, a visit to a small restaurant should be planned. English, French, Dutch and German are spoken in reception.

Facilities

Six modern, well maintained sanitary blocks provide washbasins (open and in cabins), free preset showers. Facilities for disabled visitors. Baby room. Laundy facilities. Motorcaravan services. Well stocked shop. Bar, restaurant, snack bar and takeaway. At Camping Floréal 2: heated outdoor swimming pool. New wellness facilities with sauna and jacuzzi (1/4-15/10). Professional entertainment team (during local school holidays). Sports field. Volleyball. Tennis. Minigolf. Pétanque. Dog shower. WiFi. Mobile homes to rent. Off site: Mountain bike and canoe hire 300 m. Riding and bicycle hire 1 km.

Open: All year.

Directions

From E25/A26 take exit 50 and follow N89 southwest to La Roche. In La Roche follow signs for Houffalize (beside Ourthe river). Floréal Group Camping 1 is 1.5 km. along this road. Note: go to camping 1 not 2. GPS: 50.17600, 5.58600

Charges guide

Per unit incl. 2 persons	
and electricity	€ 17.05 - € 23.05
extra person	€ 3.60
child (3-11 yrs)	€ 2.60
dog (max. 1)	€ 3.25

Manhay
Camping Domaine Moulin de Malempré
Rue Moulin De Malempré No 1, B-6960 Manhay (Luxembourg) T: 086 455 504.
E: info@camping-malempre.be **alanrogers.com/BE0730**

This pleasant countryside site, very close to the E25, is well worth a visit and the owners will make you very welcome (English is spoken). The reception building houses the office and a small shop, above which is an attractive bar and restaurant with open fireplace. The 140 marked touring pitches are separated by small shrubs and gravel roads on sloping terrain. All have 10A electricity, 90 have water and drainage as well and the site is well lit. There is a little traffic noise from the nearby E25 (however it is not too intrusive).

Facilities

Modern toilet facilities include some washbasins in cubicles and family bathrooms on payment. The unisex unit can be heated and has a family shower room. Unit for disabled visitors. Baby room. Laundry. Motorcaravan services. Shop for basics. Baker calls daily. Bar, restaurant and takeaway (July/Aug and weekends). Heated swimming and children's pools (28/5-30/9). TV. Boules. Playground. WiFi over site (free). Off site: Riding 6 km.

Open: 1 March - 11 November.

Directions

From E25/A26 (Liege-Bastogne) exit 49. Turn onto N651 (southwest) towards Manhay. After 220 m. turn sharp left (east) towards Lierneux. Follow signs for Malempré and site. GPS: 50.29498, 5.72317

Charges guide

Per unit incl. 2 persons	
and electricity	€ 20.00 - € 30.00
extra person	€ 3.75

Neufchâteau

Camping Spineuse

Rue de Malome 7, B-6840 Neufchâteau (Luxembourg) T: 061 277 320. E: info@camping-spineuse.be
alanrogers.com/BE0675

This delightful Dutch owned site lies about 2 km. from the town centre. It is on low lying, level grass, bordered by a river, with trees and shrubs dotted around the 87 pitches. Seasonal units take just 14 pitches leaving 73 for touring units, all with 10/16A electricity. One corner of the site is particularly secluded, but the whole place has the feel of a peaceful garden. There is unfenced water on site and a footbridge over the river with no guard rails. The attractive main building houses reception, and a pleasant bar/bistro with a friendly, family atmosphere.

Facilities

Toilet facilities in the central building and in a new block (open mid May to Sept) are neat and clean with preset showers, open washbasins in main block, cubicles with shower and washbasin in new block. Very limited facilities for disabled campers (none for wheelchair users). Washing machine and dryer. Motorcaravan services. Small shop for basics (July/Aug). Bistro/bar and takeaway (April-Oct). Large inflatable pool (June-Sept). Tennis. Boules. Two playgrounds and playing field with volleyball court. Fishing. Mobile homes to rent. Free WiFi over part of site. Off site: Shops, bars and restaurants in Neufchâteau 2 km.

Open: All year.

Directions

Neufchâteau is just off E25/E411 (Luxembourg, Liège, Brussels) at exits 26-28. Site is 2 km. southwest of Neufchâteau on the N15 towards Florenville. There are three sites fairly close together, this is the last one on the left hand side. GPS: 49.83287, 5.41743

Charges guide

Per unit incl. 2 persons and electricity	€ 20.00
extra person	€ 3.50
child (0-6 yrs)	€ 2.00
dog	€ 1.25

Rendeux

Camping Floréal le Festival

89 route de la Roche, B-6987 Rendeux (Luxembourg) T: 084 477 371. E: camping.festival@florealgroup.be
alanrogers.com/BE0733

Floréal le Festival is a member of the Floréal group, attractively located in the wide wooded valley of the River Ourthe. There are 360 pitches here and the site is open all year. Pitches are of a good size and each is surrounded by hedges. Most have electrical connections. On-site amenities include a small supermarket, a bar (which also provides takeaway meals) and a restaurant. Sports amenities are good and include a football field, volleyball and tennis. Furthermore, the region is ideal for walking and mountain biking, and the site's managers will be pleased to recommend routes.

Facilities

Three traditional toilet blocks have washbasins (open and in cabins), free showers, baby bath and facilities for disabled visitors. Washing machines and dryers. Supermarket. Bar. Takeaway. Restaurant. Play area. Tennis. Volleyball. Football. Mobile homes for rent. WiFi. Off site: Walking and cycle tracks. Riding 500 m. Bicycle hire 1 km. Grottes de Hotton. La Roche-en-Ardennes.

Open: All year.

Directions

From Namur, head south on N4 as far as Marche-en-Famenne. Here, join westbound N86 to Hotton, then southbound N822 to Rendeux. From here follow signs to site. GPS: 50.22469, 5.52603

Charges guide

Per unit incl. 2 persons and electricity	€ 13.95 - € 19.90
extra person	€ 3.60

Tellin

Camping Parc la Clusure

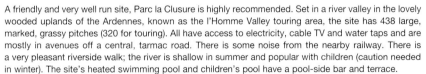

Chemin de la Clusure 30, B-6927 Bure-Tellin (Luxembourg) T: 084 360 050.
E: info@parclaclusure.be alanrogers.com/BE0670

A friendly and very well run site, Parc la Clusure is highly recommended. Set in a river valley in the lovely wooded uplands of the Ardennes, known as the l'Homme Valley touring area, the site has 438 large, marked, grassy pitches (320 for touring). All have access to electricity, cable TV and water taps and are mostly in avenues off a central, tarmac road. There is some noise from the nearby railway. There is a very pleasant riverside walk; the river is shallow in summer and popular with children (caution needed in winter). The site's heated swimming pool and children's pool have a pool-side bar and terrace.

Facilities

Three excellent sanitary units, one heated in winter, include some washbasins in cubicles, facilities for babies and children, and for disabled campers. Motorcaravan services. Well stocked shop, bar, restaurant, snack bar and takeaway (all Easter-1/11). Outdoor pools (1/5-13/9). Bicycle hire. Tennis. New playgrounds. Organised activity programme. Fishing (licence essential). WiFi over site (free). Barrier card deposit (€ 20). Max. 1 dog in July/Aug.

Open: All year.

Directions

Site is signed north at the roundabout off the N803 Rochefort-St Hubert road at Bure, 8 km. southeast of Rochefort. GPS: 50.09647, 5.2857

Charges guide

Per unit incl. 2 persons and electricity	€ 20.00 - € 37.00
extra person (over 2 yrs)	€ 4.00 - € 7.00
dog (max. 1)	€ 4.00 - € 5.00
Camping Cheques accepted.	

FREE Alan Rogers Travel Card
Extra benefits and savings - see page 12

Sainte Cécile
Camping de la Semois

Rue de Chassepierre 25, B-6820 Sainte Cécile (Luxembourg) T: 061 312 187.
E: info@campingdelasemois.be **alanrogers.com/BE0714**

La Semois is an attractive family site, located on the banks of the Semois river in the south of the Belgian Ardennes. This is a tranquil spot and an ideal base for walking, mountain biking and canoeing. The 110 touring pitches are grassy with good shade, but not always level. They are unmarked, but all have 10A electricity. Motorised vehicles are parked at the site entrance to create a tranquil and safe environment. A shallow brook runs through the site and forms a popular play area for children, along with a well equipped playground. The site is most suited to tents and small motorcaravans as the entry road is narrow and steep. Canoeing is very popular and the site owners rent out canoes and will undertake to collect canoeists from points along the river. Children will enjoy the mini-farm with donkeys, goats and Vietnamese pot-bellied pigs. Accommodation to rent on site includes three yurts, two teepees, two large Sahara tents, a Moroccan tent and a Romany-style caravan. There are three sanitary blocks, two of which are basic prefabricated units. The third unit is new and adjoins the reception/bar area. A pleasant terrace by the bar overlooks the site. The villages of Saints Cécile and Chassepierre are both within walking distance. Chassepierre has drawn many artists over the years, thanks to its Baroque church and attractive setting.

Facilities

Three sanitary buildings. Covered dishwashing area with hot water. Shop and bar (all season). Café/snack bar (July/Aug). Canoe hire. Play area. Trampoline. Children's farm. Games room. Activity programme. Accommodation to rent. Free WiFi in bar area. Off site: Villages of Chassepierre and Ste Cécile. Orval Monastery. Walking and cycling trails. Fishing. Riding 2 km. Sedan (Europe's largest castle) 28 km.

Open: 1 April - 1 October.

Directions

Approaching from Brussels (A4), take exit 23A and head for Transinne, Maissin and Paliseul on N899. Continue as far as Menuchenet and then take N89 to Bouillon. Beyond Bouillon take N83 to Florenville and Ste Cécile is 20 km. The site is well signed from here. GPS: 49.723073, 5.25625

Charges guide

Per unit incl. 2 persons and electricity	€ 21.00 - € 29.00
extra person	€ 4.00
child (3-17 yrs acc. to age)	€ 2.50 - € 3.50
dog (max. 1)	€ 2.50

Tel: 0032 - (0)61 312 187
info@campingdelasemois.be
www.campingdelasemois.be

Tintigny
Camping De Chênefleur

Norulle 16, B-6730 Tintigny (Luxembourg) T: 063 444 078. E: info@chenefleur.be
alanrogers.com/BE0715

Camping De Chênefleur is an excellent family run site situated beside the Semois river. With a total of 223 pitches (196 for touring), it would make an ideal site for a stopover or equally for a longer stay. It is attractively laid out in an informal, park-like style with 6A electricity available to all pitches. Some are separated by hedges, others are arranged in more open space and a few are available along the river bank. Fred Lemmers, the owner, has developed a generally peaceful and quiet environment with entertainment organised for children in high season.

Facilities

Two new fully refurbished sanitary blocks, one with facilities for children. Washing machine and dryer. Shop. Bar. Restaurant. Heated outdoor swimming pool (25/4-15/9). Two play areas with beach volleyball court. Full entertainment programme in season. Bicycle hire. Max. 2 dogs. WiFi (charged). Off site: Riding 17 km. Luxembourg City 40 km.

Open: 1 April - 1 October.

Directions

From Liège follow E25 towards Luxembourg and continue on E411. Take exit 29 Habay-La-Neuve and continue to Etalle. From Etalle follow N83 to Florenville. Drive through Tintigny and follow site signs. GPS: 49.68497, 5.52050

Charges guide

Per unit incl. 2 persons and electricity	€ 19.50 - € 32.00
extra person (over 3 yrs)	€ 4.00 - € 5.50
dog	€ 4.00 - € 5.00

Camping Cheques accepted.

For latest campsite news, availability and prices visit
alanrogers.com

Virton

Camping Colline de Rabais

Clos des Horles 1, B-6760 Virton (Luxembourg) T: 063 422 177. E: info@collinederabais.be

alanrogers.com/BE0710

Colline de Rabais is a large site on a hill top looking out over the surrounding wooded countryside. The Dutch owners offer a warm welcome and are slowly making improvements to the site while maintaining its relaxed atmosphere. There are around 217 pitches for touring units, all with 16A electricity (some long leads needed), plus 37 mobile homes and bungalows for rent and a few tour operator tents. Various activities are organised throughout the season. The adjacent forest is open to walkers and cyclists alike – you can just keep on going without seeing another person. The French border is only 10 km. to the south if you fancy a taste of France, whilst the Duchy of Luxembourg is about 30 km. to the east and its capital city is less than an hour's drive away. A similar distance to the northwest along country roads is the town of Bouillon, which has an interesting ruined castle and from where you can explore the green hillsides and valleys of the Ardennes and perhaps take a canoe trip along a section of meandering river.

Facilities	Directions
Three toilet blocks, one modernised with shower/washbasin cubicles and an en-suite room for disabled visitors. Cleaning and maintenance can be variable and not all blocks are open in low season. Washing machines and dryers. Shop (1/4-31/8). Bar/restaurant and takeaway (Apr-Oct). Small outdoor swimming pool (15/5-15/9) with wood decking for sunbathing. Bicycle hire. Free WiFi over site. Off site: Fishing 1 km. Shops, bars and restaurants in Virton 2 km. Riding 3 km.	Virton is 39 km. southwest of Arlon on E25/E411 Luxembourg-Brussels/Liège motorway. From exit 29 head for Virton. After Etalle, turn west for Vallée de Rabais, right at sports complex and at crossroads turn right up hill to site at end of road. From exit 31 take N82 for 22 km, then turn right for Vallée de Rabais and left to site. GPS: 49.58015, 5.54773

Open: All year.

Charges guide

Per unit incl. 2 persons	€ 18.50 - € 25.00
extra person (over 2 yrs)	€ 3.00 - € 4.50
dog	€ 4.00 - € 5.00

FREE Alan Rogers Travel Card
Extra benefits and savings - see page 12

CAPITAL: NAMUR

The province of Namur is known as The Land of the Valleys and visitors delight in its beautiful gardens, historic caves and two citadels.

The province is divided by the many waterways, including the Meuse, Lesse, Rocq, Semois, Samson and Sambre, which carve the landscape into a series of extraordinary valleys and feed its lush hillsides. Namur's legendary caves are both a testament to prehistoric times and a focus of more recent archaeological interest. The region is a paradise for nature lovers with its leafy forests, nature and animal parks, and evidence of the past in the form of medieval castles, monasteries and citadels.

The beautiful water gardens of the Château d'Annevoie are a 20-minute drive along the River Meuse, and there are many more parks and gardens: Frewr, Chevetogne, Bambois, where you can enjoy a relaxing stroll and admire the fauna. The Brasserie du Bocq in Purnode has been brewing beer since 1858, and visitors can sample a glass after their guided tour. The Meuse, whose banks are populated with local fishermen, meanders through hamlets of modest cottages and is shaded by dramatic overhanging rocks, while further downstream, heavy barges line the basins near the barrages.

Places of interest

Han-sur-Lesse: world famous caves, wild animal park and Museum of the Subterranean World.

Rochefort: Gallo-Roman villa Malagne, ruins of the Castle of the Counts, abbey brewery, two tourist trains.

Philippeville: star-shaped landscaped streets around a central square; 10 km. of subterranean passageways, some open to the public.

Dinant: citadel via cable-car, abbey, imposing rock and cave, La Merveilleuse.

Namur: citadel de Namur, home of L'Impériale mustard, textiles, several good museums.

Attractions

Vents d'Houyet: not-for-profit initiative with an educational programme at L'Académie du Vent (The Wind Academy), teaching children about the benefits of sustainable wind energy.

Architectural Route of Hamois, Natoye: use the superbly illustrated guide to discover the vernacular architecture of the Condroz region, by bicycle or by car.

Ciney: railroad Bocq, a museum tourist train linking the cities of Ciney and Yvoir (Purnode) via the Valley of Bocq, tributary of the Meuse.

Auvelais: weekend barge cruises on the Sambre.

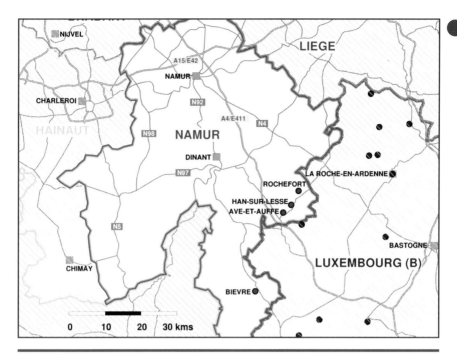

Ave-et-Auffe

Camping Le Roptai

Rue du Roptai 34, B-5580 Ave-et-Auffe (Namur) T: 084 388 319. E: info@leroptai.be

alanrogers.com/BE0850

This family site in the heart of the Ardennes, within easy reach of Dinant and Namur was established in 1932. In a rural wooded setting with its own adventure playground in the trees, it is a good site for an active holiday, especially in high season when there is a weekly programme, including rock climbing, abseiling, mountain biking and potholing. There are 108 good sized, grassy, touring pitches on sloping ground, most with 6A electricity. Other amenities include a swimming pool, a well stocked shop and a bar/snack bar. There are excellent footpaths around the site and the owner and staff will be pleased to recommend routes. The pretty little village of Ave is just 1 km. from le Roptai, and the larger village of Han-sur-Lesse is around 4 km. away. There is an evening market at Han, as well as world famous caves.

Facilities

Sanitary facilities include an excellent suite for babies and disabled visitors. Five other blocks of varying styles are kept clean and offer basic facilities. Shop, bar/snack bar with takeaway (all 1/7-31/8). Swimming pool and paddling pool (1/7-31/8). Play area. Activity programme (July/Aug). Bicycle hire. WiFi over part of site (charged). Mobile homes for rent. Off site: Fishing 6 km. Riding 10 km.

Open: 1 February - 31 December.

Directions

From E411 (Brussels-Luxembourg) motorway take exit 23 (Wellin-Han-sur-Lesse) and follow signs for Han-sur-Lesse. Continue 1 km. to Ave and turn left at the church, following signs to the site (1 km. further). GPS: 50.11128, 5.13376

Charges guide

Per unit incl. 2 persons
and electricity   € 25.00 - € 33.00

FREE Alan Rogers Travel Card
Extra benefits and savings - see page 12

Bièvre

Camping les 3 Sources

Rue de la Wiaule 20, B-5555 Bièvre (Namur) T: 061 730 051. E: info@3sources.be

alanrogers.com/BE0713

Les 3 Sources can be found between the pilgrimage village of Beauraing and Bouillon. The campsite is run by a Dutch family and is well located for exploring the Belgian Ardennes. The site boasts a number of springs, three of which feed some large ponds, which are well stocked with carp and other coarse fish. A small fee is charged for fishing, and this is used to fund the addition of fresh fish stock. The site extends over 2.5 hectares and has 150 pitches. A number of these are occupied by seasonal units, or by mobile homes, chalets and fully equipped tents (many available for rent).

Facilities

New sanitary building (with heating and air conditioning). Play area. Three fishing ponds (small charge). Activity and entertainment programme. Accommodation for rent. Off site: Supermarkets, shops and post office within 1 km. Cycle and mountain bike trails. Riding. Bison ranch 10 km. Caves of Han-sur-Lesse. Castles and fortresses.

Open: All year.

Directions

The campsite is close to N95, which runs parallel to the Brussels-Luxembourg motorway. Take the exit from N95 just north of Bièvre and the site is well signed. GPS: 49.944925, 5.011002

Charges guide

Per unit incl. 2 persons	
and electricity	€ 15.00 - € 19.00
extra person	€ 3.00 - € 4.00

Han-sur-Lesse

Camping le Pirot

Rue de Charleville, B-5580 Han-sur-Lesse (Namur) T: 084 377 280. E: han.tourisme@skynet.be

alanrogers.com/BE0860

Le Pirot is an attractive, rather basic site on an island in the River Lesse, on the edge of the pleasant village of Han. Because of the access, it is more suitable for small caravans, motorcaravans and tents. Camping de La Lesse, its sister site nearby, caters for larger units. Bars, restaurants and shops are within walking distance of both sites. There are just 18 grass pitches for touring units, 17 with electricity hook-ups, and two areas for tents. There are views across both branches of the river.

Facilities

A fairly old but characterful wooden building at the end of the camping area houses adequate sanitary facilities, including washbasins in cabins with hot and cold water and controllable showers. There are no facilities for disabled visitors, no chemical disposal and no on-site motorcaravan services. Communal barbecue area (no barbecues on pitches). Off site: Bicycle hire 200 m. Shops, bars, restaurants and small supermarket, 'tram safari', caves and museums all within walking distance.

Open: 1 April - 30 September.

Directions

Han is 55 km. southeast of Namur. From E411 Brussels - Luxembourg motorway take exit 23 (Wellin, Han-sur-Lesse) and follow signs for Han-sur-Lesse. Site is on left immediately before main river bridge. Camping de La Lesse is signed 100 m. further along on right. GPS: 50.125693, 5.186678

Charges guide

Per unit incl. 2 persons	
and electricity	€ 15.00 - € 17.00
extra person	€ 3.50 - € 4.00

Rochefort

Camping les Roches

Rue du Hableau, 26, B-5580 Rochefort (Namur) T: 084 211 900. E: campingrochefort@lesroches.be

alanrogers.com/BE0845

Camping les Roches has been recently renovated and can be found close to the centre of Rochefort, in the heart of the Ardennes. Despite its proximity to the town centre, this is a tranquil site, close to the large Parc des Roches. The 76 grassy touring pitches all have 16A electricity, water and drainage. They are of a good size on sloping ground. The adjacent tennis courts and municipal swimming pool are free to campers. During peak season, an entertainment team organises a range of activities for adults and children, including archery and accompanied cycle tours.

Facilities

Two modern, well maintained toilet blocks, heated when required, have washbasins in cabins and preset showers. Family room with shower, children's bath and WC. Excellent unit for disabled visitors. Bar with basic snacks (July/Aug). Games/TV room. Playground. Activity and entertainment programme (July/Aug). Free Internet access and WiFi (charged) in reception. Off site: Swimming pool and tennis (free). Minigolf. Bicycle hire, restaurants and shops in Rochefort 500 m. Caves at Han-sur-Lesse 6 km. Golf 20 km. Walking and cycle tracks.

Open: Easter - All Saints' week.

Directions

Rochefort is 50 km. southeast of Namur. From E411 motorway leave at exit 22 for Rochefort and continue east on N911 to Rochefort. Cross the river and take the first road on the left (rue au Bord de l'Eau) and follow signs to the site. GPS: 50.159585, 5.226185

Charges guide

Per unit incl. 2 persons	
and electricity	€ 22.50 - € 25.00
extra person	€ 4.00
child (4-11 yrs)	€ 3.00

For latest campsite news, availability and prices visit

alanrogers.com

CAPITAL: BRUGES

Belgium's only coastal province with 67 km. of coastline. In the west, the River IJzer meets the sea at Nieuwpoort, while the north is characterised by its flat polders and to the south lie the West Flemish hills.

Farming, fishing and bustling city centres; sea, hills and forest; industry and handicrafts, art and religion, gastronomy and provincial dishes – all are found in abundance in the land of contrasts that is the Westhoek region. The popular seaside town of De Panne is a coastal gem; its beach is the widest on the Flemish Coast and its many attractions are a magnet for visitors in high season. The region of the Leie marries a fascinating industrial heritage with contemporary living. Whether you prefer to cycle or walk, you can look forward to a world of discovery.

Oostende is a cosmopolitan city with a rich past where you can shop to your heart's content. It boasts a harbour and marina, international airport, numerous hotels, casino and busy nightlife. Sights include: the Earth Explorer science theme park, three-mast sailing ship, Mercator, Fort Napoleon, the Japanese Garden and James Ensor House. Bruges, one of the most beautiful cities in Europe, was classed as a UNESCO World Heritage Centre in 2000. As you weave your way along winding alleys and over romantic canals, it isn't difficult to imagine yourself here in medieval times.

Places of interest

Koekelare: the Fransmansmuseum about Belgian seasonal workers in France, and the Käthe Kollwitz gallery.

Het Zwin, Knokke-Heist: bird and nature reserve with unaccompanied or guided walks in the salt marshes.

The River Leie: 150 km. of navigable waterways meandering between Northern France and Gent, perfect for a cruise or a shorter trip by hired craft.

Castle of Loppem: neo-gothic monument with original architecture and interiors, features a rich art collection, a romantic park and a labyrinth.

Kortrijk: many monuments and historic buildings, including World Heritage Sites the Belfort and the Begijnhof; museums, parks, gardens and modern architecture.

Attractions

Boudewijn Seapark: zoo, dolphinarium and amusement park; seals, sea lions and birds of prey will keep you entertained.

Museum Constant Permeke, Jabbeke: more than 150 works by the great Flemish expressionist.

Butterfly Garden, Knokke-Zoute: 350 specimens of 35 different species of tropical butterflies, exhibited in their various life stages.

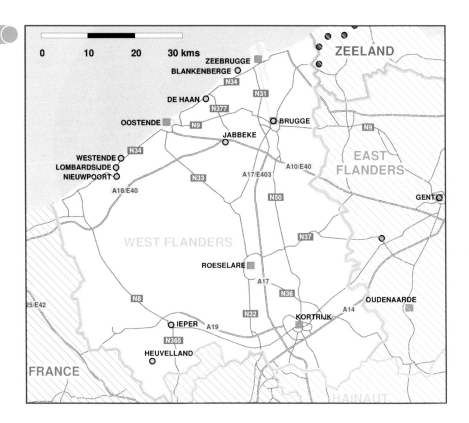

Blankenberge
Camping Bonanza 1

Zeebruggelaan 137, B-8370 Blankenberge (West Flanders) T: 050 416658. E: info@bonanza1.be

alanrogers.com/BE0546

Camping Bonanza 1 is a modern, family site within walking distance of a good beach, and close to the centre of the important resort of Blankenberge, home to Belgium's only sea pier. Pitches here are grassy and are generally without shade. All have 10A electrical connections. A separate area for tents is available at the rear of the site. The centrally located toilet blocks are well maintained (a small charge is made for hot showers). On-site amenities include the friendly Azura bar/bistro, with a terrace overlooking the well appointed playground for children.

Facilities

A clean and well maintained central sanitary unit has facilities for disabled visitors (key access). Laundry with washing machines and dryer. Motorcaravan services. Bar/bistro with varied menu and takeaway meals. Play areas. Pétanque. WiFi (charged). Off site: Supermarket 500 m. Sports centre 700 m. Fishing and covered swimming pool 900 m. Beach 20 mins. walk. Bruges 13 km. Hiking and cycle tracks.

Open: 27 March - 27 September.

Directions

From west (France) leave A10 motorway at exit 7 (Loppem), taking N397 towards Zedelgem and join N31 northbound. Continue to N371 exit (Blankenberge). Follow N371 and at second roundabout turn right on N335 (Zeebruggelaan). Site is east of Blankenberge town centre on Zeebruggelaan and is well signed.
GPS: 51.31168, 3.15354

Charges guide

Per unit incl. 2 persons and electricity	€ 29.00 - € 42.00
extra person	€ 5.50 - € 6.00
child (2-12 yrs)	€ 3.50 - € 4.00
dog	€ 4.00

For latest campsite news, availability and prices visit
alanrogers.com

Brugge
Camping Memling
Veltemweg 109, B-8310 Brugge (West Flanders) T: 050 355 845. E: info@campingmemling.be
alanrogers.com/BE0580

This traditional site is ideal for visiting Brugge (or Bruges). The 100 unmarked pitches (69 for touring units, 20 hardstanding) are on level grass, with gravel roads and trees and hedges providing some shade. Electricity (10A) is available to all pitches. There is a separate area for 40 tents. Bars, restaurants, local shops and supermarkets are within walking distance. Brugge itself has a network of cycle ways and for those on foot, a bus stops near the campsite and runs into the centre. Reservation in June, July and August is necessary. Visitors with large units should always telephone in advance to ensure an adequate pitch.

Facilities

A new toilet block provides washbasins (open and in cabins) and spacious showers. Laundry with washing machine and dryer. Bread can be ordered from reception. Small, rather old reception room with TV and piano. WiFi over site (charged). Dogs are not accepted in July/Aug. Off site: Municipal swimming pool (all year) and park nearby. Supermarkets 250 m. Bicycle hire and golf 2 km.

Open: All year.

Directions

From R30 Brugge ring road take exit 6 onto N9 towards Maldegem. At second set of traffic lights (opposite McDonald's), turn right, then immediately left. Site is 400 m. on right. GPS: 51.20692, 3.26294

Charges guide

Per unit incl. 2 persons	
and electricity	€ 21.60 - € 27.00
extra person	€ 5.00

De Haan
Camping Ter Duinen
Wenduinesesteenweg 143, B-8420 De Haan (West Flanders) T: 050 413 593. E: info@campingterduinen.be
alanrogers.com/BE0578

Ter Duinen is a large, seaside holiday site with 120 touring pitches and over 700 privately owned static holiday caravans. The pitches are laid out in straight lines with tarmac access roads and the site has three immaculate toilet blocks. Other than a bar and a playing field, the site has little else to offer, but it is only a 600 m. walk to the sea and next door to the site is a large sports complex with a sub-tropical pool and several sporting facilities. Opportunities for riding and golf (18-hole course) are close by. It is possible to hire bicycles in the town. Access to the beach is via a good woodland footpath. There is a main road and tramway to cross, but there are designated pedestrian crossings. Cycling is very popular in this area and there are numerous good cycle paths, including one into the centre of De Haan (1.5 km). The best places to visit for a day trip are Ostend with the Atlantic Wall from WWII, Knokke (which holds many summer festivals) and Bruges.

Facilities

Three modern toilet blocks have good fittings, washbasins in cubicles (hot and cold water) and showers (€ 1.20). Baby bath. Facilities for disabled visitors. Laundry facilities with two washing machines and a dryer, irons and ironing boards. Motorcaravan services. Shop. Snack bar and takeaway. Internet room (charged). Off site: Bicycle hire and sea with sandy beach 600 m. Riding 1 km. Golf 3 km. Boat launching 6 km. A bus for Bruges stops 200 m. from the site, a tram for the coast 400 m.

Open: 15 March - 15 October.

Directions

On E40/A10 in either direction take exit 6 (De Haan, Jabbeke). Follow N377 towards Haan-Bredene, at roundabout go towards Vlissegem. After 4 km. go straight on at junction. Turn right after a further 1.5 km. Site is in 750 m. GPS: 51.28318, 3.05753

Charges guide

Per unit incl. 4 persons	
and electricity	€ 19.00 - € 28.00
extra person	€ 3.50
child (under 10 yrs)	€ 3.00

Camping Cheques accepted.

FREE Alan Rogers Travel Card
Extra benefits and savings - see page 12

Heuvelland

Camping Ypra

Pingelaarstraat 2, Kemmel, B-8956 Heuvelland (West Flanders) T: 057 444631. E: camping.ypra@skynet.be

alanrogers.com/BE0573

This is a peaceful, rural site less than a kilometre walk from a pretty Flemish village with cafés, bars, shops and a tourist information office. The site extends up the slopes of Kemmelberg, the highest point in West Flanders. The 230 seasonal pitches are on the upper part of the site, while 50 grass touring pitches are by the site entrance on firm, level ground. There are an additional 20 hardstandings for motorcaravans, and a separate tent field. All the pitches have 6A electric hook-up available. English, Dutch, French and German are spoken.

Facilities

The sanitary facilities are located in five traditional blocks across the site (two can be heated) and have modern showers and toilets. Those by the touring area have facilities for disabled campers. Laundry with washing machines and dryers. Shop for basics. Bar and snack bar. Minigolf. Fishing. Tennis courts. Play area. Children's entertainment (July/Aug). WiFi. Off site: Bus stop at site entrance for Ieper and Poperinge. Kemmel village with banks, shops, cafés and restaurants 1 km. Bicycle hire 1 km. Riding 5 km. Walking and cycling.

Open: 1 March - 30 November.

Directions

From N33 Poperinge bypass turn south onto N304 at roundabout (Reningelst). Pass through Reningelst and Klyte towards Kemmel. Turn right at site sign at edge of Kemmel. GPS: 50.78477, 2.81958

Charges guide

Per unit incl. 2 persons and electricity	€ 22.00
extra person	€ 4.00
child (4-12 yrs)	€ 1.90
dog	€ 1.90

Ieper

Camping Jeugdstadion

Bolwerkstraat 1, B-8900 Ieper (West Flanders) T: 057 217 282. E: info@jeugdstadion.be

alanrogers.com/BE0570

Camping Jeugdstadion is a small municipal site that has had a substantial facelift in recent years. It is well maintained, clean and neat, and has 40 touring pitches, 18 of which are hardstands, all with 10A electricity, plus a separate grassy area for 70 tents. The site entrance barrier links to the automated booking system, so even when there are no staff on site, it is still possible to gain access at the 24-hour reception. This also allows all-year use by motorcaravans.

Facilities

The heated sanitary block has some washbasins in cubicles and free hot showers. One toilet for disabled campers. Three sinks for dishwashing outside. Motorcaravan services. Bicycle hire. Free WiFi in reception. Off site: Sports complex adjacent. Indoor and outdoor swimming pools 500 m. Very large comprehensive playground. Minigolf. During school holidays these facilities are extensively used by local children and can therefore be fairly busy and lively.

Open: 1 March - 12 November.

Directions

From N336 (Lille) at roundabout by Lille Gate, turn left on Picanolaan and first right into Leopold III Laan. Jeugdstadion entrance is on right. Use roadside parking and book in at the Kantine inside the gates. Alternatively go to the vehicle gate and walk through site to reception. GPS: 50.84682, 2.89748

Charges guide

Per unit incl. 2 persons and electricity	€ 18.00 - € 27.00
extra person	€ 4.00
child (6-12 yrs)	€ 2.50
dog	€ 1.00

For latest campsite news, availability and prices visit
alanrogers.com

Jabbeke

Recreatiepark Klein Strand

Varsenareweg 29, B-8490 Jabbeke (West Flanders) T: 050 811 440. E: info@kleinstrand.be

alanrogers.com/BE0555

In a convenient location just off the A10 motorway and close to Bruges, this site is in two distinct areas divided by an access road. The main part of the site offers a lake with a marked off swimming area, a sandy beach, water slides and boating (no fishing). The touring section has 137 large pitches on flat grass separated by well trimmed hedges; all have electricity and access to water and drainage. Some leisure facilities for children are provided on this part of the site, along with a spacious bar and snack bar with takeaway (seasonal). The main site with all the privately owned mobile homes is closer to the lake, so has most of the amenities. These include the main reception building, restaurants, bar, minimarket, and sports facilities. This is a family holiday site and offers a comprehensive programme of activities and entertainment in July and August. Klein Strand is an ideal base from which to visit Bruges (by bus, every 20 minutes) and Ghent (by train from Bruges).

Facilities	Directions
Single modern, heated, toilet block with good sized showers (charged) and vanity style washbasins. Baby room. Basic facilities for disabled campers. Laundry facilities. Additional toilet facilities with washbasins in cubicles behind touring field reception (open July/Aug). Motorcaravan services. Bar and snack bar. Play area. Fun pool for small children. In main park: European and Chinese restaurants, bar and snack bar, takeaways. Shop (Easter-end Aug). Tennis. Sports field. Water ski school; water ski shows (Sundays in July/Aug). Bicycle hire. WiFi.	Jabbeke is 12 km. southwest of Bruges. From A18/A10 motorways, take exit 6/6B (Jabbeke). At roundabout take first exit. In 650 m. on left-hand bend, turn left to site in 600 m. Main reception is on left but in high season continue to touring site on right in 200 m. GPS: 51.18448, 3.10445

Open: All year.

Charges guide

Per unit incl. up to 4 persons and electricity	€ 22.00 - € 39.00
dog	€ 2.00

DON'T LOOK ANY FURTHER
LARGE PITCHES, ALL FACILITIES!

Klein Strand

IN THE MIDDLE OF EVERYWHERE!
Varsenareweg 29, Jabbeke
only 9 km from Bruges (good bus connection)
near Ostend, Ypres & Ghent
www.kleinstrand.be

He likes Klein Strand, so will you!

Lombardsijde

Camping De Lombarde

Elisabethlaan 4, B-8434 Lombardsijde Middelkerke (West Flanders) T: 058 236 839. E: info@delombarde.be

alanrogers.com/BE0560

De Lombarde is a spacious, good value holiday site between Lombardsijde and the coast. It has a pleasant atmosphere and modern buildings. The 380 pitches (150 for touring) are set out in level, grassy bays surrounded by shrubs, all with 16A electricity, long leads may be needed. Vehicles are parked in separate car parks. There are many seasonal units and 21 holiday homes, leaving 170 touring pitches. There is a range of activities and an entertainment programme in season. This is a popular holiday area and the site becomes full at peak times. A pleasant stroll of one kilometre takes you into Lombardsijde. There is a tram service from near the site entrance to the town and the beach.

Facilities	Directions
Three heated sanitary units are of an acceptable standard, with some washbasins in cubicles. Facilities for disabled visitors. Large laundry. Motorcaravan services. Shop, restaurant/bar and takeaway (1/4-31/8 and school holidays). Tennis. Boules. Fishing lake. TV lounge. Entertainment programme for children. Outdoor fitness equipment. Playground. WiFi in bar. ATM. Torch useful.	From Westende, follow tramlines. From traffic lights in Lombardsijde, turn left following tramlines into Zeelaan. Proceed to crossroads and tram stop, turn left into Elisabethlaan. Site is on right after 200 m. GPS: 51.15644, 2.75329

Open: All year.

Charges guide

Per unit incl. 1-6 persons and electricity	€ 18.40 - € 33.20
No credit cards.	

Nieuwpoort

Kompas Camping Nieuwpoort

Brugsesteenweg 49, B-8620 Nieuwpoort (West Flanders) T: 058 236 037.
E: nieuwpoort@kompascamping.be **alanrogers.com/BE0550**

Not far from Dunkerque and Calais and convenient for the A18 motorway, this large, well equipped and well run site with 1056 pitches caters particularly for families. There are many amenities including a heated pool complex, a range of sporting activities, play areas and a children's farm. The 469 touring pitches, all with 10A electricity, are in regular rows on flat grass in various parts of the site; 120 also have a water point and waste water drainage. With many seasonal units and caravan holiday homes, the site becomes full during Belgian holidays and in July and August. A network of footpaths links all areas of the site. Gates to the rear lead to a reservoir reserved for sailing, windsurfing and canoeing (canoes for hire) during certain hours only. Although the site is vast, there is a sense of spaciousness thanks to the broad stretch of landscaped leisure areas. The site is well fenced with a card-operated barrier and a night guard. The area is a paradise for cyclists with access to over 200 km. of cycle-friendly routes.

Facilities

Five modern, clean and well maintained toilet blocks include washbasins in cubicles, controllable showers and excellent facilities for families, young children and disabled visitors. Laundry facilities. Motorcaravan services. Supermarket, bakery, restaurant, takeaway and café/bar (all daily, w/ends low season). Swimming pools (heated and supervised) with slide, paddling pool and pool games (17/5-14/9). Bicycle hire. Tennis. Extensive adventure playgrounds. Multisports court. Entertainment programme in July/Aug. WiFi over site (charged).

Open: 28 March - 12 November.

Directions

From Dunkerque on A18 (E40) take exit 3. At roundabout take fourth exit (small road). At junction turn left on N356. At T-junction, turn right on N367. Site is in 300 m. GPS: 51.12965, 2.77222

Charges guide

Per unit incl. 4 persons and electricity	€ 25.90 - € 39.90
dog	€ 2.90
Largest unit accepted 2.5x8 m.	

Camping Cheques accepted.

Amidst Flanders battlefields and significant sites and monuments of the Great War

BELGIAN COAST　　　　　WESTENDE • NIEUWPOORT　　KOMPAS Camping

TEL. WESTENDE: +32 (0)58-22 30 25
TEL. NIEUWPOORT: +32 (0)58-23 60 37　　　HOLIDAY ... EXPERIENCE IT AT KOMPAS CAMPING

W W W . K O M P A S C A M P I N G . B E

Westende

Kompas Camping Westende

Bassevillestraat 141, B-8434 Westende (West Flanders) T: 058 223 025. E: westende@kompascamping.be
alanrogers.com/BE0565

Camping Westende is a large holiday site near the sea. The beach is only a short walk away and there is easy access to the coastal tram service. Of the 435 pitches, half are taken by seasonal caravans plus 43 rental units, leaving some 100 touring pitches on grass with 10A electricity, plus a group of 77 large (150 sq.m) serviced pitches with water and electricity. The site is well cared for with a range of amenities for children, including a play barn. The shop, bar and restaurant are grouped around reception. One end of the site is leased to a firm providing rental accommodation in mobile homes. Adjacent are a large holiday rental complex and a barrier operated motorcaravan area. Ostend is only 15 km. away and offers a wide variety of activities. There is easy access to the cycle path network.

Facilities

Four toilet blocks are modern, recently renovated and very clean. One block is due for refurbishment. Good facilities for children and disabled visitors in one block. Shop, bar, restaurant and takeaway (high season and w/ends). Adventure playground. Play barn. Sports area. Boules. Entertainment and activities programme for children (July/Aug). Bicycle hire. WiFi throughout (charged).

Open: 28 March - 11 November.

Directions

From the E40 take exit 4 to Middelkerke (3-4 km). At the church turn left on N318 to Westende. After Westende church take the fourth turn right to the site (signed). GPS: 51.15787, 2.7606

Charges guide

Per unit incl. 4 persons and electricity	€ 25.90 - € 39.90

Camping Cheques accepted.

For latest campsite news, availability and prices visit
alanrogers.com

CAPITAL: LUXEMBOURG CITY

Tourist Office

Luxembourg Tourist Office
122 Regent Street, London W1B 5SA
Tel: 020 7434 2800
Fax: 020 7734 1205
Email: tourism@luxembourg.co.uk
Internet: www.luxembourg.co.uk

The Grand Duchy of Luxembourg is a sovereign state, lying between Belgium, France and Germany. Divided into two areas, the spectacular Ardennes region in the north and the rolling farmlands and woodland in the south, it is bordered on the east by the wine growing area of the Moselle Valley.

From wherever you are in Luxembourg, you are always within easy reach of the capital, Luxembourg-Ville, home to about one fifth of the population. The city was built upon a rocky outcrop, and has superb views of the Alzette and Petrusse Valleys. Those who love the great outdoors must make a visit to the Ardennes, with its hiking trails, footpaths and cycle routes that take you through beautiful winding valleys and across deep rivers, a very popular region for visitors. If wine tasting takes your fancy, then head for the Moselle Valley, particularly if you like sweet, fruity wines. From late spring to early autumn, wine tasting tours take place in cellars and caves. The Mullerthal region, known as the 'Little Switzerland', lies on the banks of the River Sûre. The earth is mostly made up of soft sandstone, so through the ages many fascinating gorges, caves and formations have emerged.

Population

537,000

Climate

A temperate climate prevails, the summer often extending from May to late October.

Language

Letzeburgesch is the national language, with French and German also being official languages.

Telephone

The country code is 00 352.

Money

Currency: The Euro
Banks: Mon-Fri 08.30/09.00-12.00 and 13.30-16.30.

Shops

Mon 14.00-18.30. Tues to Sat 08.30-12.00 and 14.00-18.30 (grocers and butchers at 15.00 on Sat).

Public Holidays

New Year; Carnival Day mid-Feb; Easter Mon; May Day; Ascension; Whit Mon; National Day 23 June; Assumption 15 Aug; Kermesse 1 Sept; All Saints; All Souls; Christmas 25, 26 Dec.

Motoring

Many holidaymakers travel through Luxembourg to take advantage of the lower fuel prices, thus creating traffic congestion at petrol stations, especially in summer. A Blue Zone area exists in Luxembourg City and various parts of the country (discs from tourist offices) but meters are also used.

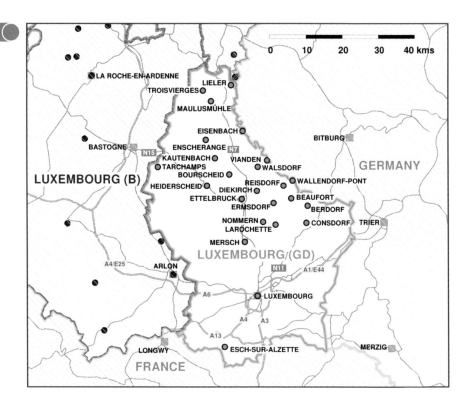

Beaufort

Camping Plage Beaufort

87 Grand-Rue, L-6310 Beaufort T: 836 099 300. E: camplage@pt.lu

alanrogers.com/LU7840

Plage Beaufort is an all-year-round site run by the Syndicat d'Initiative et du Tourisme. It is a little off the main tourist route but there is some nice countryside in the area known as Little Switzerland. The site has 312 pitches, 109 of which are taken by privately owned mobile homes and chalets, leaving around 200 for touring units. The terrain is undulating with some terracing and some pitches are hidden away in quiet corners. Pitch sizes do vary but all have 10A electricity. In summer the area provides for cycling, tennis and other sporting facilities, with the main attraction of the site being the excellent municipal swimming pool adjacent (included in price).

Facilities	Directions
Four toilet blocks, some heated, provide an interesting mix of facilities with baby room and facilities for disabled visitors. All are spotlessly clean. Motorcaravan services. Recycling. Snack bar. Several small basic playgrounds. Bicycle hire. Internet access. Off site: Municipal swimming pool adjacent. The village has a variety of shops, and a 'buvette' serves food and drink, just outside at the far end of the site. Fishing 4 km. Golf and riding 10 km.	Beaufort is midway between Diekirch and Echternach. From Reisdorf take CR128 for 5 km. and site is north of town centre, opposite the pharmacy. GPS: 49.8399, 6.28945

Open: All year.

Charges guide

Per unit incl. 2 persons and electricity	€ 18.00 - € 22.50
extra person (from 4 yrs)	€ 5.50
dog	€ 3.00

For latest campsite news, availability and prices visit

alanrogers.com

Berdorf

Camping Bon Repos

39 rue de Consdorf, L-6551 Berdorf T: 790 631. E: irma@bonrepos.lu

alanrogers.com/LU7820

In the Petite Suisse region of Luxembourg, an area of limestone gorges which is popular with climbers and hikers, this attractive and peaceful family run site would make a good base from which to explore the eastern side of this tiny country. Located at the edge of the village of Berdorf, the site is gently sloping, with a central tarmac roadway. The 56 pitches for touring are mostly arranged in bays of four, each on a small terrace, and all have a 16A electric hook-up. Most are fairly open, a few have a little shade. A separate area is provided for tents. The tourist town of Echternach is just 6 km. away.

Facilities	Directions
Modern and clean main sanitary building provides all the usual facilities. Smaller unit (without showers) by the tent field. Both units can be heated. Further en-suite unit. Reception (open 09.30-10.00, 19.00-20.00) sells wine, beer and soft drinks. TV and games room. Playground. Baker calls. Gas supplies. Dogs are not accepted. WiFi. Off site: Hotels for drinks and meals, and municipal sports complex with indoor swimming pool are a few minutes walk away. Bus stop 100 m. Supermarket 5 km.	Berdorf is 6 km. west of Echternach, the site is signed from village centre towards Consdorf. The entrance is just after a left-hand bend, take care. GPS: 49.819486, 6.347491

Open: 1 April - 7 November.

Charges guide

Per unit incl. 2 persons and electricity	€ 20.80
extra person	€ 6.00
child (3-13 yrs)	€ 2.00

10% reduction for pitch and adults in low season.

Bourscheid

Camping Um Gritt Castlegarden

Buurschtermillen 10, L-9164 Bourscheid T: 990 449. E: umgritt@castlegarden.lu

alanrogers.com/LU7930

Camping Um Gritt is a family run campsite with friendly Dutch owners. It is located at the foot of a castle in the heart of the Ardennes, in the beautiful wooded valley of Bourscheid. It has a long season, open from April until the end of October. There are 98 reasonably level, unmarked pitches, many with little shade, including about 40 long stay pitches. All have 16A Europlug. They are laid out in a sunny, grassy meadow along the banks of the shallow River Sûre. This is an ideal place to cool off on a hot day, bathing, fishing, messing around in small boats or having a drink in the small bar/restaurant.

Facilities	Directions
There are five modern toilet blocks with all necessary facilities. Washing machine and dryer. Bread delivery. Small bar, restaurant and takeaway. Club for children and some family entertainment (July/Aug). Small playground. Volleyball. Mountain bike hire. Walking and hiking maps. WiFi throughout (charged). Off site: Lake swimming 20 minutes. Paragliding from 'point de vue Gringlay', organised from the site. Tennis and canoeing close by. Supermarket 10 mins walk. Railway station approx. 4 km.	From Ettelbruck, take N7. At roundabout take 2nd exit onto N27. Turn left onto CR308. Follow signs to Bourscheid Moulin. Cross over bridge and site is signed to left. Follow co-ordinates, not address or postcode. GPS: 49.91015, 6.08635

Open: 1 April - 31 October.

Charges guide

Per unit incl. 2 persons and electricity	€ 18.50 - € 22.50
extra person	€ 4.00 - € 5.00
child (3-14 yrs)	€ 2.00 - € 2.50

Consdorf

Camping la Pinède

33 rue Burgkapp, L-6211 Consdorf T: 790 271. E: sit.consdorf@internet.lu

alanrogers.com/LU7630

La Pinède is a pleasant municipal site in the Mullerthal region, situated adjacent to the municipal sports field. The site provides 110 individual, hedged, grassy spaces for touring units, all with 10A electricity, plus 39 pitches housing static units. There is no shop on site but all necessary shops and services are in the town within walking distance. A baker calls Monday to Saturday (not on Wednesday in low season). The immediate area is popular for cycling and hiking and the River Moselle and vineyards are an easy day trip by car. Guided walks are organised in high season.

Facilities	Directions
Sanitary facilities provide washbasins and showers in a building which can be heated in cool weather. A further small, modern unit is situated at the far end of the site. Extra facilities are to the rear of the bar. Gas supplies. Café/bar. Small adventure-style playground. Minigolf. Tennis. Football field. Bicycle hire. Internet access. Off site: Golf 6 km. Fishing 9 km. Echternach 10 km.	Consdorf is southwest of Echternach. From N14 Diekirch-Grevenmacher, turn left onto CR121 signed Consdorf. Site is in the town centre near sports stadium (well signed). GPS: 49.780873, 6.332062

Open: 15 March - 15 November.

Charges guide

Per unit incl. 2 persons and electricity	€ 18.70
extra person	€ 4.90
child	€ 2.50

FREE Alan Rogers Travel Card
Extra benefits and savings - see page 12

Diekirch
Camping Bleesbrück

Bleesbrück 1, L-9359 Diekirch T: 803 134. E: info@camping-bleesbruck.lu
alanrogers.com/LU7730

Camping Bleesbrück a family run site, is centrally located in rolling countryside, ideal for exploring the Ardennes and the Eifel. The surrounding farmland and forests lie within the Our, a natural park which can be explored on foot or by bicycle. The main site is enclosed by trees and offers 144 shaded and unshaded touring pitches with electricity (10A). There is a separate 30-pitch naturist area, screened off at the far end of the main site. The Blees flows past and offers opportunities for the angler. Entertainment is available for adults and children. Both electric and standard bicycles can be hired on site, and guided walks and cycle routes run past the site.

Facilities

Two sanitary units, one a separate unit for the naturist site, include washbasins in cabins, baby room and facilities with access for disabled visitors. Washing machine and dryer. Motorcaravan services. Bar. Terraced restaurant (seats 60). Takeaway (snacks). TV and games room. Sports field. Large playground. Outdoor table football. Fishing. Bicycle and E-bike hire. Accommodation includes huts, mobile homes, apartments and chalets. WiFi (charged). Off site: Shop and petrol station at entrance.

Open: 1 April - 15 October.

Directions

Via Belgium: Bastogne-N15 towards Ettelbrück-Diekirch-Bleesbruck. The site is located between Diekirch and Vianden. The entrance is beside the Q8/GULF petrol station (roundabout). GPS: 49.87286, 6.18923

Charges guide

Per unit incl. 2 persons and electricity	€ 22.30
dog	€ 2.60

Diekirch
Camping de la Sûre

Route de Gilsdorf, L-9234 Diekirch T: 809 425. E: tourisme@diekirch.lu
alanrogers.com/LU7870

The municipal Camping de la Sûre is within walking distance of the centre of Diekirch, a town that is brimming with things to see and do. Located on the banks of the Sûre, this site offers 204 flat grass pitches, of which 175 are for touring, most with 10A electricity. One large building close to the entrance houses the reception and excellent sanitary facilities, all of which were in pristine condition at the time of our visit. A path for walking and cycling runs alongside the campsite; maps are available in the Syndicat d'Initiative (Tourist Office) in the town centre. Diekirch, with its modern and ancient history, including recently discovered Roman remains, is well worth a visit.

Facilities

Heated modern facilities including showers and communal washbasins. Baby room and suite for disabled visitors. Laundry. New reception area. Bar and snack bar. Large play area. Children's entertainment (July/Aug). Boules. Fishing. Bicycle hire. WiFi in bar. Off site: Diekirch has all leisure facilities within walking distance of site.

Open: 17 March - 18 December.

Directions

Follow signs (official camping signs, not site name) from centre of Diekirch. GPS: 49.86602, 6.16477

Charges guide

Per unit incl. 2 persons and electricity	€ 19.50
extra person	€ 6.00
child (3-14 yrs)	€ 2.25
dog	€ 2.00

Eisenbach
Camping Kohnenhof

Kounenhaff 1, L-9838 Eisenbach T: 929 464. E: kohnenhof@pt.lu
alanrogers.com/LU7680

Nestling in a valley with the River Our running through it, Camping Kohnenhof offers a very agreeable location for a relaxing family holiday. From the minute you stop at the reception you are assured of a warm and friendly welcome. There are 105 pitches, 80 for touring, all with 6/16A electricity. Numerous paths cross through the wooded hillside so this could be a haven for walkers. A little bridge crosses the small river over the border to Germany. The river is shallow and safe for children (parental supervision essential). A large sports field and play area with a selection of equipment caters for younger campers.

Facilities

Heated sanitary block with showers and washbasins in cabins. Facilities for disabled visitors. Motorcaravan services. Laundry. Bar, restaurant, takeaway (open all season). Baker calls daily. TV room. Sports field with play equipment. Boules. Bicycle hire. Golf weeks. Discounts on six local 18-hole golf courses. WiFi over site.

Open: 1 April - 31 October.

Directions

Take N7 north from Diekirch. At Hosingen, turn right onto the narrow and winding CR324 signed Eisenbach. Follow site signs from Eisenbach or Obereisenbach. GPS: 50.01602, 6.13600

Charges guide

Per unit incl. 2 persons and electricity	€ 19.90 - € 29.90
extra person	€ 5.00
Camping Cheques accepted.	

For latest campsite news, availability and prices visit
alanrogers.com

Enscherange

Camping Val d'Or

Um Gaertchen 2, L-9747 Enscherange T: 920 691. E: valdor@pt.lu

alanrogers.com/LU7770

Camping Val d'Or is one of those small, family run, countryside sites where you easily find yourself staying longer than planned. Set in four hectares of lush meadowland under a scattering of trees, the site is divided into two by the tree-lined Clerve river as it winds its way slowly through the site. A footbridge goes some way to joining the site together and there are two entrances for vehicles. There are 76 marked, level grass touring pitches, all with electricity (6A Europlug) and with some tree shade. Cars are parked away from the pitches. There are open views of the surrounding countryside with its wooded hills. The site's Dutch owners speak good English. Credit cards are not accepted.

Facilities

Next to the reception is a heated sanitary block where some facilities are found, others including some showers are located under cover, outside. Showers are token operated. Laundry room. Gas supplies. Bar (all day in high season). Takeaway (high season except Sundays). Swimming and paddling in river. Three play areas (one with waterways, waterwheel and small pool). Bicycle hire. WiFi (free). Max. 1 dog. Off site: Fishing and golf 10 km.

Open: 29 March - 1 November.

Directions

From A26/E25 (Liège - Luxembourg) take exit 54 to Bastogne, then N84/N15 (Diekirch) for 15 km. At crossroads left towards Wiltz following signs for Clervaux. Go via Wiltz into Weidingen, 500 m. after VW garage turn right on Wilderwiltz rd. In Wilderwiltz follow signs for Enscherange then site signs. GPS: 50.00017, 5.99106

Charges guide

Per unit incl. 2 persons and electricity	€ 16.00 - € 22.00

Ermsdorf

Camping Neumuhle

Reisdorferstrasse 27, L-9366 Ermsdorf T: 879 391. E: info@camping-neumuhle.lu

alanrogers.com/LU7810

Camping Neumuhle is located at Ermsdorf, at the heart of Luxembourg close to Diekirch. It is surrounded by the Mullerthal and some delightful countryside, known as Little Switzerland. Pitches here are spacious and all have electricity. This is great walking country and the long-distance hiking track GR5 (North Sea-Riviera) passes close to the site. Walking maps are available for loan at reception. There are 85 touring pitches all with 6A electricity and 20 chalets to rent. The site is terraced with level grass pitches separated by small hedges. The restaurant and covered terrace overlook the swimming pool and a small shop sells all basic provisions. Other on-site amenities include a large adventure playground.

Facilities

The central sanitary block is modern and clean, but has no facilities for disabled visitors. Shop (July/Aug). Restaurant with covered terrace and snack bar. Takeaway (July/Aug). Swimming pool (May-Aug). Boules. Adventure play area. Entertainment and activity programme. Kids' club (July/Aug). Bicycle hire. WiFi over site (charged).

Open: 15 March - 31 October.

Directions

Ermsdorf is northeast of the city of Luxembourg. From Diekirch, head south on CR356 and site is well signed from Ermsdorf. From Reisdorf follow Ermsdorf road. Site is before village. GPS: 49.8391, 6.225

Charges guide

Per unit incl. 2 persons and electricity	€ 19.75
extra person	€ 5.50

Esch-sur-Alzette

Camping Gaalgebierg

Boite Postale 20, L-4001 Esch-sur-Alzette T: 541 069. E: gaalcamp@pt.lu

alanrogers.com/LU7700

Occupying an elevated position on the edge of town, near the French border, this site is run by the local camping and caravan club. On a hilltop and with a good variety of trees, most pitches have shade. Of the 150 grass pitches marked out by trees, 100 are for tourers, the remainder being occupied by seasonal units. There are some gravel pitches set aside for one night stays, plus four all-weather pitches for motorcaravans. All pitches have 16A electricity and TV points.

Facilities

The toilet block can be heated and has some washbasins in cubicles, hot showers and separate facilities for babies and disabled visitors. Laundry. Key-card entry system. Motorcaravan services. Gas available. Small bar, snack bar and takeaway (all year; on demand in low season). Playground. Bicycle hire. Boules. Entertainment and activity programme in high season. WiFi over site (charged). Off site: Restaurant within walking distance. Shops, bars and restaurants in Esch 2 km.

Open: All year.

Directions

Esch is 18 km. southwest of Luxembourg City. Site is signed from centre of town. From motorways take exit 5 for Esch Centre, turn left (Schifflange) at T-junction in 1 km. to avoid town centre then right after railway crossing, ahead at traffic lights and follow signs to site. GPS: 49.48492, 5.98657

Charges guide

Per unit incl. 2 persons and electricity	€ 14.95 - € 33.25
extra person	€ 2.80 - € 4.00

FREE Alan Rogers Travel Card
Extra benefits and savings - see page 12

Ettelbruck

Camping Ettelbruck

88, Chemin du Camping 88, L-9022 Ettelbruck T: 812 185. E: ellen.ringelberg@gmx.de

alanrogers.com/LU7910

This agreeable, good value municipal site is situated on a hilltop overlooking the town. It is quietly located about 1 km. from the centre of Ettelbruck, with a nice atmosphere and well tended gardens and grass. The modern main building includes reception, an excellent restaurant and a 'salle de séjour' (with library and TV). The 136 marked pitches, 130 for touring, are accessed from tarmac roads and have electricity available (16A). Reception provides good tourist information and English is spoken. There is a welcome cup of coffee on arrival.

Facilities

A new sanitary unit using solar energy provides washbasins in cabins and hot showers. Provision for disabled campers. Laundry. Dishwasher. Motorcaravan services. Restaurant. Snack bar and takeaway (evenings). Breakfasts can also be served. Baker calls daily at 09.00 (order day before). Playground. Entertainment in season. Daily baking session for children and afternoon tea twice a week for parents. Electric car hire. WiFi (charged).

Open: 1 April - 15 October.

Directions

Site is signed on the western outskirts of Ettelbruck off the N15 and approached via a short one-way system. GPS: 49.846073, 6.082022

Charges guide

Per unit incl. 2 persons and electricity	€ 26.40
extra person	€ 7.50
child (8-12 yrs)	€ 3.50

Heiderscheid

Camping Fuussekaul

4 Fuussekaul, L-9156 Heiderscheid T: 268 8881. E: info@fuussekaul.lu

alanrogers.com/LU7850

This site lies in the rolling wooded hills of central Luxembourg, not far from the lakes of the Sûre river dam. Of the 370 pitches, 220 of varying sizes are for touring units, all have 6/16A electricity connection. There are some super pitches with private electricity and water. The site consists of winding roads, some sloping, along which the pitches are set in shaded areas. The touring area (separate from the chalets and seasonal pitches) is well equipped with modern facilities, although there is no provision for visitors with disabilities.

Facilities

Four excellent sanitary blocks provide showers (token € 1), washbasins (in cabins and communal) and children and baby rooms with small toilets, washbasins and showers. Laundry. Parking and service area for motorcaravans. Well stocked shop. Bar. Restaurant and takeaway. Swimming pool (1/5-1/10). Beauty salon. Playgrounds. Cross-country skiing when snow permits. Bicycle hire. Children's club. WiFi over most of site (charged). Off site: Bus stops outside site entrance. Riding 500 m.

Open: All year.

Directions

Take N15 from Diekirch to Heiderscheid. Site is on left at top of hill just before reaching the village. Motorcaravan service area is signed on the right. GPS: 49.87750, 5.99283

Charges guide

Per unit incl. 2 persons and electricity	€ 20.00 - € 32.00
extra person	€ 3.00
child (under 4 yrs)	€ 1.00 - € 2.00

Heiderscheid

Naturistencamping De Reenert

4 Fuussekaul, L-9156 Heiderscheid T: 268 8881. E: info@reenert.lu

alanrogers.com/LU7860

Naturistencamping de Reenert is located at Heiderscheid, in the natural park of the Haute-Sûre. Visitors report to the reception at Camping Fuussekaul opposite, where they are given the code to enter the site. There are 95 large flat pitches, all with electricity (6/10A). Amenities include a newly built, heated swimming pool with lounge area and meeting rooms for campers, and a small children's outdoor play area. An extensive entertainment programme including sports, games, body painting and many other activities is run during the high season. Visitors are welcome to use the bar, restaurant, sauna, tennis court and shop at Fuussekaul (where fresh bread is baked daily).

Facilities

One modern block and one prefabricated unit provide excellent facilities, including one family shower and three low level showers. New heated indoor pool with sanitary facilities and clubhouse. Aqua gym (May-Sept. free). Play area. Entertainment/meeting room. Shop, bar, restaurant, sauna, tennis, bicycle hire at Fuussekaul. Caravan holiday homes for rent. WiFi (charged).

Open: All year.

Directions

Take N15 from Deikirch to Heiderscheid. Site is on right at top of hill just before the village – check in at Fuussekaul on left. GPS: 49.87788, 5.99364

Charges guide

Per unit incl. 2 persons and electricity	€ 20.00 - € 25.00
extra person	€ 3.00
Camping Cheques accepted.	

For latest campsite news, availability and prices visit

alanrogers.com

Kautenbach
Camping Kautenbach
An der Weierbach, L-9663 Kautenbach T: 950 303. E: info@campingkautenbach.lu

alanrogers.com/LU7830

Kautenbach is situated in the heart of the Luxembourg Ardennes and was established over 60 years ago. Although in an idyllic location, it is less than a mile from a railway station with regular trains to Luxembourg City to the south. There are 135 touring pitches here, mostly of a good size and with reasonable shade. All pitches have electrical connections (10A). This is excellent walking country with many tracks around the site. The site managers will be happy to recommend walks for all abilities. Kautenbach has an attractive bistro style restaurant, specialising in local cuisine, as well as a large selection of whiskies! The site has direct river access and fishing is popular (small charge applicable). During the high season, a wide range of activities are organised along with a lively children's club.

Facilities

Three toilet blocks with open style washbasins and showers, baby changing. Facilities for disabled visitors (key). Laundry. Shop for basics (1/4-31/10, bread to order). Restaurant, bar/snack bar (all season). Direct river access. Fishing. Play area. Mobile homes, safari tents and camping pods for rent. Internet café. Off site: Walking and cycle trails. Railway station 1 km. Caves at Consdorf. Cathedral at Echternach. Chateau Bourscheid. Vianden. Clervaux.

Open: 20 January - 20 December.

Directions

Head south from Namur on the A4 and then join the N4 (exit 15). Continue on the N4 to Bastogne and then join the N84 towards Wiltz. Follow signs to Kautenbach on the CR331 and the site is well signed from here. GPS: 49.95387, 6.0273

Charges guide

Per unit incl. 2 persons and electricity	€ 23.80 - € 25.35
extra person	€ 6.40
child (2-12 yrs)	€ 4.20
dog	€ 2.50

Camping Kautenbach
An der Weierbaach
L-9663 Kautenbach
Luxemburg

Tel.:(+352) 950303 • Fax.:(+352) 950093
info@campingkautenbach.lu
www.campingkautenbach.lu

Ideal for young families, seniors, bikers & hikers •
Cool Pod's, fully furnished Safari Tents & Mobile Homes •
Eco-friendly •
Possibility to fish •

Open from 20 January till 20 December

Larochette
Camping Birkelt
1 Um Birkelt, L-7633 Larochette T: 879 040. E: info@irisparc.com

alanrogers.com/LU7610

This is very much a family site, with a great range of facilities provided. It is well organised and well laid out, set in an elevated position in attractive, undulating countryside. A tarmac road runs around the site with 427 large grass pitches (280 for touring), some slightly sloping, many with a fair amount of shade, on either side of gravel access roads in straight rows and circles. Two hundred pitches have electricity, 134 serviced ones have 16A, the remainder 10A. An all-weather swimming pool complex is beside the site entrance (free for campers) and entertainment for children is arranged in high season. The site is very popular with tour operators (140 pitches). On site, all signage is in four languages including English.

Facilities

Three modern heated sanitary buildings well situated around the site include mostly open washbasins (6 cabins in one block). Facilities (including accommodation to rent) for wheelchair users. Baby baths. Washing machines and dryers. Motorcaravan services. Shops. Coffee bar. Restaurant with terrace. Swimming pool with sliding cupola (heated all season). Outdoor pool for toddlers. Play areas. Trampolines. Volleyball. Minigolf. Tennis. Bicycle hire. Riding. Internet points. Free WiFi over site.

Open: 27 March - 1 November.

Directions

From N7 (Diekirch-Luxembourg City), turn onto N8 (CR118) at Berschblach (just past Mersch) towards Larochette. Site is signed on the right 1.5 km. from Larochette. Approach road is fairly steep and narrow. GPS: 49.78508, 6.21033

Charges guide

Per unit incl. 2 persons and electricity	€ 19.50 - € 36.00
with water and drainage	€ 22.50 - € 39.00
extra person	€ 4.25

Camping Cheques accepted.

FREE Alan Rogers Travel Card
Extra benefits and savings - see page 12

Larochette
Camping Auf Kengert
Kengert, L-7633 Larochette-Medernach T: 837186. E: info@kengert.lu
alanrogers.com/LU7640

A friendly welcome awaits you at this peacefully situated, family run site, 2 km. from Larochette, which is 24 km. northeast of Luxembourg City, providing 180 individual pitches, all with electricity (16A Europlug). Some in a very shaded woodland setting, on a slight slope with fairly narrow access roads. There are also eight hardened pitches for motorcaravans on a flat area of grass, complete with motorcaravan service facilities. Further tent pitches are in an adjacent and more open meadow area. There are also site owned wooden chalets for rent. This site is popular in season, so early arrival is advisable, or you can reserve.

Facilities

The well maintained sanitary block in two parts includes a modern, heated unit with some washbasins in cubicles, and excellent, fully equipped cubicles for disabled visitors. The showers, facilities for babies, additional WCs and washbasins, plus laundry room are located below the central building which houses the shop, bar and restaurant. An additional block is planned for 2015. Motorcaravan services. Gas supplies. Indoor and outdoor play areas. Solar heated swimming pool (Easter-30/9). Paddling pool. WiFi (free). Off site: Bicycle hire 3 km.

Open: 1 March - 8 November.

Directions

From Larochette take the CR118/N8 (towards Mersch) and just outside town turn right on CR119 towards Schrondweiler, site is 2 km. on right. GPS: 49.79992, 6.19817

Charges guide

Per unit incl. 2 persons and electricity	€ 22.00 - € 33.00
extra person	€ 10.00 - € 15.50
child (4-17 yrs)	€ 4.00 - € 5.00
dog	€ 1.50

Lieler
Camping Trois Frontières
Hauptstrooss 12, L-9972 Lieler T: 998 608. E: info@troisfrontieres.lu
alanrogers.com/LU7880

On a clear day, it is possible to see Belgium, Germany and Luxembourg from the campsite swimming pool, hence its name: Trois Frontières. Corinne and Erwin Levering own and manage the site themselves and all visitors receive a personal welcome and immediately become part of a large, happy family. There are 112 touring pitches on slightly sloping fields divided by pine trees which give some shade. All have 6-10A electricity. Most of the facilities are close to the entrance, leaving the camping area quiet, except for the play area. The restaurant/takeaway provides good quality food at reasonable prices, served either inside or on the pleasant terrace. A member of the TopCamp group.

Facilities

Toilet block including suite for visitors with disabilities, plus baby bath and changing station, and family bathroom. More WCs in second building (down some steps). Laundry. Covered, heated swimming pool (1/4-31/10). Play area. Boules. Games room. Bicycle hire. WiFi (free). Off site: Shops 2.3 km. Golf 8 km. Clervaux 12 km. Riding 15 km.

Open: All year.

Directions

Take N7 northward from Diekirch. 3 km. south of Weiswampach turn right onto CR338 to Lieler (site signed here). Site is on right as you enter the village. GPS: 50.12340, 6.10517

Charges guide

Per unit incl. 2 persons and electricity	€ 23.00 - € 30.50
extra person	€ 7.50 - € 8.00

Luxembourg
Camping Kockelscheuer
22 route de Bettembourg, L-1899 Luxemburg T: 471 815. E: caravani@pt.lu
alanrogers.com/LU7660

Camping Kockelscheuer is 4 km. from the centre of Luxembourg City and quietly situated (but there can be some aircraft noise at times). On a slight slope, there are 161 individual pitches of good size, either on flat ground at the bottom of the site or on wide flat terraces with easy access, all with 16A electricity. There is also a special area for tents, with picnic tables and, in the reception building, a tent campers' lounge. For children, there is a large area with modern play equipment on safety tiles and next door to the site is a sports centre. There is a friendly welcome, charges are reasonable and English is spoken.

Facilities

Two fully equipped, identical sanitary buildings, both very clean. Washing machines. Motorcaravan services. Shop (order bread the previous day). Snack bar. Restaurant in adjacent sports centre also with tennis, squash etc. Rest room. No entry or exit for vehicles (reception closed) 12.00-14.00. WiFi (charged). Off site: Bus 200 m. every 10 mins. to Luxembourg. Golf 200 m. Bicycle hire 5 km.

Open: Week before Easter - 31 October.

Directions

Site is SSW of Luxembourg City on the N31 to Bettembourg. From the south, exit A4 at junction signed Kockelscheuer onto N4. In 2 km. turn right (Kockelscheuer and campsite) and continue to follow the signs. GPS: 49.57180, 6.10900

Charges guide

Per unit incl. 2 persons and electricity	€ 17.00
extra person	€ 4.25

For latest campsite news, availability and prices visit
alanrogers.com

Maulusmühle
Camping Woltzdal

Maison 12, L-9974 Maulusmühle T: 998 938. E: info@woltzdal-camping.lu

alanrogers.com/LU7780

Set by a stream in a valley, Camping Woltzdal is one of the many delightful sites in the Ardennes, a region of wooded hills and river valleys that crosses the borders of Belgium, France and Luxembourg. The site has 79 flat touring pitches, set on grass amongst fir trees; all with 4A electricity and 20 of which also have water and waste water. They are fairly open and have views of the surrounding wooded hills. A railway passes the site on the far side of the stream, but there are only trains during the day. This is a family run site with a small, friendly bar/restaurant.

Facilities	Directions
The site boasts a new state-of-the-art toilet block with solar-powered water heating (access is by smart key with deposit). Large family bathrooms and facilities for disabled visitors. Laundry room. Service points for motorcaravans. Reception and small shop are in the large house at the entrance where there is also a bar and a restaurant/snack bar with terrace. Children's library/activity room. WiFi throughout (charged). Play area. Boules. Mountain bike hire. Entertainment programme for children in high season. Off site: Fishing and golf 6 km. Riding 20 km.	Site is 6 km. north of Clervaux on the CR335 road. Leave Clervaux towards Troisvierge (N18). After 1 km. take right fork to Maulusmühle on CR335. Site is signed on right just before Maulusmühle village. Steep turn onto campsite road. GPS: 50.091283, 6.027833

Open: Easter - 30 October.

Charges guide

Per unit incl. 2 persons and electricity	€ 20.00 - € 23.20
extra person	€ 7.00

Mersch
Camping Krounebierg

12 rue du Camping, L-7572 Mersch T: 329 756. E: contact@campingkrounebierg.lu

alanrogers.com/LU7580

Situated on a hillside with views over the Mersch valley this is an attractive site for stopovers or longer stays. It is close to the town of Mersch with good facilities and transport links but the site has a pleasant rural ambience. There are 177 pitches, 137 for touring, including 12 hardstandings. All are level, grassy and of a good size, with 10A electricity, and separated by hedges. A stylish, modern building at the site entrance houses reception, shop, bar and restaurant and has an elevated terrace overlooking the open-air children's pool. Campers can also use the town's indoor pool, adjacent to the site, at a reduced rate.

Facilities	Directions
Five traditional, clean sanitary blocks are heated and have free hot showers. Facilities for disabled visitors. Well stocked shop. Modern bar and restaurant/takeaway. Outdoor paddling pool. Games room with TV, darts etc. Play area. Football field. Badminton. Daily activity programme (July/Aug). Internet and WiFi. Off site: Close to Mersch with good transport links into Luxembourg City.	From A7 motorway take exit 3. Turn left onto rue de la Chapelle and left again onto rue Quatre-Vents. Site is well signed from this point. GPS: 49.743573, 6.089781

Open: 1 April - 31 October.

Charges guide

Per unit inc. 2 persons and electricity	€ 29.95 - € 42.65
extra person	€ 4.20

Nommern
Europacamping Nommerlayen

Rue Nommerlayen, L-7465 Nommern T: 878 078. E: info@nommerlayen-ec.lu

alanrogers.com/LU7620

Situated at the end of its own road, in the lovely wooded hills of central Luxembourg, this is a top quality site with fees to match, but it has everything! A large, central building housing most of the services and amenities opens onto a terrace around an excellent swimming pool complex with a large fun pool and an imaginative water playground. The 367 individual pitches (100 sq.m) are on grassy terraces, all have access to electricity (2/16A) and water taps. Pitches are grouped beside age-appropriate play areas and the facilities throughout the campsite reflect the attention given to families in particular. Interestingly enough the superb sanitary block is called Badtemple (having been built in the style of a Greek temple).

Facilities	Directions
A large, high quality, modern sanitary unit provides some washbasins in cubicles, facilities for disabled visitors, family and baby rooms and a sauna. Private bathrooms for rent. Laundry. Motorcaravan services. Supermarket. Restaurant. Snack bar. Bar (all 1/4-1/11). Swimming pool complex (1/5-15/9) and new covered and heated pool (26/4-1/11). Fitness programmes. Bowling. Playground. Entertainment in season. Bicycle hire. WiFi (free).	Take the 118 road between Mersch and Larochette. Site is signed 3 km. north of Larochette towards the village of Nommern on the 346 road. GPS: 49.78472, 6.16519

Open: 1 March - 1 November.

Charges guide

Per unit incl. 2 persons and 16A electricity	€ 23.50 - € 48.50
extra person (over 2 yrs)	€ 5.50
dog	€ 3.00

FREE Alan Rogers Travel Card
Extra benefits and savings - see page 12

Reisdorf

Camping de la Sûre

23 route de la Sûre, L-9390 Reisdorf T: 836 246. E: reisdorfcamp@gmail.com

alanrogers.com/LU7650

Camping de la Sûre is on the banks of the river that separates Luxembourg and Germany. It is a pleasant site close to Reisdorf with 120 numbered pitches (all with 10A Europlug). These are not separated but are marked with lovely beech and willow trees that provide some shade. There are caravan holiday homes in a fenced area towards the back of the site, leaving the prime pitches for touring units. The site is surrounded by trees on the hillsides and from Reisdorf visits can be made to Vianden Castle or Trier (oldest German city) just across the border.

Facilities

Modern, clean sanitary facilities have been completely refurbished and include family shower room, sanitary facilities for children and disabled visitors. Laundry. Motorcaravan services. Small shop. New bar and restaurant. Takeaway. Playground. Sports field. Canoeing. Fishing. WiFi throughout (free). Off site: Town centre within easy walking distance. Cycle ways abound. Bicycle hire 200 m. Riding 5 km. Golf 8 km.

Open: 1 April - 30 October.

Directions

From the river bridge in Reisdorf, take the road to Echternach, de la Sûre is the second campsite on the left. GPS: 49.87003, 6.26750

Charges guide

Per unit incl. 2 persons	
and electricity	€ 14.00 - € 20.00
extra person	€ 5.00
child (under 14 yrs)	€ 2.50
dog	€ 2.50

Tarchamps

Camping Um Bierg

Um Bierg 32, L-9689 Tarchamps T: 993 217. E: umbierg@pt.lu

alanrogers.com/LU7500

This well maintained and attractive small site is set on a hillside overlooking the small village of Tarchamps. The upper area has two terraces with 90 generously sized, level grass pitches for tourers, all with 6A electricity. Large units may find access challenging. The lower area is for seasonal caravans. Once pitched, cars must be left at the car park by the entrance, and this adds to the overall feeling of peace and serenity. There is a small swimming pool, and a bar/restaurant where evening meals must be ordered in advance. The friendly and helpful owners bake their own bread, which is sold on site. The lack of dedicated facilities and steps to the toilet blocks make this site unsuitable for disabled visitors.

Facilities

The prefabricated toilet block in the touring area has immaculately clean showers and toilets. A second block is adjacent to reception. Both can be heated and are accessed by steps. Laundry facilities. Heated swimming pool (July/Aug). Entertainment for children. WiFi. Off site: Small village of Tarchamps (no facilities) 300 m. Riding 2 km. Fishing, sailing and boat launching 7 km.

Open: 15 March - 30 September.

Directions

From Belgium N84 from Bastogne towards Wiltz and Diekirch. Once in Luxembourg this road becomes the N15. Through village of Doncols and then follow campsite signs. GPS: 49.946507, 5.801023

Charges guide

Per unit incl. 2 persons	
and electricity	€ 16.50 - € 19.75
extra person	€ 4.00 - € 5.25
child (under 12)	€ 2.50 - € 3.00
dog	€ 2.00

For latest campsite news, availability and prices visit

alanrogers.com

Troisvierges
Camping Walensbongert

Rue de Binsfeld 32, L-9912 Troisvierges T: 997 141. E: wbongert@pt.lu

alanrogers.com/LU7510

Camping Walensbongert is just 300 metres from all the facilities of Troisvierges, a large village with banks, bars, restaurants and shops. It is owned by the local tourist office, and the village swimming pool, with its restaurant and bar, is located at the heart of the site – campers enjoy a concessionary daily rate of € 2.50. The 151 level, grass touring pitches are separated by hedges and vary in size from 80-100 sq.m. They are in both open and shady areas and all have 10A electricity. The main sanitary block is accessed by a staircase, but new well equipped disabled facilities are provided at ground level. This site with its waymarked walks will suit anyone who wants to enjoy the peace of the countryside, although the site can be lively in high season. There is a bus stop within 300 m. and a railway station within 600 m. of the entrance. All transport costs only € 4.00 for a 24-hour ticket to anywhere within Luxembourg.

Facilities
Unusual rotunda style building (one flight of stairs) contains hot showers, toilets, laundry and washing up facilities. Facilities for disabled visitors at ground level (key access and unmarked door). Heated indoor and outdoor swimming pools (July/Aug), indoor pool closed 21/8-15/9. Playing field adjacent. Play area. Activity programme (July/Aug). WiFi throughout (charged). Off site: Waymarked walks directly from site. Walking leaflets and maps from reception (€ 3). Troisvierges 300 m. Public transport within walking distance. Riding 4 km. Lake and fishing 5 km.

Open: 1 April - 30 September.

Directions
Site is signed from the main street of Troisvierges, 300 m. downhill from village centre. GPS: 50.118885, 6.001523

Charges guide
Per unit incl. 2 persons	
and electricity	€ 17.80 - € 19.50
extra person	€ 4.95 - € 5.50
child (4-14 yrs)	€ 2.35 - € 2.60
dog (max. 2)	€ 2.50

You will find Camping Walensbongert situated along a small river in the beautiful Luxembourg Ardennes. Splendid area for rambling. Small village with swimming pools, shops and railway station within walking distance.

Rue de Binsfeld 32bis • L-9912 Troisvierges • Luxembourg • Tel.: +352-997141
www.walensbongert.lu • wbongert@pt.lu • GPS: N 50.118885 / E 6.001523

Vianden
Camping du Moulin

Route de Bettel, L-9415 Vianden T: 834 501. E: info@campingdumoulin.lu

alanrogers.com/LU7520

A popular site set on lightly wooded, level ground alongside the River Our, Camping du Moulin is conveniently located with good road access. The 150 touring pitches (all with 10A connections, four with hardstanding) are numbered but not separated. One terrace of about 20 pitches is alongside the river, with the remainder on a level grassy area slightly above. The site itself has a bar and snack bar; in addition there is a service station with a small supermarket nearby. A pleasant 1.5 km. walk, mostly alongside the river, takes you into the charming and historic town of Vianden with its cobbled streets, castle and cable car.

Facilities
Two modern, clean sanitary blocks with free hot showers and hot water to sinks. Private bathroom (€ 7/day). Facilities for disabled visitors. Laundry facilities. Shop, bar overlooking the river, snack bar (all season). Games room with TV, snooker, darts and books. Play area. Daily activities with dedicated team (July/Aug). Fishing. WiFi (charged). Off site: Close to the historic town of Vianden with its quaint streets, fortified walls and cable car up to the castle.

Open: 27 April - 2 September.

Directions
From N17 Diekirch to Vianden road turn right onto N178 in village of Fouhren. Camping du Moulin is clearly visible on right in valley when approaching Vianden. GPS: 49.926553, 6.220129

Charges guide
Per unit incl. 2 persons	
and electricity	€ 22.50 - € 27.50
extra person	€ 7.50 - € 8.00
child (3-14 yrs)	€ 4.00 - € 4.50
dog	€ 1.50

FREE Alan Rogers Travel Card
Extra benefits and savings - see page 12

Vianden
Camping Op dem Deich

Rue Neugarten, L-9401 Vianden T: 834 375. E: ellen.ringelberg@gmx.de

alanrogers.com/LU7530

A friendly, relaxed site in a most convenient location only a short riverside walk from the medieval town of Vianden with its fortified walls and cobbled streets. This riverside site is partly set in a former orchard where the fruit trees remain to offer shade. The 100 level grassy touring pitches are numbered but not separated and campers using the popular riverside pitches will need long electricity cables to reach the 16A supply. There is no shop, bar or restaurant on site, but it is a very short walk into Vianden, where all facilities can be found.

Facilities

Two clean, modern shower blocks can be heated. A single storey building houses both the reception area and the main shower block. Facilities for children. Ramped access for disabled visitors. Washing machine and dryer. Daily entertainment (July/Aug). TV room. Playground. Fishing. WiFi (charged). Gas barbecues only. Off site: Vianden with shops, bar, restaurants and castle 1 km. Indoor swimming pool 1 km. Bicycle hire 2 km. Riding 5 km.

Open: 1 April - 15 October.

Directions

Take N17 from Diekirch towards Vianden. Turn right onto N178 at Fouhren. Cross river bridge at edge of Vianden and take first left (rue Moenchkelterhaus) and then follow signs to site. GPS: 49.932086, 6.215676

Charges guide

Per unit incl. 2 persons and electricity	€ 23.10
extra person	€ 6.50
child (4-8 yrs)	€ 2.70
dog	€ 2.50

Wallendorf-Pont
Camping Du Rivage

Echternacherstroos 7, L-9392 Wallendorf-Pont T: 836 516. E: voogt@pt.lu

alanrogers.com/LU7800

Du Rivage is a small site located on the edge of Wallendorf Pont by a bend in the River Sûre. The owners are friendly and helpful and run a canoe hire business and bicycle hire from the site. The 70 level, grassy touring pitches (all with 6A electricity, long cables needed) are open and undefined. The site is ideal for active families who will enjoy the kayaking, cycling and fishing. For a small charge, the wellness centre and Internet facilities in the adjacent hotel can be accessed. Motorcaravans over 6 m. are not accepted as the ground becomes soft in wet weather and the site roads are unsuitable.

Facilities

A modern heated sanitary block with free hot showers, but no facilities for disabled visitors at present. Further small block with cold showers. Bread and milk. Small play area. Bicycle hire. Kayak and canoe hire. Bar and takeaway (1/5-30/9). WiFi (free). Off site: Hotel next door with Internet and wellness by arrangement. Bus stop by entrance. ATM 2 km.

Open: 14 April - 1 October.

Directions

Take N10 Diekirch to Echternach road. Site is between road and river near centre of Wallendorf Pont and is clearly signed. GPS: 49.8737, 6.29041

Charges guide

Per unit incl. 2 persons and electricity	€ 24.00 - € 26.75
extra person	€ 6.50
child (2-12 yrs)	€ 3.50

Walsdorf
Beter-Uit Vakantiepark Walsdorf

Tandlerbaach, L-9465 Walsdorf T: 834 464. E: walsdorf@beter-uit.nl

alanrogers.com/LU7540

A beautifully presented site set in a quiet wooded valley. The 110 touring pitches are set in terraces alongside a small stream. The pitches are a good size at 100 to 170 sq.m, each with mature hedges and 4A electricity. The site buildings are modern and very well maintained. There are 40 mobile homes for rent but these are discreetly placed on the upper terracing. This Dutch-owned and managed site is popular and lively in high season but quiet and peaceful at other times.

Facilities

Immaculate, well equipped sanitary block has facilities for children and disabled visitors. Hot showers (first 5 mins. free). Small shop (limited hours in low season). Pleasant bar with terrace, restaurant and takeaway (all open all season). Bicycle hire (high season). Mountain bikes planned. Club room with TV. Full entertainment programme (July/Aug). Ball game field. Volleyball. Trampoline. WiFi planned (charged). Off site: Historic town of Vianden with castle. Walsdorf village nearby. Nordic walking track from site. Walking and cycling.

Open: 21 April - 6 October.

Directions

From N17 Vianden/Diekirch road. Site is signed at Tandel village. GPS: 49.916976, 6.178501

Charges guide

Per unit incl. 2 persons and electricity	€ 16.25 - € 26.25
extra person	€ 3.00 - € 6.00
child (under 12 yrs)	free - € 3.00
dog	€ 2.50

CAPITAL: AMSTERDAM

Tourist Office

Netherlands Board of Tourism
PO Box 30783, London WC2B 6DH
Tel: 020 7539 7958
Fax: 020 7539 7953
Email: info-uk@holland.com
Internet: www.holland.com/uk

With vast areas of the Netherlands reclaimed from the sea, nearly half of the country lies at or below sea level. The result is a flat, fertile landscape, criss-crossed with rivers and canals. Famous for its windmills and bulb fields, it also boasts some of the most impressive coastal dunes in Europe.

There is more to the Netherlands than Amsterdam and the bulb fields. Granted, both are top attractions and no visitor should miss the city of Amsterdam with its bridges, canals, museums and listed buildings or miss seeing the spring-time riot of colour that adorns the fields and gardens of South Holland. This is a country with a variety of holiday venues ranging from lively seaside resorts to picturesque villages, idyllic old fishing ports and areas where nature rules. The Vecht valley is an area of natural beauty which centres around the town of Ommen. Giethoorn is justly dubbed the 'Venice of the North'. The Alblasserwaard polder offers the chance to discover the famed windmills of Kinderdijk, cheese farms and a stork village. The islands of Zeeland are joined by amazing feats of engineering, particularly the Oosterschelde storm surge barrier. Island hopping introduces lovely old towns such as Middelburg, the provincial capital Zierikzee with its old harbour and the quaint old town of Veere.

Population

16.8 million

Climate

Temperate with mild winters and warm summers.

Language

Dutch. English is very widely spoken, so is German and to some extent French. In Friesland a Germanic language, Frisian, is spoken.

Telephone

The country code is 00 31.

Money

Currency: The Euro
Banks: Mon-Fri 09.00-16.00/17.00.

Shops

Mon-Fri 09.00/09.30-17.30/18.00.
Sat to 16.00/17.00. Later closing hours in larger cities.

Public Holidays

New Year; April Fools Day 1 April; Good Fri; Easter Mon; Queen's Birthday 30 April; Labour Day; Remembrance Day 4 May; Liberation Day 5 May; Ascension; Whit Mon; SinterKlaas 5 Dec; Kingdom Day 15 Dec; Christmas 25, 26 Dec.

Motoring

There is a comprehensive motorway system but, due to the high density of population, all main roads can become very busy, particularly in the morning and evening rush hours. There are many bridges which can cause congestion. There are no toll roads but there are a few toll bridges and tunnels notably the Zeeland Bridge, Europe's longest across the Oosterschelde.

CAPITAL: ASSEN

From traditional small villages to vibrant cities, Drenthe embraces a diverse landscape. With a rich history, Neolithic stones, festivals, and friendly, hospitable people – no wonder it's so popular with Dutch holidaymakers.

Drenthe, unlike many other parts of the Netherlands, has been a sparsely populated rural area since medieval times. Except for some industry in Assen and Emmen, the lands in Drenthe are mainly used for farming. This province is epitomised by stillness and an affinity with nature, which affords so many opportunities for hiking, cycling and boating. Quiet though it may be, you're never far away from one of the lively old cities with their vibrant shops and restaurants.

Drenthe is divided into three regions, each with its own special character. In northern and central Drenthe, the large lakes – Leekstermeer, Paterswoldsmeer and Zuidlaardermeer – with their many attractions are popular with watersports enthusiasts. In southwestern Drenthe, the Dwingelderveld and the Drents-Friese Wold National Parks with their thousands of acres of fens, heathland and forest will capture the imagination of walkers and cyclists alike. In this area, there are constant reminders of the ancient landscapes as you experience everything that the countryside has to offer. Nearby are the flourishing cities of Meppel and Hoogeveen for more lively pursuits. And finally in the southeast there are the immense moorland areas with their many dolmens reflecting man's presence here prior to the Bronze Age.

Places of interest

Assen: internationally renowned Drents Museum, modern shopping centre and beautiful countryside.

Emmen: a mix of urban vitality and rural serenity, with a great zoo.

Hondsrug Hunze Valley - Forest of Gieten-Borger: vast forests surrounded by charming medieval villages, meadows and ancient hedgerows.

Open-air Museum Orvelte: museum village with many historic attractions.

Attractions

Assen TT circuit: test your skills at kart racing, drive your own car or sail a boat. Young persons' driving licences are available.

Borger Hunebed Centre: takes you back to prehistoric times, when the first peasants settled in Drenthe and erected the impressive stone monoliths called Hunebedden.

Attractions Park Drouwenerzand: rides and activities for all ages - a combination of games, education and refreshment all under one roof!

Prison Museum Veenhuizen: interactive museum tracing the history of crime and punishment in the Netherlands from 1600 to the present day.

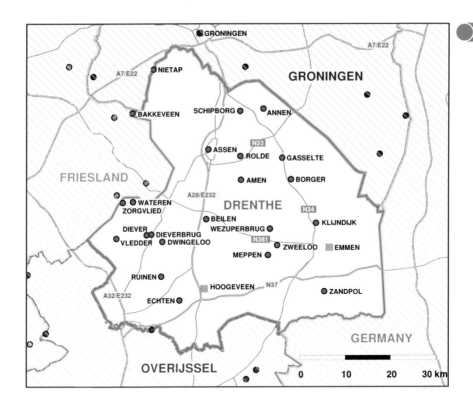

Amen

Vakantiepark Diana Heide

Amen 53, NL-9446TE Amen (Drenthe) T: 0592 389 297. E: info@dianaheide.nl

alanrogers.com/NL5795

Diana Heide is in a beautiful location on the edge of the Drentsche National Park and is surrounded by vast and varied forests. In recent years, this 30-acre site has seen a real metamorphosis. The natural setting here is complemented by many modern amenities. Although one half of the terrain is dedicated to camping, the other half has been designated as a nature reserve. There are 325 spacious touring pitches here (110-200 sq.m), all with 10A electricity, water and drainage. Diana Heide is very family friendly and there is an outdoor swimming pool, a playground, sports fields, a private rowing and fishing pond and a children's theatre. In high season, there is an activity and entertainment programme for young children, and a separate programme for teenagers. There is a convivial restaurant with a large outdoor terrace and a snack bar. A small supermarket is well stocked and sells fresh bread. There is good access to the surrounding forests, with their ponds, woods and heaths. An ideal site for hiking and cycling or maybe walking the dog.

Facilities

Toilet blocks with good provision. Private sanitary facilities for rent at toilet block. Facilities for disabled visitors. Launderette. Shop. Restaurant. Snacks. Outdoor pool. Sports fields. Pond for boating and fishing. Activities for all ages. Children's theatre. Bicycle hire. Chalets and cabins for rent. WiFi over site (charged). Off site: Emmen Zoo. Aerial adventure park. Walking and cycle routes.

Open: 1 April - 31 October.

Directions

Approaching on A28 (Zwolle-Groningen motorway) take exit 31 towards Hooghalen. Follow signs to Grolloo and Amen, and then follow signs to the site. GPS: 52.93161, 6.58666

Charges guide

Per unit incl. 2 persons and electricity	€ 20.00 - € 25.00
dog	€ 3.00

FREE Alan Rogers Travel Card
Extra benefits and savings - see page 12

Annen

Naturistencamping De Groenlanden

De Bulten 14-16, NL-9468 TD Annen (Drenthe) T: 0592 272 711. E: contact@degroenlanden.nl

alanrogers.com/NL6142

De Groenlanden is a pretty naturist site located near the De Drentsche Aa National Park. This immaculately kept site has six separate areas arranged in circles, each comprising around 120 spacious pitches. All are 100-120 sq.m. with 6A electricity (ten with water and drainage), and are shaded by tall trees. There is a large children's field and play area at the centre of the site, which is overlooked by most pitches, in addition to a small lake with a beach. The lake has a safe, enclosed area for younger children to swim. The site is largely car free and the access gate could be difficult for large units.

Facilities

Pyramid toilet block with preset hot showers (5 minutes), open style washbasins and facilities for babies and disabled visitors. Launderette. Canoes, rowing boats and windsurfers for hire. Boules. Volleyball. Trampoline. Basketball. Play area. Evening entertainment and activities. Naturist guided walks. Balloon rides. WiFi. Off site: Shops, markets and restaurants in Assen, Groningen and Emmen. Bicycle hire 3 km. Golf 10 km.

Open: 1 April - 1 November.

Directions

Take the A28 from Hoogeveen and exit at Assen. Follow N33 towards Emmen and then N34 towards Annen Zuidlaren. Take the exit at Annen, turn right, continue past the BP garage and take the second right towards the antique farm. The site is 2 km. on the right. GPS: 53.065707, 6.757681

Charges guide

Per unit incl. electricity	€ 28.40 - € 31.00
dog	€ 2.60

Assen

Vakantiepark Witterzomer

Witterzomer 7, NL-9405 VE Assen (Drenthe) T: 0592 393 535. E: info@witterzomer.nl

alanrogers.com/NL6153

Attractively located in a century old area of woodland and fields in the province of the Hunebedden, this is an attractive, large and well organised site. The Hunebedden are prehistoric monuments, built of enormous granite boulders and older than Stonehenge. The 600 touring pitches at Witterzomer are on grass with a woodland setting, with varying degrees of shade and 4-10A electricity. Most also have water, a drain and TV connections and some have private sanitary facilities. All of the amenities here are of excellent quality and are particularly targeted at families.

Facilities

Good heated toilet blocks include separate facilities for babies and disabled visitors, as well as family bathrooms. Laundry. Shop (1/4-30/9). Restaurant/bar and takeaway (1/4-28/10). Heated outdoor swimming pool (25/4-2/9). Sports field and games room. Tennis. Bicycle hire. Minigolf. Lake with beach and fishing. Internet and WiFi throughout (charged). Max. 2 dogs. Off site: Several nature parks. Assen 4 km. Golf 6 km. Groningen 30 km.

Open: All year.

Directions

Site is 4 km. southwest of Assen. From A28 exit 33 follow N371 (Balkenweg) to Assen. After 200 m. turn right (Europaweg) and again after 200 m. to the right onto Witterhoofdweg. Follow this road for 2 km. (under A28) to the site. GPS: 52.9802, 6.5053

Charges guide

Per unit incl. 2 persons and electricity	€ 18.50 - € 27.00
extra person	€ 4.00
No credit cards.	

Bakkeveen

Camping De Drie Provinciën

Bakkeveenseweg 15, Eén-West, NL-9343 TB Bakkeveen (Drenthe) T: 0516 541 201.
E: info@dedrieprovincien.nl **alanrogers.com/NL6155**

This is a uniquely located, park like site on the border of the provinces of Groningen, Friesland and Drenthe, right on the edge of the beautiful Bakkefeansterdunen nature reserve. The site is the perfect base for hiking, cycling and otherwise enjoying the relaxed natural environment. There are 140 good sized pitches with electricity, all separated by hedges and many sheltered by trees, including 36 large ones (up to 160 sq.m) with water and drainage. There is a pretty café/restaurant with a garden terrace near the reception. The restaurant is perfect for a cup of coffee, a light lunch or a good evening meal.

Facilities

Three well appointed toilet blocks. Launderette. Bar/restaurant. Fishing. Bicycle hire. WiFi over site (charged). Off site: Swimming pool at Bakkeveen, 4 km. Walking and cycling through the Bakkefeansterdunen nature reserve. An ancient defensive walk along the Friesland and Drenthe border. Shopping in Haulerwijk, 4 km.

Open: 1 April - 1 October.

Directions

From Drachten take A7 (Groningen), then take exit 33 to E22. Turn right on N388 (Niebert). Continue through Niebert and follow signs to Carolieweg for 2 km. and through a series of bends. Take N979 past Zevenhuizen and turn right in to Bakkeveenseg. Follow signs to the site. GPS: 53.0875, 6.31434

Charges guide

Per unit incl. 2 persons and electricity	€ 17.90
extra person	€ 4.45

For latest campsite news, availability and prices visit
alanrogers.com

Beilen
Camping Vorrelveen
Vorrelveen 10, NL-9411 VP Beilen (Drenthe) T: 0593 527 261. E: info@campingvorrelveen.nl
alanrogers.com/NL6134

In comparison with the larger (and justifiably popular) campsites in Drenthe, Camping Vorrelveen is a small site which reflects the pleasant countryside. It is located next to a working farm and enjoys beautiful views. There are just 28 spacious pitches, all with 6A electricity, and the owners do their best to ensure a very personal, tranquil atmosphere. For example, your bread for breakfast will be delivered to your pitch and, in the evening, you can order home made pizzas. This is a prime example of a small, uncomplicated rural campsite. Vorrelveen is an ideal place for a peaceful, relaxing holiday.

Facilities	Directions
Single toilet block includes a family shower. The same building houses a large room for meals and socialising. Essential supplies kept at the farmhouse. Motorcaravan services (with pitches on hardstanding). Play area with cable track and children's fort. Pétanque. Bicycle hire. WiFi throughout. Three new chalets for hire. Off site: Fishing 800 m. The museum villages of Orvelte and Kabouterland (Pixieland).	Take exit 30 from the A28 following signs to Smilde. Turn right at the third bridge towards Hijken and then immediately turn left towards Vorrelveen. After a further 3 km. the site is on the left. GPS: 52.88000, 6.44200

Open: 1 April - 30 September.

Charges guide

Per unit incl. 2 persons and electricity	€ 18.00
dog	free - € 1.00

Borger
Recreatiepark Hunzedal
De Drift, NL-9531 Tk Borger (Drenthe) T: 0599 234 698. E: info@vakantiegevoel.nl
alanrogers.com/NL6145

Recreatiepark Hunzedal is a large park with holiday homes, touring pitches, rental units and seasonal guests. It is in beautiful natural surroundings, close to the moors of Drenthe. It has over 250 touring pitches, 80 with water, 6-16A electricity, waste water and cable. Pitches are laid out in circular bays, off hardcore access roads on grassy fields taking around ten units. Level pitches are numbered and with shade to the back from mature trees and shrubs. Close to the touring pitches is a large water area with play equipment and a sandy beach. The reception building houses a sub-tropical pool. Hunzedal is ideal for families with children looking for an active holiday.

Facilities	Directions
Three fully equipped toilet blocks for tourers with toilets, washbasins (open style and in cabins) and preset showers. Family shower rooms. Baby room. En-suite facilities for disabled visitors. Laundry. Motorcaravan services. Shop. Bar/restaurant. Snack bar. Sub-tropical pool. Minigolf. Sun beds and sauna. Playgrounds. Adventure hall. WiFi (charged). Off site: Zoo in Emmen. Camp Westerbork.	On A28 in either direction take exit 32 and continue east on N33. At the crossroads with the N34, turn South towards Borger. In Borger follow the site signs. GPS: 52.92322, 6.8034

Open: 3 April - 31 October.

Charges guide

Per unit incl. 5 persons and electricity	€ 18.00 - € 50.00
extra person	€ 4.00

Diever
Camping Wittelterbrug
Wittelterweg 31, NL-7986 PL Diever (Drenthe) T: 0521 598 288. E: info@wittelterbrug.nl
alanrogers.com/NL6148

Camping Wittelterbrug is a well established, family friendly site with a central location between the Drents-Friese Wold and the Dwingelderveld. This is excellent cycling and walking country (cycle hire is available on site). Pitches are in long lanes off paved access roads on good sized, grassy fields. All are equipped with electricity (10A), water and drainage (a small charge is made for hot showers). On-site amenities include two indoor heated pools and a café/snack bar serving takeaway meals. In peak season, there is a lively activity and entertainment programme, including special activities for children.

Facilities	Directions
Two blocks for tourers with controllable, hot showers and open style washbasins. Baby room. Facilities were not adequate for wheelchair users. Bar provides meals, takeaways, drinks and ice. Covered swimming pool and children's pool. Playground. Bowling alley. Bicycle hire. WiFi (charged). Accommodation for rent. Off site: Shops and restaurants in Dwingeloo and Diever. Fishing. Golf 8 km. Walking and cycle tracks.	Approaching from the south (Amersfoort and Zwolle), use A28 motorway and leave at Meppel. Continue north on N371 to Diever, and follow signs to the site. GPS: 52.824973, 6.318356

Open: 1 April - 31 October.

Charges guide

Per unit incl. 2 persons, electricity, water and waste water	€ 17.00 - € 21.00
extra person (over 1 year)	€ 3.25 - € 3.65
dog	€ 3.00 - € 3.60

FREE Alan Rogers Travel Card
Extra benefits and savings - see page 12

Diever
Camping Diever
Haarweg 2, NL-7981 LW Diever (Drenthe) T: 0521 591 694. E: info@camping-diever.nl
alanrogers.com/NL6180

Camping Diever is just outside the quiet, rural village of Diever and close to the Drents-Friese Wold nature reserve. A special attraction in Diever is the open-air theatre where they perform a Shakespearean play all summer. Camping Diever has 210 touring pitches, all with 10A electricity, arranged informally around the site between the trees and separated by natural greenery. Some of the ground is sandy with some grass areas off sand access roads. The village of Diever is an easy 15 minute walk. This whole area is excellent for long walks and cycling tours.

Facilities

Three toilet blocks (one heated) provide toilets, washbasins (open style and in cabins) and preset hot showers with key for hot water. Family shower. Baby room. Laundry facilities. Fresh bread and basics from reception. Recreation hall with games machine, billiards, library and fireplace. Playing field. Bicycle hire. Adventure play island. No charcoal barbecues. Torch useful. WiFi (charged). Off site: Shakespeare Theatre, Diever 1 km.

Open: 1 April - 30 September.

Directions

On A28, take exit 31 and continue on N381 towards Drachten. At Hoogersmilde, turn south on N371 towards Meppel. Turn towards Diever and follow site signs. GPS: 52.86675, 6.32018

Charges guide

Per unit incl. 2 persons and electricity	€ 23.90 - € 30.90
extra person (under 10 yrs)	€ 6.15
child	€ 3.70

Dieverbrug
Landgoed 't Wildryck
Groningenweg 13, NL-7981 LA Dieverbrug (Drenthe) T: 0521 591 207. E: info@wildryck.nl
alanrogers.com/NL6139

Landgoed 't Wildryck offers camping on a large, 32-hectare estate in one of the most beautiful parts of Holland. Behind the site is the Drents-Friese Wold national park, with two others nearby (De Weerribben and the Dwingelderhei). 't Wildryck has just 59 touring pitches up to 140 sq.m, all with 10A electricity and private sanitary facilities (shower, toilet and washbasin) in attractively built little houses. The site is landscaped with low trees and pitches are on three level areas, some in the open, others with shade from mature trees and partly separated by fir trees. Site roads can become dusty in dry weather.

Facilities

Private sanitary facilities with basin, toilet and shower at each pitch. Baby room combined with toilet for disabled visitors. Small shop. Restaurant with bar for simple meals (closed Tues). Indoor heated pool with paddling pool. Tennis. Bicycle hire. Playground and indoor play attic. WiFi (charged). Torch useful. Barbecues are not permitted. Off site: Fishing 200 m. Lake beach and riding 5 km.

Open: All year.

Directions

Take exit 31 on A28 and continue west on N381 towards Drachten. At Hoogersmilde, turn south on N371 towards Meppel. Site is signed on this road. GPS: 52.863493, 6.353008

Charges guide

Per unit incl. 2 persons and electricity	€ 15.00 - € 29.00
extra person (over 3 yrs)	€ 4.00

Dwingeloo
Camping Torentjeshoek
Leeuweriksveldweg 1, NL-7991 SE Dwingeloo (Drenthe) T: 0521 591 706. E: info@torentjeshoek.nl
alanrogers.com/NL6141

Camping Torentjeshoek is situated next to the Planetron attraction in the Dwingelderveld National Park. The partly car-free site is attractively landscaped with trees and shrubs and has 260 pitches, with 160 for tourers. The numbered and level touring pitches are well laid out and well spaced on circular, grassy fields between mature fir and spruce trees. There is shade around the fields and all pitches have 10A electricity, water, waste water and cable. An open-air, heated public pool adjacent to the site has free entry for campers. The site has a snack bar and in high season an entertainment team provides various activities.

Facilities

Two toilet blocks (main block to the front and a smaller block to the back) with toilets, washbasins (open style and in cabins) and free, preset hot showers. Toilets for children. Family shower room. Baby room. Facilities for disabled visitors. Laundry. Motorcaravan services. Basics from reception. Bar with terrace and TV. Snack bar (weekends). Boules. Bicycle hire. Animal farm. Playground. Recreation hall (entertainment in high season). WiFi. Off site: Riding 1 km. Lake beach and fishing 2.5 km.

Open: 1 April - 31 October.

Directions

On A28, take exit 29 for Dwingeloo and follow signs for the town. Site is signed in Dwingeloo and is next to the Planetron. GPS: 52.819048, 6.360644

Charges guide

Per unit incl. 2 persons and electricity	€ 19.20 - € 27.85
extra person	€ 2.00 - € 4.00
dog	€ 3.00

For latest campsite news, availability and prices visit
alanrogers.com

Dwingeloo
Camping Meistershof

Lheebroek 33, NL-7991 PM Dwingeloo (Drenthe) T: 0521 597 278. E: info@meistershof.nl

alanrogers.com/NL6147

Meistershof is a small, interesting site with only 157 pitches, all for tourers. Developed on a former farm, the buildings have retained their original style, which gives the site a rustic look and feel. This, and the fact that the site is partly car free, ensures a relaxing holiday in beautiful, natural surroundings. The numbered pitches are all level and arranged on grassy fields with paved access lanes. They are separated by a variety of hedges and have shade from mature trees, and 10A electricity. There are 40 pitches with electricity, water and drainage; some have hardstandings or private sanitary facilities.

Facilities	Directions
New, stylish toilet block at the centre of the site with superb facilities. Toilets, washbasins (open style and in cabins) and controllable hot showers (charged). Toilets and washbasins for children. Facilities for disabled visitors. Family shower room. Baby room. Laundry. Shop for basics. Snack bar. Playing field. Playground and covered play area. Minigolf. Boules. Excursions into Dwingelderveld. WiFi (charged).	From the A28 take exit 29 (Dwingeloo) and continue towards town. Site is signed before Dwingeloo and is in the village of Lheebroek. GPS: 52.845746, 6.427469

Open: 1 April - 30 September.

Charges guide

Per unit incl. 2 persons and electricity	€ 21.00 - € 22.00
extra person	€ 4.10

Dwingeloo
RCN Camping De Noordster

Noordster 105, NL-7991 PB Dwingeloo (Drenthe) T: 0521 597 238. E: noordster@rcn.nl

alanrogers.com/NL6158

RCN de Noordster can be found in the Dutch National Park Dwingelderveld, a beautiful expanse of moorland in the northern Netherlands. Hours of long walks though fields of purple heather and deep into ancient forests are possible here. All the pitches are well shaded, under large trees and surrounded by colourful shrubs. A range of mobile homes and chalets is available for rent, including some units specially adapted for visitors with disabilities. There are several children's playgrounds here, including a skateboard park. Other leisure amenities include an outdoor pool (with waterslide), children's and toddlers' pools and various water games.

Facilities	Directions
Five clean, modern toilet blocks. Launderette. Restaurant, bar, café and takeaway. Bakery and supermarket. Fun paddling pool. Evening entertainment. Play area. Minigolf. Sports hall. Multisports field. Bicycle and go-kart hire. Skateboard track with half pipe. WiFi. Off site: Heated outdoor pool (adjacent). Planetarium at Dwingeloo 3 km.	Site is 3 km. south of Dwingeloo, reachable from A28 (via N855) and A32 (via N371). In town centre follow the camping signs. GPS: 52.81337, 6.378926

Open: All year.

Charges guide

Per unit incl. 2 persons and electricity	€ 16.50 - € 24.00
dog	€ 4.95 - € 7.50

Echten
Vakantiepark Westerbergen

Oshaarseweg 24, NL-7932 PX Echten (Drenthe) T: 0528 251 224. E: info@westerbergen.nl

alanrogers.com/NL6150

Vakantiepark Westerbergen is beautifully situated in the picturesque region of Drenthe. The campsite is divided into two different areas, the campsite itself and the residential park. There are 373 pitches of which 335 are for touring. All pitches have electricity (6-16A) and most are equipped with water, drainage and cable TV connections. Mostly on a separate field, the marked pitches are of a good size. In the centre of the site there is a fishing pond. During holiday times an entertainment team organises activities, for example survival exercises, children's theatre, treasure hunts, discos and much more. The site's swimming pool is heated and covered. There is also an outside water play area for little ones.

Facilities	Directions
One new and two renovated toilet blocks are clean and neat with hot showers, toilets and individual washbasins. Facilities for disabled visitors and for babies. Laundry facilities. Motorcaravan services. Shop (April-Oct). Restaurant. Snack bar. Bar and terrace. Indoor swimming pool. Indoor and outdoor play areas. Multisports court. Minigolf. Laser game. Archery. Tennis. Bicycle hire. Fishing. WiFi throughout (charged). Off site: Golf 4 km.	From the A28 (Hoogeveen/Groningen) take exit for Zuidwolde and Echten (25). At crossing turn left towards Echten and at T-junction turn right (de Leeuweveenseweg), then left (de Echtenseweg) towards Echten. At T-junction turn left (follow signs for site) and in the village turn left and site is 1 km. GPS: 52.70300, 6.37640

Open: 23 March - 26 October
(mobile home accommodation, all year).

Charges guide

Per unit incl. up to 4 persons and electricity	€ 15.50 - € 21.00

FREE Alan Rogers Travel Card
Extra benefits and savings - see page 12

Gasselte
Camping De Lente van Drenthe

Houtvester Jansenweg 2, NL-9462 TB Gasselte (Drenthe) T: 0599 564 333. E: info@delentevandrenthe.nl
alanrogers.com/NL6124

De Lente van Drenthe is located on the edge of the Gieten-Borger forest. Along with its attractive situation amidst forests and moorland, it is also just a short walk (200 m) from 't Nije Hemelriek. This is a large lake, with a maximum depth of 1.3 m, crystal clear water and a fine sandy beach. There is direct access to the many cycle, mountain bike and walking routes in the area. There are around 100 pitches for touring units here, all with 6A electricity and cable TV connections. The pitches are of a good size (a minimum of 100 sq.m). Electricity, water and drainage are available on 25 touring pitches.

Facilities

Good modern toilet blocks, including a family shower room. Basic essentials from reception. Small restaurant, bar, snack bar (1/4-15/9). Heated outdoor swimming pool (1/5-15/9). Playground. Sports field. Tennis. Minigolf. Bicycle and go-kart hire. Nordic walking. Games room. Entertainment for children (high season). Max. 2 dogs. WiFi throughout (charged). Off site: Beach 200 m.

Open: 29 March - 25 October.

Directions

Site is 3 km. west of Gasselte. From the N34 (Borger-Gieten) take exit for Gasselte and follow signs to Nije Hemelrijk and site.
GPS: 52.97652, 6.75608

Charges guide

Per unit incl. 2 persons and electricity	€ 17.50 - € 20.50

Klijndijk
Vakantiecentrum De Fruithof

Melkweg 2, NL-7871 PE Klijndijk (Drenthe) T: 0591 512 427. E: info@fruithof.nl
alanrogers.com/NL6131

Vakantiecentrum de Fruithof is an immaculately kept site that is attractively landscaped with different varieties of shrubs and trees. The site is fairly open and has attractive pitches on well kept grassy lawns with access from tarmac roads. They are separated by fir trees and low hedges, providing lots of privacy. De Fruithof has 450 level, numbered pitches (250 for tourers), all with 6A electricity, water, cable and drainage. To the front of the site is an open-air pool with a paddling pool and large water slide. At the centre of the site is a large lake with sandy beaches and some play equipment.

Facilities

Four toilet blocks have toilets, washbasins (open style and in cabins) and free, preset hot showers. Washbasins for children. Family shower room. Baby room. Facilities for disabled campers. Laundry. Motorcaravan services. Shop (bread to order). Bar, restaurant and snack bar. Open-air swimming pool (heated) with water slide and paddling pool. Lake with sandy beach. Playing field. Tennis. Bicycle hire. Playground. Entertainment team (high season and school holidays). WiFi (free). Off site: Emmen zoo.

Open: 8 April - 26 September.

Directions

On N34 take the exit for Emmen-Noord and turn immediately left towards Klijndijk. Follow site signs from there. GPS: 52.828868, 6.857342

Charges guide

Per unit incl. 2 persons and electricity	€ 19.50 - € 29.50
extra person (over 2 yrs)	€ 4.65
dog (max. 1)	€ 2.75

Meppen
Vakantieoord De Bronzen Emmer

Mepperstraat 41, NL-7855 TA Meppen (Drenthe) T: 0591 371 543. E: info@bronzenemmer.nl
alanrogers.com/NL6129

De Bronzen Emmer is in the centre of three nature reserves, close to the German border in the southwestern part of Drenthe. The 180 level and grassy touring pitches are attractively laid out and average 100 sq.m. in size. All have 10A electricity and are shaded by mature trees. There are 60 fully serviced pitches. To the front of the site are a heated indoor pool and paddling pool with a small slide and an open-air paddling pool. Here also are a sauna, sunbeds, recreation hall, small café and a playground. This is a good site for a family holiday or for those who enjoy walking and cycling.

Facilities

Two well placed, traditional style toilet blocks (one heated) with toilets, washbasins (open style and in cabins) and free, preset hot showers. Laundry. Motorcaravan services. Small shop for basics, small restaurant with bar and open-air terrace, takeaway (all open 1/5-31/8). Heated indoor swimming pool (20x10 m) with paddling pool and open air paddling pool (20/4-25/10). Sauna and sun beds. Bicycle hire. Playing field. Fishing. Tennis. Playground. Activity team in high season. WiFi throughout (free). Off site: Riding 150 m. Fishing 7 km.

Open: 29 March - 26 October.

Directions

On A28, take exit 31 (Beilen) and continue east on N381 road towards Emmen. Before Emmen turn south towards Meppen and follow site signs. GPS: 52.778987, 6.686323

Charges guide

Per unit incl. 2 persons incl. electricity	€ 19.50 - € 27.20
extra person (over 3 yrs)	€ 3.60
dog (max. 2)	€ 4.00

For latest campsite news, availability and prices visit
alanrogers.com

Nietap
Watersportcamping Cnossen Leekstermeer

Meerweg 13, NL-9312 TC Nietap (Drenthe) T: 0594 512 075. E: info@cnossenleekstermeer.nl

alanrogers.com/NL6185

Camping Cnossen Leekstermeer is a great site for nature lovers and watersports enthusiasts. There is a very extensive fleet of canoes, sailing boats, motorboats and rowing boats with windsurfing and sailing schools available. There are 140 touring pitches (125-175 sq.m), 110 with 6-16A electricity, water and drainage, and 30 tent pitches on the nature camping field. All pitches are on level, grassy fields with shade from mature trees and bushes, and there are three hardstandings. The site is situated in the centre of a nature reserve, which is still being extended, offering many opportunities for walking and cycling, and only 20 km. from the bustling town of Groningen. To the rear of the site is a pasture for sheep and horses, with a separate field with water, electricity and drainage taking around 20 large units. At the front of the site is a restaurant (with reception) and an open air terrace, plus a marina. Pitches here have marvellous views over the Leekstermeer and it is possible to moor your own boat in the marina.

Facilities	Directions
Two toilet blocks, one central and CO_2 neutral, a smaller one to the back, with underfloor heating, washbasins in cabins and free, preset hot showers. Extra services at the marina. Facilities for children and disabled visitors. Family shower rooms. Baby room. Laundry. Motorcaravan services. Bar/restaurant. Numerous sailing boats, canoes and rowing boats for hire. Windsurfing and sailing schools. Play area. WiFi (charged). Off site: Groningen 18 km.	From the A7 take exit 34 (Leek) and continue south towards Leek, then Nietap. Site is signed Leekstermeer. GPS: 53.175752, 6.423177

Open: 1 April - 1 November.

Charges guide

Per unit incl. 2 persons and electricity	€ 20.20 - € 28.30
extra person (over 4 yrs)	€ 4.30
dog	€ 2.00

Rolde
Camping De Weyert

Balloërstraat 2, NL-9451 AK Rolde (Drenthe) T: 0592 241 520. E: info@deweyert.nl

alanrogers.com/NL6144

Camping De Weyert is located within the Drentsche Aa National Park. This is a good choice for nature lovers, close to the holiday village of Rolde. There are 70 good sized touring pitches on two level, grassy fields (the larger one used as an ice-skating rink in winter). All have water, electricity (4/6A), drainage and cable TV connections. Alternatively, it is possible to rent a Hooiberghut (Hay store), a traditional chalet, unique to this area, which can accommodate up to four people. On-site amenities include a café and well designed children's playgrounds, in addition to a large indoor playroom. Drenthe is famous for its Hunebedden (dolmens). A stone's throw from the site is one of the most famous Hunebedden groups. This is great country to explore by bicycle and many excellent routes lead from the site.

Facilities	Directions
Two modern, heated toilet blocks with controllable hot showers, open style washbasins and a baby room. Cafeteria. Covered playground. WiFi over part of site (charged). Activity and entertainment programme. Mobile homes and Hooiberghuts for rent. Off site: Zoo at Emmen. Theme park at Slagharen. Excellent cycle routes. Nearest shops 1 km. Golf 7 km.	Take N33 from Assen to Gieten/Veendam. Then take the exit to Rolde. In Rolde follow signs to Balloo and site is on the right. GPS: 52.99081, 6.641711

Open: 1 April - 31 October.

Charges guide

Per unit incl. 2 persons and electricity	€ 18.20 - € 25.80
extra person	€ 3.90
child (2-10 yrs)	€ 2.40

FREE Alan Rogers Travel Card
Extra benefits and savings - see page 12

Ruinen

Camping Ruinen

Oude Benderseweg 11, NL-7963 PX Ruinen (Drenthe) T: 0522 471 770. E: info@camping-ruinen.nl

alanrogers.com/NL6160

Camping Ruinen, under new ownership, is a large, spacious site with 230 pitches, 197 for touring set within the woods of Drenthe. All pitches have electricity (6/10A Europlug) and include 105 serviced pitches also with water and drainage. The numbered pitches are over 100 sq.m. in size and are on large, grassy fields. They are separated by hedges and in the shade of trees. At this comfortable site you can relax by cycling or walking through the woods or over the moors, or join organised trips in groups on a regular basis. A brand new, central complex, also housing reception, includes a swimming pool, an indoor play room, a bar, restaurant and takeaway. Local attractions for children include Speelstad Oranje, a very large play-town and Ponypark Slagharen, a theme park. Adult activities include a Whisper Tour by boat through the De Weerlibben National Park or a visit to the water town of Giethoorn.

Facilities

Three modern toilet blocks provide washbasins (open style and in cabins), child size toilets and baths and a baby room. Facilities for disabled visitors. Laundry. Motorcaravan services. Shop. Restaurant with children's menu. Newly opened bar. New swimming pool. Play areas between pitches. Giant chess. Boules. Minigolf. Bicycle hire. Entertainment in high season. Petting farm. WiFi on part of site. Off site: Riding 400 m. Fishing 3 km.

Open: 1 April - 1 October.

Directions

From Zwolle follow A28 north and take exit 28. At the roundabout take the first exit. Turn left under the motorway. When you arrive in Ruinen follow site signs from there. GPS: 52.77492, 6.36993

Charges guide

Per unit incl. 2 persons and electricity	€ 16.20 - € 23.50
extra person	€ 4.00
dog	€ 3.50

Schipborg

Camping De Vledders

Zeegserweg 2a, NL-9469 PL Schipborg (Drenthe) T: 0504 091 489. E: info@devledders.nl

alanrogers.com/NL6130

Camping De Vledders is set in the centre of one of the most beautiful nature reserves in Holland, between the Drentse Hondsrug and the Drentsche Aa river. This attractive site is landscaped with many varieties of trees and shrubs. There are 150 touring pitches (all with 6A electricity) on rectangular, grassy fields, separated by well kept hedges. The level pitches are around 100 sq.m. in size with some shade provided at the back from mature trees and hedges. Static units and seasonal pitches are on separate fields. In one corner of the site there is an attractive lake with sandy beaches. Boating, swimming and even windsurfing are possible on the lake.

Facilities

Two refurbished, heated sanitary blocks with some washbasins in cabins and controllable hot showers. Family shower rooms. Baby room. En-suite facilities for disabled visitors. Motorcaravan services. Shop for basics. Snack bar. TV in reception. Lake with fishing, boating, windsurfing. Football field. Riding. Nordic walking. Playground. Some entertainment for children (high season). Bicycle hire. Torch useful. WiFi over site (charged). Off site: Golf 10 km. Sub-tropical pool in Zuidlaren. Sprookjeshof theme park in Zuidlaren.

Open: 1 April - 30 October.

Directions

From the A28 take exit 35 and continue towards Zuidlaren. Just before Zuidlaren follow signs for Schipborg and then site signs. GPS: 53.079267, 6.665617

Charges guide

Per unit incl. 2 persons and electricity	€ 19.70 - € 23.65
extra person (over 1 yr)	€ 3.35
dog (max. 2)	€ 2.95

No credit cards.

For latest campsite news, availability and prices visit
alanrogers.com

Vledder
Recreatiecentrum De Adelhof

Vledderweg 19, NL-8381 AB Vledder (Drenthe) T: 0521 381 440. E: info@adelhof.nl
alanrogers.com/NL6125

With a fine location close to the large nature reserves of the Drents-Friese Wold and Het Land van Oost, Recreatiecentrum De Adelhof is an ideal base for a cycling holiday in Drenthe, with miles of cycle tracks in the area. This is also a good site for anglers with a well stocked fishing lake. De Adelhof has 140 spacious touring pitches spread over several fields. The pitches are surrounded by bushes and shrubs to ensure privacy. They are generally around 100 sq.m. and all have electricity. Several attractive children's play areas have been created in each of the fields. One field in particular is reserved for families with dogs. On site, there is a lively activity programme in high season.

Facilities	Directions
Four toilet blocks with all the usual facilities (one open in winter, cleaning can be variable). Small shop (1/5-1/9). Café/restaurant and snack bar (6/4-26/10). Large fishing lake with carp. Children's farm. Play areas. All-weather tennis. Minigolf. Bicycle and go-kart hire. Football field. Internet access. WiFi throughout (charged). Professional entertainment team (spring holidays and high season). Off site: Municipal outdoor pool (1/5-1/9, charged). **Open:** All year.	Vledder is 10 km. northeast of Steenwijk. From A38 motorway take the Steenwijk exit and follow N855 north to Frederiksoord and Vledder. The site is just before the village to the right. GPS: 52.85178, 6.19845

Charges guide	
Per unit incl. 2 persons and electricity	€ 24.00
extra person	€ 3.50

Wateren
Molecaten Park Het Landschap

Schurerslaan 4, NL-8438 SC Wateren (Drenthe) T: 0521 387 244. E: hetlandschap@molecaten.nl
alanrogers.com/NL6152

Het Landschap is ideal for those who enjoy peace and relaxation, although there are plenty of activities available too. There are facilities for several sports, minigolf and an open-air theatre. In good weather, swimming is possible in the three-hectare lake with its sandy beaches and an island. Alternatively, in poor weather there is an indoor, heated swimming pool. The 200 touring pitches are spacious, all with 6A electricity (some with 10A), TV connections and water (shared between two). The grass camping areas are surrounded by trees and some climbing frames are provided for children.

Facilities	Directions
Toilet block with WCs, showers (on payment) and washbasins in cabins. Baby room. Well stocked shop. Bar. Restaurant. Snack bar with takeaway. Heated indoor swimming pool with paddling pool. Play area, bouncy castle and a few climbing frames. Sports field. Horse and pony riding. Minigolf. Boules. Lake swimming. Fishing. Bicycle and tricycle hire. Mountain bike hire. Entertainment team in high season. Miniclub. WiFi (charged). **Open:** 21 March - 31 October.	From Diever follow signs for Zorgvlied. The site is on the right immediately before Zorgvlied. GPS: 52.92227, 6.26731

Charges guide	
Per unit incl. 2 persons and electricity	€ 17.50 - € 25.00
serviced pitch	€ 6.00
dog (max. 2)	€ 4.35

Wezuperbrug
Molecaten Park Kuierpad

Oranjekanaal NZ 10, NL-7853 TA Wezuperbrug (Drenthe) T: 0591 381 415.
alanrogers.com/NL5790

Professionally run, this all year round site is suitable as a night stop, or for longer if you wish to participate in all the activities offered in July and August. The site itself is in a woodland setting on the edge of the village. The 550 flat and grassy pitches for touring units (with 900 in total) are of reasonable size. All have 4/6/10A electricity and 45 are fully serviced with electricity, TV aerial point, water and drainage. On-site activities include canoeing, windsurfing, water chutes and the dry ski slope, which is also open during the winter so that the locals can practise before going en-masse to Austria.

Facilities	Directions
Eleven sanitary blocks, including a new one, with hot showers. Facilities for disabled visitors. Laundry. Motorcaravan services. Supermarket (1/4-15/9; bread all year). Restaurant and bar with TV. Takeaway. Indoor pool (all year). Outdoor heated pool (1/5-15/9). Whirlpool. Internet access. Dry ski slope. Play areas. Minigolf. Lake with beach. Boat rental. New high rope adventure park with 517 m. zip wire. WiFi throughout (charged). **Open:** 1 April - 31 October.	From A28 take exit 31 (Beilen) onto N381. Exit Westerbork onto N374. After 2 km. turn right to Wezuperbrug. Site is on left after 2 km. GPS: 52.84005, 6.72593

Charges guide	
Per unit incl. 2 persons and electricity	€ 20.00 - € 36.20
extra person	€ 6.00
No credit cards.	

FREE Alan Rogers Travel Card
Extra benefits and savings - see page 12

Zandpol
Recreatiecentrum Zandpol
Stieltjeskanaal 14, NL-7764 AJ Zandpol (Drenthe) T: 0591 553 002. E: info@zandpol.nl
alanrogers.com/NL6137

De Zandpol is an attractively landscaped site with many varieties of trees and shrubs and fairly open pitches (some with shade at the back). Pitching is on level, grassy areas, each taking 12-15 units, with access from tarmac roads. The numbered pitches are 120 sq.m. in size and partly separated by hedges and bushes. There are 27 pitches with 10A electricity, water and waste water. All fields have some play equipment. To the front of the site is a small animal farm, and next to it a heated, open-air pool and small paddling pool. Central to the site is a comfortable garden café, more like a living room, with a library, darts, billiards and open-air terrace.

Facilities

One traditional, but adequate, toilet block (key access) with toilets, open style washbasins, and free, preset hot showers. Children's toilet. Baby room. Motorcaravan services. Laundry facilities. Basics from reception. Restaurant with library for light meals with open-air terrace. Solar heated open-air pool with paddling pool. Tennis. Minigolf. Bicycle hire. Playground. WiFi (charged). No groups of young people and no bikers allowed. Off site: Lake with sandy beach and fishing 100 m.

Open: 26 March - 14 October.

Directions

From Emmen, go south on N34 towards Coevorden. At crossing with A37, turn east towards Klazienaveen. At crossing with N853, turn south towards Schoonebeek. Site is signed in Zandpol. GPS: 52.693085, 6.854525

Charges guide

Per unit incl. 2 persons	
and electricity	€ 19.25 - € 22.75
extra person (over 2 yrs)	€ 3.75
dog	€ 3.00

Zorgvlied
Rekreatiepark Groot Bartje
De Gavere 1, NL-8437 PE Zorgvlied (Drenthe) T: 0521 387 249. E: info@vakantiegevoel.nl
alanrogers.com/NL6165

This park is aimed very much at those who enjoy riding. The site has 35 stables available, so you can bring your own horse. Riding trips through the countryside are organised, and site staff will follow you with picnic baskets. Groot Bartje has 100 touring pitches on three circular, grassy fields and two smaller fields to the side. The middle field has 36 spacious, level pitches on grass, with shade from mature trees. All are equipped with 16A electricity, water, waste water and cables.

Facilities

One good toilet block with underfloor heating, toilets, washbasins and preset hot showers (5 minutes free). Baby room. Facilities for disabled visitors. Laundry with washing machines and dryers. Basics and bread from reception. Bar/restaurant and snack bar (daily in season). Pool (15x10 m) with slide and paddling pool. Tennis. Riding. Bicycle hire. Playground. Torch useful. WiFi (charged). Off site: Riding 3 km. Fishing 5 km. Golf 10 km. Boat launching 20 km.

Open: 1 April - 1 November.

Directions

On A28, take exit 31 Westerbork and continue on N381 towards Drachten. At Hoogersmilde, turn south onto N371 towards Meppel. Follow through Diever and in the centre of Diever, turn northwest towards Oude Willem, Wateren and Zorgvlied. GPS: 52.92359, 6.250609

Charges guide

Per unit incl. 2 persons	
and electricity	€ 13.00 - € 38.00
extra person	€ 6.00

Zweeloo
Camping De Knieplanden
Hoofdstraat 2, NL-7851 AA Zweeloo (Drenthe) T: 0591 371 599. E: camping.knieplanden@planet.nl
alanrogers.com/NL6133

Camping De Knieplanden is a small site, close to the German border. Taken over by the Eefting family in 2005, it has 65 touring pitches on five grassy fields and 16 mobile homes in a separate area. Touring pitches are laid out in circular bays surrounded by high hedges. The level pitches are numbered and have 4/8A electricity. To the front of the site is an open-air public pool with water slide and paddling pool. Central on the site is a café and small restaurant where you can enjoy basic meals. Also here is the recreation hall, where activities for children are organised in high season and school holidays.

Facilities

New toilet block with roomy facilities at the centre of the site, and a single, basic but heated toilet block with toilets, washbasins (open style and in cabins) and free, preset hot showers. Laundry with washing machines. Bar/restaurant with simple meals (daily in season). Playing field. Tennis. Minigolf. Boules. Playground. Some entertainment in high season. WiFi. Torch useful. Off site: Bicycle hire 500 m.

Open: All year.

Directions

On A28, take exit 31 (Beilen) and continue east on N381 towards Emmen. Before Emmen, turn south towards Zweeloo and follow site signs. GPS: 52.794719, 6.724373

Charges guide

Per unit incl. 2 persons and electricity	€ 22.00
extra person	€ 3.75
child (0-12 yrs)	€ 3.25

CAPITAL: ALMERE

When you hear that Flevoland is a new, man-made flat polder, you may imagine a dull, desert-like landscape whipped by the west wind, but you couldn't be more wrong!

You will be surprised by the variation in the landscape of Flevoland. Traditional farmhouses with patchworks of fields lie side by side with deep forests, dramatic open spaces and nature reserves thronging with wildlife. The Oostvaardersplassen, for example, is the largest wetland nature reserve in the Netherlands and a paradise for birds. Most of this area is made up of vast lakes and a pristine wetland. Although Flevoland is a new province, the region itself has a long history and what once was water, is now an attractive residential and recreational area with a growing population.

A visit to Schokland brings into focus the age-old Dutch struggle against water. It was evacuated some 150 years ago due to the threat of flooding by the waters of the then Zuiderzee (now the IJsselmeer). When the northeast polder was drained, Schokland relinquished its status as an island, and now only a raised area remains as a reminder of its unique past, which is traced in the local museum.

Places of interest

Almere: young, modern city with some stunning architecture; currently with 130,000 inhabitants and still growing.

Emmeloord: the centre point of the Noordoost-polder with all amenities. The 65 m. high Polder Tower offers breathtaking views and has a carillon of 48 bells.

Urk: characteristic old fishing harbour.

Attractions

Museum Nieuwland, Lelystad: traces the development of Flevoland and shows the way of life of its inhabitants when it was an island.

Lakes and beaches: the lakes of Flevoland are shallow and safe for children. There is also deeper water for all types of watersports.

Bataviastad: retail outlet with top brands, plus museums and Batavia wharf.

Walibi World: theme park promising fun and entertainment for the whole family.

Aviodome: national aviation theme park.

Farms: the fertile land of the Flevoland polder produces quality regional products on sale at many farms.

Landscape art: five large works of landscape art, including Reims Cathedral, 'constructed' from trees.

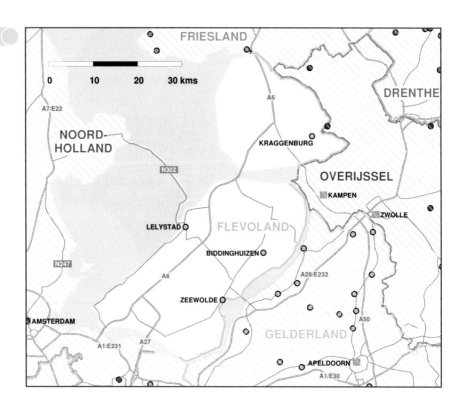

Biddinghuizen
Molecaten Park Flevostrand

Strandweg 1, NL-8256 RZ Biddinghuizen (Flevoland) T: 0320 288 480. E: flevostrand@molecaten.nl
alanrogers.com/NL6212

Flevostrand is a family site with direct access to Lake Veluwe's sandy beach. All pitches are situated on spacious, grass fields offering ideal opportunities for children to play. You can choose between the area inside the dyke (with 10A electricity) or the beach site (6A electricity) directly at the waterfront. The site has a large marina with a pier and slipway, from where boat launching is possible (boat hire is available). There are various play areas and heated indoor and outdoor pools, and a full bar/restaurant with terrace enjoying beautiful views over the lake.

Facilities

Well maintained toilet blocks provide clean facilities with open style washbasins, preset showers and a baby room. Bar/restaurant and terrace, and takeaway (all 1/4-30/9). Indoor pool and outdoor pool with paddling pool (all heated). Games room with air hockey and billiards. Tennis courts. Play areas. Beach volleyball. Bicycle and boat hire. Marina with slipway, surf school and sailing school. WiFi over site (charged). Max. 2 dogs per pitch. Mobile homes and chalets to rent. Off site: Walking and cycling. Walibi Holland theme park. Harderwijk.

Open: 29 March - 1 November.

Directions

From A28 motorway take exit 26 (Harderwijk, Lelystad) and follow signs to Lelystad (N302). After you have crossed the bridge (4.5 km), take first right turn at the roundabout towards Kampen (Harderdijk). Follow road to Kampen and turn right after 3 km. Site is well signed. GPS: 52.385401, 5.629088

Charges guide

Per unit incl. 2 persons	
and electricity	€ 17.00 - € 32.00
extra person	€ 3.90
child (2-10 yrs)	€ 2.90
dog	€ 3.90

For latest campsite news, availability and prices visit
alanrogers.com

Kraggenburg
Recreatiepark De Voorst

Leemringweg 33, NL-8317 RD Kraggenburg (Flevoland) T: 0527 252 524. E: devoorst@vdbrecreatie.nl
alanrogers.com/NL6042

Recreatiepark De Voorst is on the polder beside the Zwolsevaart canal from where there is easy access to the Zwarte Meer and the IJsselmeer lakes. The level pitches are 100 sq.m. and arranged on well kept, grassy fields, some under trees with shade, others more open. Some pitches have views over the canal where it is possible to moor small boats (boat ramp available). The touring fields vary in size and all have a small play area. All 200 touring pitches have 4A electricity. To the rear of the site is a separate area for privately owned mobile homes.

Facilities

Several toilet blocks with toilets, washbasins (open style and in cabins) and controllable, hot showers (token). Baby room. Motorcaravan services. Playing field. Playgrounds. Tennis. Boules. Fishing. Bicycle hire. Water bikes for rent. Boat launching. Off site: Restaurant and open-air pool 100 m. Beach and sailing 10 km.

Open: 1 April - 1 October.

Directions

From the A6 take exit 13 and continue east on N352 towards Kraggenburg. Site is signed at the roundabout on the edge of Kraggenburg.
GPS: 52.675597, 5.8921

Charges guide

Per unit incl. 2 persons and electricity	€ 22.50
extra person	€ 3.00
dog	€ 2.50

Lelystad
Camping 't Oppertje

Uilenweg 11, NL-8245 AB Lelystad (Flevoland) T: 0320 253 693. E: info@oppertje.nl
alanrogers.com/NL6206

Located on the banks of a beautiful lake, Het Bovenwater, and adjacent to the natural park of De Oostvaardersplassen, this site provides campers with peace and space, albeit with opportunities for various watersports on the lake. The site appeals primarily to young families, but also to retired couples. There are 70 touring pitches on one or two grassy fields and a designated area for campervans next to reception (all with 6A electricity). Some wooden cabins and a few caravans are available for rent, and 25 pitches have been designated for large tents in a separate field. There is no restaurant, but the site provides a barbecue hut with TV.

Facilities

Modern heated toilet block with controllable hot showers (€ 0.50) and facilities for babies and disabled visitors. Dishwashing (€ 0.20). Motorcaravan services. Direct lake access (sailing, windsurfing and fishing). Basketball. Trampoline. Dogs are not accepted. Off site: Shops and restaurants in Lelystad 4 km. Watersports centre. Walking and cycling. Riding. Golf.

Open: 1 April - 2 October.

Directions

Approaching using A6 take exit 10 to Lelystad (N309). This is the Larserdreef. After 2.5 km. and just before a sharp right-hand bend, turn left (Buizerdweg). After 1.5 km. turn right at the Uilenweg. The site is at the end of this road.
GPS: 52.48542, 5.41468

Charges guide

Per unit incl. 2 persons and electricity	€ 20.00 - € 21.00

Zeewolde
Erkemederstrand Camping Horeca Jachthaven & Dagrecreatie

Erkemederweg 79, NL-3896 LB Zeewolde (Flevoland) T: 0365 228 421. E: info@erkemederstrand.nl
alanrogers.com/NL6200

Erkemederstrand is a leisure park in Flevoland with direct access to the Nuldernauw where there is a sandy beach, a lake and a forest. It provides a campsite for families, a marina, an area for youngsters to camp, a camping area for groups and a recreation area for day visitors. The campsite itself is divided into two areas: one before the dyke at the waterfront and one behind the dyke. The pitches are spacious (125-150 sq.m) and most have electricity, water and drainage. The focal point of the site and marina is the De Jutter beachside restaurant.

Facilities

Six neat, clean and heated toilet blocks (access by key; exclusively for campers). Washbasins in cabins, showers and family bathrooms (some charges for hot water). Laundry facilities. Well stocked supermarket, bar, restaurant and takeaway (all open all season). Several play areas and children's farm. Watersports facilities and lake swimming. Fishing. Football pitch. Minigolf. Bicycle hire. Entertainment programme. WiFi (charged). Beach and shower for dogs. Off site: Golf 9 km. Riding 10 km.

Open: 28 March - 26 October.

Directions

From A28 (Utrecht-Zwolle) take exit 9 (Nijkerk, Almere) and follow N301 to Zeewolde. Cross the bridge and turn right following signs to site. From Amsterdam/Almere, take exit 5 and follow N27 (becomes N305) to Zeewolde. Then take N301 to Nijkerk. From bridge turn right and follow signs to site. GPS: 52.27021, 5.48871

Charges guide

Per unit incl. 2 persons and electricity	€ 27.00
extra person	€ 3.25

FREE Alan Rogers Travel Card
Extra benefits and savings - see page 12

Zeewolde
Camping Het Groene Bos

Groenewoudse Weg 98, NL-3896 LS Zeewolde (Flevoland) T: 036 523 6366. E: info@hetpolderbos.nl
alanrogers.com/NL6214

Camping Het Groene Bos is a pleasant rural site, located at the edge of a vast forest, the Horsterwold, in the province of Flevoland. There is a real sense of space and nature here. This immaculately kept site has 80 large, grassy touring pitches (well distributed over the site and up to 200 sq.m) most with 6-10A electricity. The forest is ideal for walking, cycling and riding, with many miles of marked tracks. Unusually, it's possible to bring your own horse to the site and then discover the Zeebodemtrail, a route of over 80 km. with facilities for horses along the way. On site, the children's farm is undeniably a popular feature. Zeewolde (3 km. away) is an attractive town and provides good opportunities for many water activities with a fine beach and a marina.

Facilities

One central, modern toilet block has preset hot showers, family rooms, baby room and facilities for disabled visitors. Play area. Giant chess. Bar with library, TV and children's games. Boules. Children's farm. Stabling for horses. Bicycle and go-kart hire. Motorcaravan services. WiFi (charged). Off site: Golf (18 holes) 1.5 km. Bicycle hire 2 km. Zeewolde with all usual facilities, beaches and a marina 3 km. Dolfinarium marine park. Walibi World theme park. Ancient towns of Harderwijk and Elburg.
Open: 1 April - 20 October.

Directions

The site is located just west of Zeewolde. Leave the A28 Amersfoort-Zwolle motorway at exit 9 and follow the signs Zeewolde. The campsite is well signed. GPS: 52.340118, 5.505473

Charges guide

Per unit incl. 2 persons	
and electricity	€ 16.90 - € 20.90
extra person	€ 3.50
dog	€ 2.00

Zeewolde
RCN Camping Zeewolde

Dasselaarweg 1, NL-3896 LT Zeewolde (Flevoland) T: 0365 221 246. E: zeewolde@rcn.nl
alanrogers.com/NL6215

This site, a member of the RCN group, has been developed on reclaimed land in the Polderland in the province of Flevoland. There is direct lake access, and the site is split into inner and outer dykes. In the outer dyke area, there are grassy, sunny touring pitches (most with 10A electricity, water and drainage) close to the lake and its sandy beach, as well as Zeewolde's marina. The marina is a great centre for sailing, fishing and windsurfing. It also has a friendly beach bar. The inner dyke pitches are also grassy but are enclosed by hedges and have mature trees to provide more shade.

Facilities

Modern sanitary block at the beach pitches with facilities for disabled visitors and children. Dog shower. Launderette. Restaurant with lake views. Bar. Beach bar. Bakery and supermarket. Beach with swimming area for toddlers. Play areas. Open-air and covered pools (heated). Multisports field. Mountain bike track. Tennis courts. Bicycle hire. Go-kart hire. Jetty and beach for catamarans. 5-a-side football. Climbing wall (6.5 m). WiFi over site (charged). Accommodation to rent. Off site: Sailing boat hire (adjacent). Walking and cycle tracks. Riding 5 km. Golf 10 km.
Open: All year.

Directions

Take the Zeewolde exit from A28 and follow the road for 5 km. crossing a bridge. After crossing the bridge, at the roundabout take the N701 to Zeewolde. Follow this road for 6 km. The campsite will be on your right. GPS: 52.31167, 5.54356

Charges guide

Per unit incl. 2 persons	
and electricity	€ 18.50 - € 29.50
extra person	€ 3.90
dog	€ 4.95

CAPITAL: LEEUWARDEN

Friesland is a unique province where Frisian is spoken and written widely, alongside Dutch. The many lakes are a Mecca for tourists and not just lovers of watersports.

Friesland has a strong agricultural history, with a vast network of canals, ditches and streams dividing the fields and pastures. These lead not only to magnificent Frisian lakes, picturesque villages and beautiful countryside vistas but also to the 11 Frisian cities with designated historical status. Typical of the Frisian landscape are its strong vertical elements – steeples, windmills, masts and sails; the vast tracts of land and enormous skies are among its main attractions, together with the forests of Gaasterland and the cliffs of the IJsselmeer. But do not forget the four islands in the Waddenzee that also belong to this province: Vlieland, Terschelling, Ameland and Schiermonnikoog, all accessible by ferry from the mainland.

The 11 Frisian cities are all worth a visit. The historic Hanseatic Bolsward, the pilgrimage town of Dokkum, the former university city of Franeker, the fishing town of Harlingen, the picturesque Hindeloopen, the canal city IJlst, the capital Leeuwarden, small Sloten, bustling lakeside Sneek, the old Stavoren and the picturesque town Workum. Moving from city to city you will take in the many cultural and historical sights while being captivated by some of the most beautiful corners of the Frisian countryside.

Places of interest

Leeuwarden: city with 575 national monuments, home to 'De Elfstedentocht' the traditional 200 km. skating tour – there is also an alternative route for cyclists.

Schiermonnikoog: island and national park, with only a few areas closed to the public. Feel the wind in your hair and savour the tang of the tidal flats.

Hindeloopen: city surrounded by water on three sides, with charming narrow streets, bridges, shops, canals and a popular marina.

Makkum: known worldwide for its pottery – the oldest in the Netherlands.

Moddergat: 50 small fishermen's cottages are a feature of this picturesque town.

Attractions

The Fries Museum, Leeuwarden: the largest regional museum in the Netherlands, combining art, culture and history under one roof.

Fries Scheepvaart Museum, Sneek: maritime museum tracing the history of Frisian shipping from the 17th to the 20th century.

Sneekweek: home to the country's largest watersport event, with the famous race of the 'skûtsjes', a week-long regatta with historic sailing ships representing the different towns of Friesland.

Bolsward: visit the distillery of Sonnema and sample the national drink 'Berenburg'.

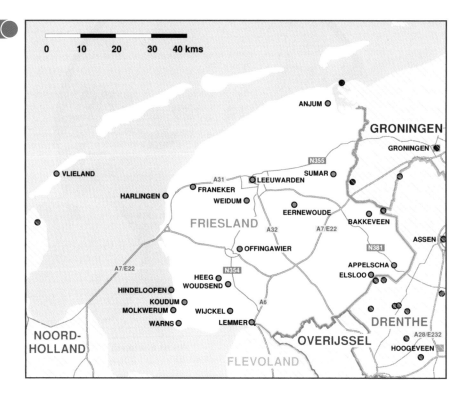

Anjum
Landal Esonstad
Oostmahorn 29B, NL-9133 DT Anjum (Friesland) T: 0519 329 555. E: esonstad@landal.nl
alanrogers.com/NL6051

Esonstad is a member of the Landal group and is attractively located on the Lauwersmeer, close to the Schiermonnikoog ferry. There is an impressive range of facilities, including an all-weather tennis court, indoor pool and indoor play barn. This open site is situated on the edge of the National Park, in a landscape of lakes, forests and dykes – ideal for wildlife and watersports enthusiasts. It extends over five hectares and comprises 129 spacious pitches (100 sq.m) all with 16A electricity and a private water supply close by. Many pitches are close to the water. There are some tent pitches on a separate field and a few hardstandings.

Facilities
The modern, clean toilet block has vanity-style washbasins, preset hot showers, a baby room and facilities for disabled visitors. Washing machine. Shop, restaurant/bar (all 27/3-1/11). Indoor heated swimming pool with separate paddling pool (27/3-1/11). Whirlpool. Solarium. Sauna and Turkish bath. Indoor play barn. Games room. Tennis. Golf. Site ferry to Schiermonnikoog. WiFi (charged). Off site: 18-hole pitch & putt course. Old windmill at Anjum. Nature museum at Dokkum.

Open: 27 March - 2 November.

Directions
Follow A28 motorway to Meppel and then A32 towards Heerenveen and Drachten (A7). On A7 take the exit to Buitenpost (N358). In Buitenpost follow signs to Lauwersoog as far as Anjum. In Anjum turn right to Oostmahorn and follow signs to Landal Esonstad. GPS: 53.37909, 6.162332

Charges guide

Per unit incl. 2 persons	
and electricity	€ 16.00 - € 31.00
extra person	€ 5.25
dog	€ 5.50

For latest campsite news, availability and prices visit
alanrogers.com

Appelscha
Camping Alkenhaer

Alkenhaer 1, NL-8426 EP Appelscha (Friesland) T: 0516 432 600. E: info@campingalkenhaer.nl

alanrogers.com/NL6085

Alkenhaer is a pleasant and peaceful family campsite near Appelscha in the southeast part of Friesland, and close to the province of Drenthe. Located between the beautiful natural parks of Drents-Friese Wold and Fochteloërveen, the focus is very much on space and nature. The 240 pitches, 90 for touring, are dispersed over spacious marked fields and are all equipped with 10A electricity. The fields only take a few units, making camping here cosy. Shade is provided by mature trees. There are separate hardstanding areas for mobile homes and large caravans. On-site amenities include a large football field, a volleyball court, a well equipped playground and a children's pool.

Facilities	Directions
Two modern toilet blocks have open style washbasins and preset hot showers. Facilities for children and baby room. Washing machine. Motorcaravan services. Bar, restaurant and snack bar (1/4-30/9). Children's pool. Play equipment. Football. Volleyball. Riding. Bicycle hire. WiFi over site (charged). Off site: Outdoor swimming pool. Golf 1 km. Fishing 2 km. National parks. Appelscha.	From A28 take exit 31 and follow N381 towards Drachten/Appelscha. Take the exit for Appelscha, then follow signs to the site. GPS: 52.94579, 6.362007
Open: 1 April - 31 October.	

Charges guide

Per unit incl. 2 persons and electricity	€ 17.50 - € 20.50
extra person	€ 2.50

Bakkeveen
Molecaten Park 't Hout

Duurswouderweg 11, NL-9243 KA Bakkeveen (Friesland) T: 0516 541 287. E: thout@molecaten.nl

alanrogers.com/NL6020

Camping 't Hout is a holiday paradise for children with its covered playground, indoor play paradise, open-air fun pool with paddling pool and animal farm. The site is in the woods, just outside the interesting village of Bakkeveen. It has 250 touring pitches on seven well cared for grassy fields, all with cable. Of these, 130 have 10A electricity, water, waste water and a numbered parking place. Other pitches have 4A electricity. The central building next to the pool also houses a bakery selling croissants, pizza and bread rolls, a shop and there is an open-air terrace for drinks.

Facilities	Directions
Four modern, heated toilet blocks have washbasins in cabins, and free, preset hot showers (6 min. hot water). Facilities for babies and children. Family shower rooms. Laundry. Shop for basics. Central building with snack bar, bread shop and terrace. Open-air fun pool (10x5 m) with slide and paddling pool (heated July/Aug). Air cushions. Volleyball. Basketball. Skelter hire. Covered playground. Indoor play palace. Canoe hire. Children's theatre. WiFi.	On A28 in either direction, take exit Beilen-Noord and continue on N31 towards Drachten. Take the exit Wijnjewoude/Bakkeveen after 35 km. and then follow the site signs. GPS: 53.078665, 6.252913
Open: 1 April - 30 September.	

Charges guide

Per unit incl. 2 persons and electricity	€ 16.50 - € 27.50
extra person	€ 4.00

Bakkeveen
Camping de Ikeleane

Duerswâldmer Wei 19, NL-9243 KA Bakkeveen (Friesland) T: 0516 541283. E: info@ikeleane.nl

alanrogers.com/NL6021

Camping de Ikeleane (Frisian for Oak Lane) has a rural setting, 14 km. southeast of the pleasant town of Drachten. This is a much loved part of Friesland, where forests alternate with dunes and heathland. De Ikeleane is a good base for exploring this Frisian countryside on foot or bicycle (bicycle and go-kart hire on site) and has wonderful views over the countryside. This is a well equipped site with 200 pitches, 79 for touring, all with 6/10A electricity, and 67 with water and drainage. Children will enjoy the football and volleyball pitches and the indoor play barn. The entertainment team organises a variety of activities, including ballooning, cycling and volleyball matches.

Facilities	Directions
Three toilet blocks with open style washbasins, controllable hot showers (card operated), family showers, baby room and facilities for disabled visitors. Bar, restaurant (small meals) and snack bar. Washing machine. Motorcaravan services. Play barn. Football. Volleyball. Bicycle and go-kart hire. Entertainment. WiFi. New luxury chalets and caravans for rent. Twin-axle caravans are not accepted.	From A7 Heerenveen-Groningen motorway, take exit 30 and follow N381 towards Oosterwolde. After 500 m. turn left to Ureterp and follow this road (N917) to Bakkeveen. In village bear right to Wijnjewoude. Site is 1 km. to the left. GPS: 53.071158, 6.242742
Open: 1 April - 31 October.	

Charges guide

Per unit incl. 2 persons and electricity	€ 18.50 - € 22.00
extra person	€ 3.00

FREE Alan Rogers Travel Card
Extra benefits and savings - see page 12

Bakkeveen
Recreatiecentrum De Waldsang
Foarwurkerwei 2, NL-9243 JZ Bakkeveen (Friesland) T: 0516 541 255. E: info@waldsang.nl
alanrogers.com/NL6035

Camping on the Waldsang is camping in the green heart of Friesland. Close to the site are numerous woodlands, dunes and moors, which makes it an ideal base for long walks and cycling tours. De Waldsang has 115 touring pitches (up to 120 sq.m) on separate fields from the static units. Pitching is on rectangular, level, grassy fields off gravel access lanes, partially shaded by mature trees. Most pitches have 16A electricity, and some 30 also have water and waste water. A canal runs alongside the site and some road noise can be heard.

Facilities	Directions
Two modern toilet blocks with toilets, washbasins and preset, hot showers (6 minutes free). Laundry. Motorcaravan services. Shop (daily in season). Bar and restaurant with snack bar and open-air terrace (daily in season). TV and video room. Fishing. Entertainment team in high season. Canoe hire. Bicycle hire. Playground. WiFi throughout (charged). Off site: Bus stop outside site. Open-air public pool in Bakkeveen (free for campers).	On A28 in either direction, take exit Beilen-Noord and continue on N31 towards Drachten. Take the exit Wijnjewoude/Bakkeveen after 35 km. and then follow the site signs. GPS: 53.085483, 6.250033

Charges guide

Per unit incl. 2 persons and electricity	€ 16.00 - € 24.00

Open: 1 April - 1 October.

Eernewoude
Camping It Wiid
Koaidijk 10, NL-9264 TP Eernewoude (Friesland) T: 0511 539 223. E: info@wiid.nl
alanrogers.com/NL6055

Camping It Wiid is surrounded by water and has easy access to the famous Frisian lakes. On site, it is possible to rent sailing boats and motorboats or you can moor your own. The site has 300 touring pitches, all with 4–16A electricity. Of these, 90 have water, waste water and cable as well. Pitching is on level, grassy fields with shade from mature trees and hedges. To the far edge of the site is a spit of land where you can camp surrounded by water, and from where there are great views over the Fokkesloot water. Cars are parked away from pitches.

Facilities	Directions
Two new, heated toilet blocks with washbasins and preset, hot showers. Baby room. Facilities for children and disabled visitors. Laundry. Motorcaravan services. Well stocked shop. Bar/restaurant and takeaway. Open-air pool with 65 m. water slide and fun paddling pool. Boat rental. Sailing school. Football. Volleyball. Basketball. Fishing. Bicycle hire. Tennis. Playground. Entertainment programme in high season. WiFi (charged). Off site: Fishing 100 m. Bicycle hire 2 km.	From channel ports you can either go north from Amsterdam via A7/E22 through Leeuwarden towards Drachten, or east from Amsterdam via A6, onto A7 at sign for Leeuwarden/Groningen, then onto N31 at sign for De Haven/Drachten. On N31 take exit for Earnewald and follow site signs. GPS: 53.1268, 5.946183

Charges guide

Per unit incl. 2 persons and electricity	€ 28.25 - € 29.75
extra person	€ 6.25
Camping Cheques accepted.	

Open: 1 April - 1 October.

Elsloo
Camping Wilhelminahoeve
Canada 3, NL-8424 SR Elsloo (Friesland) T: 0516 516 651. E: scheepstra@hetnet.nl
alanrogers.com/NL6023

Camping Wilhelminahoeve is set in a pleasant, rural location at the heart of the Drents-Friese Wold with a number of important attractions close at hand. The site is beside a lake and has a pleasant beach. There are just 39 pitches here, divided between two large, car-free fields and one smaller field. All pitches have 6A electricity and some have shade. Grass play areas have been created in the centre of the large fields. There are also two apartments for rent. On-site amenities include a convivial restaurant/snack bar with a terrace. The surrounding countryside is best explored by bicycle, with miles of excellent tracks. The site managers will be pleased to recommend routes.

Facilities	Directions
Small but adequate toilet blocks with washbasins and showers. Bar with TV. Snack bar/restaurant. Play area. Entertainment and activity programme. Apartments for rent. Off site: Shops and restaurants in Assen. Zoo at Emmen. Walking and cycling.	Approaching from the north (Assen A28) take the southbound N371 as far as Smilde. Shortly beyond this village, turn right towards Appelscha, from where site is well signed. GPS: 52.934816, 6.287884

Charges guide

Per unit incl. 2 persons and electricity	€ 14.50
extra person	€ 4.25

Open: All year.

For latest campsite news, availability and prices visit
alanrogers.com

Franeker
Recreatiepark Bloemketerp

Bug. J. Dijkstraweg 3, NL-8800 AA Franeker (Friesland) T: 0517 395 099. E: info@bloemketerp.nl

alanrogers.com/NL6075

Camping Bloemketerp can be found within walking distance of the interesting and historic town of Franeker. There are 120 sheltered and good sized pitches here. These are dispersed around several camping fields. The park also has a range of holiday homes for rent. There is a well equipped sports centre adjacent, with sub-tropical indoor swimming pool, canoe rental and bicycle hire. Campers are allowed free access to this centre (fitness, tennis, squash, racquetball, sauna and massage). The park boasts an attractive, friendly restaurant (with sun terrace) offering both a set menu and buffet options. Some road noise can be heard, but it is not too intrusive.

Facilities

One large toilet block with controllable, hot showers (€ 0.50), open style washbasins and facilities for disabled visitors. Laundry. Motorcaravan services. Restaurant (with buffet option). Takeaway meals. Sports centre full facilities. Play area. Ten-pin bowling. Recreation team (high season). Canoe hire. WiFi over site (charged). Accommodation for rent. Off site: Adjacent sub-tropical swimming pool (free).

Open: All year.

Directions

Franeker is near the A31 between the head of the Afsluitdijk and capital of Friesland, Leeuwarden. Take exit 20 towards Franeker then follow signs to Bloemketerp. GPS: 53.189683, 5.553333

Charges guide

Per unit incl. 2 persons and electricity	€ 20.50 - € 23.45
extra person	€ 3.50

Harlingen
Camping De Zeehoeve

Westerzeedijk 45, NL-8862 PK Harlingen (Friesland) T: 0517 413 465. E: info@zeehoeve.nl

alanrogers.com/NL6080

Superbly located, directly behind the sea dyke of the Wadden Sea and just a kilometre from the harbour of Harlingen, De Zeehoeve is an attractive and spacious site. It has 300 pitches (125 touring units), all with 16A Europlug connection and 20 with water, drainage and electricity. There are 16 hardstandings for motorcaravans and larger units. Some pitches have views over the Harlingen canal where one can moor small boats. An ideal site for rest and relaxation, for watersports or to visit the attractions of Harlingen and Friesland. After a day of activity, one can wine and dine in the site's recently modernised restaurant or at one of the many pubs in the town.

Facilities

Three sanitary blocks include open style washbasins with cold water only, washbasins in cabins with hot and cold water, controllable showers (on payment). Family showers and baby bath. Facilities for disabled visitors. Cooking hob. Launderette. Motorcaravan services. Bar/restaurant (July/Aug). Play area. Bicycle hire. Boat launching. Pedalo and canoe hire. Fishing. Entertainment (July/Aug). B&B. Hikers' cabins and boarding houses. WiFi (charged).

Open: 1 April - 15 October.

Directions

From Leeuwarden take A31 southwest to Harlingen, then follow site signs. GPS: 53.16237, 5.41688

Charges guide

Per unit incl. 2 persons and electricity	€ 22.50
extra person	€ 4.25
child (4-11 yrs)	€ 3.25
dog	€ 3.50

Heeg
Watersport Camping Heeg

De Burd 25A, NL-8621 JX Heeg (Friesland) T: 0515 442 328. E: wch@watersportcampingheeg.nl

alanrogers.com/NL6026

Watersport Camping Heeg is a welcoming and comfortable site, ten minutes walk from the centre of Heeg, an old fishing town that is now mainly a focus for watersports. Heeg is a bustling resort with many opportunities for dining and shopping. The campsite is on the lake and has a small sandy beach and a jetty for 90 boats with a trailer ramp. There are 200 attractive, level pitches on grass (with 4A electricity) off gravel access roads. With 120 numbered pitches for touring (100 sq.m) and three hardstandings there are lovely views over the lake from the front rows.

Facilities

Two toilet blocks, one at the front, a second, newer one towards the back, with toilets, washbasins (open style and in cabins) and controllable, hot showers (€ 0.50). Baby room. Laundry with washing machines and dryers. Kiosk for basics. Bar. Playground. Dutch tub for hire. Small sandy beach. Lake for swimming and sailing. Sailing, surfing and kite surfing lessons. Canoe and sail boat hire.

Open: 1 April - 1 October.

Directions

From the A6, take exit 17 (Lemmer) and continue west on the N359. At Balk, turn north on N928 towards Woudsend and turn north again on N354. Exit for Heeg and follow site signs. GPS: 52.967369, 5.594594

Charges guide

Per unit incl. 2 persons and electricity	€ 23.80
extra person	€ 5.60
child (under 13 yrs)	€ 3.00

FREE Alan Rogers Travel Card
Extra benefits and savings - see page 12

Hindeloopen
Camping Hindeloopen

Westerdijk 9, NL-8713 JA Hindeloopen (Friesland) T: 0514 521 452. E: info@campinghindeloopen.nl

alanrogers.com/NL6050

Hindeloopen is one of the 11 historic cities of Friesland and this site is nearby. The delightful city retains plenty of old maritime charm. Situated directly behind the embankment of the IJsselmeer, the site has 136 touring pitches (out of 650), all of which have 6/16A electricity (Europlug), water and drainage. There are 15 hardstandings for motorcaravans and large caravans. The pitches are 90-100 sq.m. in size and arranged in groups that are separated from each other by high hedges. The lake here is not deep and from its banks there are wonderful views of the town of Hindeloopen and the surrounding countryside.

Facilities

Two basic toilet blocks include showers and washbasins in cabins. Facilities for children. Baby room. Facilities for disabled visitors. Laundry. Freezer for ice packs. Motorcaravan services. Shop (daily in July/Aug). Café/restaurant and snack bar (daily in July/Aug). Play area with bike course. Football pitch. Tennis. Bicycle hire. Fishing. Surfing school. Boat launching and boat rental. Children's club (open 6 weeks during July/Aug). Free WiFi over site. Dogs are not accepted. Off site: Riding 5 km.

Open: 28 March - 1 November.

Directions

From Lemmer follow the N359 northwest to Hindeloopen and from there, campsite signs. GPS: 52.93492, 5.40430

Charges guide

Per unit incl. 2 persons, water, waste water and electricity	€ 19.00 - € 24.50
extra person	€ 3.00
child (3-12 yrs)	€ 2.00

Koudum
Camping De Kuilart

Kuilart 1, NL-8723 CG Koudum (Friesland) T: 0514 522 221. E: info@kuilart.nl

alanrogers.com/NL5760

De Kuilart is a well run, modern and partly car-free site by Friesland's largest lake. With its own marina and many facilities, it attracts many watersports enthusiasts. There are around 543 pitches, 310 for touring units, all with electricity (6/16A), water, drainage, WiFi and TV connections, and 34 new pitches with private sanitary facilities. The restaurant provides beautiful views over Lake Fluessen.

Facilities

Four modern, heated sanitary blocks well spaced around the site with showers on payment and most washbasins (half in private cabins) have only cold water. Launderette. Motorcaravan services. Gas supplies. Restaurant/bar, supermarket, indoor pool with 3 sessions daily (all open 30/3-4/11). Sauna and solarium. Sports field. Play areas. Tennis. Bicycle hire. Fishing. Animation team (high season). Internet access. Lake swimming area. Marina. Windsurfing, boat hire and boat shop. Car hire. WiFi over site (charged). Off site: Riding and golf 4 km.

Open: All year.

Directions

Site is southeast of Koudum, on the Fluessen lake. Follow the camping sign off the N359 Bolsward-Lemmer road. GPS: 52.90250, 5.46620

Charges guide

Per unit incl. 2 persons and electricity	€ 17.50 - € 37.80
extra person	€ 4.70
dog	€ 3.50

Special weekend rates at B.Hs.

Camping Cheques accepted.

Leeuwarden
Camping De Kleine Wielen

De Groene Ster 14, NL-8926 XE Leeuwarden (Friesland) T: 0511 431 660. E: info@dekleinewielen.nl

alanrogers.com/NL5750

Camping De Kleine Wielen is named after a small lake of the same name that lies in the 1,000 hectare nature and recreation area of De Groene Ster. The campsite is adjacent to the lake – possible activities include boating on the lake or cycling and walking around this beautiful area of forest, grassland and ponds. The site provides 360 pitches, of which 220 are for touring units. The remaining pitches are used for privately owned mobile homes and three for hire. All the touring pitches have 4A electricity and many have wonderful views over the water and surrounding countryside.

Facilities

Four basic toilet blocks provide washbasins in cabins and preset showers (coin operated). Maintenance is variable. Facilities for disabled visitors. Motorcaravan services. Shop and bar (all season). Café/restaurant and takeaway (all season). Playground. Sports pitch. Minigolf. Lake with beach. Fishing. Rowing boats. Surf boards. Extensive recreation programme in July/Aug. WiFi throughout (charged). Off site: Golf 1 km. Boat launching 2 km.

Open: 1 April - 1 October.

Directions

From the N355 turn off east towards Leeuwarden and follow campsite signs. GPS: 53.21650, 5.88703

Charges guide

Per unit incl. 2 persons and electricity and car	€ 20.25 - € 22.75
extra person	€ 4.25 - € 4.75

For latest campsite news, availability and prices visit

alanrogers.com

Lemmer
Watersportcentrum Tacozijl

Plattedijk 20, NL-8531 PE Lemmer (Friesland) T: 0514 562 003. E: info@tacozijl.com

alanrogers.com/NL6060

The area around Lemmer is wonderful for people who enjoy watersports and this site is just a stone's throw away from the Gaasterlandse lakes and not too far from the IJsselmeer. Tacozijl has 190 pitches of which 110 are for touring units (most with 4/6A Europlug). The pitches are level and on well maintained grass, directly beside the marina. A new field at the rear of the site has around 50 back-to-back pitches, without shade, but with views over the water, plus a dedicated hardstanding area for motorcaravans. From the pitches located around a bay on the marina, you can almost jump into your boat from your tent or caravan and sail away.

Facilities	Directions
New modern toilet block with toilets, showers, washbasins with cold water and washbasins in cabins with hot and cold water. Laundry. Motorcaravan services. Shop. Two restaurants and bar (all year). Snack bar. Some play equipment. Tennis. Fishing. Bicycle hire. Marina and boat launching. Boat hire. WiFi (first hour free). Off site: Beach 500 m. Riding 10 km.	On the A6 north of Almere, take exit for Lemmer and follow the N379 westwards. Remain on the N370 through Lemmer and site is on the right immediately after crossing bridge on the outskirts of the town. GPS: 52.85125, 5.68223

Open: All year.

Charges guide

Per unit incl. 2 persons and electricity	€ 17.65
extra person	€ 3.40

Molkwerum
Camping 't Séleantsje

't Séleantsje 2, NL-8722 HE Molkwerum (Friesland) T: 0514 681 395. E: info@camping-seleantsje.nl

alanrogers.com/NL6038

Camping 't Séleantsje is located just behind the IJsselmeer dykes, which makes it an ideal base for enjoying all kinds of watersports and fishing. The site rents a variety of canoes and motorboats and it is possible to get everything you need for fishing (including the permit) 200 m. down the road. The site is divided into a section for mobile homes and one for tourers. The 80 touring pitches are on a single large field without separation or shade. The grassy pitches are level and there is access from paved roads. There are just 26 pitches with 2/6A electricity and 20 with electricity, water and drainage. Across the road are 18 hardstanding motorcaravan pitches with 6A electricity.

Facilities	Directions
The single toilet block has open style washbasins (cold water only) and preset, hot showers (with token). Facilities for disabled visitors. Laundry. No shop but bread to order. Café and snack bar (15/4-15/9). Motorboat and canoe hire. Bicycle hire. Full entertainment programme for children (high season). Card nights, line dancing and bingo. Off site: Beach and sailing 100 m. Shop 200 m.	From the A6 take exit 17 for Lemmer and continue east on N359 until you can turn south towards Bakhuizen, then Warns and Molkwerum. Site is signed in Molkwerum. GPS: 52.903581, 5.395985

Open: 1 April - 1 November.

Charges guide

Per unit incl. 2 persons and electricity	€ 27.80 - € 38.30
extra person	€ 3.70

Offingawier
RCN De Potten

De Potten 2-36, NL-8626 GG Offingawier (Friesland) T: 0515 415 205. E: potten@rcn.nl

alanrogers.com/NL6048

De Potten is a good choice for lovers of watersports. This campsite is located on a peninsula on the Sneekermeer. The site has its own marina with boat launching facilities (charge applies). All manner of water transport is on offer here: motorboats, rowing boats, sailing boats, canoes, and more besides! Sailing lessons are organised (from eight years old), and include special family sessions. Pitches here are large and grassy, with limited shade. Many have fine views across the lake. There are chalets (with wooden terraces) for rent, which also have great lake views.

Facilities	Directions
Clean toilet facilities with preset showers, washbasins and cabins and toilets. Launderette. Restaurant with lake view, bar and snack bar. Bakery. Sports area. Play area with giant chess and draughts. Tennis. Minigolf. Trampolines. Boats, bicycles and go-karts for hire. Sailing school for children (from 8 years) and for adults. Boat launching and mooring facilities. WiFi (charged). Off site: Swimming in Sneekermeer. Sneek (village) 5 km.	On the eastern side of the Sneek ring road, take the exit to Offingawier. After 2 km. turn right towards Paviljoenwei and you will soon see the site entrance on your left. GPS: 53.029729, 5.724236

Open: 15 March - 31 October.

Charges guide

Per unit incl. 2 persons and electricity	€ 18.50 - € 29.50
dog	€ 4.95 - € 7.50

FREE Alan Rogers Travel Card
Extra benefits and savings - see page 12

Friesland

Sumar

Recreatiecentrum Bergumermeer

Solcamastraat 30, NL-9262 ND Sumar (Friesland) T: 0511 461 385. E: info@bergumermeer.nl

alanrogers.com/NL6040

Recreatiecentrum Bergumermeer's location beside the Bergum lake, makes it ideal for lovers of watersports, with sailing, surfing and canoeing available, as well as swimming from two sandy beaches. There is also a large, heated indoor swimming pool with fun paddling pool and an indoor play paradise. The site provides 270 good sized, flat touring pitches for both caravans and tents, some having attractive views over the Prinses Margrietkanaal and the surrounding countryside, others with views over the lake. All pitches are fully serviced with 10A electricity, water and drainage, and there are ten large hardstandings.

Facilities

Three sanitary buildings offer private cabins, family showers, baby bath and facilities for children and disabled visitors. Launderette. Freezer. Shop. Bar/restaurant. Pancake restaurant. Heated indoor pool. Solarium. Play area. Children's farm. Tennis. Minigolf. Fishing. Sailing dinghies, motorboats and canoes for hire. Entertainment programme in high season. Club space with disco. Bicycle hire. Boat launching. Beach. WiFi over site (charged). Off site: Riding 5 km. Golf 19 km.

Open: 27 March - 31 October.

Directions

Either go north from Amsterdam via A7/E22 through Leeuwarden towards Drachten, or east from Amsterdam via A6, onto A7 (Leeuwarden, Groningen), then onto N31 (De Haven/Drachten) and in either case onto N356 towards Bergum following site signs. GPS: 53.19127, 6.12428

Charges guide

Per unit incl. 2 persons and electricity	€ 18.00 - € 31.00
extra person	€ 6.25

Vlieland

Kampeerterrein Stortemelk

Kampweg 1, NL-8899 BX Vlieland (Friesland) T: 0562 451 225. E: info@stortemelk.nl

alanrogers.com/NL6029

Camping Stortemelk is located on the West Frisian island of Vlieland, separated from a broad sandy beach by high dunes. The island is car (and caravan) free, therefore this is a traditional tent campsite. Pitching is haphazard, partly on the grassy dunes with some good views of the campsite. Most fields are slightly sloping and special long sand pegs are needed (these can be provided at reception). There are specific fields for youngsters and groups. A number of attractive, traditionally-styled chalets are available for rent. On-site amenities include De Bolder, a convivial café/restaurant, which is the base for concerts, as well as the campsite's activity programme. Strict rules apply for night rest. There is a large car park in Harlingen and a frequent ferry service to Vlieland (advance booking essential). Upon arrival in Vlieland, your luggage can be transported to the campsite by horse and cart (for a small fee). Alternatively, a bus service is available. There is only one small village on the island, Oost-Vlieland, easily accessible by bicycle.

Facilities

Five modern toilet blocks are well distributed over the site and provide open style washbasins, preset hot showers, attractive children's facilities and a baby room. Facilities for disabled campers. Supermarket. Café/restaurant. Playgrounds. Volleyball. Some entertainment is provided. Direct beach access. WiFi over site (free). Off site: Shops and restaurants in Oost-Vlieland. Walking and cycle tracks across the island. Riding and bicycle hire 1 km. Watersports.

Open: 1 April - 1 October.

Directions

Harlingen can be reached from the A7 or A31 motorways. In Harlingen, follow signs to ferry port and large car park, where you must leave your vehicle. The ferry journey lasts around 1.5 hours and there is a connecting bus and luggage service on the island. GPS: 53.304397, 5.079616

Charges guide

Per unit incl. 2 persons and electricity	€ 22.40
extra person	€ 6.80
child (under 10 yrs)	€ 3.50

The natural dune campground of Stortemelk on Wadden-isle Vlieland, only one dune away from the North-sea-beach, offers room for tents, travel sleepers, completely furnished rental tents and tent houses. Grand café the Bolder – with terrace, friendly priced meals and live music – and a varied cultural and sport program make this campsite a very attractive place to be for both young and old. Camping Stortemelk, open from April 1st until October 1st, also has beautiful nostalgic isle cottages. Close to the sea and available throughout the whole year. During their stay all guest of Stortemelk have free entrance to swimming pool Flidunen.

Kampweg 1 - 8899 BX Vlieland - Tel. +31(0)562 45 12 25 - info@stortemelk.nl

Warns

Camping De Weyde Blick

It Sou 29, NL-8721 GX Warns (Friesland) T: 0514 681 428. E: hbreimer@cs.com

alanrogers.com/NL6028

Camping De Weyde Blick comprises two slightly sloping camping areas divided by a pasture with sheep, giving the site a truly rural feel. The area behind reception is mainly for mobile homes, the other terrain is reserved for touring units. There are 35 touring pitches, of which 15 have 4/6A electricity, water and drainage. They are on both sides off a long, gravel and grass access road in groups of two to six units, with three hardstandings for motorcaravans and large units to one end. The site is fairly open, although some shade is provided by tall bushes.

Facilities	Directions
One toilet block on the touring field has toilets, washbasins (both open style and in cabins; cold water only), and controllable hot showers. Children's toilet. Baby room. Laundry. Bar/restaurant with small terrace for simple meals (15/4-30/9). Open-air pool (10x5 m) with paddling pool. Some entertainment organised. Off site: Sailing and fishing 2 km. Riding 5 km.	From the A6, take exit 17 for Lemmer and continue west on N359 road. Turn south towards Bakhuizen and from there towards Warns and follow site signs. GPS: 52.870209, 5.412588

Open: 1 April - 1 November.

Charges guide

Per unit incl. 2 persons and electricity	€ 13.30
child (0-11 yrs)	€ 1.50
extra person	€ 2.65

Weidum

Camping WeidumerHout

Dekemawei 9, NL-9024 BE Weidum (Friesland) T: 0582 519 888. E: welkom@weidumerhout.nl

alanrogers.com/NL5715

Camping WeidumerHout is a member of the Karaktervolle Groene Campings group, literally 'characterful green campsites'. It has a superb rural location, close to the historic village of Weidum. There are 48 well spaced pitches (150 sq.m) with 10A electricity and two with hardstanding. The owner makes sure that all visitors can enjoy the great views over either the countryside or the river that runs past the site. The site has been developed on a farm that dates back to 1867 and has a tranquil, historic atmosphere. The site's fully equipped sauna (charged) will add to your relaxation – owner Eddy de Boer will describe the benefits of a good sauna.

Facilities	Directions
Heated sanitary block with toilets, showers and washbasins. Baby room. Washing machine and dryer. Bar and restaurant (all year). Sauna. Solarium. Library. Bicycle hire. Beach access plus fishing and boat launching. Canoe hire. WiFi throughout (free). Fitness equipment. Torch useful. Off site: Shop and bus stop 800 m. Riding 5 km. Sailing 8 km. Golf 12 km.	From Leeuwarden head south on the A32 and follow signs for Weidum. Just before entering the village, the site is on the right. GPS: 53.14906, 5.76166

Open: All year, excl. Christmas - 1 January.

Charges guide

Per unit incl. 2 persons and electricity	€ 21.50
extra person (over 2 yrs)	€ 5.75
dog	€ 2.00

Wijckel

Camping 't Hop

Meerenstein 1, NL-8563 AV Wijckel (Friesland) T: 0514 602 436. E: info@campingthop.nl

alanrogers.com/NL6044

Camping 't Hop, in addition to 60 seasonal pitches and 35 permanent pitches, provides 60 touring pitches (about 100 sq.m), all with 6A electricity and 32 fully serviced. There are a few hardstandings. The site is adjacent to the Menno van Coehoorn forest and only a few yards from Sloter lake with an open connection to it for boats. The site is divided into 11 areas, each with around ten pitches. The seasonal pitches are in a separate area. The focal point of the site is an adventure play area, together with the pride of the site, a café which offers a varied menu and is definitely recommended.

Facilities	Directions
Excellent toilet block near reception provides toilets, some washbasins in cabins, and controllable hot showers (€ 0.50). Baby room. Facilities for disabled visitors. Motorcaravan services. Laundry with washing machines and dryers. Café/bar serving small meals. Covered swimming pool and paddling pool. Tennis. Bicycle and canoe hire. Playground. Entertainment programme for youngsters in season. Off site: Boat launching, fishing, beach and sailing 500 m. Riding 3 km.	On the A6 from Joure travelling south towards Almere, take exit 17 (Lemmer, Balk) and follow the N359 to Balk. Following site signs, turn right then left after 1 km. GPS: 52.89361, 5.6224

Open: 1 April - 30 September.

Charges guide

Per unit incl. 2 persons and electricity	€ 24.50
extra person	€ 4.75
child (2-10 yrs)	€ 4.00
dog	€ 1.75

FREE Alan Rogers Travel Card
Extra benefits and savings - see page 12

Woudsend

Aquacamping De Rakken

Lynbaen 10, NL-8551 NW Woudsend (Friesland) T: 0514 591525. E: info@derakken.nl
alanrogers.com/NL6027

Located between the three largest Frisian lakes, Slotermeer, Heegermeer and Sneekermeer, De Rakken is a great choice for both nature and watersports enthusiasts. Just two minutes on foot from the site, Woudsend is a good watersports resort with a wealth of catering facilities and places of interest (including mills and churches). The site offers boat moorings as well as bicycle, electric boat and car hire. The 50 touring pitches are of a reasonable size and all have 6A electricity, with 15 on hardstanding. Accommodation for rent on site includes hikers' cabins and attractive chalets. The site is open all year.

Facilities

Four heated toilet blocks include preset hot showers, open style washbasins, a baby room and facilities for disabled visitors. Play area with volleyball. Petting zoo. Tennis. Fishing. Marina. Boat launching. Electric boats for rent. Hiker cabins and chalets for rent. WiFi. Off site: The charming old town of Woudsend with good shops and restaurants. The Frisian lakes. Watersports. Golf 10 km.

Open: All year.

Directions

Take A6 northbound (Heerenveen) and a few kilometres past Lemmer take the exit to Woudsend (N354). At the roundabout before Woudsend, go left (N928, Balk) then turn right at next roundabout. Follow signs to the site. GPS: 52.94651, 5.62768

Charges guide

Per unit incl. 2 persons and electricity	€ 17.50 - € 29.50
dog	€ 1.00

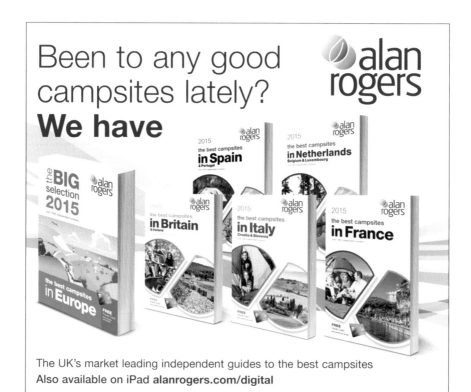

For latest campsite news, availability and prices visit
alanrogers.com

CAPITAL: ARNHEM

Once the scene of heavy fighting during WWII, Gelderland is now a province with much to offer the tourist in Achterhoek, Veluwe, Rivierenland, Arnhem and Nijmegen.

The Achterhoek is a region of forests, estates, castles, streams and picturesque villages, a perfect destination for the cyclist and the hiker. De Hoge Veluwe National Park is one of the Netherlands' oldest and largest national parks with no less than 5,500 hectares of woodland, heathland, lakes and drift sands. Together with the Kröller-Müller Museum and the sculpture garden, it is a unique alliance of nature, art and architecture. Rivierenland (Riverland) is a rural area that has developed around the traditional activities of farming and handicrafts. Many of the old mills, castles, fortifications and art galleries are well worth a visit.

The cities of Arnhem and Nijmegen have evolved from a fascinating and occasionally turbulent history. While they are located only 20 km. from each other, their attractions, shops, landscapes, culture and gastronomy couldn't be more different. Not surprisingly, there is great rivalry too, as you can see when their football clubs meet! Arnhem is a very green city with several parks and the estate of the Rosendaal Castle (former residence of the dukes of Gelre), while Nijmegen is an ancient city where you can still glimpse remains dating from the Roman period to the Middle Ages.

Places of interest

Hanseatic cities: along a sparkling river, the IJssel, lie the beautiful medieval gems of Hasselt, Kampen, Zwolle, Hattem, Deventer, Zutphen and Doesburg.

Museum Castle Wijchen: an extensive archaeological collection is housed in Wijchen's picturesque castle.

Rural Cuijk: attractions include horse driving, vineyards, tea garden and even a home theatre in a hayloft; sample the delicious local produce at the farm shops.

Zutphen: a comprehensive selection of shops, markets, restaurants, pubs, museums and galleries.

Attractions

Koningin Julianatoren: family fun park in Apeldoorn.

Tivoli Amusement Park: a small park for younger children with magic shows, circus workshops and minigolf.

Dolfinarium Harderwijk: Europe's largest marine park with performing dolphins, sea lions and seals, enjoyed by 1 million visitors annually.

Kasteel Doorwerth: a 13th-century fairytale castle and museum, with its own moat and resident ghost.

The Liberation Route: follow the path of allied forces through the Arnhem/Nijmegen region in 1944 and 1945.

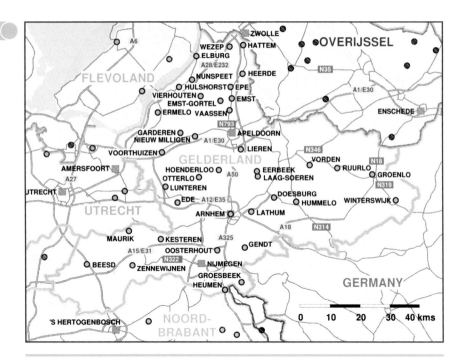

Arnhem
Camping Warnsborn

Bakenbergseweg 257, NL-6816 PB Arnhem (Gelderland) T: 0264 423 469. E: info@campingwarnsborn.nl
alanrogers.com/NL5830

Camping Warnsborn is a small, well maintained site set in the grounds of an attractive estate owned by the Gelderland Trust for natural beauty. Located on the outskirts of the historical city of Arnhem and set amongst 3.5 hectares of undulating woodland, this site really has something for everyone. There are 90 hardstanding pitches for tourers (6A electricity) arranged in either open grassy fields or surrounded by trees, with a separate secluded area for backpackers and small tents. On-site facilities include a good play area with a large sandpit and guided walks through the surrounding countryside.

Facilities

Modern heated toilet block including facilities for babies, families and disabled visitors. Washing machines and dryers. Well stocked shop, bread to order. TV room/library. Playground with large sandpit. Bicycle hire. Boules. Hikers' cabins. WiFi over site (charged).

Open: 1 April - 31 October.

Directions

From Utrecht follow the A12 and take exit N224 following signs towards Arnhem Noord/Burgers zoo. Follow signs to the site. GPS: 52.0072, 5.87135

Charges guide

Per unit incl. 2 persons and electricity	€ 18.30 - € 20.80

Arnhem
DroomPark Hooge Veluwe

Koningsweg 14, NL-6816 TC Arnhem (Gelderland) T: 0264 432 272. E: info@droomparkhoogeveluwe.nl
alanrogers.com/NL5850

Its situation at the entrance to the Hoge Veluwe national park with its moors, forests, sand drifts, walking routes and cycle paths, makes this a highly desirable holiday base with great appeal for families with children of all ages. The site itself is well managed and attractively laid out with 260 touring pitches, including 120 fully serviced places of 300 sq.m. All have electricity (4-16A), are numbered and laid out in small fields divided by hedging. Some are traffic free, so cars must be left in a nearby car park.

Facilities

Three excellent, heated sanitary blocks with all facilities. Launderette. Motorcaravan services. Gas. Supermarket. Restaurant. Takeaway. TV room. Heated outdoor and indoor pools, and paddling pool. Many small play areas. Recreation hall. Activity/play area for older children. Football pitch, skateboard loop, cycle track. Bicycle and pedal go-kart hire. Boules. Wellness and gym. WiFi.

Open: All year.

Directions

Leave A12 motorway at exit 25 (Oosterbeck) and follow signs for Hoge Veluwe. Site is on right in 6 km. From the A50, take exit 21 to Schaarsbergen and follow signs. GPS: 52.03102, 5.86680

Charges guide

Per unit incl. 2 persons and electricity	€ 15.00 - € 28.00
extra person	€ 3.00 - € 5.00

For latest campsite news, availability and prices visit
alanrogers.com

Arnhem

Oostappen Vakantiepark Arnhem

Kemperbergerweg 771, NL-6816 RW Arnhem (Gelderland) T: 0264 431 600. E: info@vakantieparkarnhem.nl
alanrogers.com/NL6310

Vakantiepark Arnhem is a wooded site in the Veluwe region of the Netherlands, close to the Hoge Veluwe National Park. The 750 pitches are partly in the sun and partly in the shade of tall trees and there are 500 for touring units, some with hardstanding. This is a perfect base for visiting the national park, the Kröller-Müller museum or the outdoor museum. You could also go riding or play golf nearby, or experience the silence high up in the air in a glider from Terlet airport. There is also plenty to do on the site including tennis and minigolf. Expect some road noise from the motorway to the east of the site.

Facilities

Modern sanitary blocks (may be under pressure in high season) provide free hot showers, facilities for disabled visitors and a baby room. Fully equipped launderettes. Motorcaravan services. Supermarket. Restaurant with waiter service. Takeaway food. Bar. Tennis. Minigolf. Sports field. Boules. Open-air theatre. Several playgrounds. Adventure pond. Swimming pool and paddling pool. Entertainment programme in high season. Bicycle hire. Off site: Arnhem for shopping. Burgers Zoo. Kröller-Müller museum. Airborne museum. Riding and golf. Gliding. Balloon trips and boat trips.

Open: 1 April - 26 October.

Directions

From the A50 take exit 21 for Schaarsbergen. Go to Schaarsbergen and follow the Recreatiepark Arnhem signs. GPS: 52.02428, 5.85874

Charges guide

Per unit incl. 2 persons and electricity	€ 15.00 - € 29.00

Beesd

Camping Betuwestrand

A Kraalweg 40, NL-4153 XC Beesd (Gelderland) T: 0345 681 503. E: info@betuwestrand.nl
alanrogers.com/NL5860

A pleasant site for a night stop or a longer stay, conveniently situated just off the A2/E25 motorway (Utrecht - 's Hertogenbosch, exit 14). It is a large site with 154 pitches for tourers on well cared for, grassy lawns (all with 10A electricity and drainage), in addition to its 400 well established permanent units. The touring pitches are in four distinct areas with many situated around the edges of an attractive lake with a large sandy beach and pleasant views. For families with young children there are various areas away from the water with play areas, as well as many facilities for older children. An area of the lake is cordoned off for swimming with a slide and diving boards and it is also suitable for water skiing and wakeboarding. The lake is also used by the public. Gelderland is the part of the Netherlands famous for fruit growing, situated between the rivers Maas and Waal and worthy perhaps of further consideration by British visitors. Local excursions could include the Flipje Museum (jam and marmalade) and the Glasmuseum in Leerdam.

Facilities

The toilet blocks are of a good standard and include family rooms and facilities for disabled visitors. Hot water is on payment in both showers and washbasins (in individual cabins). Laundry facilities. Motorcaravan services. Shop. Restaurant (open to the public). Bar/TV room. Room for young people. Play area. Good lake fishing. Tennis. WiFi over site (charged). Dogs are permitted on a small field for touring units only. Off site: Bicycle hire 500 m. Golf 3 km.

Open: 28 March - 27 September.

Directions

Site is 25 km. SSE of Utrecht, clearly signed from both directions on the E25 road between Utrecht and 's Hertogenbosch. Take the exit 14 (Beesd) and site is 200 m. GPS: 51.898623, 5.184541

Charges guide

Per unit incl. up to 2 persons and electricity	€ 25.00 - € 32.50
extra person	€ 4.80

Less 20% in low season.
Special weekend or weekly prices. No credit cards.

Teen family campsite　　　**www.betuwestrand.nl**

Doesburg
Camping IJsselstrand

Eekstraat 18, NL-6984 AG Doesburg (Gelderland) T: 0313 472 797. E: info@ijsselstrand.nl

alanrogers.com/NL6332

This campsite calls itself a recreation village on the river, and the name suits it perfectly. It has 700 pitches in total, with a mix of permanent and touring pitches. The 200 touring pitches are set on sunny, grassy fields and around the marina and beach area. There are 46 pitches with private sanitary facilities (shower, washbasin, toilet) and 18 hardstandings for motorcaravans. Central to the campsite is a covered water complex, including a pool, a jacuzzi and slide. This can be opened in summer. There is a large play area and, for bad weather, there is enough room for all in a pleasant indoor playground.

Facilities

Modern sanitary facilities are plentiful. Supermarket (15/3-2/11). Covered swimming pool. Large indoor and outdoor play areas. Riding. Sandy beach. Marina and floating restaurant. Pedalos and canoes for hire. Entertainment team. Free WiFi. Chalets, lodges and tents for hire. Off site: Ancient, fortified town of Doesburg. Walking and cycling in the Achterhoek Châteaux countryside. Veluwe forest is 30 minutes away by car.

Open: All year.

Directions

Site is 25 km. northeast of Arnhem. From A12 take exit 27 onto the A348 towards Zutphen, then right onto N317 for 4 km. to Doesberg. Take third exit from the roundabout (Zomerweg) for 1.2 km. then the third exit again (Eekstraat) and site is 1 km. on left. GPS: 52.02848, 6.16292

Charges guide

| Per unit incl. 2 persons and electricity | € 19.25 - € 31.75 |
| extra person | € 4.00 |

Ede
Camping Zuid Ginkel

Verlengde Arnhemseweg 97, NL-6718 SM Ede (Gelderland) T: 0318 611 740. E: info@zuidginkel.nl

alanrogers.com/NL5855

This is a small, attractive, family site, located in the heart of the Veluwe, in a natural setting perfect for nature lovers and families with young children. This car-free site has 158 spacious and grassy pitches, all equipped with water and 6A electricity. Some also have drainage (for a small charge). Chalets are also available for rent throughout the year. On-site amenities here include a children's playground with table tennis and a playhouse. With its 1,600 km. of marked cycle tracks, the Veluwe region has the most extensive cycle network in Europe.

Facilities

Modern and heated sanitary blocks. Facilities for babies. Launderette. Play area. Dairy products available from reception. Bicycle hire. Library. Play house. WiFi within touring area (charged). Off site: Restaurant and takeaway (outside campsite gates, from 1 April). Restaurants and shops in the nearby town of Ede. Cinemec, the largest cinema complex in The Netherlands. Burgers zoo. Open air museum. Kröller-Müller museum.

Open: 29 March - 31 October.

Directions

Follow A12 motorway towards Arnhem/Oberhausen and take exit 25 (Oosterbeek). Then take N224 towards Ede for 8 km. Site will be on your right. GPS: 52.0377, 5.73374

Charges guide

Per unit incl. 2 persons and electricity	€ 18.00 - € 20.00
extra person	€ 4.00
child (under 12 yrs)	€ 2.00

Ede
Recreatiepark 't Gelloo

Barteweg 15, NL-6718 TH Ede (Gelderland) T: 0318 618 282. E: info@gelloo.nl

alanrogers.com/NL6340

Recreatiepark 't Gelloo is an attractive family park that is popular with nature lovers, young families and those looking for peace and quiet. This is a comfortable site where quality is a priority. There are 420 pitches, 150 for tourers (all with 6A electricity), and 55 of these have water and drainage. The recreational facilities are also very good and include an indoor swimming pool. The site is close to the town of Ede and in the area there are theme parks such as Pretpark Julianatoren and, as this is right in the centre of the Hoge Veluwe region, plenty of nature reserves. Member of the Topparken Group.

Facilities

One centrally located toilet block with good, clean facilities. Baby rooms in ladies' section. Two units for disabled campers (key access). Motorcaravan services. Shop. Restaurant (high season and weekends). Takeaway. Heated indoor pool (all season). Bicycle hire. Indoor and outdoor play areas. Tennis. Entertainment for children in high season. Free WiFi over site. Chalets to rent. Off site: Ede 4 km. Fishing and riding 5 km. Golf 15 km.

Open: 21 March - 25 October.

Directions

From the A30 take exit 3 (de Stroet, Lunteren) towards Lunteren, then signs towards Ede. Site is signed. GPS: 52.07451, 5.66816

Charges guide

Per unit incl. up to 4 persons and electricity	€ 17.00 - € 31.00
extra person	€ 6.00
dog (max. 2)	€ 5.00

Eerbeek

Landal Coldenhove

Boshoffweg 6, NL-6961 LD Eerbeek (Gelderland) T: 0313 659 101. E: coldenhove@landal.nl

alanrogers.com/NL5827

Coldenhove is a member of the Landal group and is an attractive campsite within the acclaimed natural region of the Veluwe, some 20 km. from Arnhem. This is a well equipped site with a good range of on-site amenities. There are 180 marked and shady pitches of 100 sq.m (electricity 4-10A and TV connections), located in the woods, half a kilometre from the main activity centre, and providing a quiet, relaxing atmosphere. Leisure facilities are grouped together near the site entrance and include an indoor swimming complex, an indoor playground, minigolf and a mini-scooter track. There are several good playgrounds for children, with sand pits and a trampoline.

Facilities

Modern toilet blocks. Shop, bar, restaurant and takeaway (all season). Indoor heated pool, (all season). Beauty salon. Minigolf. Play areas. Boules. Basketball court. Activity and entertainment programme. WiFi (charged). Accommodation for hire. Off site: Open-air swimming pool at Apenheul. The sumptuous Paleis Het Loo. Apeldoorn and Arnhem. Golf 7.5 km.

Open: 13 March - 6 November.

Directions

Approaching on A50 motorway, between Arnhem and Apeldoorn, take the Loenen/Eerbeek exit. At the first roundabout follow directions to Dieren, and then follow signs to Coldenhove. GPS: 52.091692, 6.034281

Charges guide

Per unit incl. 2 persons and electricity	€ 18.00 - € 38.00
extra person	€ 5.25

Elburg

Recreatieoord Veluwe Strandbad

Flevoweg 5, NL-8081 PA Elburg (Gelderland) T: 0525 681 480. E: info@monda.nl

alanrogers.com/NL6325

Recreatieoord Veluwe Strandbad is beside the Veluwe lake and it makes an ideal base for an active holiday on the water, either here or on the larger IJsselmeer lake. The site has a few touring fields set amongst a large number of static units and from some there are views over the lake. The 110 touring pitches are all level and on grass, with tarmac access roads. Most have 6A electricity, water, waste water and cable connections. Central on the site is a welcoming bar/restaurant with a terrace from where there are views to the lake. An indoor pool (10x10 m) with a paddling pool is also here.

Facilities

Two good, modern toilet blocks (heated) serve the touring area, with toilets, washbasins (open style and in cabins), baby room and facilities for disabled visitors. Laundry facilities. Motorcaravan services. Bar/restaurant. Beach shop. Indoor pool. Indoor games room. Tennis. Boat launching. Fishing. Children's activity programme. Bicycle hire. Skateboard park. Boules. Playground. WiFi over site (charged). Dogs not accepted. Payment card required for toilet blocks, pool and laundry facilities.

Open: All year.

Directions

Via the N309 or N306 enter Elburg from the northwest and site is on the right. GPS: 52.455576, 5.821251

Charges guide

Per unit incl. 2 persons and electricity	€ 14.00 - € 24.00
extra person	€ 3.50

No credit cards.

Emst

Camping De Veluwse Wagen

Oranjeweg 67, NL-8166 JA Emst (Gelderland) T: 0578 661 628. E: info@veluwse-wagen.nl

alanrogers.com/NL6305

De Veluwse Wagen is attractively landscaped with different sorts of trees and bushes. This small, car-free site is behind a pancake restaurant of the same name. It has immaculately kept pitches on four level, grassy fields, taking 25 touring units in total. Electricity is available to all and the numbered pitches are level and with some hardstanding. With access from gravel roads, the camping areas are separated by mature trees on two fields which give shade to some pitches. The remainder of the site is occupied by privately owned mobile homes. De Veluwse Wagen is in beautiful natural surroundings, near the Royal woodland and hunting grounds, the Vierhouterbos and the Gortel moors.

Facilities

The single toilet block is behind the restaurant with toilets, open style washbasins and controllable, hot showers (4 minutes free hot water). Washing machines and dryers. Bar/restaurant. Playing field. Riding. Bicycle hire. Boules. Animal farm. WiFi over site (charged). No cars allowed on site. Off site: Kievitsveld lake with sandy beach 2 km.

Open: 1 April - 1 November.

Directions

From A50, take exit 27 (Epe) and continue towards Emst. Site is signed from the roundabout in Emst, on the road towards Gortel. GPS: 52.322486, 5.958097

Charges guide

Per unit incl. 2 persons and electricity	€ 18.25 - € 20.25
extra person	€ 3.75
child (2-12 yrs)	€ 3.25

FREE Alan Rogers Travel Card
Extra benefits and savings - see page 12

Emst

Camping De Zandhegge

Langeweg 14, NL-8166 GT Emst (Gelderland) T: 0578 613 936. E: info@zandhegge.nl

alanrogers.com/NL6320

De Zandhegge is a comfortable, family site under private ownership on the edge of the woodlands of the Veluwe. Close to the site are moors and the IJsselvallei for beautiful tours. The site has 225 pitches, of which 52 are for tourers. Most of the touring pitches are in a separate field to the front of the site in the shade of mature trees, with more to the rear. Pitching is on grassy fields approached by gravel access lanes and all pitches have 16A electricity, water, waste water and cable. Access to some pitches may prove difficult for large units.

Facilities	Directions
A new, central block and a second smaller block to the back provide toilets, washbasins (some in cabins) and preset, hot showers (SEP-key). Section for children with toilet, showers and washbasins. Facilities for disabled visitors. Baby room. Laundry. Snack bar with terrace. Bar (weekends and holidays). Open-air pool with paddling pool (heated). All-weather playing field. Tennis. Adventure play area. Bicycle hire. WiFi throughout (charged). Full entertainment programme for young and old. Torch useful. Off site: Riding 2 km. Beach 4 km. Fishing and golf 6 km.	From the A50 take exit 27 (Epe/Nunspeet) and turn left towards Emst at the traffic lights. Take first right (site is signed) and follow to the end. GPS: 52.330159, 5.961609

Charges guide

Per unit incl. 2 persons and electricity	€ 18.00 - € 25.00
extra person (over 2 yrs)	€ 3.00 - € 3.75
dog	€ 2.75

No credit cards.

Open: 1 April - 2 October.

Emst-Gortel

Camping De Wildhoeve

Hanendorperweg 102, NL-8166 JJ Emst-Gortel (Gelderland) T: 0578 661 324. E: info@wildhoeve.nl

alanrogers.com/NL6285

Camping De Wildhoeve is an exceptional, welcoming, privately owned site with many amenities of the type one would normally find on larger holiday camps. The well maintained site is located in woodland and has 400 pitches with 330 for tourers. Pitching is in several areas, mostly in the shade of mature conifers. Partly separated by trees and bushes, the level pitches are numbered and all have electricity, water and drainage. Behind reception is an octagonal-shaped, indoor sub-tropical pool with a large water slide and fun paddling pool. Next to reception is a water adventure playground with a small beach.

Facilities	Directions
Four well placed, heated blocks with toilets, washbasins (open style and in cabins) and free, preset hot showers. Special section for children. Baby room. Family shower room. Facilities for disabled children. Laundry facilities. Shop, grand café/restaurant. Snack bar. Indoor and outdoor pools with slides and paddling pool. Water adventure playground. Bicycle hire. Tennis. Open-air theatre. WiFi over site (charged). Dogs are not accepted. Off site: Fishing 4 km. Riding 5 km. Apeldoorn.	From the A28, take exit 15 (Epe/Nunspeet). Go east towards Epe and at lights turn south towards Emst. Continue straight ahead at roundabout in Emst. Turn right at church, into Hanendorperweg. Site is on the right after 3.5 km. GPS: 52.31369, 5.92707

Charges guide

Per unit incl. 2 persons and electricity	€ 21.00 - € 37.75
extra person	€ 5.00

Camping Cheques accepted.

Open: April - September.

Epe

Recreatiepark De Veldkamp

Veldkampweg 2, NL-8162 PV Epe (Gelderland) T: 0578 614 348. E: info@develdkamp.nl

alanrogers.com/NL6315

Recreatiepark De Veldkamp is a relatively small site with only 110 pitches, of which 50 are for tourers. The site is attractively landscaped with many varieties of shrubs, flowers and trees and is set behind a traditional pancake restaurant. The pitches are on several well kept, level, grassy fields and all have 4A electricity. Some are more open, others are in the shade of mature trees and separated by shrubs and trees. A shallow, circular pool is centrally located, with a small island, a paddling pool, slide and flume. Behind reception is a large play room with bar, books and games.

Facilities	Directions
One central toilet block provides toilets, washbasins in cabins and free, controllable hot showers. Family shower room. Baby room. Laundry facilities. Reception stocks basics. Pancake restaurant. Open-air pool with slide and flume. Play field. Indoor activity room. Bicycle hire. Boules. Playground. Entertainment hall. Dogs are not accepted. Off site: Riding and bicycle hire 2 km. Beach 6 km.	From the A50, take exit 27 (Epe) and continue west on N309. Site is signed from the N309. GPS: 52.340932, 5.940227

Charges guide

Per unit incl. up to 4 persons	€ 17.00 - € 27.00
extra person	€ 3.50

Open: 26 March - 30 October.

For latest campsite news, availability and prices visit

alanrogers.com

Epe
RCN Camping De Jagerstee
Officiersweg 86, NL-8162 NR Epe (Gelderland) T: 0578 613 330. E: jagerstee@rcn.nl
alanrogers.com/NL6356

De Jagerstee (literally – hunter's home) can be found at the heart of the Veluwe, the largest natural park in The Netherlands. Using the site as a base, there are many walks and cycle trips through the forests. The site's attractions are grouped around the open-air heated pool and the two touring areas (in total 200 pitches) are on either side. Twenty pitches are fully serviced (10A electricity). Rented bungalows occupy the remainder of the site. To the rear of each pitch are large trees and shrubs which provide some welcome shade on hot summer days.

Facilities

Four modern toilet blocks all have family rooms and baby facilities. Launderette. Restaurant, bar, café, takeaway. Bakery and supermarket. Outdoor swimming pool. Sports hall. Open-air theatre. Play area. Minigolf. Beach volleyball. 5-a-side football pitch. Bicycle and go-kart hire. Mobile homes and chalets for rent. WiFi over site (charged). Off site: Village of Epe 500 m. Royal Palace 't Loo and Apenheul (primate park) 15 km.

Open: All year.

Directions

Take exit 15 (Epe/Nunspeet-Oost) off A28 motorway and follow N792. Take the second exit off the first roundabout after 7.5 km. (Tongerenseweg). Take left after 1.2 km. (Koekenbergweg) and then after a further 1.2 km. turn right into Officiersweg and follow signs to the site. GPS: 52.363483, 5.957991

Charges guide

Per unit incl. 2 persons and electricity	€ 17.00 - € 24.75

Ermelo
Camping & Bungalowpark Haeghehorst
Fazantlaan 4, NL-3852 AM Ermelo (Gelderland) T: 0341 553 185. E: haeghehorst@ardoer.com
alanrogers.com/NL6342

The swimming complex with an indoor and outdoor pool is spectacular here. The 45 m. long water slide with separate splash pool and Tube Sensation is one of the main attractions at Camping and Bungalowpark Haeghehorst. The 283 touring pitches have 6/10A electricity and are around 100 sq.m. They are laid out in several fields and shaded by trees and hedges. About one third of the site is occupied by private bungalows. There are 23 mobile homes for rent. This site provides plenty of activities for the whole family. A member of the Ardoer Group.

Facilities

Two modern, heated toilet blocks, one with a wellness centre, have designated facilities for disabled visitors and children. Shop, restaurant, takeaway (April-Oct). Bar. Swimming pools. Bicycle hire. Accommodation to rent. Tennis. Riding. Free WiFi over site. Dogs are only accepted in bungalow area. Off site: Fishing, golf and riding 5 km.

Open: All year.

Directions

From the A28 take exit 12 (Ermelo, Harderwijk-Ermelo West) onto the N303. After 200 m. turn right and follow road for 2.2 km. Take second exit at the roundabout. Site is signed. GPS: 52.31332, 5.62995

Charges guide

Per unit incl. 2 persons and electricity	€ 19.00 - € 33.00
extra person (over 2 yrs)	€ 4.00 - € 5.00
No credit cards.	

Ermelo
Camping De Kriemelberg
Drieerweg 104, NL-3052 MC Ermelo (Gelderland) T: 0341 552 142. E: info@kriemelberg.nl
alanrogers.com/NL6354

Camping De Kriemelberg lies in a wooded area, close to the moors of Ermelo. You can access the forest directly from this family site where you can cycle and enjoy walks. The site has 90 touring pitches, all with 6-10A electricity, and some with water and cable connection. The pitches are on average 100 sq.m. and are spread out under the trees in open fields. The recreation programme here is run in high season by a Christian organisation (Het Baken) and everyone is welcome to participate in the activities such as sports tournaments and treasure hunts. A natural pool with a beach area has recently been constructed. Due to its central location, there are plenty of day trips to enjoy. These include places such as Royal Palace 't Loo in Epe, De Apenheul (to see monkeys) and Walibi World theme park.

Facilities

New, heated sanitary block with fun family bathrooms. Baby room. Washing and ironing area. Small shop. Bar. Snack bar (high season). Play area. Sports pitch. Volleyball. Trampoline. Bicycle hire. Activity programme in high season. WiFi over site (charged). Off site: Fishing and boating on Veluwemeer. Riding 7 km. Royal Palace 't Loo.

Open: 15 March - 25 October.

Directions

The site is 30 km. northeast of Amersfoort. From the A28 exit 10, 11 or 12 head for Ermelo on N303. The site is signed on the southeast edge of the town off N303 (2 km). GPS: 52.28814, 5.64708

Charges guide

Per unit incl. 2 persons	€ 16.90 - € 20.65
extra person	€ 2.00

FREE Alan Rogers Travel Card
Extra benefits and savings - see page 12

Garderen

Camping De Hertshoorn

Putterweg 68-70, NL-3886 PG Garderen (Gelderland) T: 0577 461 529. E: hertshoorn@ardoer.com

alanrogers.com/NL5820

Although this is quite a large site, this is not immediately apparent with its woodland location. Careful design has allowed both single pitches in little glades and groups on cleared grassy areas with plenty of gentle shade. Some 330 of the pitches are for tourers and all have electricity (10A), water, drainage and cable TV connection, and there is a central area for tents. Cars must be parked at the entrance car park. The very smart reception (more like a hotel than a campsite!) provides information packs in English, with a pleasant restaurant at the rear which the owners call 'a living room for guests'.

Facilities

Four excellent toilet blocks provide heated facilities with a variety of cabins and showers. Well equipped laundry. Gas supplies. Motorcaravan services. Supermarket. Restaurant (closed Mondays). Snacks. Indoor heated swimming pool and indoor and outdoor heated paddling pools. Tennis. Children's farm. Play areas. Indoor playground. Entertainment for children in high season. Klimbos (similar to Go Ape). Bicycle hire. WiFi throughout (charged). Tree tents for rent. Dogs are not accepted. Off site: Riding 2 km. Golf 6 km. Beach 10 km.

Open: 30 March - 28 October.

Directions

From A1/E30 between Amersfoort and Apeldoorn, take Garderen exit no. 17. Turn right on N310 towards Garderen. Cross the N344, through village and site is signed on Putten road.
GPS: 52.23642, 5.68977

Charges guide

Per unit incl. 2 persons and electricity	€ 19.00 - € 32.00
extra person	€ 5.00

No credit cards.

Gendt

Camping Waalstrand

Waaldijk 23A, NL-6691 MB Gendt (Gelderland) T: 0481 421 604. E: info@waalstrand.nl

alanrogers.com/NL5823

Camping Waalstrand lies just outside the village of Gendt. It is stretched out along the banks of the River Waal and backed by a dyke separating the river from the town. Many of the pitches have good views of the various boats plying the river. Surrounding the campsite is an excellent nature reserve, the Gelderese Poort, an extensive delta of river dunes, lowland forests and meadows with many walks and cycle routes. This is a quiet campsite with no organised entertainment. There are 150 medium size, level, unshaded, grassy pitches with 90 for touring units. All pitches are fully serviced with 6A electricity and a TV hook-up. Access is good for large outfits.

Facilities

Modern clean toilet block with all necessary facilities. Washing machine/dryer. Outdoor swimming pool. Café. Terrace. Play area. Boules. Large chess set. Small sandy river beach and boat ramp. Bicycle hire. Motorcaravan services. Fishing. WiFi (charged). Dogs are welcome in a small area of the site and limited to one dog per pitch. Off site: Arnhem. Nijmegen, the Netherlands' oldest city.

Open: 1 April - 1 October.

Directions

Leave A15 motorway at Bemmel between Nijmegen and Arnhem, signed Gendt (7 km). Site is signed from Gendt. GPS: 51.87597, 5.98897

Charges guide

Per unit incl. 2 persons and electricity	€ 26.00
extra person	€ 5.00

No credit cards.

Groenlo

Marveld Recreatie

Eishofweg 6, NL-7141 DH Groenlo (Gelderland) T: 0544 466 000. E: info@marveld.nl

alanrogers.com/NL6420

This large, high quality holiday park lies on the outskirts of Groenlo in the Achterhoek, (Back Country) a region of the Netherlands rich in nature and history. The site is level with several separated, grassy camping fields surrounded by mature trees. There are 330 touring pitches and a further 300 permanent holiday homes. Three main touring fields are serviced by modern, heated toilet blocks. In addition, 34 pitches have individual sanitary cabins. The site is pleasantly landscaped and, in spite of its size, does not give an impression of overcrowding.

Facilities

Three modern, heated toilet blocks servicing the three touring fields include facilities for babies and disabled visitors. Individual sanitary cabins on full service pitches. Supermarket. Restaurant and snack bar. Launderette. Hairdressing salon. Outdoor pool and sub-tropical swim paradise. Tennis and squash courts. Sauna and sun beds. Bicycle hire. Pitch and putt golf. Bowling. Fishing. Rowing. Disco. WiFi over site (charged). Off site: Arnhem. Zutphen.

Open: All year.

Directions

From Arnhem take A12 to A18, towards Doetinchem. Continue on N18 to Groenlo. The site is 1.5 km. southeast of Groenlo, signed from the ring road. GPS: 52.03477, 6.63163

Charges guide

Per unit incl. 2 persons and electricity	€ 25.10
extra person	€ 3.70

Camping Cheques accepted.

For latest campsite news, availability and prices visit
alanrogers.com

Groesbeek
Camping De Oude Molen
Wylerbaan 2A, NL-6561 KR Groesbeek (Gelderland) T: 0243 971 715. E: camping@oudemolen.nl
alanrogers.com/NL6346

The family site of De Oude Molen is set in the countryside of Gelderland on the edge of the town of Groesbeek, close to the German border. There are 340 pitches of which 140 are for touring and these are spread out over several fields divided by hedges. Pitches are about 100 sq.m. with 6A electricity and water. The whole site has large trees around it, offering shade and privacy. The excellent facilities here include a heated outdoor swimming pool with slide and paddling pool, a sauna, sunbed and a whirlpool.

Facilities
Heated sanitary block includes family bathrooms. Facilities for babies and children with a jungle theme. Launderette. Dog shower. Reception with shop. Bistro bar and snack bar (high season). Heated outdoor swimming pool and paddling pool. Sunbathing area with loungers. Sauna with showers. Private cabins with whirlpool. Sun bed. Play area. Animal field. Entertainment. Free WiFi over part of site. Off site: Wellness centre by entrance. Golf 800 m.
Open: April - October.

Directions
The site is 10 km. southeast of Nijmegen, on the northern part of Groesbeek. From A73 take exit 3 to Groesbeek and follow the site signs. GPS: 51.78435, 5.93462

Charges guide
Per unit incl. 2 persons
and electricity €19.90 - €34.05
extra person €3.95

Hattem
Molecaten Park Landgoed Molecaten
Koeweg 1, NL-8051 PM Hattem (Gelderland) T: 0384 447 044. E: landgoedmolecaten@molecaten.nl
alanrogers.com/NL6357

Landgoed Molecaten can be found amongst old beech and oak trees on the southern side of the fortified town of Hattem. This is a tranquil site with large pitches, surrounded by a variety of mature trees which provide plenty of privacy and shade, perfect for those seeking peace and quiet. There are 130 hectares of woodland, flora and fauna here. Children can safely explore the woods – ideal for hide and seek. A pair of owls have been resident here for many years and are often seen at twilight. Accommodation to rent is a Boshuus, a specially designed chalet for four people, perfect for walkers and cyclists. Narrow access makes this site unsuitable for large units.

Facilities
Two toilet blocks are centrally located. Some washbasins in cabins, large family shower room (hot water on payment key). Toilet facility only for disabled visitors (key access). Washing machine and dryer. Snack bar/takeaway with terrace. Play areas. Volleyball. Bicycle hire. GPS tours. Activity and entertainment programme (under 12s; high season). WiFi over site (charged). Off site: Cycling and walking tracks. Walibi Holland. Harderwijk and dolphinarium. Riding 1 km. Golf 15 km.
Open: 29 March - 30 September.

Directions
From the A50 motorway take exit 30 and follow signs towards Apeldoorn (Hattem/Hessenweg). Then follow directions to Hattem. Upon arrival here, continue ahead on to Hessenweg. Site is signed from here. GPS: 52.466955, 6.058115

Charges guide
Per unit incl. 2 persons
and electricity €16.00 - €18.00
extra person €2.90
child (2-10 yrs) €1.90

Hattem
Molecaten Park De Leemkule
Leemkuilen 6, NL-8051 PW Hattem (Gelderland) T: 0384 441 945. E: deleemkule@molecaten.nl
alanrogers.com/NL6358

De Leemkule is a Molecaten park and can be found deep in the Veluwe woods. The camping area here is spacious and 150 comfort pitches (all with Europlugs, electricity, water and drainage) are available. Hikers' cabins (for short term rentals) are set in beautiful, mature woodland. There is a real sense of nature here – sightings of rabbits and roe deer are common, particularly early in the morning. The mature Veluwe woods provide welcome shade in high summer, but there are also some sunnier pitches in fields at the centre of the site. There are also gypsy wagons (4 persons) and bungalows (2-12 persons) for rent.

Facilities
One large sanitary block serves the touring area. Facilities for children and babies. Restaurant and bar (27/3-1/11), takeaway (27/3-1/11). Supermarket. Indoor pool with children's pool (16/1-31/12) and whirlpool, sauna, Turkish bath, solarium (charged). Heated outdoor pool (8/5-1/9). Tennis. Play areas. Activity and entertainment programme including club for children. Bicycle hire. Dogs are not accepted. WiFi (charged). Off site: Harderwijk village. Golf 3 km. Fishing 5 km. Riding 7 km.
Open: 27 March - 1 November.

Directions
Take exit 17 from the A28 motorway, and follow directions as far as Wezep. At the roundabout in Wezep remain on N308 and continue ahead onto Stationsweg. The site is well signed. GPS: 52.455587, 6.040238

Charges guide
Per unit incl. 2 persons
and electricity €19.50 - €24.50
extra person €3.90
child (2-10 yrs) €2.90

FREE Alan Rogers Travel Card
Extra benefits and savings - see page 12

Heerde

Molecaten Park De Koerberg

Koerbergseweg 4/1, NL-8181 LL Heerde (Gelderland) T: 0578 699 810. E: dekoerberg@molecaten.nl

alanrogers.com/NL6355

Molecaten Park De Koerberg is located in the extensive Veluwe region. This is a spacious site with 132 large, well shaded touring pitches set on sheltered fields in the woods. Special hiker's pitches and simple cabins are available. Accommodation to rent includes a fully equipped De Waard tent and bungalows for 4-6 persons. The new reception and site restaurant are welcoming and form the centre of the complex. The restaurant offers a tempting range of local dishes (including takeaway meals). Breakfast can be delivered to your pitch if you wish. A bowling centre is also available and is great fun for a night out with a difference.

Facilities

One large, heated sanitary block in the touring area has facilities for babies and families. Shop. Bar, restaurant and takeaway. Heated, outdoor swimming pool. Play area. Tennis. Football. Bowling alley. WiFi throughout (charged). Entertainment and activity programme. Tents and bungalows to rent. Off site: Beach, golf and riding 3 km. Fishing and boat launching 5 km. Cycle and walking tracks. Kröller-Müller museum.

Open: 1 April - 1 November.

Directions

Heading south from Zwolle, leave A50 motorway at exit 28 and follow signs to Heerde. Then follow signs to the site. GPS: 52.40965, 6.051149

Charges guide

Per unit incl. 2 persons	
and electricity	€ 19.25 - € 25.25
extra person	€ 3.90
child (2-10 yrs)	€ 2.90
dog (max. 1)	€ 3.90

Heumen

Recreatiecentrum Heumens Bos

Vosseneindseweg 46, NL-6582 BR Heumen (Gelderland) T: 0243 581 481. E: info@heumensbos.nl

alanrogers.com/NL5950

Heumens Bos covers 17 hectares of woodland and grassed fields providing 165 level touring pitches arranged in groups of ten or twelve. All pitches have electricity (6A) and cable connections, and cars are parked away from the units allowing plenty of recreational space. The site is situated beside miles of beautiful woods, criss-crossed by cycle paths, in a tranquil, rural setting. Heumens Bos is open over a long season for touring families and all year for bungalows. One small section for motorcaravans has some hardstandings. The restaurant offers a wide menu and also has a new terrace.

Facilities

The main, good quality sanitary building, plus another new block, are modern and heated, providing showers on payment. Rooms for families and disabled visitors. Smart launderette. Motorcaravan services. Gas supplies. Shop. Bar, restaurant and snack bar. Heated outdoor swimming pool (1/5-30/9). Bicycle hire. Tennis. Boules. Glade area with play equipment on sand and grass. Activity and excursion programme (high season). Large wet weather room. WiFi over site (charged). Off site: Riding 300 m. Fishing 2 km. Golf 6 km.

Open: All year.

Directions

From A73 (Nijmegen-Venlo) take exit 3 (4 km. south of Nijmegen) and follow site signs. GPS: 51.76915, 5.82050

Charges guide

Per unit incl. 2 persons	
and electricity	€ 18.00 - € 30.00
extra person (over 3 yrs)	€ 4.00
dog (max. 1)	€ 4.00

Special low season weekends (incl. restaurant meal) and special deal for over 55 yr. olds.

Hoenderloo

Veluwecamping De Pampel

Woeste Hoefweg 35, NL-7351 TN Hoenderloo (Gelderland) T: 0553 781 760.
E: info@veluwevakantieparken.nl **alanrogers.com/NL5840**

Camping De Pampel has the most congenial atmosphere and caters both for families (great facilities for children) and for those seeking peace and quiet. This is enhanced by its situation deep in the forest, with nine hectares of its own woods to explore. There are 280 pitches (20 seasonal) with 6-16A electricity. You can choose to site yourself around the edge of a large, open field with volleyball in the middle, or pick one of the individual places which are numbered, divided by trees and generally quite spacious.

Facilities

Toilet facilities are excellent, and the new Sani Plaza has to be seen. Laundry. Well stocked shop (1/4-1/10). Restaurant. Snack bar (July/Aug, otherwise weekends only). Swimming pool and new fun paddling pool with water canon (heated by solar panels; open 1/4-31/10). Play area. Pets' corner. Sports area. Indoor play area. Dogs are not accepted. WiFi throughout (free). Off site: Riding 1 km. Golf 10 km. Fishing 15 km.

Open: All year.

Directions

From A50 Arnhem-Apeldoorn road take Hoenderloo exit and follow signs. GPS: 52.11885, 5.90569

Charges guide

Per unit incl. 2 persons	
and electricity	€ 20.00 - € 37.00
extra person	€ 4.25 - € 5.25
child (1-11 yrs)	€ 3.25 - € 4.25

For latest campsite news, availability and prices visit
alanrogers.com

Hulshorst
DroomPark Bad Hoophuizen

Varelseweg 211, NL-8077 RB Hulshorst (Gelderland) T: 0341 451 353. E: m.budding@droomparken.nl
alanrogers.com/NL6343

Centrally located on the shores of Veluwemeer in the beautiful Veluwe region, between Harderwijk and Nunspeet, Camping DroomPark Bad Hoophuizen is a good family site. There are currently 550 touring pitches, most with water, 6/10A electricity and cable TV connections. This is a spacious site with a choice of pitches of varying sizes and locations. Several types of rented accommodation are also on offer. The recently reconstructed café/restaurant has an attractive conservatory and lakeside terrace, from where you can enjoy beautiful sunsets across the Veluwemeer.

Facilities

Eight well maintained, prefabricated-type sanitary blocks with modern facilities including baby rooms and facilities for disabled campers. Restaurant. Snack bar. Shop. Indoor pool. Free entry to the sub-tropical swimming pool (De Brake) in Nunspeet. Bicycle hire. Canoes, kayaks, pedaloes and boats for hire. Tennis. Free WiFi over site. Indoor play area. Off site: Ferry across the Veluwemeer.

Open: 25 March - 30 October.

Directions

From A28 motorway, take exit 13 towards Lelystad (N302). After 2 km. turn right towards Hierden and Hulshorst. In Hulshorst follow signs to the site (to the left). GPS: 52.382711, 5.708323

Charges guide

Per unit incl. 2 persons and electricity	€ 18.50 - € 35.50
extra person	€ 3.00 - € 5.00

Hummelo
Parkcamping De Graafschap

Loenhorsterweg 7C, NL-6999 DT Hummelo (Gelderland) T: 0314 343 752. E: info@camping-degraafschap.nl
alanrogers.com/NL5865

De Graafschap is an attractive, family friendly site located on the outskirts of the beautiful Kruisbergse forest between Doetinchem and Hummelo, a large green area perfect for hiking, mountain biking and cycling enthusiasts. Pitches here are all of a good size, on average 125-150 sq.m. There are 65 touring and 65 permanent pitches on several well kept grassy fields, all with electricity (6A), water, drainage and cable TV connection (charged). There is a cosy canteen offering snacks and drinks and a small shop in the reception for all your daily essentials. Finnish Kotas and mobile homes are for rent all year round.

Facilities

Two heated sanitary blocks with free hot water and baby room. Launderette. Motorcaravan services. Small shop. Canteen. Playground. Boules. WiFi (charged). Off site: Shops and restaurants in Doetinchem 2 km. Bronckhorst, local historic village. House Verwolde Castle. Cycling and walking routes through Kruisbergse forest.

Open: All year.

Directions

Take the A12 from Arnhem towards Oberhausen and exit at A348 to Zutphen. Continue to the end and then follow N317 towards Doesburg/Doetinchem into Laag Keppel. At the intersection turn left into Hummelo and first right towards Hengelo. Follow signs to the site. GPS: 51.9912, 6.27960

Charges guide

Per unit incl. 2 persons and electricty	€ 18.35 - € 22.15

No credit cards.

Hummelo
Camping Jena

Rozegaarderweg 7, NL-6999 DW Hummelo (Gelderland) T: 0314 381457. E: info@campingjena.nl
alanrogers.com/NL5875

Camping Jena is an attractive, rural site on the edge of the vast forests and estate of Enghuizen. There are 175 spacious pitches (min. 100 sq.m), all for touring, with 6/10A electricity. In one area they are enclosed by hedges, shrubbery and trees, providing plenty of privacy; in other areas they are more open. For younger visitors there is a sports field, a recreation room, play equipment and a BMX track. Adults will appreciate the Golden Carp (the region's oldest hotel and restaurant) in Hummelo, just 2 kilometres away. This is an exceptionally peaceful site with many cycle routes and footpaths on the doorstep.

Facilities

Two clean sanitary blocks. Facilities for disabled visitors. Laundry. Small shop with bread. Café. Takeaway. Free WiFi in café. Off site: Motorcaravan service point at entrance. Supermarket and Golden Carp hotel/restaurant in Hummelo 2 km. Walking and cycling routes. Fishing and golf 2 km. Riding 8 km.

Open: 29 March - 26 October.

Directions

From A12 junction 27 (Arnhem/Zutphen) take exit for Doesburg N338. After Angerlo turn right onto the N317, then left on N314 for a short distance towards Hummelo. Site is signed on right. GPS: 51.993182, 6.256247

Charges guide

Per unit incl. 2 persons and electricity	€ 16.35 - € 19.10
extra person	€ 3.50

No credit cards.

FREE Alan Rogers Travel Card
Extra benefits and savings - see page 12

Kesteren
Camping Betuwe

Hoge Dijkseweg 40, NL-4041 AW Kesteren (Gelderland) T: 0488 481 477. E: info@campingbetuwe.nl

alanrogers.com/NL6275

Camping Betuwe is in the Neder-Betuwe municipality of Gelderland, a rich agricultural region of fruit plantations and tree nurseries. This long established park is undergoing a complete transformation. As well as the many seasonal pitches, there are spacious pitches for touring units and tents, with 16A electricity, adjacent to the new toilet facilities. A full and varied entertainment programme is offered during the high season. There are two lakes, one with a sandy beach and play area and the other being a well stocked fishing lake. This site is suitable for all ages, for those seeking peace and tranquillity in rural surroundings, and for families with young children and teenagers.

Facilities

New sanitary facilities have washbasins in cubicles and hot showers (key operated). No facilities for children or disabled visitors. Well stocked shop, takeaway, bar and restaurant (weekends only in low season). High class restaurant/brasserie (all year). Playgrounds. Lakeside beach and swimming. Well stocked fishing lake. Bicycle hire. Dogs (max. 2) are allowed. Public transport is 5 min. walk away. WiFi (charged). Only gas barbecues permitted. Riding. Off site: Golf 20 km.

Open: 15 March - 27 October.

Directions

Leave A15 at exit 35 and take N233 towards Kesteren. After 2 km. turn left then right onto N320. After 1 km. turn right at signpost and then first right. Site is on left in 1 km. New entrance 200 m. past old entrance (closed). GPS: 51.93753, 5.54589

Charges guide

Per unit incl. 2 persons and electricity	€ 21.00 - € 27.00
extra person	€ 5.00
dog	€ 5.00

Laag-Soeren
Vakantiedorp De Jutberg

Jutberg 78, NL-6957 DP Laag-Soeren (Gelderland) T: 0313 619 220. E: jutberg@ardoer.com

alanrogers.com/NL6344

What makes De Jutberg attractive is the relaxed atmosphere, the friendly staff and the natural setting of the site. This is a typical Dutch Veluwe campsite with curved paths and different types of pitches, 145 in total. They range from luxury pitches with all the modern comforts of water, drainage, electricity and cable TV, to rather more natural pitches without any services. Some pitches are a distance from the toilet blocks. Almost all are surrounded by trees or hedges providing shelter and privacy. The site is set in a rural environment so there is not much lighting. Adjacent to the touring pitches are several areas occupied by private chalets, all hidden in their own wooded glades.

Facilities

Four modern toilet blocks include facilities for families and babies. No facilities for disabled visitors. Freezer. Shop, restaurant and takeaway (1/4-31/10). Bar. Bicycle hire. Swimming pool with sliding roof (1/4-31/10). Large play area. Nature hut. Activities daily in high season. Free WiFi over site. Wooden huts and teepees to rent. Off site: Riding 1 km. Fishing 2 km. Golf 10 km.

Open: All year.

Directions

De Jutberg is 15 km. northeast of Arnhem, signed from the N786 between Dieren and Laag-Soeren. GPS: 52.07089, 6.0764

Charges guide

Per unit incl. 2 persons and electricity	€ 17.00 - € 33.00
extra person (over 2 yrs)	€ 2.50 - € 4.75
dog	€ 4.00

Lathum
Recreatiepark Rhederlaagse Meren

Marsweg 2, NL-6988 BM Lathum (Gelderland) T: 0313 632 211. E: R.Stokman@succesparken.nl

alanrogers.com/NL6328

Recreatiepark Rhederlaagse Meren is situated on the shore of the Rhederlaag, a 300-acre leisure lake with sandy beaches, boating and watersports. The 500 pitches, 125 for touring, are separated by hedges and are right on the lakeside; all have 10A electricity. There is an entertainment programme for both children and adults during high season. In the evening you can relax in the site's restaurant or enjoy a snack in the cafeteria. Families with young children will enjoy the beach and play areas, while teenagers can try their hand at some of the many watersports activities.

Facilities

One clean, heated sanitary block has basic but adequate facilities (none for children or disabled visitors). Outdoor heated swimming pool (1/5-1/10). Well stocked shop, bar and restaurant (weekends only out of high season). Play area. Lake swimming. Fishing. Tennis court. Watersports. Bicycle hire. WiFi over site (charged). Off site: Veluwe National Park 2 km. Riding 10 km. Golf 15 km.

Open: All year.

Directions

From A12 exit at exit 27 (Arnhem/Zutphen). Take exit Westervoort and follow signs for Doesburg (N338). Turn left just after Lathum village. GPS: 51.994348, 6.029896

Charges guide

Per unit incl. 4 persons and electricity	€ 28.00 - € 32.00
extra person	€ 10.00

Lieren
Recreatiecentrum De Bosgraaf

Kanaal Zuid 444, NL-7364 CB Lieren (Gelderland) T: 0555 051 359. E: bosgraaf@ardoer.com

alanrogers.com/NL6338

With a real park-like feel, this green site has spacious grass pitches in wooded surroundings. It is a delightful site for quiet relaxation. There are 194 touring pitches (6/10A electricity), half of which have private sanitary facilities for rent. In addition, there are privately owned chalets and mobile homes, also set in the woods. In the summer months the site is mostly organised for campers with children. The large children's pool with its water slides is very popular, as is the paddling pool. The play areas are numerous and varied and in high season there are organised activities. A member of the Ardoer group.

Facilities	Directions
Four modern toilet blocks include facilities for families and babies. Private toilet facilities for 94 pitches are rather basic. Launderette. Shop (10/4-15/9). Bar. Restaurant (3/4-20/9). Sauna. Large sports field with adventure playground. Small animal farm. Fishing. Bicycle hire. WiFi over part of site (charged). Accommodation for hire. Dogs are not accepted. Off site: Golf and fishing 1 km. Riding 2 km. Bus to Apeldoorn in summer.	From the A1 take exit for Apeldoorn-Zuid and Beekbergen and turn left towards Dieren. After 600 m. turn right towards Dieren. Follow the canal for 5 km. to reach site. GPS: 52.14842, 6.03828

Open: 21 March - 25 October.

Charges guide

Per serviced pitch incl. 2 persons and electricity	€ 24.00 - € 30.00
incl. own sanitary facility	€ 27.00 - € 37.00
extra person	€ 5.00

No credit cards.

Lunteren
Camping De Rimboe

Boslaan 129, NL-6741 KG Lunteren (Gelderland) T: 0318 482 371. E: info@campingderimboe.com

alanrogers.com/NL6331

Camping De Rimboe is set in 10.5 hectares of sloping fields and mature woodland. The 140 touring pitches (90-150 sq.m) are either on grass, which has both sun and shade, or in the woods where there is an opportunity for free camping. All have a water point and 4/6A electricity. This is a peaceful site where visitors can relax, appreciate the natural environment and explore the area by foot or bicycle. As a contrast, the lively resort towns of Lunteren, Ede and Bardeveld are a short distance away. The site's recreational space provides opportunities for a variety of games and sports.

Facilities	Directions
Heated sanitary facilities. Washing machines and dryers. Clubhouse. Picnic tables. Recreation space. Volleyball. Sand quarry nature reserve. Bicycle hire. WiFi (charged). Off site: Swimming pool 800 m. (28/4-31/8). Walking and cycle routes nearby. Lunteren 2.5 km. Ede 6.8 km. Bardeveld 9.6 km.	De Rimboe is 25 km. northwest of Arnhem. From the E35 between Ede and Veenendaal turn north onto the A30. After 8 km. turn east to Lunteren. In Lunteren (Dorpstraat) follow signs for Boslaan. Site is opposite the bicycle shop. GPS: 52.09221, 5.66294

Open: 1 March - 27 October.

Charges guide

Per unit incl. 2 persons and electricity	€ 15.30 - € 17.70
dog (max. 1)	€ 2.25

Maurik
Camping De Loswal

Rijnbandijk 36, NL-4021 GH Maurik (Gelderland) T: 0344 692 892. E: info@camping-deloswal.nl

alanrogers.com/NL6280

De Loswal is a beautifully landscaped site with many fruit trees and a large marina. The 50 level touring pitches are spacious and sunny, with those close to the dyke being particularly spacious (120 sq.m). All the pitches have 6A electricity and many great views over the lake. There are four sanitary buildings of which one is new, this one being located near the entrance and reception. All the buildings are heated, tiled and well maintained. This site is good for fishing and ideal for watersports enthusiasts as you can moor your own boat here. Boat hire is available within 2 km.

Facilities	Directions
Four sanitary buildings which are kept clean and well maintained. One modern but all tiled and neat. Facilities for disabled visitors. Launderette. Small bar/restaurant with takeaway. Boat launching and marina for various types of boats. Several sandy beaches and lake swimming. Adventure play area. Fishing. Off site: Shop. Restaurant. Bar. Bicycle hire 1 km. Golf 7 km.	From the A15 take exit for Tiel/Maurik and follow signs to Maurik. Site well signed from here. From the A2 take Culemborg exit and follow N320 to Maurik (site is then well signed). GPS: 51.96328, 5.40657

Open: April - October.

Charges guide

Per unit incl. 2 persons and electricity	€ 17.60 - € 23.50
extra person	€ 3.00
dog	€ 3.00

FREE Alan Rogers Travel Card
Extra benefits and savings - see page 12

Maurik
Camping Eiland van Maurik

Eiland van Maurik 7, NL-4021 GG Maurik (Gelderland) T: 0344 691 502. E: receptie@eilandvanmaurik.nl
alanrogers.com/NL6290

Camping Eiland van Maurik is beside a lake in the centre of an extensive nature and recreation park in the Nederrijn area. These surroundings are ideal for all sorts of activities – swimming, windsurfing, water-skiing or para-sailing, relaxing on the beach or fishing. There is even an animal farm for the children. The site has 265 numbered, flat pitches, all fully serviced (10A electricity). You could enjoy pancakes in the Oudhollandse restaurant with its views over the water. There is direct access from the site to the lakeside beach.

Facilities

The three toilet blocks for tourers include washbasins (open style and in cabins), controllable showers and a baby room. Launderette with iron and board. Shop. Bar/restaurant/pizzeria (all season). Play areas (one indoors). Playing field. Tennis. Minigolf. Bicycle hire. Go-karts. Water-skiing. Sailing and motorboat hire. Para-sailing. Animal farm. Entertainment in high season (incl. riding). Off site: 18-hole pitch and putt 1 km.

Open: 1 April - 1 October.

Directions

From the A2 take the Culemborg exit towards Kesteren and follow signs for Eiland Maurik. From the A15 take exit 33 Tiel towards Maurik and follow signs. GPS: 51.97656, 5.43013

Charges guide

Per unit incl. 2 persons
and electricity   € 20.00 - € 35.00
No credit cards.
Camping Cheques accepted.

Nieuw Milligen
Landal Rabbit Hill

Grevenhout 21, NL-3888 NR Nieuw Milligen (Gelderland) T: 0577 456 431. E: rabbithill@landal.nl
alanrogers.com/NL5822

You will soon discover the reason for Landal Rabbit Hill's name. Wildlife abounds on this friendly site which is located deep within the heavily forested Veluwe, close to Nieuw Milligen. The cities of Apeldoorn, Amersfoort and Arnhem are all within easy reach. There are 140 large, well shaded pitches. All have 10/16A electricity and cable TV connections. You will be impressed with the facilities, which include an excellent indoor pool with slides and other features. There is also a wonderful indoor play area with an impressive range of games. This is also home to the site's popular children's club.

Facilities

Two modern, heated sanitary blocks are clean and central to the touring fields. Free controllable hot showers and some washbasins in cabins. Large family room. Facilities for disabled visitors. Washing machines and dryers. Motorcaravan services. Well stocked shop and café/restaurant with takeaway (all year). Indoor (all year) and outdoor (1/5-30/9) pool complex. Indoor and outdoor playgrounds. Mobile homes and chalets for rent. Dogs are not accepted. Bicycle hire. WiFi (charged).

Open: All year.

Directions

Approaching from the west (Amersfoort) use the A1 motorway as far as the Nieuw Milligen exit, and then join the northbound N302. Site is signed to the right within the village. GPS: 52.218673, 5.785503

Charges guide

Per unit incl. 2 persons
and electricity   € 18.00 - € 45.00
No credit cards.

Nunspeet
Molecaten Park De Hooghe Bijsschel

Randmeerweg 8, NL-8071 SH Nunspeet (Gelderland) T: 0341 252 406. E: dehooghebijsschel@molecaten.nl
alanrogers.com/NL6359

A family focused campsite with direct access to Lake Veluwe, this site is understandably popular with windsurfers, sailors and fishermen. The lake is shallow and therefore also ideal for younger children. The two large camping fields are car-free and are bordered by hedges and mature trees. The 123 grassy touring pitches all have 6/10A electricity. There is plenty of space for children to safely play in the middle of the fields. There is a marina and pier (with a slipway) – ideal for boat launching, and also a lakeside beach. In high season, free courses are organised for children (up to 12 years) to try out watersports.

Facilities

Two toilet blocks have facilities for babies and for disabled visitors. Restaurant and bar with terrace and lake view, takeaway. Small shop. Heated outdoor swimming pool with children's pool (8/5-1/9), whirlpool. Direct lake access. Beach with play area. Volleyball. Tennis. Play areas. Bicycle and boat hire. Boat launching. Windsurfing and sailing tuition. Activity and entertainment programme. WiFi throughout (charged).

Open: 29 March - 30 September.

Directions

Take exit 14 from the A28 motorway and follow signs to Elspeet/Nunspeet on N310. In Nunspeet, continue ahead onto Elspeterweg/N310. On the outskirts of Nunspeet, take first exit on Vreeweg. The site is signed from here. GPS: 52.392054, 5.735056

Charges guide

Per unit incl. 2 persons
and electricity   € 18.50 - € 28.00
No credit cards.

For latest campsite news, availability and prices visit
alanrogers.com

Nunspeet
Camping De Tol

Elspeterweg 61, NL-8071 PB Nunspeet (Gelderland) T: 0341 252 413. E: info@camping-detol.nl
alanrogers.com/NL6361

Camping De Tol is a very attractive family owned and run campsite in the wooded Veluwe area, close to the town of Nunspeet. Its 188 touring pitches (80-100 sq.m; all with 4-10A electricity) are arranged in groups of six around a large leisure lake with floating play equipment. The campsite is organised with families in mind, and there is a choice of lake swimming or the heated outdoor pool, and a range of organised activities in high season. In the evening, why not relax on the terrace with a drink, then enjoy an excellent meal from the restaurant?

Facilities	Directions
Three sanitary blocks with some washbasins in cubicles (hot water on payment). En-suite unit for disabled campers (key access). Bar, restaurant and takeaway (July/Aug). Large lake with floating play equipment and beach. Outdoor heated swimming pool (1/5-mid Sept). Sports field. Minigolf. Bicycle hire. WiFi over site (charged). Dogs are not accepted. Off site: Golf and riding 2 km. Beach and fishing 4 km.	From A28 exit at exit 14 take N310 towards Elspeet. Site is 1 km. on the left. GPS: 52.35571, 5.786941

Charges guide

Per unit incl. 2 persons and electricity	€ 16.50 - € 25.50
extra person (over 3 yrs)	€ 3.50

Open: 29 March - 28 October.

Oosterhout
Camping De Grote Altena

Waaldijk 39, NL-6678 MC Oosterhout (Gelderland) T: 0481 481 200. E: info@campingdegrotealtena.nl
alanrogers.com/NL6395

This campsite occupies a scenic location on the River Waal. It has 160 pitches in total, half of which are situated immediately beside the river with fabulous views. There are 25 permanent and 60 seasonal pitches, plus 70 for touring with 6A electricity, water and drainage. A separate field, with a fish pond, is available for short stays. The playground with open-air chess and trampoline is popular with children. De Grote Altena is ideal for nature lovers who enjoy peace and space. The attractive cities of Arnhem and Nijmegen are both within easy reach.

Facilities	Directions
Three sanitary buildings are modern and well maintained with free hot showers and facilities for babies. Laundry facilities. Shop, bar, restaurant and takeaway (all season). Bicycle hire. Playground. Fishing. Direct river access. Open-air chess. Small, riverside beach. Boat launching. WiFi over site (charged). Off site: Restaurant. Nearest shops in Oosterhout 1 km. Supermarket in Elst 4 km. Arnhem and Nijmegen.	From Arnhem or Nijmegen follow A325, and leave at Ressen Tiel/Rotterdam exit (A15). After 2.6 km. take exit 38 to Elst/Oosterhout. Turn left after 500 m. at petrol station, turn right, then follow signs to site. GPS: 51.87585, 5.80752

Charges guide

Per unit incl. 5 persons and electricity	€ 26.00
extra person	€ 4.50
dog	€ 3.00

Open: 6 April - 6 October.

Otterlo
Droompark De Zanding

Vijverlaan 1, NL-6731 CK Otterlo (Gelderland) T: 0318 596 111. E: info@zanding.nl
alanrogers.com/NL5780

De Zanding is a highly rated, family run site that offers almost every recreational facility, either on site or nearby, that active families or couples might seek. As soon as you turn the corner to this impressive site, children will want to investigate the play equipment by the lake. There are many sporting options and organised high season programmes for all ages. There are 463 touring pitches spread around the site (all with electricity), some individual and separated, others in more open spaces shaded by trees. Some serviced pitches are in small groups between long stay units and there is another area for tents.

Facilities	Directions
First class sanitary facilities are housed in five modern blocks that are clean, well maintained and well equipped. Good provision for babies and disabled guests. Laundry. Kitchen. Motorcaravan services. Gas. Supermarket. Restaurant/bar. Lake beach and swimming. Fishing. Tennis. Minigolf. Boules. Five play areas. Bicycle hire. Organised activities. WiFi over site (charged). Off site: Riding 1 km. Golf 25 km.	Leave A12 Utrecht-Arnhem motorway at Oosterbeek at exit 25 and join N310 to Otterlo. Then follow camping signs to site, watching carefully for entrance. GPS: 52.09310, 5.77757

Charges guide

Per unit incl. 2 persons and electricity	€ 25.00 - € 38.00
extra person	€ 8.00
dog	€ 4.00
Camping Cheques accepted.	

Open: All year.

FREE Alan Rogers Travel Card
Extra benefits and savings - see page 12

Otterlo
Camping Beek en Hei

Heideweg 4, NL-6731 SN Otterlo (Gelderland) T: 0318 591 483. E: info@beekenhei.nl
alanrogers.com/NL5835

Camping Beek en Hei, located in the heart of the Veluwe nature reserve, offers space, tranquillity and beautiful scenery. There are 150 pitches within four camping areas, including an open plan family field and a touring area with tall hedges and secluded pitches, all with 6A electricity. If you prefer something a little more natural, there are pitches on the edge of the campsite in the forest and an opportunity to get back to nature with wild camping in the heart of the forest. On site facilities include a play area and treasure hunts and games with the local ranger. A lake with a beach is also within walking distance.

Facilities

One clean, heated prefabricated unit in each area has showers (€0.50) and baby changing. Facilities for disabled visitors in some blocks. Motorcaravan services. Launderette. Shop with basics in reception. Library/TV room. Well maintained play areas. Organised children's activities (July/Aug). Bicycle hire. Winter cabins. WiFi over site (charged). Off site: Shops and restaurants in Otterlo. Walking and cycling routes Kröller-Müller museum.

Open: All year.

Directions

Take A12 from Utrecht-Arnhem, exit at Veenendaal and continue towards Renswoude. Take the N224 towards Arnhem-Ede for 9 km, continue on the N304 for Otterlo then follow signs for the site. GPS: 52.0918, 5.77020

Charges guide

Per unit incl. 2 persons and electricty	€ 19.75
extra person	€ 4.50
child (under 12 years)	€ 3.25

Otterlo
Camping De Wije Werelt

Arnhemseweg 100-102, NL-6731 BV Otterlo (Gelderland) T: 0318 591 201. E: wijewerelt@ardoer.com
alanrogers.com/NL6350

Camping De Wije Werelt offers all the facilities you need for a very comfortable holiday. The 170 touring pitches all have water and drainage, 10A electricity, cable, and WiFi. The site is surrounded by forest – the home of many wild animals and there are numerous good cycling and walking routes. This peaceful site is very child friendly and extremely popular with families during school holidays. There are plenty of activities for children on site including a playground for younger children and an area with different play equipment for older children. There is also a heated, outdoor swimming pool with paddling pool.

Facilities

Heated toilet block includes washbasins in cabins. Family wash cabins and facilities for children. Baby room. Launderette with ironing facilities. Microwave. Well stocked shop. Bar. Restaurant. Snack bar and takeaway. TV room. Playground, bouncy castle and climbing frames. Sports field. Boules. Entertainment in high season. Bicycle and tricycle hire. Recreation area. Miniclub. Electronic games. WiFi over site (charged). Off site: Riding 500 m. Fishing 1 km. Golf 20 km.

Open: 21 March - 25 October.

Directions

The site is north of Arnhem. From the A1 take exit 17 south onto the N310 and the site is signed to the right after Otterlo and De Zanding. GPS: 52.08656, 5.76945

Charges guide

Per serviced pitch incl. 2 persons, electricity, water and waste water	€ 22.00 - € 36.25
extra person	€ 5.00
dog (max. 1)	€ 4.00

Ruurlo
Camping Tamaring

Wildpad 3, NL-7261 MR Ruurlo (Gelderland) T: 0573 451 486. E: info@camping-tamaring.nl
alanrogers.com/NL6423

Camping Tamaring is a small, tranquil site, ideal for those seeking a natural setting with plenty of space. It is located close to the natural parks of Beekvliet and Grote Veld. There are 120 large pitches here (100-150 sq.m) on 3.5 acres, spread over four fields. One field has pitches separated by hedges, creating a private atmosphere. A separate field caters for tents with a covered picnic area and children's hide-out. All pitches have electricity connections (10A) and Europlugs. There are also two bungalows (for six persons) and two mobile homes for rent.

Facilities

New modern, heated sanitary block with facilities for babies and disabled visitors. Launderette. Small shop. Reception with terrace. Bar. Outdoor swimming pool. Bicycle hire. DVD hire. Boules. Indoor reading area. Play areas. WiFi. Off site: Shops and restaurants in Ruurlo. Medieval city of Zutphen. Ruurlo Castle and maze. Beautiful gardens in Ruurlo, Harfsen and Vorden. Outdoor swimming pool with water slides.

Open: 1 April - 31 October.

Directions

From Arnhem take A348 towards Zutphen, continue on N348 and then N314 to bypass Zutphen. At roundabout take N319 through Vorden to N312 for Ruurlo. Site is 1.5 km. north of Ruurlo on N312 towards Lochem. GPS: 52.102836, 6.441553

Charges guide

Per unit incl. 2 persons and electricity	€ 17.60 - € 19.75
extra person	€ 3.90 - € 4.25

Vaassen

Camping De Helfterkamp

Gortelseweg 24, NL-8171 RA Vaassen (Gelderland) T: 0578 571 839. E: info@helfterkamp.nl

alanrogers.com/NL5845

Helfterkamp is a pretty, family friendly site located between the historical royal estate of Het Loo and the Ijssel Valley. With 14 hectares of land and making good use of traditional farm buildings, it offers an appealing, natural farming environment. There are 195 sheltered, grassy touring pitches with electricity (6/16A), arranged around the edges of green fields with children's play areas in the centre of some. A barn has been refurbished to create a craft centre for children. There is also a small farm for children. The site is on the outskirts of the Het Loo crown estate, the largest country estate in the Netherlands.

Facilities

Three modern, heated toilet blocks are clean and have facilities for children and disabled visitors. Laundry facilities. Motorcaravan services. Small shop with bread to order. Recreation barn including TV, shuffleboard and organised craft sessions. Play areas. Sports field. Children's entertainment (high season). Bicycle hire. WiFi over site (charged). Off site: Vaassen. Julianatoren (amusement park in Apeldoorn). Riding 1 km. Fishing 5 km. Golf 12 km. Het Loo royal crown estate.

Open: 16 February - 31 October.

Directions

From the A50 to Apeldoorn take exit 26 (Vaasen). Following signs to Vaasen centre, pass through traffic lights. Continue for 2 km, turning right into Gortelseweg. The site entrance is 500 m. to the right. GPS: 52.2908, 5.94535

Charges guide

Per unit incl. 2 persons	€ 17.50 - € 20.50
extra person	€ 4.00
electricity per kWh	€ 0.40

Vierhouten

Recreatiepark Samoza

Plaggeweg 90, NL-8076 PM Vierhouten (Gelderland) T: 0577 411 283. E: info@samoza.nl

alanrogers.com/NL6295

Recreatiepark Samoza is hidden in woodland and surrounded by moorland, water and sand dunes. The site has some 300 touring pitches, scattered around the site on various fields and between static units and seasonal guests. The level pitches are 100 sq.m. in size, most in the shade of mature trees and all with electricity (4A), water and cable connections. There are 50 fully serviced pitches (10A electricity) for motorcaravans. To the front of the site is a welcoming indoor pool (25x10 m). Next to that is a heated outdoor pool with a large sun terrace and an open grass area.

Facilities

Several solar-heated toilet blocks close to the touring pitches provide toilets, open style washbasins and free, preset hot showers. Baby room. Facilities for disabled campers. Laundry. Motorcaravan services. Well stocked shop. Bar with open air terrace (daily). Restaurant. Indoor and outdoor pools and paddling pool. Boules. Bicycle hire. Tennis. Basketball. Riding. Animal farm. WiFi over site (charged). Off site: Golf 4 km.

Open: 29 March - 27 October.

Directions

From the A28, take exit 14 (Nunspeet/Elspeet) and continue towards Elspeet. Turn towards Vierhouten and follow site signs. GPS: 52.348376, 5.824406

Charges guide

Per unit incl. 2 persons and electricity	€ 29.00 - € 32.65
extra person	€ 3.65 - € 4.20
No credit cards.	

Voorthuizen

Recreatiepark De Boshoek

Harremaatweg 34, NL-3781 NJ Voorthuizen (Gelderland) T: 0342 471 297. E: info@deboshoek.nl

alanrogers.com/NL6337

Camping de Boshoek is a spacious, family oriented campsite, which forms a part of a large leisure park which includes bungalows for rent and private chalets. There are 130 touring pitches of 100-120 sq.m., all equipped with 10A electricity, water, drainage and cable TV connections. They are in various fields, each with its own play area and including two car-free areas, with a central area for general use. There are eight pitches reserved for campers. Rented accommodation includes comfortable safari tents. Children will enjoy the playground with its giant slide. There is also a pony club and a children's farm.

Facilities

One clean, heated toilet block has free showers and some washbasins in cubicles. Good facilities for children and disabled visitors. Some private sanitary facilities to rent on pitches. Shop. Restaurant, bar, snack bar. Large swimming complex. Large adventure play area. Pony riding and lessons. Minigolf. 10-pin bowling. Short golf. Tennis. Children's farm. Entertainment and children's club. Hairdresser. Bicycle hire. WiFi over part of site (charged).

Open: 23 March - 27 October.

Directions

From A1 take exit 16 and on to Voorthuizen. In Voorthuizen at first roundabout turn right and drive through the village. Then take first turn right (Bosweg). At the end turn left to the site entrance on the right (500 m). GPS: 52.187556, 5.630976

Charges guide

Per unit incl. 2 persons and electricity	€ 22.00 - € 45.00
extra person	€ 5.00
No credit cards.	

FREE Alan Rogers Travel Card
Extra benefits and savings - see page 12

Gelderland

Voorthuizen
Recreatiecentrum Ackersate
Harremaatweg 26, NL-3781 NJ Voorthuizen (Gelderland) T: 0342 471 274. E: ackersate@ardoer.com
alanrogers.com/NL6336

This is a sophisticated, wooded site with 150 touring pitches out of a total of 490, all with electricity. The swimming pool has a fun pool with slides, a large pool for young children, imaginatively designed, separate pool for length swimming and even a flume. Also popular, is the cosy restaurant/bar. There is a play club for children, a playing field and a petting farm. Other activities available include minigolf, table tennis and a pool table. A member of the Ardoer Group.

Facilities	Directions
Three toilet blocks are conveniently situated around the touring areas. En-suite unit for disabled campers. Laundry. Well stocked shop. Bar with TV. Snack bar/takeaway. Heated indoor pool. Play area. Entertainment for younger children (high season). Bicycle hire. WiFi over site. Accommodation for hire. Max. 1 dog per pitch. Off site: Golf 3 km. Fishing and riding 10 km. **Open:** 27 March - 27 October.	From the A1 between Amersfoort and Apeldoorn, take exit 16 N303 to Voorthuizen then onto the N344 towards Garderen. The site is signed soon after leaving Voorthuizen. GPS: 52.18692, 5.62458

Charges guide

Per unit incl. 2 persons and electricity	€ 22.50 - € 36.50
extra person	€ 5.00
dog (max. 1)	€ 5.00

Vorden
Camping 't Meulenbrugge
Mosselseweg 4, NL-7251 KT Vorden (Gelderland) T: 0575 556 612. E: info@meulenbrugge-vorden.nl
alanrogers.com/NL6335

Camping 't Meulenbrugge is an open, attractive site attached to a working farm and approached by a bridge over the Baakse Brook. The emphasis at this site is centred on the enjoyment of nature, with no constructed leisure facilities. The 109 touring pitches are spacious and arranged on large grassy fields with tall trees around the edges offering some shade. All have electricity (10/16A) and Europlugs. There are also 94 serviced pitches with electricity, water and drainage and some hardstandings for awnings. Fishing is available on site in the Baakse brook and there are many marked walking and cycling trails from the site. Cars are parked away from the pitches.

Facilities	Directions
Two modern, heated toilet blocks (hot water payment card). Free use of fridge. Launderette. Motorcaravan services. No shop but fresh bread daily. Play area. Bicycle hire. Free bike parking. Boules pitch. Fishing. WiFi over part of site (charged). Caravans for rent. Off site: Shops, restaurants and a bank in Vorden 2 km. Many marked walking and cycling routes. Heated, outdoor swimming pool in de Dennen. Historic city of Zutphen. **Open:** 15 March - 1 November.	From Zutphen follow N319 to Vorden. In Vorden, follow signs towards Ruurlo. After 1 km. turn left at an S-shaped bend (Mosselseweg). After 400 m. turn right to the site. GPS: 52.106653, 6.355264

Charges guide

Per unit incl. 2 persons and electricity (plus meter)	€ 16.50 - € 18.50
extra person	€ 4.50
No credit cards.	

Wezep
Camping De Heidegaard
Heidehoeksweg 7, NL-8091 BC Wezep (Gelderland) T: 0383 761 382. E: info@campingdeheidegaard.nl
alanrogers.com/NL5805

De Heidegaard is a well established site in woodland, close to the bustling town of Zwolle and the IJssel river. The site is landscaped with shrubs and flowers and the buildings are constructed of wood which gives the site a rustic, Western-style atmosphere. Most of the 160 touring pitches are pleasantly located in the shade of mature trees. A further 150 serviced pitches (8-10A electricity) are located on two large fields with newly planted trees. Access roads are tarmac and most pitches have 4A electricity. There are also plans to further develop a lake and its small sandy beach. Some train noise can be heard.

Facilities	Directions
Four toilet blocks (one recently added) are well placed around the site, with toilets, washbasins in cabins, free, preset hot showers, bathroom and baby room. Facilities for disabled visitors. Laundry. Small shop with fresh bread. Tavern for meals and drinks with terrace. Snack bar. Indoor pool with paddling pool. Small lake with sandy beach. Play field. Bicycle hire. Boules. Entertainment in season. Off site: Fishing 5 km. Beach and golf 8 km. Riding 10 km. **Open:** 1 April - 30 October.	From the A28 take exit 17 and continue southeast towards Wezep. Site is signed in Wezep (note: site is called Heidegaard, not Heidehoek, on road signs). GPS: 52.449647, 5.989791

Charges guide

Per unit incl. 2 persons and electricity	€ 18.50 - € 21.50
extra person (over 3 yrs)	€ 5.00
dog	€ 3.75

Winterswijk
Camping Vreehorst

Vreehorstweg 43, NL-7102 EK Winterswijk (Gelderland) T: 0543 514 805. E: info@vreehorst.nl
alanrogers.com/NL6400

Camping Vreehorst is a tranquil site with modern facilities, located within the Winterswijk National Park and close to the nature reserve at De Bekendelle. There are 200 pitches here, all of which are super pitches (100-140 sq.m, with water, drainage, 10A electricity, TV and WiFi connections). Of these, 22 pitches are available with private bathrooms or hardstandings. On-site amenities include an outdoor swimming pool and a paddling pool, a playground with a bouncy castle, and a sports field with artificial grass. In peak season, an activity and entertainment programme is on offer for children under 11 years.

Facilities

Luxury heated sanitary buildings with family showers, baby room and a private sauna. Fresh bread and newspapers. Outdoor swimming pool. Paddling pool. Play area with bouncy castle. Multisports field. Animal farm with wallabies. Activity programme in high season. Bicycle hire. WiFi. Off site: Shops, cafés, restaurants, cinema and covered pool in Winterswijk. Cycle and walking tracks. Fishing 2 km. Golf 5 km.

Open: 30 March - 28 October.

Directions

Take the A12 and A18 motorways to Varsseveld and then N318 towards Aalten and Winterswijk. Around 2 km. before Winterswijk, and 600 m. beyond Miste, turn right (Breukinkweg). Follow signs from there. GPS: 51.949217, 6.691141

Charges guide

Per unit incl. 2 persons and electricity	€ 19.00 - € 27.00
with own sanitary unit	€ 26.00 - € 36.00

Winterswijk
Camping Het Wieskamp Winterswijk

Kobstederweg 13, NL-7113 AA Winterswijk-Henxel (Gelderland) T: 0543 514 612. E: info@wieskamp.nl
alanrogers.com/NL6405

Camping Het Wieskamp Winterswijk is a quiet and luxurious campsite, located between two streams in the eastern section of the Achterhoek. There are two camping fields with a total of just 28 touring pitches, all with private sanitary units, TV and Internet connections and 16A electricity. The first field, Esch, has just six pitches, and is well shaded by mature trees and shrubs. The second field, Waliën, is sunnier and hosts 22 pitches, including two hardstandings for mobile homes. There is an excellent restaurant, which attracts many visitors from far and wide. The prevailing ambience is relaxed, with a play area for children on the terrace. The remainder of the large site is occupied by 273 permanent summer homes, 15 of which are for rent.

Facilities

Private sanitary units on all pitches. Launderette. Restaurant and snack bar. Outdoor, heated pool and paddling pool. Sand-based adventure playground. Model railway. Small animal farm. Bowling centre. Bicycle hire. Free WiFi over site. Off site: Golf 1 km. Fishing and riding 2 km. Shops and restaurants in Winterswijk 2 km.

Open: 1 April - 4 November.

Directions

Approaching from the west (Arnhem) use A12, A18 and N318 as far as Winterswijk. At Winterswijk take the road to Vreden (Germany) and follow signs to site (2 km). GPS: 51.9865, 6.74299

Charges guide

Per unit incl. 2 persons, electricity and sanitary unit	€ 20.00 - € 30.00
extra person	€ 3.50

Winterswijk
Recreatiepark Het Winkel

De Slingeweg 20, NL-7115 AG Winterswijk (Gelderland) T: 0031 543 513025. E: info@hetwinkel.nl
alanrogers.com/NL6412

Recreatiepark Het Winkel is a friendly family campsite in the middle of unspoilt countryside, surrounded by woodland in the Achterhoek region. The generous pitches (100 for touring) are serviced with 10A electricity, water and drain. Some meadow areas (without electricity) are only used for tents. Eight chalets are available to rent. There are large open spaces for leisure and sporting activities and a wide range of facilities for all the family. Cycling, running and walking routes start from the site. The Achterhoek region has the most extensive network of cycle paths in the Netherlands.

Facilities

Eight modern sanitary units and a beautifully presented block for children. Private en-suite facilities to rent for 8 touring pitches. Shop and bar (both open all year). Restaurant/takeaway (1/4-30/9). Swimming and paddling pools (heated 1/5-15/9) with water slide, sauna and solarium. Indoor play area for children. Bicycle hire. Tennis. Small animal park. WiFi (charged). Off site: Fishing 1 km. Riding 2 km. Golf 4 km.

Open: All year.

Directions

Site is 60 km. east of Arnhem close to the border with Germany. From Winterswijk take N319 southeast for 2 km. then turn right onto De Slingeweg. Site is on outskirts of Winterswijk Brinkheurne. GPS: 51.952137, 6.736899

Charges guide

Per unit incl. 2 persons and electricity	€ 19.00 - € 27.00
extra person	€ 3.25

FREE Alan Rogers Travel Card
Extra benefits and savings - see page 12

Winterswijk
Vakantiepark De Twee Bruggen

Meenkmolenweg 13, NL-7109-AH Winterswijk (Gelderland) T: 0543 565 366. E: info@detweebruggen.nl
alanrogers.com/NL6425

De Twee Bruggen is a spacious recreation park set in the Achterhoek countryside. The 350 touring pitches (all with 10/16A electricity) are divided between several fields of varying sizes. Although the fields are surrounded by tall trees, the ground is open and sunny. Beyond the touring area, 71 chalets set in well tended grounds, are for rent. Indoor and outdoor swimming pools can be enjoyed by children and adults. At the indoor pool there is a covered terrace and, for relaxation, a sauna and jacuzzi. Adjacent to the pool is a small, open-air theatre, where shows are staged in high season. This campsite is suited to families looking for a relaxing holiday with many leisure activities. A variety of mobile homes and chalets are for rent. The German border is within 20 minutes of the site.

Facilities	Directions
Three modern, well maintained sanitary buildings include showers and washbasins in private cabins. Fourteen pitches have private sanitary facilities. Washing machines and dryers. Motorcaravan services. Supermarket. Bar, restaurant and takeaway (all year). Heated outdoor pool (30/4-15/9). Heated indoor pool (all year). Paddling pool. Sauna. Jacuzzi. Solarium. Sports field. Tennis courts. Bicycle hire. Minigolf. Bowling. Playground. Deer field. Free WiFi over site. Max. 2 dogs. Off site: Distance to fishing and beach 500 m. Riding 2 km. Golf 15 km.	From Arnhem, take the A12 then A18 towards Varsseveld which will turn onto the N18. In Varsseveld follow signs for Aalten (N318). In Aalten follow signs for Winterswijk. Drive through Aalten and site is signed after 4 km. GPS: 51.94961, 6.6477

Open: All year.

Charges guide

Per unit incl. 2 persons and electricity	€ 18.00 - € 43.00
extra person	€ 2.00 - € 3.00
dog	€ 3.00

Zennewijnen
Campingpark Zennewijnen

Hermoesestraat 13, NL- 4062 PP Zennewijnen (Gelderland) T: 0344 651 498.
E: info@campingzennewijnen.nl **alanrogers.com/NL5872**

Camping Park Zennewijnen is attractively located amongst apple and pear trees, which are a beautiful sight when the white and pink blossom is out. There are 150 pitches of which 46 are for touring. They are spacious and comfortable, all with 10A electricity, and the toilet facilities are clean and modern. Breakfast, snacks, evening meal and drinks are provided in the cosy bar/restaurant. There is plenty to do on site, with a swimming pool, a playground, a petting zoo and even a fishing pond. In high season there is an evening entertainment programme. Also in the area you can try canoeing on the Linge, follow bicycle and hiking routes and visit historic forts and castles. Wooden cabins and roulottes are available for rent and bed and breakfast is offered.

Facilities	Directions
The heated toilet block has showers and washbasins in private cubicles. Baby changing room. Bathroom for disabled visitors. Laundry facilities. Motorcaravan services. Shop selling fresh farm foods, bar, snack bar and takeaway (all 5/3-31/10). Outdoor swimming pool and paddling pool. Fishing. Playground. WiFi throughout (charged). Accommodation to rent. Off site: Bicycle hire 2 km. Riding 5 km. Walking and cycling trails. Shops, bars and restaurants in Tiel.	From A15 take exit 32 (Tiel West) and join N834 southeast. At second roundabout, turn right into Schaarsdijkweg and at next roundabout turn left onto Doctor JM den Uyllaan. Continue on this road and site is on the right. GPS: 51.85464, 5.40714

Open: 15 March - 31 October.

Charges guide

Per unit incl. 2 persons and electricity	€ 19.00 - € 22.50
extra person	€ 3.25
dog (max. 1)	€ 3.00

Campingpark Zennewijnen
Ton en Jeannette Coenraads
Hermoesestraat 13
4062 PP Zennewijnen
Tel: +31 (0) 344 65 14 98
E-mail: info@campingzennewijnen.nl

For latest campsite news, availability and prices visit
alanrogers.com

CAPITAL: GRONINGEN

Groningen is a traditional province with medieval churches, typical man-made mounds called 'terpen' or 'wierden', cosy country pubs, ancient mills and farms.

The Groningen terp landscape is one of the oldest man-made landscapes in the northwest of Europe. Some 600 years ago, Groningen was made up of vast swamps and salt marshes that lay boggy and deserted. In order to survive, inhabitants constructed terps, or artificial hills, to protect themselves from the rising water. These pre-date the first dykes, which were constructed in the Middle Ages. At the Wierdenland museum you can find out what it was like for the people who lived here in days gone by, and why Ezinge was also referred to as the Pompeii of the north.

Groningen City is the cultural centre of the north; with its rich seam of architecture, design, theatre and music it has become a flourishing centre for the arts. You can explore the city on foot, by bicycle, by pedal boat and even in a canoe! There are countless eye-catching buildings, and leading architects such as Starck, Koolhaas, and Hejduk have all left their mark here. The Lauwersmeer National Park is a must for watersports enthusiasts, and whether you are sailing, canoeing or surfing, its immense stretches of open water guarantee room to manoeuvre, even in high season. There are plenty of moorings, with four marinas, special jetties and several recreational islands to choose from.

Places of interest

Groningen City: comic strip heroes in the Stripmuseum, the 500-year-old Martini Tower and the famous Groningen Museum.

Bourtange: star-shaped fortified town and open-air museum, sympathetically restored to its original state. Within the ramparts are traditional shops and museums, and good restaurants in the picturesque market square.

Ter Apel: a famous monastery dating from 1465, located on the old trade route between Münster and the city of Groningen.

Attractions

The Seal Sanctuary, Pieterburen: sick and weak seals are taken in and nursed back to health. View the seals and take a look in the sanctuary's kitchen to see what they are fed.

The Fraeylemaborg, Slochteren: a beautifully preserved Groningen estate house.

The salt marshes: north of Westernieland, a reminder of how the Groningen countryside looked before the construction of dykes.

The Reitdiep Valley: reflects 2,500 years of habitation and man's struggle against the sea. Its ancient villages and meandering roads make an ideal route for the fit cyclist.

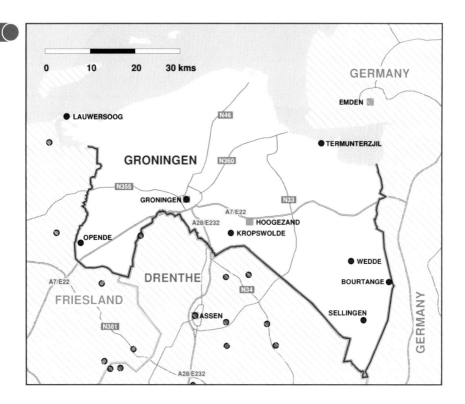

Bourtange
Camping 't Plathuis
Bourtangerkanaal Noord 1, NL-9545 VJ Bourtange (Groningen) T: 0599 354 383. E: info@plathuis.nl
alanrogers.com/NL6110

Camping 't Plathuis is beautifully located in the fortified village of Bourtange. This small town dates back to the times of the invasion of the Bishop of Münster in the 1600s. The site has 92 touring pitches, most on well established, grass fields with shade from the mature trees that surround the site. On the newest area at the back of the site there are 22 serviced pitches with 6-16A electricity, water and drainage, including 14 with cable TV. There are four hardstandings available for motorcaravans. There are plans to further extend the site. To the front of the site is a lake for swimming and fishing with a sandy beach.

Facilities

Single older style, but neat and adequate, heated toilet block with toilets, washbasins (open style and in cabins) and coin-operated, controllable, hot showers. Second prefabricated block in the new field. Family shower rooms. Baby room. Facilities for disabled visitors. Laundry facilities. Shopping service for basics. Bread to order. Bar. Snack bar. Lake for swimming and fishing. Canoe hire. Playground. WiFi (charged). Off site: Village of Bourtange.

Open: 1 April - 31 October.

Directions

From A7 take exit 47 for Winschoten and continue on N367 towards Vlagtwedde. In Vlagtwedde turn on N368 towards Bourtange. Site is on right 200 m. after entering village. GPS: 53.0093, 7.1844

Charges guide

Per unit incl. 2 persons	€ 17.00 - € 20.50
extra person	€ 4.00
child (3-10 yrs)	€ 2.50
dog	€ 2.00

For latest campsite news, availability and prices visit
alanrogers.com

Groningen
Camping Stadspark
Campinglaan 6, NL-9727 KH Groningen (Groningen) T: 0505 251 624. E: info@campingstadspark.nl
alanrogers.com/NL5770

The Stadspark is a large park to the southwest of the city, well signed and with easy access. The campsite is within a park with many trees and surrounded by water. It has 200 pitches with 150 for touring units, of which 75 have 6A electricity and 30 are fully serviced with electricity, water and drainage. Several hardstandings are available for large units and motorcaravans. The separate tent area is supervised directly by the manager. The grass areas are car free. Buses for the city leave from right outside and timetables and maps are provided at reception. Groningen is a lively city with lots to do.

Facilities

Two sanitary blocks provide hot showers, washbasins and toilets. One is new and the other has been refurbished to a good standard. Family shower and baby room. Motorcaravan services. Shop (15/3-15/10). Restaurant, café, bar and takeaway (1/4-15/9). Bicycle hire. Volleyball. Fishing. Canoeing. WiFi (free). Off site: Riding and golf 5 km. Boat launching 6 km.

Open: 15 March - 15 October.

Directions

From Assen on A28 turn left on the A7 towards Drachten. Follow signs for Stadspark and the campsite. GPS: 53.20090, 6.53570

Charges guide

Per unit incl. 2 persons and electricity	€ 21.00
extra person	€ 3.00
child (2-12 yrs)	€ 1.50

Kropswolde
Camping Meerwijck
Strandweg 2, NL-9606 PR Kropswolde (Groningen) T: 0598 323 659. E: info@meerwijck.nl
alanrogers.com/NL5775

This large lakeside site (23 hectares) has 500 pitches (200 for touring units) and is beautifully located on the beaches of the Zuidlaardermeer. The touring pitches are arranged on several separate fields away from the mobile homes and seasonal guests, either in circular bays or in long rows from paved access lanes. All touring pitches have electricity (6A), water, waste water and cable TV connections. This site is ideal for youngsters as there is direct access to the sandy beaches and there is an indoor heated swimming pool with a paddling pool. In high season an entertainment team provides games and excursions for youngsters and adults.

Facilities

Three modern and clean toilet blocks for touring units with hot showers (six minutes), washbasins (open style and in cabins), family bathrooms, baby rooms and facilities for disabled visitors. Laundry facilities. Small supermarket. Bar and snack bar. Indoor pool (15x20 m) with paddling pool. Playing field. Multisports court. Playgrounds. Animal farm. Tennis. Fishing. Bicycle hire. Marina. Activity team in high season. Lake with sandy beaches. WiFi throughout (charged). Off site: Restaurant at the beach. Riding 3 km.

Open: 30 March - 29 September.

Directions

On A7 to and from Groningen, take exit for Foxhol and continue south towards Kropswolde. Cross the canal and the railway and turn right at next roundabout towards the site. GPS: 53.14316, 6.68916

Charges guide

Per unit incl. 2 persons and electricity	€ 20.00 - € 27.00
extra person	€ 4.00
boat trailer	€ 2.50

Lauwersoog
Camping Lauwersoog
Strandweg 5, NL-9976 VS Lauwersoog (Groningen) T: 0519 349 133. E: info@lauwersoog.nl
alanrogers.com/NL6090

The focus at Camping Lauwersoog is very much on the sea and watersports. One can have sailing lessons or hire canoes and there is direct access to the beach from the site. There are 450 numbered pitches with 250 for tourers; 140 have water, drainage, electricity and cable connections. The pitches are on level, grassy fields (some beside the beach), partly separated by hedges and some with shade from trees (cars parked separately). A building in the marina houses a restaurant, bar, shop, laundry and an adventure playground. It also provides beautiful views over the Lauwersmeer. The site's restaurant specialises in seafood and even the entertainment programmes for all ages have a water theme.

Facilities

The two toilet blocks for touring units provide washbasins, preset showers and child size toilets. Facilities for disabled visitors. Laundry. Campers' kitchen. Motorcaravan service. Shop. Restaurant (all year), bar and snack bar including takeaway service (1/4-1/10). Play area with bouncy castle. Minigolf at the beach. Sailing school. Canoe hire. Surfing lessons (July/Aug). Riding. Bicycle and go-kart hire. Boules. WiFi. Entertainment programme (July/Aug).

Open: All year.

Directions

Follow N361 from Groningen north to Lauwersoog and then follow site signs. GPS: 53.40205, 6.21732

Charges guide

Per unit incl. 2 persons and 10A electricity	€ 20.00 - € 34.50
with full services	€ 22.50 - € 37.50
extra person (over 1 yr)	€ 4.75

Camping Cheques accepted.

FREE Alan Rogers Travel Card
Extra benefits and savings - see page 12

Opende

Camping 't Strandheem

Parkweg 2, NL-9865 VP Opende (Groningen) T: 0594 659 555. E: info@strandheem.nl

alanrogers.com/NL6120

Camping 't Strandheem has 330 quite large, numbered pitches (110 sq.m) some with hardstanding and suitable for motorcaravans. All with electricity (4/10A), there are 180 used for touring units, partly separated by low hedges but without much shade. Of these, 45 pitches have water points, drainage and cable TV connections. The Bruinewoud family will give you a warm welcome. The reception building houses an attractive bar, a full restaurant, a disco for teenagers and a shop. The site has a lot to offer, especially for youngsters with a full entertainment programme in high season with water games in the lake next to the site, a games area and an indoor pool.

Facilities	Directions
Two modern toilet buildings have washbasins, controllable showers, child size toilets and washbasins, a good baby room and fully equipped bathroom. Facilities for disabled campers. Launderette. Motorcaravan service. Shop. Bar and restaurant. Café and snack bar. Covered swimming pool (5x5 m) with separate paddling pool, slide and sun terrace. Playgrounds. Indoor play hall. Minigolf. Fishing. Bicycle hire. Boules. Lake with beach (€ 1 p/p per day). Recreation programme (July/Aug). Free WiFi in reception.	Follow A7 west from Groningen towards Heerenveen and take exit 31. Follow campsite signs from there. GPS: 53.15278, 6.19138

Open: 1 April - 1 October.

Charges guide

Per unit incl. 2 persons and electricity	€ 18.50 - € 27.50
with private sanitary facility	€ 28.00 - € 37.00

Sellingen

Camping De Papaver

Beetserweg 58A, NL-9551 VH Sellingen (Groningen) T: 0599 324 274. E: info@campingdepapaver.nl

alanrogers.com/NL6105

De Papaver is located in a large nature reserve near the village of Sellingen, north of the city of Emmen. It is an oasis of calm and tranquillity and is an ideal base for a cycling or walking holiday. There are 130 good sized touring pitches, most of which have 4/6A electrical connections. De Papaver is situated on a peninsula and is surrounded by a 50 hectare lake. There are several sandy beaches around the lake and these are good for swimming, canoeing and windsurfing. During school holidays a large number of activities are organised for children, including campfires, building rafts, tree climbing and canoeing.

Facilities	Directions
Two sanitary buildings with family shower rooms. Facilities for disabled campers. Shop with fresh bread daily. Restaurant and takeaway. Swimming pool with jet stream. Lake and sandy beach. Sauna and wellness centre (Turkish bath, solarium, relaxation room). Games room. Free hand-carts for moving luggage and go-karts. Canoes, pedaloes and cycles for hire. Activities and entertainment. New tents for rent. WiFi (charged).	Head towards Hoogeveen on A28. Then, take A37 and N34 to Emmen. Bypass Emmen (on eastern side) and drive to Ter Apel (N391). In Ter Apel, follow signs to Sellingen and follow the campsite signs. GPS: 52.939014, 7.093

Open: 1 April - 31 October.

Charges guide

Per unit incl. 2 persons and electricity	€ 16.50 - € 22.25
extra person (over 2 yrs)	€ 3.50

Sellingen

Campingpark De Barkhoorn

Beetserweg 6, NL-9551 VE Sellingen (Groningen) T: 0599 322510. E: info@barkhoorn.nl

alanrogers.com/NL6115

Camping De Barkhoorn is located in the Westerwolde, southeast of Groningen. The campsite is surrounded by vast forests and heathland interspersed with beautiful ponds. It offers camping in a tranquil setting on spacious, verdant pitches with shade to the back provided by tall trees. A car-free site, there are 152 touring pitches (13 are comfort pitches), all with 10A electricity, and hardstandings for motorcaravans outside the gate. This is a pleasant family campsite, ideal for families with children, and for those who enjoy walking and cycling. The German border is nearby.

Facilities	Directions
Four older style, but clean sanitary buildings including one without hot water have showers, open style washbasins and preset hot showers. Private facilities to rent. Facilities for disabled visitors. Launderette. Bar/restaurant and terrace (Fri-Sun). Snack bar also sells basics. Play areas. Recreation lake with beach. Sports field. Minigolf. Tennis. Bowling and other activities. Bicycle hire. Fishing. Canoeing. WiFi over site (charged). Cabins to rent.	Follow signs from Zwolle, Hoogeveen and Emmen for Ter Apel. Sellingen is on the main road between Ter Apel and Winschoten, 2 km. from the centre of Sellingen. Follow site signs from the village. GPS: 52.946406, 7.131192

Open: 30 March - 27 October.

Charges guide

Per unit incl. 2 persons and electricity	€ 15.00 - € 25.50

For latest campsite news, availability and prices visit
alanrogers.com

Termunterzijl
Camping Zeestrand Eems-Dollard

Schepperbuurt 4A, NL-9948 PP Termunterzijl (Groningen) T: 059 660 1443.
E: info@campingzeestrand.nl **alanrogers.com/NL6101**

Camping Zeestrand is a well kept site in the far northeast of Holland on the Eems estuary, which forms the border with Germany, close to a sandy beach. The site has 120 average size pitches with 65 for touring, electricity (6/10A) available. Most pitches are unmarked and laid out on an open, level field but a few have hard standing. The campsite is surrounded by trees giving most pitches good shade. The nearby town of Delfzijl lies next to the World Heritage Wadden Sea and is an ideal spot for sailing and boating. It also has a small beach and many shops, bars and other attractions.

Facilities

Three toilet blocks with all necessary facilities including those for babies. Washing machine and dryer. Snack bar with covered terrace and TV. Bread to order. Play areas. Multisport area. Games room. Activities for adults and children mid July to mid Aug. WiFi (free in snack bar, charged on pitches). Off site: Beaches, canoeing, fishing. Many walking and cycling routes. Delfzijl, some shops 12.5 km, boat trips to German island of Borkum. Groningen 40 km.

Open: 28 March - 2 November.

Directions

Leave the E22 motorway about 22 km. east of Groningen. Take N362 northeast for about 14 km. and then follow local roads towards Termunterzijl to the campsite in just under 8 km.
GPS: 53.30169, 7.0306

Charges guide

Per unit incl. 2 persons and electricity	€ 16.10
extra person	€ 4.30
child (2-16 yrs)	€ 3.40

Wedde
Camping Wedderbergen

Molenweg 2, NL-9698 XV Wedde (Groningen) T: 0597 561 673. E: info@wedderbergen.nl
alanrogers.com/NL6100

Camping Wedderbergen is a well established, modern site. Its focus is being changed from seasonal to touring pitches. There are now 233 touring pitches, all with 10A electricity, water, waste water and cable. A separate area provides hardstandings for larger units and motorcaravans. This is supported by a toilet block in front of the touring fields. There are some views over the Westerwoldsche river and shade in some areas from mature trees. Pitches at the front of the site have a jetty for small boats. To the back of the site is a large expanse of water with a sandy beach. The only disadvantage is a public road that runs through the site (some road noise).

Facilities

Toilet block for touring units with toilets, washbasins in cabins and preset hot showers (hot water with key). Family shower rooms. Baby room. Facilities for disabled campers. Laundry. Motorcaravan services. Well stocked shop. Bar, canteen and snack bar. Recreation lake with sandy beach. Playing field. Bicycle hire. Fishing. Tennis. Playgrounds. Bouncy cushion. WiFi (charged). Off site: Sub-tropical pool.

Open: April - October.

Directions

On A7 from either direction take exit 47 for Winschoten and continue towards Vlagtwedde. Passing through Wedde, follow the site signs.
GPS: 53.08611, 7.08291

Charges guide

Per unit incl. 4 persons	€ 19.50 - € 29.50
extra person	€ 4.00 - € 5.00
dog	€ 4.00

FREE Alan Rogers Travel Card
Extra benefits and savings - see page 12

CAPITAL: MAASTRICHT

Limburg has a range of attractive landscapes: the green hills in the south, a large area of waterland at its heart, the scenic countryside of Peel and Maas, and the marshes and dunes in the north.

Limburg's multi-faceted landscape – woodland, peat moorland, sand dunes and marl plateaux – offers endless opportunites for the active holidaymaker. The extensive cycle network, ferries across the River Maas and delightful mountain bike trails are all waiting to be enjoyed. The numerous marked trails passing by nature reserves and areas of outstanding natural beauty are a gift for hikers and cyclists alike who can pause to admire some of the most beautiful areas of Limburg.

Limburg offers a taste of the good life – its shopping, fine dining, and wealth of tourist attractions, coupled with the locals' warm hospitality will make your visit an experience to remember. Maastricht is believed to be the oldest city in the Netherlands. It has grown from a Roman settlement on the banks of the Meuse to a thriving city with a large student population and a reputation for cordiality – the number of beautiful cafés that line its streets may have something to do with that. With its wealth of romantic streets, picturesque squares and historical architecture, there are plenty of opportunities for sightseeing.

Places of interest

Maastricht: Bonnefanten Museum, classic paintings in a spectacular building by Aldo Rossi; Thiessen Wijnkoopers is the oldest wine house in the country.

Baarlo: typical village along the Maas with four castles, and the former home of the CoBrA artist, Tajiri.

Thorn: known as the white town, because many buildings are white limed, it has intimate courtyards, streets cobbled with Maas stone, mosaic floors and a beautiful abbey church.

Valkenburg: tourist town in the middle of the hills with various attractions including marl caves.

Attractions

Old mill: the Friedesse mill in Neer is mentioned in a document dating from 1343. Open Sundays from May to September.

Montfort Castle: dating from 1260 and for centuries one of the largest castles in the Netherlands, impressive ruins with visitors' centre in a restored tower.

Wijlre: the oldest brewery in the Netherlands in a beautiful location. Discover the ancient history of Brand beer, one of Limburg's treasures.

Stef's house, Brunssum: recreates life in a mining village using film footage and photographs, historical artifacts and props from a television series.

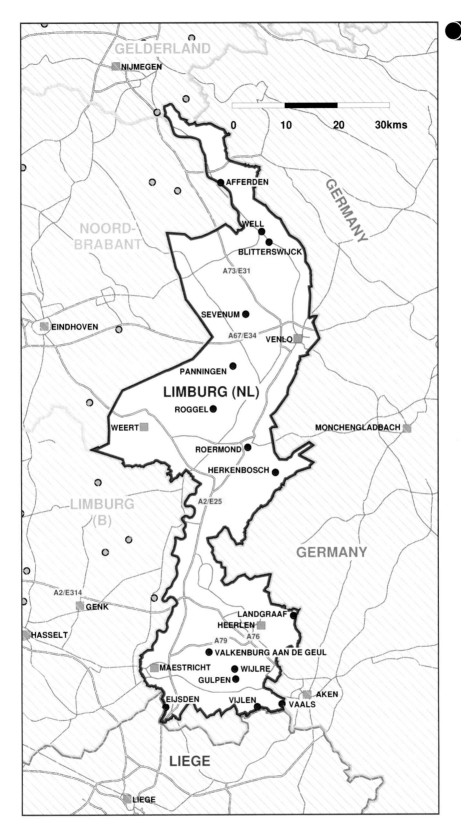

FREE Alan Rogers Travel Card
Extra benefits and savings - see page 12

Afferden

Camping Roland

Rimpelt 33, NL-5851 EK Afferden (Limburg) T: 0485 531 431. E: info@campingroland.nl

alanrogers.com/NL5892

Family run Camping Roland is a quiet site in an attractive region between the River Maas and the German border. The surroundings are made up of dunes, woods, moorland and lakes. Pitches here are divided into two groups, each with its own charm. All 90 spacious, grassy pitches have 6A electricity, water, drainage and cable TV connections. Swimming, sailing, fishing, mountain biking and hiking are amongst the activities on offer here. The swimming pool features a 40 m. water slide and a large sun terrace. This region has many signed cycle routes both around the site and on the far side of The Maas, reached by ferry.

Facilities

Two well maintained, attractive sanitary blocks with showers (token). Laundry with washing machines and dryers. No facilities for disabled visitors. Shop (1/4-12/9). Cafeteria, restaurant and bar with billiards and large screen TV (15/3-20/9). Swimming pool with water slide and terrace. Fishing pond. Large playground. Sports field. Entertainment and activity programme. Tennis. WiFi over site (charged). Off site: Two golf courses at Bleijenbeek (discounted green fees can be arranged with the site).

Open: All year.

Directions

From A73 Nijmegen-Venlo motorway, take exit 2 (Rijkevoort) and follow A77. Then, join N271 towards Bergen. After a further 5 km. (at Afferden) site is signed to left. Continue for 1.5 km. and site is on left just past windmill. GPS: 51.635117, 6.034203

Charges guide

Per unit incl. 2 persons and electricity	€ 19.00 - € 27.00
extra person (over 3 yrs)	€ 4.00

Blitterswijck

Camping 't Veerhuys

Veerweg 7, NL-5863 AR Blitterswijck (Limburg) T: 0478 531 283. E: info@campingveerhuys.nl

alanrogers.com/NL6532

Camping 't Veerhuys is a quiet site extending along the Maas river, opposite the Maasduinen National Park (reached on foot and cycle ferry) in northern Limburg. The 80 touring pitches are grassy and equipped with 6/10A electricity and water. All have panoramic views over the Maas. The site features a cosy bar and a well known restaurant, Tanty Jet (discount for campers) with a terrace with views over the river, where you can enjoy a quiet drink and a meal. The MaasHopper, a boat taking passengers and bicycles, calls in three times a week, stopping at several locations from where you can return on foot or by bike, if you wish. There are various watersports available including water skiing (lessons available), banana rides, wake boarding, swimming and fishing. A recreational park and indoor pool are 500 m.

Facilities

One basic, but clean and heated, sanitary block is behind the restaurant. It has all necessary facilities including those for children and disabled visitors. Showers are charged (SEP key) and washbasins are open style. Laundry with washing machine and dryer. Traditional bar and restaurant with terrace and snacks. Paddling pool. Play areas. Trampoline. Bicycle hire. WiFi over site (charged). No charcoal barbecues. Off site: Supermarket 500 m.

Open: 1 April - 31 October.

Directions

Site is 18 km. northwest of Venlo. From A73 take exit 9 towards Wanssum. Turn right at the roundabout and then left in Wanssum. Follow signs to Blitterswijck. The site is signed from there. GPS: 51.5309, 6.11805

Charges guide

Per unit incl. 2 persons and electricty	€ 21.95 - € 22.45
extra person	€ 3.45

Eijsden

Camping De Oosterdriessen

Oostweg 1a, NL-6245 LC Oost-Maarland (Limburg) T: 0434 093 215. E: info@oosterdriessen.nl

alanrogers.com/NL6595

This friendly site can be found in the southern Netherlands, around 5 km. south of the city of Maastricht, and 3 km. from the village of Eijsden. The site enjoys an attractive lakeside setting on the Pieterplas, with its own private beach and with opportunities for watersports. The 230 touring pitches here are grassy and most have 6A electricity. A special area is reserved for hikers and cyclists, and a reduced charge applied (maximum two nights stay). There is also a broad, grassy area for sport and leisure. Given its lakeside situation, this is a popular site with anglers (small fee charged). Credit cards are not accepted.

Facilities

Single traditional style toilet block with preset showers. Facilities for disabled visitors. Baby room. Laundry. Small shop, fresh bread to order. Bar with TV. Café with terrace. Adventure play area. Bicycle hire. Fishing. Sports field. Direct lake access. Activity and entertainment programme (high season). Four log cabins for rent. WiFi (free).

Open: 27 April - 24 September.

Directions

From the north (Maastricht) take southbound A2 and proceed to Oost Maarland. From here, follow signs to lake and site. GPS: 50.799689, 5.70636

Charges guide

Per unit incl. 2 persons and electricity	€ 21.20 - € 23.20
extra person	€ 5.00

For latest campsite news, availability and prices visit
alanrogers.com

Gulpen
Terrassencamping Gulperberg Panorama
Berghem 1, NL-6271 NP Gulpen (Limburg) T: 0434 502 330. E: info@gulperberg.nl
alanrogers.com/NL6530

Gulperberg Panorama is just three kilometres from the attractive village of Gulpen, midway between the interesting cities of Maastricht and Aachen. The 322 touring pitches are large and flat on terraces overlooking the village on one side and open countryside on the other. Many have full services. English is spoken in reception, although all written information is in Dutch (ask if you require a translation). Gulperberg Panorama is a haven for children. During the high season there is a weekly entertainment programme to keep them occupied. The site is not suitable for visitors with disabilities. Dogs are restricted to one section of the campsite.

Facilities	Directions
Four sanitary blocks have good facilities. Family shower room and baby room. Laundry. Shop (27/4-31/8). Bar. Takeaway. New restaurant with terrace. Swimming pool (29/4-15/9). Three play areas. Bouncy cushion. TV and games room. Extensive entertainment programme for children plus family entertainment. WiFi over site (charged). Off site: Golf and bicycle hire 3 km. Fishing 4 km. Riding 5 km. Further afield are caves, museums and Maastricht with its wide range of shops. Beach 15 km.	Gulpen is east of Maastricht. Take N278 Maastricht-Aachen. Site is signed just as you enter Gulpen at the traffic lights. Turn right and follow camping signs for 3 km. GPS: 50.80673, 5.89413

Open: Easter - 31 October.

Charges guide

Per unit incl. 2 persons and electricity	€ 22.00 - € 32.00
extra person (over 2 yrs)	€ 3.00 - € 4.00

Camping Cheques accepted.

Gulpen
Camping Osebos
Reymerstokker dorpsstraat 1, NL-6271 PP Gulpen (Limburg) T: 0434 501 611. E: info@osebos.nl
alanrogers.com/NL6590

Family run, Camping Osebos is a quiet, attractive and well kept terraced site with a southerly aspect in the Dutch mountains. There are 215 touring pitches, all with electricity, 90 of which have fresh water, waste water and TV connections. They are level, grassed and set in rows on terraces or in groups, on the lower part of the site. From the pitches there are extensive views of the surrounding countryside with its rolling, partially tree-clad hills. There is walking and cycling directly from the site and many pretty villages to visit in this attractive, less well known, southern part of Holland close to Belgium and Germany.

Facilities	Directions
Three heated sanitary blocks contain free showers, washbasins (open and in cabins), family showers and a new, separate children's/baby facility. Laundry facilities, washing machine, dryer plus ironing. Motorcaravan services. Shop, bar/restaurant, takeaway (22/4-31/10). Outdoor swimming pool, paddling pool. Play areas. Children's entertainment in summer. Sports pitch. Bicycle hire. Max. 2 dogs. Off site: Fishing 2 km. Golf 7 km.	Site is between Maastricht and Aachen, just south of N278. Leave E25/A2 at exit 54 (Europaplein) and head east towards Aachen on N278. In 3.5 km. after Margraten, on the descent to Gulpen, turn south towards Beutenaken. After 400 m. at bottom of hill, site is to the right. GPS: 50.80669, 5.87078

Open: 1 April - 28 October.

Charges guide

Per unit incl. 2 persons and electricity	€ 15.00 - € 25.00

Herkenbosch
Oostappen Vakantiepark Elfenmeer
Meinweg 1, NL-6075 NA Herkenbosch (Limburg) T: 0475 531 689. E: info@vakantieparkelfenmeer.nl
alanrogers.com/NL5940

Situated in the Meinweg National Park, this large site with facilities on a holiday camp scale caters well for families with children of all ages. Of the 800 grassed pitches (averaging 90 sq.m) 400 are for touring units. They are level, separated into enclosures of various sizes by hedges and most have 4A electricity and fresh water. There is ample tree shade over the site, grassed places to sunbathe and a wealth of activities to keep children busy. Beside reception, the main building houses a restaurant/bar with terrace on the first floor, a supermarket and other eating and drinking establishments.

Facilities	Directions
Four toilet blocks are clean and well maintained, with individual washbasins with cold water, baby room and toilets for disabled campers. Supermarket. Restaurant/bar (30/4-30/10). Takeaway (July/Aug). Swimming pools (May-Oct). Organised sports (July/Aug. and school holidays). Fishing lake. Large playground. Mini zoo. Minigolf. Bowling alley. Bicycle hire. WiFi (charged).	From Roermond take Wassenberg road to southeast (to find this exit you can also follow white signs to Roerstreek industrial estate); pass turning on right to Herkenbosch after 6 km. and turn left to site 1 km. further on. GPS: 51.162121, 6.091442

Open: 2 April - 1 November.

Charges guide

Per unit incl. 2 persons and electricity	€ 14.00 - € 28.00

FREE Alan Rogers Travel Card
Extra benefits and savings - see page 12

Landgraaf
Camping De Watertoren

Kerkveldweg 1, NL-6374 LE Landgraaf (Limburg) T: 0455 321 747. E: info@campingdewatertoren.nl
alanrogers.com/NL6575

De Watertoren is situated near the village of Landgraaf in the rolling hills of South Limburg. Surrounded by the trees and shrubs of the adjacent forest, the site focuses on families with children under 12 years old, nature lovers and those who are seeking peace and quiet. There are 120 touring pitches on grass with varying degrees of shade, spread out over several small fields. The German village of Ubach Palenberg is very close and a delightful cycle track crosses the border. The interesting cities of Aachen (20 minutes), Maastricht and Valkenburg (both less than half an hour) are easily reached. Several annual music festivals are held nearby. Tourist information and advice are available at reception.

Facilities

Comfortable, heated toilet block providing all facilities, accessed by key card (€ 30 deposit). Family shower room. Motorcaravan services. Bar and snack bar (weekends only in low season). Small shop. Daily fresh bread and the famous Limburgse vlaai in high season and during holidays. Two swimming pools (15/5-1/9). Play area. Recreation team (high season). Bicycle hire. Sports field. Boules. Free WiFi over part of site.

Open: All year.

Directions

From A2 motorway exit 47 follow signs for Brunssum. From Brunssum follow signs to Landgraaf passing golf course. Continue to Europaweg Noord, later Europaweg Zuid. Follow the small brown campsite signs. GPS: 50.9104, 6.07327

Charges guide

Per unit incl. 2 persons and electricity	€ 18.00 - € 25.00
extra person (over 2 yrs)	€ 3.50

Panningen
Camping & Speelparadijs Beringerzand

Heide 5, NL-5981 NX Panningen (Limburg) T: 0773 072 095. E: info@beringerzand.nl
alanrogers.com/NL6525

The history of this friendly site dates back more than 100 years to when it was established as a holiday resort for members of the Lazarist religious congregation. The park and its historic building (now the Patershof restaurant) have, for the last 40 years, been developed as a holiday paradise for young families. Beringerzand is set amongst the lovely villages and small lakes of the wooded area between the De Peel Natural Park and the Muse river. The 21-hectare site offers 375 spacious touring pitches, all with electricity (10A), TV, water and waste water, arranged around the edges of green fields. There are currently also 140 privately owned chalets. The fields have been very well designed and include various activity areas appropriate to different age groups.

Facilities

Four heated toilet blocks include bathrooms for children and fully equipped launderette. Well stocked supermarket, bar, restaurant and takeaway. Games and TV rooms. Indoor and outdoor swimming pools (no lifeguard). Tennis. Minigolf. Pétanque. Adventure play areas. Bicycle hire. Small BMX track. Outdoor chess. Riding. Fishing. Kids' club and evening entertainment. WiFi over site (charged).

Open: 27 March - 1 November.

Directions

From A67 between Eindhoven and Venlo take exit 38 (direction Helden). At lights turn right to Koningslust and after 2 km. turn right again to site following camping signs. GPS: 51.34897, 5.96101

Charges guide

Per unit incl. 2 persons and electricity (plus meter)	€ 33.75

No credit cards.

Roermond
Resort Marina Oolderhuuske

Oolderhuuske 1, NL-6041 TR Roermond (Limburg) T: 0475 588 686. E: info@oolderhuuske.nl
alanrogers.com/NL6515

When staying on this interesting site, which is part of a resort complex, you know you are on holiday. The site is situated at the end of a peninsula, on a low lying spit of land and overlooks wild stretches of open water and the River Maas. There are 220 pitches, 80 of which are for touring. All have electricity (6-16A) water and drainage, are level, grassed and many are waterside – no pitch lies more than 60 m. from the water. There are numerous cycling routes from the site, either directly overland or via the passenger/cycle ferry that crosses the Maas.

Facilities

One floating block and two prefabricated units provide toilets, free showers, washbasins and outside sinks. Motorcaravan services. Shop and bar (weekends and high season), restaurant with terrace, snacks and takeaway. Small indoor swimming pool, gym, sauna, steam bath, solarium. Sports fields. Tennis. Playgrounds. Bicycle hire. Boat launching. High season entertainment. Barrier deposit € 50. WiFi throughout (charged).

Open: 1 April - 31 October.

Directions

From Maastricht on A2 (Maastricht-Eindhoven) take Roermond exit. In Roermond (centrum) follow signs for Eindhoven, just after Muse bridge (Maasbrug) right to Hatenboer/de Weerd. Follow brown signs to Marina Oolderhuuske. GPS: 51.19195, 5.94942

Charges guide

Per unit incl. up to 4 persons and electricity	€ 24.00 - € 36.00

For latest campsite news, availability and prices visit
alanrogers.com

Roggel
Recreatiepark De Leistert

Heldensedijk 5, NL-6088 NT Roggel (Limburg) T: 0475 493 030. E: info@leistert.nl

alanrogers.com/NL6550

This large, long established site in the wooded Limburg province of south Holland has 1,200 pitches, of which 750 are touring pitches. With its varied amenities, the site would be a good choice for families with small children and teenagers. Most of the pitches are not separated, but are arranged in hedged groups with tall, mature trees. They are serviced with electricity (4-10A), cable TV connections, water and drainage. A recreation programme is organised for all ages in high season.

Facilities

Five toilet blocks are fully equipped, with good facilities for children. Covered plaza with supermarket, bar, restaurant, snack bar, games and TV room and disco, indoor pool, sauna, gym and massage. Outdoor pool (both pools with lifeguard). Minigolf. Tennis. Adventure playground. Rowing, fishing and sandy beach. Bicycle hire. Mini zoo. Gas refill at supermarket. Activity programme (high season). WiFi.

Open: 1 April - 1 November.

Directions

From Eindhoven (A2) take A67 (Venlo) and exit for Asten Meijel. At Roggel roundabout turn left on N562 (Helden) to site. From Nijmegen take A73 (Venlo), then N273 (Maastricht). In Neer turn right towards Roggel and on to site. GPS: 51.274105, 5.931971

Charges guide

Per unit incl. 2 persons	
incl. electricity	€ 18.00 - € 42.00

Sevenum
De Schatberg

Midden Peelweg 5, NL-5975 MZ Sevenum (Limburg) T: 0774 677 777. E: info@schatberg.nl

alanrogers.com/NL6510

In a woodland setting of 96 hectares, this friendly, family run campsite is more reminiscent of a holiday village, with a superb range of activities that make it an ideal venue for families. Look out for the deer! A large site with 1,100 pitches and many mobile homes and seasonal or weekend visitors, there are 550 touring pitches. All have electricity (6/10/16A Europlug), cable, water and drainage and average 100-150 sq.m. in size. They are on rough grass terrain, mostly with shade, but not separated. Seventy two pitches have private sanitary facilities, of which 32 also have dishwashing, fridge and gas ring, and two have a sauna and jacuzzi. Road noise can be heard in parts of this large campsite. The site is well situated for visits to Germany and Belgium, and is easily accessible from the port of Zeebrugge. The surrounding countryside offers the opportunity to enjoy nature, either by cycling or walking. For those who prefer to stay on site, the location is excellent with several lakes for fishing, windsurfing and swimming, plus an extensive range of activities and a heated outdoor swimming pool. A feature at De Schatberg is the attractive restaurant/bar area and the reception and indoor pool, manned by friendly staff.

Facilities

Five modern, fully equipped toilet blocks, plus three small wooden toilet units to save night-time walks. Family shower rooms, baby baths and en-suite units for disabled visitors. Washing machines and dryers. Motorcaravan services. Supermarket. Restaurant, bar and takeaway. Pizzeria. Pancake restaurant. Indoor pool. Outdoor pool (1/5-31/8). Trampoline. Play areas. Fishing. Watersports. Bicycle hire. Games room. Bowling. Indoor playground. Entertainment (w/ends and July/Aug). Water-ski track. No charcoal barbecues. WiFi over site (free).

Open: All year.

Directions

Site is 15 km. west-northwest of Venlo. Leave the A67 Eindhoven-Venlo motorway at Helden, exit 38. Travel north on the 277 for 500 m. and site is signed at new roundabout. GPS: 51.382964, 5.976147

Charges guide

Per unit incl. 2 persons and electricity	€ 19.60 - € 48.20
extra person	€ 4.65
Camping Cheques accepted.	

FREE Alan Rogers Travel Card
Extra benefits and savings - see page 12

Vaals

Camping Rozenhof

Camerig 12, NL-6294 NB Vijlen-Vaals (Limburg) T: 0434 551 611. E: info@campingrozenhof.nl

alanrogers.com/NL6540

Camping Rozenhof is a friendly, family run site and its hillside location offers views over a valley that has won awards for its natural beauty. This partially wooded, hilly region is popular with countryside lovers, ramblers and cyclists. Rozenhof has 68 pitches arranged on a series of small terraced, hedged meadows. There are 61 for touring units, level and mainly on grass and all with electricity (10A). A number of mature trees afford some shade. A rustic restaurant, which can become overstretched in high season, is to the left of the wide entrance. There is a large terrace and, as the site's name suggests, roses and plants are much in evidence. Behind the restaurant is a small swimming pool, and a large sandy-based playground provides ample provision for younger children when they are not out and about enjoying the countryside. In reception a range of tourist information brochures is available, including a detailed map of the immediate area showing footpaths. There is a well stocked shop including books. Well worth a day's outing are the nearby cities of Maastricht and Aachen.

Facilities

To the rear of reception, the heated modern sanitary unit houses all the usual facilities including controllable showers (tokens), washbasins (open and in cabins). Facilities for disabled visitors. Baby room and family shower room. Washing machines and dryers. Shop. Fresh bread to order. Refurbished restaurant/bar and takeaway. Gas supplies. Playground, play room and pets' corner for children. Bicycle hire. Free WiFi over part of site. Off site: Fishing 5 km. Riding 7 km. Golf 9 km.

Open: All year.

Directions

Leave A76/E314 at Knooppunt Bocholtz (not Bocholtz town) and follow N281 southwest towards Vaals for 3 km. to T-junction with N278. Turn left, then first right (Mamelisserweg) to Vijlen. In Vijlen second road to right (Vijlen Berg) and straight on for 4 km. to T-junction at far side of forest. Turn right and continue for 300 m. to site on right. GPS: 50.77021, 5.92925

Charges guide

Per unit incl. 2 persons and electricity	€ 16.00 - € 25.00
extra person (over 3 yrs)	€ 3.00
dog	€ 1.50

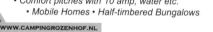

Valkenburg

Camping Vinkenhof

Engwegen 2A, NL-6305 PM Schin Op Geul (Limburg) T: 0434 591 389. E: info@campingvinkenhof.nl

alanrogers.com/NL6585

Camping Vinkenhof is a semi-rural site located at the edge of Schin Op Geul village in the attractive hilly countryside of southern Limburg. The 120 touring pitches are numbered but not delineated. Pitches are of a good size and 115 have minimum 6A electricity. There is a choice of sunny or shady pitches. A number of comfort pitches are also available. These are larger and have 10A electricity, water and drainage. Leisure facilities include a heated swimming pool and a sports field. The region of which Camping Vinkenhof forms a part is delightful with a great wealth of walking and cycling opportunities close at hand.

Facilities

Two toilet blocks, one in a new prefabricated unit with all facilities. Laundry facilities. Motorcaravan services. Busy bar/restaurant with pleasant terrace (1/4-1/10, also open to non-residents). Heated outdoor swimming pool (1/5-15/9). Paddling pool. Play area. Sports field. Entertainment and activity programme. WiFi over site (charged). Six mobile homes/chalets for rent. Off site: Walking and cycle tracks. Riding 200 m. Valkenburg 3 km. Fishing and bicycle hire 3 km. Golf 7 km. Skiing 10 km. Gerendal nature reserve.

Open: 7 March - 31 December.

Directions

Head east from Maastricht on A79 and leave at exit 4. Follow signs to Valkenburg on N29 and then take the eastbound N595 to Oud Valkenburg and Schin op Geul. From here follow signs to the site. GPS: 50.849957, 5.873107

Charges guide

Per unit incl. 2 persons and electricity	€ 16.75 - € 28.50
extra person	€ 3.50
child (2-6 yrs)	€ 2.50

For latest campsite news, availability and prices visit
alanrogers.com

Valkenburg aan de Geul
Camping Oriental

Rijksweg 6, NL-6325 PE Valkenburg aan de Geul (Limburg) T: 0436 040 075. E: info@campingoriental.nl
alanrogers.com/NL6513

Camping Oriental is an excellent family site located between Valkenburg and Maastricht. There is a mixture of 285 sunny and shaded touring pitches, all with 10A electricity and some with water, drainage and TV connections. There is also a selection of mobile homes for rent (all with TV). On-site amenities include a convivial bar, a snack bar and a well stocked shop (with fresh bread daily). There is a heated swimming pool with retractable roof, as well as a children's paddling pool. A large sports field is ideal for football, volleyball and basketball. Valkenburg has a colourful history characterised by siege and conquest. The ancient castle ruins (destroyed in 1672) can be found close to the town centre.

Facilities

Four sanitary blocks include showers and washbasins, open and in cubicles. A new block is planned. Facilities for disabled visitors. Baby room. Launderette. Dog shower. Shop. Bar. Snack bar. Heated and covered swimming pool. Paddling pool. Play areas. Large sports field. Zip wire. Boules. Mobile homes for rent. WiFi over part of site (charged). Off site: Shopping and restaurants in Valkenburg. Cycling and walking. Bicycle hire 5 km.

Open: 17 April - 1 October.

Directions

Approaching from Maastricht, take A79 motorway eastbound and take the Valkenburg exit. The site is on Rijksweg, south of the town centre, and is well signed. GPS: 50.86005, 5.77258

Charges guide

Per unit incl. 2 persons and electricity	€ 21.00 - € 27.00
extra person (over 2 yrs)	€ 3.50

No credit cards.

Vijlen
Camping Cottesserhoeve

Cottessen 6, NL-6294 NE Vijlen (Limburg) T: 0434 551 352. E: info@cottesserhoeve.nl
alanrogers.com/NL6535

The hamlet of Cottessen can be found at the end of a pretty country lane. This modern, comfortable site is surrounded by half-timbered houses, streams and forests. The heart of the site is the 17th-century farm, preserved in its original state. The atmosphere at this family site is friendly and welcoming. There are 180 good sized touring pitches, set against the hills of the Geul valley, all with electricity (6/10A Europlug) water and waste water. A number of apartments are available for rent throughout the year. Leisure amenities include a large swimming pool and separate paddling pool, and a large sports field.

Facilities

Heated toilet block with some washbasins in cabins. Baby room. Washing machine. Motorcaravan services. Supermarket. Café. Snack bar. Takeaway. Heated swimming and paddling pools (1/5-15/9). Volleyball. Football. Basketball. Play area. The recreation team regularly organises sporting activities, hiking tours and competitions. WiFi (charged).

Open: 22 March - 1 October.

Directions

From A76, take N281 exit at Bochholz. At Nijswiller take N278 towards Vaals and then head for Vijlen, and, in Vijlen, follow signs to Epen and the site. GPS: 50.759454, 5.940669

Charges guide

Per unit incl. 2 persons and electricity	€ 22.00
extra person	€ 2.35
dog	€ 3.75

Well
Vakantiepark Leukermeer

De Kamp 5, NL-5855 EG Well (Limburg) T: 0478 502 444. E: vakantie@leukermeer.nl
alanrogers.com/NL6518

Leukermeer is a pleasant holiday park in the green surroundings of the Maasduinen, with its own lakeside beaches. All 264 pitches have 10A electricity and TV connections, 225 also have fresh and waste water connections. The pitches are grassy, level and fairly open, and are arranged in groups of six or eight in hedge- and tree-lined enclosures. The site offers a wealth of water- and land-based sports facilities, as well as entertainment programmes and play areas for children. Consequently, it is a good site for families with children who are looking for an active holiday.

Facilities

Heated toilet blocks. Free hot showers, baby room, children's and family showers. Facilities for disabled visitors. Washing machine. Supermarket. Restaurant with terrace overlooking the marina, café and snack bar. Indoor and outdoor swimming pools and paddling pool (open to public). Marina. Bicycle and scooter rentals. Minigolf. Volleyball. Basketball. Activities and entertainment. Off site: Nature parks. Villages of Well and Arcen with its thermal baths and castle gardens. Cycle routes.

Open: 30 March - 29 October.

Directions

Site is 20 km. northwest of Venlo. From Nijmegen, take A73 and A77 towards Cologne. Take last exit before German border towards Nieuw Bergen (N271). Pass Nieuw Bergen and after 4.5 km. take exit to Leukermeer and follow signs to site. GPS: 51.56733, 6.06028

Charges guide

Per unit incl. 2 persons and electricity	€ 21.00 - € 42.00

Camping Cheques accepted.

FREE Alan Rogers Travel Card
Extra benefits and savings - see page 12

Limburg

Wijlre
Recreatieterrein De Gronselenput

Haasstad 3, NL-6321 PK Wijlre (Limburg) T: 0434 591 645. E: gronselenput@paasheuvelgroep.nl
alanrogers.com/NL6580

Camping Gronselenput is a small, quiet, countryside site located at the end of a narrow, tree-lined lane. It is one of five sites run by the Paasheuvel Group in Holland. Run by volunteers, it has 60 grassy level pitches, (55 for tourers, 50 with 10A electricity). With a peaceful location between a wooded hill and the River Geul (fishing allowed with permit), it is popular with visitors with younger children and those seeking a quiet site. Cars are parked separately from the camping area, thus ensuring vehicle-free space. The site is set out in a series of small hedged meadows with pitches tending to be located around the edges. Three gravel pitches are reserved for motorcaravans.

Facilities

In the sanitary block hot water for showers is free. Entry to the toilets is directly from outside. Two baby areas. Washing machines and spin dryer. Gas supplies. Shop (excellent English spoken). Bar selling pizzas with a partly covered terrace facing one of the playgrounds. Large room used for organised children's activities (July/Aug and public holidays). WiFi over site (charged). Off site: Fishing 1 km. Bicycle hire 5 km. Riding 15 km. Golf 25 km.

Open: 2 April - 1 November.

Directions

Site is near Wijlre, 10 km. northwest of Aachen. Leave A4/E314/A76 at Knooppunt Bocholtz 2 km. northwest of German border (not Bocholtz town). Follow N281 southwest for 5 km. and at junction turn right (northwest) to Wittem on N278. In Wittem, at lights turn right on N595 to Wijlre. Just after entering Wijlre site is signed to left.
GPS: 50.842167, 5.877483

Charges guide

Per unit incl. 2 persons and electricity	€ 17.00 - € 24.90
extra person	€ 2.70
dog	€ 2.50

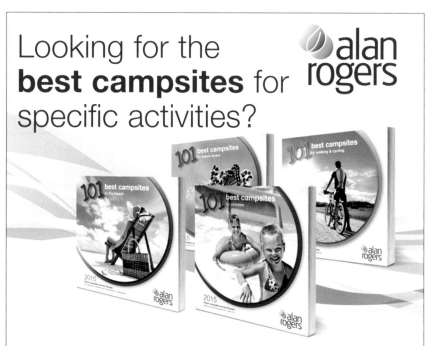

Looking for the **best campsites** for specific activities?

101 great campsites, ideal for your specific hobby, pastime or passion
Also available on iPad **alanrogers.com/digital**

For latest campsite news, availability and prices visit
alanrogers.com

CAPITAL: 'S-HERTOGENBOSCH (DEN BOSCH)

Over the years, Noord-Brabant has faced some difficult times, both economically and socially. It was here that Van Gogh painted 'De Aardappeleters', depicting a poor farming family eating their daily meal of potatoes. In recent decades, however, its fortunes have improved.

Now Noord-Brabant is the foremost industrial province of the Netherlands and a much admired economic protagonist. It has a wealth of impressive cultural sites such as the fortified towns of Grave, Megen and Ravenstein, which retain the atmosphere of ages past with their small squares, stately mansions and remains of fortifications.

The city of 's-Hertogenbosch, or Den Bosch as everyone calls it, is located in the delta of the Dommel and Aa, and owes its name and origins to the glory of Duke Henry I, who gave the settlement city rights in 1185. The impregnable ramparts, bastions and rondeaux are still intact, a testament to conflicts past. Nowadays the city is a bustling, friendly place where you can sample the sweet 'Bossche Bollen', have a dinner in a medieval hall or enjoy a night out on the town. As home to the electrical manufacturers Philips, Eindhoven and lighting are synonymous! Engineers, designers and artists collaborated on the latest lighting technology to give the old city a radiant new look.

Places of interest

Biesbosch: this national park is a green maze of rivers and islands interspersed with a network of narrow and wide creeks.

Bergen op Zoom: enjoy a stroll through this city with its many monuments, cafés and restaurants.

Tilburg: De Pont museum of contemporary art; Scryption museum dedicated to the history of writing.

Eindhoven: city of light, art and design, and sport; Van Abbe Museum of modern and contemporary art; home of PSV Eindhoven.

Breda: popular city with lots to see, especially in the areas of the Great Market and the Havermarkt.

Attractions

Safaripark Beekse Bergen: large wildlife park with more than 1,500 animals, amusements and winter skiing village.

De Efteling: one of the largest and oldest amusement parks in the Netherlands, with golf course and themed hotel.

Het Roozenhuys, Hasp: an historical site where roses have been cultivated for more than a century.

Ploegfabriek en Ploegpark, Bergeijk: the former factory of the textile company, De Ploeg; and the Mien Ruys park, with activities, tours, exhibitions and events.

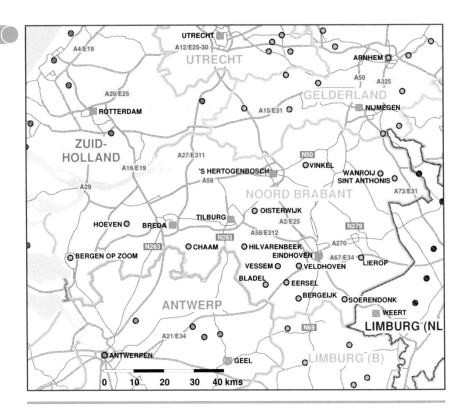

Bladel
Recreatiepark De Achterste Hoef

Troprijt 10, NL-5531 NA Bladel (Noord-Brabant) T: 0497 381 579. E: info@achterstehoef.nl
alanrogers.com/NL6710

This quite large campsite is to be found off the N284 at Bladel in Noord-Brabant. It is an ideal location for cycling and walking and is close to the Belgian border. A family oriented site, it offers good quality facilities which are well maintained and kept very clean. There are 390 touring pitches, all fully serviced and 22 with their own sanitation, sited near the lake. The touring pitches are 80-150 sq.m. in size with many amongst the trees, but some are on open meadows and some divided by young shrubs. There are also seasonal and static caravan places, but these are kept apart and mostly in one area. On entering the site you find all the main service buildings alongside reception. Opposite reception is an interestingly landscaped minigolf. To the rear of the site is a lake and beach area, with a dedicated section for swimming. Since being highly commended for families in 2012, the site has added a nine-hole golf course, a driving range, a BMX track and a large, wooded and fenced area for dog walking.

Facilities

Four sanitary blocks have showers, washbasins, both open and in cabins, a bathroom and a baby bath. Washing machine and dryer. Motorcaravan services. Supermarket, restaurant/bar and snack bar (18/4-28/9). Heated indoor (5/4-28/9) and outdoor (26/4-31/8) swimming pools. Disco. Recreation room. Football. Tennis. Bicycle hire. Watersports. Play areas (including indoor). Animal corner. Organised activities in July/Aug. Max. 2 dogs. WiFi throughout (charged).

Open: 4 April - 26 October.

Directions

Travelling east or west on N284 Eindhoven-Reusel road turn south at 2nd traffic lights in Bladel, follow camping signs to site. GPS: 51.34406, 5.226939

Charges guide

Per unit incl. 2 persons and electricity	€ 23.00 - € 36.00
with own sanitary unit	€ 31.00 - € 49.00
extra person	€ 2.00 - € 4.00

Camping Cheques accepted.

For latest campsite news, availability and prices visit
alanrogers.com

Bergeijk
Camping De Paal

Paaldreef 14, NL-5571 TN Bergeijk (Noord-Brabant) T: 0497 571 977. E: info@depaal.nl
alanrogers.com/NL5970

A really first class, family run campsite, De Paal is especially suitable for families with children up to ten years old, and in low season for those seeking a quality, peaceful site. Situated in 42 hectares of woodland, it has 580 touring pitches (up to 150 sq.m). The pitches are numbered and in meadows, separated by trees, with cars parked mainly on dedicated parking areas. All have 6A electricity, TV, water, drainage and a bin. There are 60 pitches with private sanitary facilities some of which are partly underground and attractively covered with grass and flowers. Sixteen newer pitches have a kitchen, sleeping accommodation and sanitary facilities, again partly underground. Each group of pitches has a small playground; additionally, there is a large adventure playground, more like a small desert.

Facilities

High quality sanitary facilities are ultra modern, including washbasins in cabins, family rooms and baby baths, all with lots of space. Facilities for disabled visitors. Launderette. Motorcaravan services. Underground supermarket. Restaurant (high season), bar and snack bar (all season). Indoor pool (all season, supervised in high season). Outdoor pool (May-Sept). Tennis. Play areas. Theatre. WiFi (charged). Bicycle hire. Pet zoo.

Open: Easter/1 April - 31 October.

Directions

From E34 Antwerpen-Eindhoven road take exit 32 (Eersel) and follow signs for Bergeijk and site (2 km. from town). GPS: 51.33635, 5.35552

Charges guide

Per unit incl. 2 persons	
and services	€ 31.00 - € 49.00
extra person	€ 4.00 - € 5.00
dog	€ 5.00

Bergen op Zoom
Camping Uit en Thuis

Heimolen 56, NL-4625 DD Bergen op Zoom (Noord-Brabant) T: 0164 233 391. E: info@campinguitenthuis.nl
alanrogers.com/NL5539

Camping Uit en Thuis (home and away) is a friendly, family run site close to the town of Bergen op Zoom. There is a choice of 80 sunny or shady touring pitches including eight with hardstanding. Most pitches have electricity (6A), water, drainage and cable TV connections. A number of fully equipped mobile homes are available for rent, as well as a simply furnished hikers' cabin (maximum three nights). There are also several pitches for cycle campers. On-site amenities include a popular snack bar/restaurant, which specialises in traditional Dutch cuisine (including frikandels and various schnitzels). Bergen op Zoom is a pleasant Burgundian town, which was granted city status in 1266. It is a delightful place to explore with numerous historic buildings, many surrounding the Grote Markt, including the Markiezenhof Palace, which is now home to the city's cultural centre. The city borders the Binnenschelde Lake, popular for windsurfing and other watersports.

Facilities

Three clean, modern toilet blocks have family showers, hot water (on payment) and dishwashing sinks. One block has facilities for disabled visitors and a small laundry. Café/snack bar. Half size billiard tables. Play area. Football pitch. Tennis. Volleyball. Minigolf. Activities for children up to 12 yrs. (high season). Bicycle hire. WiFi over part of site (charged). Off site: Shops and restaurants in Bergen op Zoom. Riding 1 km. Golf 2 km. Sailing 3 km. Fishing 5 km.

Open: 1 May - 1 October.

Directions

From the south (Antwerp) use A4 motorway as far as Bergen op Zoom exit, follow signs to Binnenschelde and campsite. GPS: 51.469064, 4.322337

Charges guide

Per unit incl. 2 persons	
and electricity	€ 18.50 - € 21.50
extra person	€ 3.00
child (3-10 yrs)	€ 3.00
dog	€ 3.00

Chaam
RCN Vakantiepark de Flaasbloem
Flaasdijk 1, NL-4861 RC Chaam (Noord-Brabant) T: 0161 491 654. E: flaasbloem@rcn.nl
alanrogers.com/NL6650

This is a large (100 hectares) friendly and quiet campsite set well out in the countryside. It would suit those who prefer to stay in a countryside environment, on a site providing very good facilities to keep children busy and happy. Like all successful sites it is continually developing and the latest addition is the Wildenberg, a large, vehicle-free area for tents with three Finnish nomadic huts. There are 180 level touring pitches set on grass among hedges and tall trees, and all have 10A electricity. They are spacious and shady, with a number of more open, landscaped pitches on grassy fields.

Facilities

Good sanitary facilities including those for disabled visitors. Launderette. Supermarket, bar, snack bar and bakery, restaurant with indoor garden (all open all season). Small covered pool, outdoor children's pool with water games. Games room. Library. One large and several small play areas. Mini train around the site. Multisports terrain. Tennis. Children's farm. Bicycle and go-kart hire. Mobile homes and chalets for rent (some adapted for visitors with disabilities). WiFi (charged).

Open: 28 March - 27 October.

Directions

From A58 take exit 14 (Ulvenhout/Chaam, N639) and turn right towards Chaam. After 7 km, take second exit at roundabout and join Alphensebaan. After 1.7 km. turn right; site is signed. GPS: 51.491393, 4.896464

Charges guide

Per unit incl. 2 persons and electricity	€ 16.50 - € 24.00
extra person	€ 4.25

Eersel
Recreatiepark TerSpegelt
Postelseweg 88, NL-5521 RD Eersel (Noord-Brabant) T: 0497 512 016. E: info@terspegelt.nl
alanrogers.com/NL6630

Camping TerSpegelt is a large, attractively laid out site set around three (unsupervised) lakes used for sports, non-motorised boating, swimming and fishing. The site has 855 pitches, with 481 for touring units and tents, and 70 cabins, chalets and mobile homes for rent, plus various types of tent. All touring pitches have electricity (6-16A Europlug), and 347 also have water and drainage, and some have lakeside views. We can recommend this site to families with children (pushchairs useful) and people who like to participate in organised activities (sports and outdoor activities, campfires and themed dinners).

Facilities

Five main toilet blocks, four heated by solar panels, provide toilets, washbasins (open and in cubicles) and showers. Washbasins for children. Heated baby rooms with changing mat and bath. Facilities for disabled visitors in one block. Laundry. Motorcaravan services. Supermarket, restaurant, bar, snack bar and swimming pools (all open as site). Entertainment and activities. Watersports. Climbing wall. Minigolf. Bicycle and go-kart hire. Tennis. Dogs are not accepted. WiFi (charged).

Open: 4 April - 2 November.

Directions

From Utrecht follow the A2 south towards Eindhoven, then Maastricht. Take exit for Antwerpen and follow signs for Eersel. From Eersel follow site signs. GPS: 51.33623, 5.29373

Charges guide

Per unit incl. 2 persons and electricity	€ 23.50 - € 56.50
Min. stay at some periods.	

Hilvarenbeek
Vakantiepark Beekse Bergen
Beekse Bergen 1, NL-5081 NJ Hilvarenbeek (Noord-Brabant) T: 01354 91100. E: info@libema.nl
alanrogers.com/NL5900

Centred around a large lake, Beekse Bergen campsite is part of a large leisure park complex that offers something for all the family, from the Safari Park containing over 1,000 wild animals to Speelland, which caters for children from three to eight years old. The site has 225 touring pitches, all with 4/10A electricity, 100 of which have fresh and waste water connections. They are arranged in small, level, grassy areas surrounded by hedges and mature trees. Several small sandy beaches are to be found around the lake, which can be used for, amongst other things, swimming, windsurfing and fishing.

Facilities

Sanitary facilities in the touring area include all the usual facilities with some washbasins in cabins and facilities for disabled visitors. Launderette. Supermarket. Restaurants, cafés and takeaway (weekends only in low seasons). Playgrounds. Indoor pool. Beaches and lake swimming. Watersports including rowing boats and canoe hire. Amusements. Tennis. Minigolf. Fishing. Bicycle hire. Riding. Bungalows and tents to rent. WiFi (charged).

Open: 21 March - 6 November.

Directions

From A58/E312 Tilburg-Eindhoven motorway, take exit to Hilvarenbeek on the N269 road. Follow signs to Beekse Bergen. GPS: 51.48298, 5.12800

Charges guide

Per unit incl. 2 persons and electricity	€ 15.00 - € 25.00
extra person	€ 7.00
dog	€ 4.00

For latest campsite news, availability and prices visit
alanrogers.com

Hoeven

Molecaten Park Bosbad Hoeven

Oude Antwerpsepostbaan 81b, NL-4741 SG Hoeven (Noord-Brabant) T: 0165 502 570.
E: bosbadhoeven@molecaten.nl **alanrogers.com/NL6655**

This is an ideal family site set in woodland with free access to one of Holland's most popular water parks, Splesj. Of the 900 pitches, 220 fully serviced pitches are for tourers; they are level, grassy, and mostly set in areas surrounded by mature trees with some hedge separation between pitches. There is a good restaurant with takeaway food, and with numerous play areas and a sports field there are plenty of activities for children if you can get them out of the water park complex. There are over 1,000 km. of paths and cycle tracks in the region.

Facilities	Directions
Three sanitary blocks, two modern, have all the usual facilities, showers charged by SEP key. Children's toilets and washbasins. Family shower room. Facilities for disabled visitors. Baby room. Laundry. Motorcaravan services. Small shop. Restaurant, takeaway. Covered swimming pool and outdoor pool with spectacular slide. Small lake with rowing boats and pedaloes. Train. Fishing pond. Tennis. Basketball. Playground. Indoor playground. Bicycle hire. Children's entertainment. WiFi (charged). Raised gas barbecues only. Dogs are not accepted.	From A58 exit 20 follow signs to Industrieterrein Nijverhei St Willebrord. Turn right onto Heistraat and after 2 km. take third exit onto Bovenstraat. Turn right onto Oude Antwerpsepostbaan. Site is well signed from here. GPS: 51.570494, 4.560699

Open: 28 March - 1 November.

Charges guide

Per unit incl. 2 persons and 10A electricity	€ 17.00
extra person	€ 4.00 - € 8.00
child (2-10 yrs)	€ 1.90

Lierop

Camping De Somerense Vennen

Philipsbosweg 7, NL-5715 RE Lierop (Noord-Brabant) T: 0492 331 216. E: info@somerensevennen.nl
alanrogers.com/NL6690

De Somerense Vennen is an attractive site in lovely countryside with walking, cycling and riding trails in the Somerense heartland. A very good range of activities for children are organised here, based around the Twinkle Club, which are suitable for children of all ages. There are 125 good sized touring pitches, all with electricity (4-16A) and generally well shaded. A number of mobile homes and chalets are available for rent. There is a convivial bar/restaurant, serving the best pancakes locally! The impressive swimming pool complex includes a children's area and a good range of games and play equipment.

Facilities	Directions
Two toilet blocks, the newest is small but clean and well equipped. Facilities for disabled visitors. Further toilet and shower by restaurant. Facilities for children in a separate, block are well decorated. Laundry. Swimming pool complex (can be covered). Bar, snack bar and restaurant. Riding centre. Play area. Children's club. Activity and entertainment programme. Free WiFi over site.	Use A67 Eindhoven-Venlo motorway and leave at exit 35 (Someren). In Someren go towards Lierop then follow signs to site. GPS: 51.400403, 5.675804

Open: 26 March - 30 October.

Charges guide

Per unit incl. 2 persons and electricity	€ 19.50 - € 29.50
dog	€ 4.50

Oisterwijk

Camping De Reebok

Duinenweg 4, NL-5062 TP Oisterwijk (Noord-Brabant) T: 013 528 2309. E: info@dereebok.nl
alanrogers.com/NL5905

Situated in the Noord-Brabant region of the Netherlands and open all year, Camping De Reebok is a peaceful woodland campsite in the Kampina Nature Reserve, close to the fens and forests of Oisterwijkse. There are 93 sheltered touring pitches, including some larger and better 'comfort' pitches. All have radio and television connections, electricity (16A Europlug) and are close to water and waste water. In addition there are 200 permanent annual pitches as well as mobile homes, hikers' cabins and luxury wooden bungalows to rent. Wild deer and horses can be seen from the site.

Facilities	Directions
Heated sanitary facilities with provision for families and babies. En-suite unit for disabled visitors (key access). Laundry facilities. New motorcaravan services for 2015. Shop with essentials (1/4-28/9). Bar. Restaurant, snack bar and takeaway. Large playground. Multisports field. Boules pitch. Bouncy castle. Children's entertainment (28/4-6/5 and 30/6-19/8). Games room. Gas available. Bicycle hire. WiFi over site (free). ATM. Max. 2 dogs.	From Rotterdam take A16 to Dordrecht. At Knooppunt Galder interchange follow signs for E312/A58 towards Tilburg, then A65 for Tilburg-Noord. Take exit 2 (Heukelomseweg, Oisterwijk). In Oisterwijk follow signs to recreation centre. Look for street named Duinenweg. GPS: 51.57364, 5.23202

Open: All year.

Charges guide

Per unit incl. 2 persons and electricity	€ 21.00 - € 25.00

FREE Alan Rogers Travel Card
Extra benefits and savings - see page 12

Sint Anthonis

Vakantiecentrum De Ullingse Bergen

Bosweg 36, NL-5845 EB Sint Anthonis (Noord-Brabant) T: 0485 388 566. E: ullingsebergen@ardoer.com
alanrogers.com/NL5885

Come and listen to the silence of the woods. This three-acre park is situated right next to a nature reserve where there are marvellous opportunities for walking and cycling on signed paths. Some 150 large touring pitches (100-150 sq.m) are separated by hedges and attractive medium sized trees, including silver birch. On flat grass, the pitches are arranged in rows or in groups around small play areas. This attractive site provides enough shade. More than 70 pitches have drainage and cable TV connections, 16 have water points, and all have 6A electricity. A further 150 pitches are taken by seasonal and caravan holiday homes.

Facilities

Two heated, well maintained toilet blocks provide free hot water, roomy adjustable showers and some washbasins in cabins. Baby bathroom in both blocks. Small shop. Bar (with sitting area). Restaurant and takeaway. Five play areas near pitches and two separate large ones. Games room. Three heated and guarded pools, suitable for children of all ages. Tennis courts. Dogs are not accepted.

Open: 1 April - 1 October.

Directions

From the A73 (Nijmegen-Venlo) take exit 6 (N272) at the end to St Anthonis and follow blue camping signs. GPS: 51.627731, 5.861555

Charges guide

Per unit incl. 2 persons and electricity	€ 20.00 - € 28.00
extra person (over 2 yrs)	€ 3.70

Soerendonk

Recreatiepark Slot Cranendonck

Strijperdijk 9, NL-6027 RD Soerendonk (Noord-Brabant) T: 0495 591 652. E: info@slotcranendonck.nl
alanrogers.com/NL5965

Surrounded by woodland and moors, not far from Limburg and the Belgian border, this is an attractive campsite with the appearance and ambience of a park. A large pond used for fishing is in the centre of the site. Several areas surrounded by trees and hedges accommodate caravans, motorcaravans and tents, with pitches arranged around the edges. Each pitch has 6A Europlug, cable TV connections, water and drainage. The site provides many amenities and a variety of facilities for leisure. This is an excellent area for cycling and walking. In high season, large units should telephone ahead.

Facilities

Three toilet buildings have the most modern facilities including family and baby bathrooms. Facilities for disabled visitors. Free hot water. Well stocked supermarket. Bar, restaurant and takeaway. Indoor and outdoor (15/5-31/8) swimming pools both with paddling pools (no lifeguards). Large playground. Volleyball. Two tennis courts. Football pitch. Fishing. Minigolf. Children's club and entertainment (high season). Covered playground. Bicycle hire. WiFi (charged).

Open: 27 March - 27 October.

Directions

From the A2 (Eindhoven-Weert) take exit 36 towards Soerendonk and follow blue campsite signs in village. GPS: 51.31989, 5.57434

Charges guide

Per unit incl. 2 persons and electricity	€ 20.00 - € 33.40
extra person	€ 4.90 - € 5.35
dog (max. 2)	€ 4.00

Veldhoven

Resort Molenvelden

Banstraat 25, Zandoerle, NL-5506 LA Veldhoven (Noord-Brabant) T: 0402 052 384.
E: info@vakantieparkmolenvelden.nl **alanrogers.com/NL6760**

Resort Molenvelden can be recommended as a base for those who enjoy cycling and hiking without hills, the tranquillity of nature, 'olde worlde' pubs, with unlimited modern shopping nearby. This is an attractive, well maintained site with extremely good facilities centred around a small lake. The 100 touring pitches are located in a quiet area at the rear of the site. They are level grassy, fairly open, and all have 10A electricity, fresh and waste water connections. Towards the entrance a profusion of flowers paves the way to reception, a comfortable restaurant and bar with terrace, and close by is a children's playground and pets' corner.

Facilities

Modern, well maintained sanitary block with all the usual facilities including family shower room, children's sanitary areas and baby changing room. Hot water/electricity upon payment by SEP key. Facilities for disabled visitors. Laundry facilities. Motorcaravan services. Bar. Restaurant and takeaway (July/Aug). Indoor and outdoor swimming pools. Attractive playground. Sports field. Entertainment in summer. Charcoal barbecues are not permitted.

Open: 1 April - 1 October.

Directions

Leave A2 autobahn at exit 31 Veldhoven and head southwest on Heerbaan. At third roundabout left into Sondervick then first right (Eindhovensbaan). At the end turn left into Banstaat. Site is a few hundred metres on the left. GPS: 51.408626, 5.357219

Charges guide

Per unit incl. 2 persons and electricity	€ 24.00 - € 28.35
extra person	€ 3.15 - € 5.25

Noord-Brabant

For latest campsite news, availability and prices visit
alanrogers.com

Vessem
Eurocamping Vessem

Zwembadweg 1, NL-5512 NW Vessem (Noord-Brabant) T: 0497 591 214. E: info@eurocampingvessem.com
alanrogers.com/NL5920

Eurocamping Vessem is a family run site of 50 hectares with the touring area quietly located at the bottom of the site, well away from the large outdoor swimming pool complex, playground and sports area. Of the 1,000 pitches, 600 are for tourers, they are on grass in groups surrounded by tall trees, and 400 have 6A electricity. In addition, there are 30 overnight pitches outside of the site, (18 with electricity) which are open all year. The site offers a large range of activities for children, and by carefully selecting your pitch you can almost imagine that you are camping in the forest.

Facilities	Directions
One main sanitary block is towards site entrance and one prefabricated type unit is in the touring area. They contain all the usual facilities, showers upon payment (50 cent coin). Twenty toilet-only units are spread around site. Supermarket. Snack bar. Bar. Swimming pool complex with paddling pool. Tennis courts. Minigolf. Football. Basketball. Beach volleyball. Sports/games activities. Play areas. Bouncy castle. WiFi (charged).	From E312/A58 Tilburg, Breda, take exit 8 to Kempenweg and Oirschot and follow signs to Middelbeers and Oirschot on the N395. Drive through Middelbeers and head for Vessem. After 4 km. turn right on Ellenbroek. In 2 km. turn left on Vondereind. The site is well signed from here. GPS: 51.410646, 5.276179

Open: 1 April - 30 September.

Charges guide

Per unit incl. 2 persons and electricity	€ 22.65

Vinkel
Vakantiepark Dierenbos

Vinkeloord 1, NL-5382 JX Vinkel (Noord-Brabant) T: 0735 343 536. E: info@libema.nl
alanrogers.com/NL5880

Run by the same group as Beekse Bergen (NL5900), Dierenbos is a large site with motel accommodation and a bungalow park in addition to its 500 camping pitches. These are divided into several grassy areas, many in an attractive wooded setting. There are 381 for touring units, all with electricity connections (4-10A) and some with full services (water and TV connection). A small, landscaped lake has sandy beaches and is overlooked by a large, modern play area. Some of the touring pitches also overlook the water. Campers are entitled to free entry to several attractions. The varied amenities are located in and around a modern, central complex. They include heated outdoor swimming pools, an indoor sub-tropical pool with slide and jet stream, and a ten-pin bowling alley.

Facilities	Directions
Eight toilet blocks are well situated with a mixture of clean and simple facilities (some unisex) with some warm water for washing and some individual washbasins. Baby room. Supermarket. Bar. Modern restaurant. Snack bar with takeaway (high season). Free outdoor heated swimming pools (1/6-1/9). Indoor pool (on payment). Ten-pin bowling. Tennis. Minigolf. Boules. Sports field. Bicycle hire. Pedalos. Fishing. Barbecue area. Play areas on sand.	Site is signed from the N50/A50 road between 's-Hertogenbosch and Nijmegen, 10 km. east of 's-Hertogenbosch at Vinkel. GPS: 51.70472, 5.43048

Open: 21 March - 26 October.

Charges guide

Per unit incl. 2 persons and electricity	€ 14.00 - € 28.00
extra person	€ 7.00

Wanroij
Vakantiepark De Bergen

Campinglaan 1, NL-5446 PW Wanroij (Noord-Brabant) T: 0485 335 450. E: info@debergen.nl
alanrogers.com/NL6635

Brabant is an attractive holiday region within easy reach of large cities such as Den Bosch and Nijmegen. The main attraction at this well equipped site is the large swimming lake with restaurant, snack bar and sandy beaches. There are four grades of pitch, from the relatively simple standard pitch to the luxury comfort pitches (with 10A electricity, cable TV connections, water and drainage). Visitors need not leave the site; the shop is well stocked, the Twinkle Club in high season keeps children occupied, and there is entertainment for adults. Twin-axle caravans and units over 7.75 m. are not accepted. A range of chalets and mobile homes are available to rent. An unfenced rainwater drainage channel runs through the site.

Facilities	Directions
Several modern toilet blocks are heated and well maintained. Baby room and facilities for disabled visitors (key access). Laundry. Well stocked shop. Snack bars and restaurants. Fishing. Pedalos. Bicycle hire. Adventure playground. Bowling. Pony rides. Play area. Activity and entertainment. WiFi over part of site (charged).	Go south from Nijmegen on A73. Take Boxmeer exit, follow signs to St Anthonis. Go north on D602 to Wanroj, follow site signs. GPS: 51.64029, 5.81053

Open: 1 April - 31 October.

Charges guide

Per unit incl. 2 persons	€ 18.00 - € 31.00
electricity (per kWh)	€ 0.40
dog	€ 3.50

FREE Alan Rogers Travel Card
Extra benefits and savings - see page 12

CAPITAL: HAARLEM

Beside the many historical cities and densely populated, modern residential areas, there is plenty of space for unique landscapes such as Waterland (near Amsterdam) and the Kennemer Dunes (near Haarlem).

Noord-Holland is a broad peninsula lying between the North Sea and the IJsselmeer. With more than 2.5 million people sharing an area of 2,670 sq.km, it is the country's second most populated province. In 1600, half of its surface was covered by water, then began the reclamation of land, and the construction of giant polders such as Beemster, Purmer and Schermer, a testament to the relationship between man and the sea. But there is much more to this province: forests, moors, dunes, beaches and meadows form a diverse landscape embroidered with quaint towns and charming, sleepy villages, rich in folklore and legend.

Almost the entire west coast of the province is made up of dunes and beaches. You have a choice of secluded bays or lively seaside resorts, simple pavilions or trendy beach restaurants. The east coast is bordered by the fresh water of the IJsselmeer, which offers numerous activities on its many ponds, lakes and canals. Noord-Holland's rich trading history is reflected in the elegant and vibrant cities, where there are ample opportunities to shop, visit museums and galleries, or just sit at a terrace café and watch the world go by.

Places of interest

Amsterdam: picturesque canals, 'brown cafés', restaurants, theatres and many museums make this city the cultural and artistic hub of the country.

Hoorn, Enkhuizen, Medemblik: historical cities at the IJsselmeer, formerly important sea ports, with beautiful 17th-century city centres.

Stelling van Amsterdam: a 135 km. defensive ring encircling Amsterdam, with 36 fortifications, set among beautiful landscapes and nature reserves.

Zaanstreek: the oldest industrial area of Europe with a unique heritage.

Texel: much of this island is given over to nature reserves; home to rare plants, animals and birds.

Attractions

Zuiderzeemuseum: reconstruction of an early modern Dutch fishing village in an open-air setting at Enkhuizen.

Zaansche Schans: open-air museum with working mills, old handicrafts, special features and characteristic green wooden houses.

Sprookjeswonderland: fairytale theme park for youngsters in Enkhuizen.

Naarden: fortified city with interesting walks, shopping and adventure playground at Oud Valkeveen.

Beemster: famous polder and UNESCO World Heritage Site. Visit the very interesting arboretum (free).

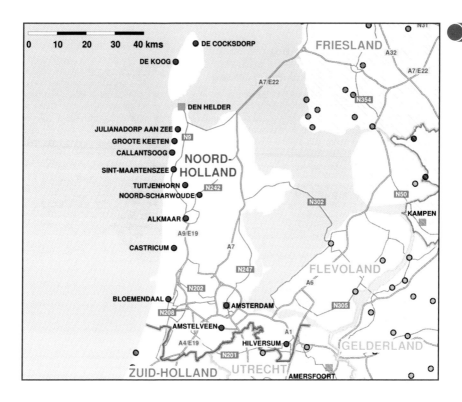

Alkmaar
Camping Alkmaar

Bergerweg 201, NL-1817 ML Alkmaar (Noord-Holland) T: 0725 116 924. E: info@campingalkmaar.nl

alanrogers.com/NL6705

Camping Alkmaar is a friendly, family run campsite on the outskirts of the charming town of Alkmaar and near the artisan village of Bergen. A short cycle ride will take you to the peaceful countryside of Noord-Holland with its dunes, wide sandy beaches, woods and unique polder landscape. Alternatively, a stroll along the canals in the picturesque heart of Alkmaar with its architecture, culture and cheese market may appeal. This is a tranquil site - there is no bar or restaurant and radios are not permitted. All 120 touring pitches have 6/10A electricity; 46 have hardstanding, and 21 are comfort pitches with water and drainage. A regular bus service runs to the town centre and the train station for connections to Amsterdam.

Facilities

New sanitary block in the touring area is clean and well maintained and has coin-operated showers and open style washbasins. Facilities for disabled visitors. Washing machine and dryer. Two motorcaravan service points. Play area. Fishing. Bicycle hire. WiFi over part of site (charged). Off site: Shops and restaurants in Alkmaar. Golf and riding 3 km. Beach 8 km. Walking and cycle trails. Batavier children's park.

Open: All year.

Directions

From the western ring road of Alkmaar (N9), turn left towards Bergen (N510). After 300 m. turn left to the site. GPS: 52.6421, 4.72329

Charges guide

Per unit incl. 2 persons and electricity (5 kWh)	€ 21.00 - € 31.00
additional electricity (per kWh)	€ 0.40
extra person	€ 4.00
dog	€ 3.00

Amstelveen

Camping Het Amsterdamse Bos

Kleine Noorddijk 1, NL-1187 NZ Amstelveen (Noord-Holland) T: 0206 416 868.
E: info@campingamsterdam.com **alanrogers.com/NL5660**

Het Amsterdamse Bos is a large park to the southwest of Amsterdam, one corner of which has been specifically laid out as the city's municipal campsite and is now under family ownership. Close to Schiphol Airport (expect some noise), it is a walk/bus and a metro ride into central Amsterdam. The site is well laid out alongside a canal, with unmarked pitches on separate flat lawns mostly backing onto pleasant hedges and trees, with several areas of paved hardstandings. It takes 400 touring units, with 100 electrical connections (10A) and some with cable TV. An additional area is for tents and groups. Some pitches can become very wet in the rain. We found the free WiFi very difficult to access.

Facilities

Three new sanitary blocks are light and airy with showers (on payment). Facilities for babies and disabled visitors. Laundry facilities. Motorcaravan services. Gas supplies. Small shop with basics. Fresh bread from reception. Cooking and dining area. Play area. Bicycle hire. Internet and free WiFi over site. Twin-axle caravans not accepted. Off site: Fishing, boating, pancake restaurant in the park. Riding 5 km.

Open: 15 March - 15 December.

Directions

Amsterdamse Bos is west of Amstelveen. From the A9 motorway take exit 6 and follow N231 to site (second traffic light). GPS: 52.29357, 4.82297

Charges guide

Per unit incl. 2 persons and electricity	€ 20.00 - € 25.00
extra person	€ 5.00 - € 5.50
child (4-12 yrs)	€ 2.50 - € 2.75
dog	€ 2.50 - € 3.00

Amsterdam

Camping Zeeburg

Zuider IJdijk 20, NL-1095 KN Amsterdam (Noord-Holland) T: 206 944 430. E: info@campingzeeburg.nl
alanrogers.com/NL5665

Camping Zeeburg is a welcoming site attractively located to the east of Amsterdam on an island in the IJmeer and, unusually, combines a sense of nature with the advantage of being just 20 minutes (5 km) from the city centre. In a sense, Zeeburg reflects the spirit of Amsterdam, claiming to be open, friendly and tolerant. The site provides 400 pitches, 350 for tents (no electricity) and 100 pitches with 10A electricity for caravans and motorcaravans, most on hardstandings and with views over the IJmeer. Tent pitches cannot be booked in advance and the maximum duration allowed on site is 14 days. Zeeburg also offers a number of colourful eco-cabins and Romany-style wagons or 'pipowagens'. The city centre can be easily accessed by bicycle (hire available on site). On-site amenities include a busy café/restaurant. There is a shop with a bakery (which claims to bake Amsterdam's best croissants), a children's farm and a canoe rental service. A swimming pool is adjacent. The wetlands of the IJmeer are well worth exploration, extending to the Diemerpark and new city of IJburg.

Facilities

Three toilet blocks are generally simple and well used, but clean. Although adequate, facilities may be stretched at peak times. Facilities for disabled visitors (key access). Shop (all year). Café/restaurant (1/4-11/11). Very small playground. Games room. Bicycle hire. Motorcaravan services. Children's petting farm. Canoe hire. Eco-cabins and wagons to rent. WiFi over site (free). Off site: Swimming pool. Buses and trains to city centre.

Open: All year.

Directions

Site is on the eastern side of Amsterdam. From the A10 (Amsterdam ring road) take exit S114 to Zeeburg. Then follow signs to the city centre and, before reaching the Piet Hein tunnel turn left and then right into the campsite. The site is well signed from the A10. GPS: 52.36532, 4.95871

Charges guide

Per unit incl. 2 persons and electricity	€ 15.00 - € 28.00
extra person	€ 5.00 - € 7.00
child (2-12 yrs)	€ 2.50 - € 3.50
dog	€ 2.00 - € 3.00

For latest campsite news, availability and prices visit
alanrogers.com

Amsterdam
Gaasper Camping Amsterdam
Loosdrechtdreef 7, NL-1108 AZ Amsterdam (Noord-Holland) T: 0206 967 326.
alanrogers.com/NL5670

Amsterdam is probably the most popular destination for visits in the Netherlands, and Gaasper Camping is on the southeast side, a short walk from a Metro station with a direct 20 minute service to the centre. The site is well kept and neatly laid out on flat grass with attractive trees and shrubs. There are 350 touring pitches in two main areas – one more open and grassy, mainly kept for tents (30 pitches with 10A connections), the other more formal with numbered pitches mainly divided by shallow ditches or hedges. Areas of hardstanding are available and all caravan pitches have electricity connections.

Facilities	Directions
Three modern, clean toilet blocks (one unisex) for the tourist sections are an adequate provision. Nine new cabins with basin and shower. Hot water for showers and some dishwashing sinks on payment. Facilities for babies. Washing machine and dryer. Motorcaravan services. Gas supplies. Supermarket (1/4-1/11), café/bar/restaurant plus takeaway (1/6-1/9). Play area on grass. Off site: Riding 200 m. Fishing 1 km. Golf 4 km. **Open:** 15 March - 1 November.	Take exit 1 for Gaasperplas-Weesp (S113) from the section of A9 motorway which is on the east side of the A2. Note: do not take the Gaasperdam exit (S112) which comes first if approaching from the west. GPS: 52.312222, 4.991389

Charges guide

Per unit incl. 2 persons and electricity	€ 19.50 - € 23.50
extra person	€ 4.75 - € 5.50

Amsterdam
Camping Vliegenbos
Meeuwenlaan 138, NL-1022 AM Amsterdam (Noord-Holland) T: 0206 368 855.
E: vliegenbos@noord.amsterdam.nl **alanrogers.com/NL5675**

Vliegenbos enjoys the best of both worlds with an appealing location in a large wood, ten minutes from the lively centre of Amsterdam and five minutes by bike from the countryside of the Waterland region, best known for its open expanses and picturesque towns such as Marken, Edam and Volendam. It extends over a 2.5 hectare site and has a good range of amenities including a restaurant, shop and recently renovated toilet blocks. Most of the 400 pitches are for tents, but there are 19 hardstandings (10A electricity) and a further 40 smaller hardstandings (no electricity).

Facilities	Directions
Renovated toilet blocks include facilities for disabled campers. Motorcaravan services. Bar/restaurant and takeaway. Shop (fresh bread daily). Free WiFi over part of site. Cabins for rent. Reservations are not accepted for touring pitches. Dogs accepted on request. Off site: Bus stop 200 m. Cycle tracks in the surrounding Waterland. Ferry terminal 15 minutes walk with regular free service to Amsterdam. **Open:** 1 April - 26 October.	Leave the A10 Amsterdam ring road at exit S116 and follow signs to Camping Vliegenbos. GPS: 52.39055, 4.928083

Charges guide

Per unit incl. 2 persons and electricity	€ 28.50 - € 30.00
extra person	€ 7.70 - € 8.70
child (2-14 yrs)	€ 5.40

Bloemendaal
Kennemer Duincamping de Lakens
Zeeweg 60, NL-2051 EC Bloemendaal aan Zee (Noord-Holland) T: 0235 411 570.
E: delakens@kennemerduincampings.nl **alanrogers.com/NL6870**

De Lakens is beautifully located in the dunes at Bloemendaal aan Zee. This site has 900 reasonably large, flat pitches of varying sizes, whose layout makes them feel quite private - some come with a ready erected hammock! There are 410 pitches for tourers (255 with 16A electricity) separated by low hedging. This site is a true oasis of peace in a part of the Netherlands usually bustling with activity. From this site it is possible to walk straight through the dunes to the North Sea. Although there is no pool, there is the sea. The reception and management are very friendly and welcoming.

Facilities	Directions
The five new toilet blocks for tourers include controllable showers, washbasins (open style and in cabins), facilities for disabled visitors and a baby room. Launderette. Two motorcaravan service points. Bar/restaurant with terrace, pizzeria and snack bar. Supermarket. Bicycle hire. Adventure playgrounds. Basketball. Entertainment in high season. Glamping-style accommodation for rent. WiFi over most of site (charged). No twin-axle caravans or large motorcaravans. No dogs. Off site: Beach within 200 m. **Open:** 27 March - 1 November.	From Amsterdam go west to Haarlem and follow the N200 from Haarlem towards Bloemendaal aan Zee. Site is on the N200, on the right hand side. GPS: 52.40563, 4.58652

Charges guide

Per unit incl. 4 persons	€ 25.60 - € 55.00
extra person	€ 5.35

FREE Alan Rogers Travel Card
Extra benefits and savings - see page 12

Callantsoog
Camping Tempelhof

Westerweg 2, NL-1759 JD Callantsoog (Noord-Holland) T: 0224 581 522. E: info@tempelhof.nl
alanrogers.com/NL5735

This first class site on the Dutch coast has 470 pitches with 220 for touring units, the remainder used by seasonal campers, with a number of static units (mostly privately owned). All touring pitches have electricity (10/16A), water, drain and TV aerial point (70-110 sq.m. but car free). Two pitches have private sanitary facilities. The grass pitches are arranged in long rows which are separated by hedges and shrubs, with access from hardcore roads. There is hardly any shade. There are facilities for many activities, including a heated indoor pool, a fitness room and tennis courts. Tempelhof is close to the North Sea beaches (1 km). A member of Leading Campings group.

Facilities

Two modern toilet blocks include washbasins (some in cabins) and controllable hot showers (SEP key). Children's area and baby room. Private bathroom (€ 50 p/w). Facilities for disabled visitors. Laundry. Motorcaravan services. Shop, restaurant, takeaway, bar, indoor heated swimming pool with paddling pool (all 22/3-3/11). Fitness room (€ 2,50). Recreation hall. Climbing wall. Tennis. Trim court. Play area. Entertainment programme (high season). WiFi over site (charged). Bicycle hire. Max. 2 dogs.

Open: All year.

Directions

From Alkmaar take N9 road north towards Den Helder. Turn left towards Callantsoog on the N503 road and follow site signs.
GPS: 52.846644, 4.715506

Charges guide

Per unit incl. 2 persons and electricity (plus meter)	€ 19.00 - € 39.00
extra person	€ 4.50
electricity (per kWh)	€ 0.35

Callantsoog
Camping De Nollen

Westerweg 8, NL-1759 JD Callantsoog (Noord-Holland) T: 0224 581 281. E: info@denollen.nl
alanrogers.com/NL6888

De Nollen is a comfortable, nine-hectare site, ideal for couples, seniors and families with younger children. There are a variety of pitches (60-120 sq.m) some basic, without connections, most with 10A electricity and comfort pitches with 10A electricity, water, drainage and cable TV. There is plenty to keep children occupied, with several playgrounds across the site, one with a large inflatable. The two nature reserves adjacent give the site a tranquil atmosphere. The Eetboey restaurant and snack bar offers simple meals and takeaway dishes. You can also eat outside on the terrace, and there is a play corner for younger children.

Facilities

Two modern toilet blocks with underfloor heating. Separate facilities for children. En-suite unit for disabled visitors. Launderette. Dog shower. Motorcaravan services. Microwave. Freezer. Supermarket. Cafeteria/snack bar and takeaway service (Thu-Sun; daily in July/Aug). Play areas. Bouncy castle. Football. Basketball. Beach volleyball. Fishing. Fridge hire. Bicycle hire. WiFi over site (charged). Off site: Beach 2 km. Riding 4 km. Golf 15 km.

Open: 28 March - 25 October.

Directions

From the Alkmaar-Den Helder road (N9) take exit for Callantsoog. Turn right at the Het Zwanenwater nature reserve. Follow small signs to the site.
GPS: 52.841381, 4.719001

Charges guide

Per unit incl. 2 persons and electricity	€ 23.00 - € 33.00
extra person	€ 4.00

Castricum
Kennemer Duincamping Geversduin

Beverwijkerstraatweg 205, NL-1901 NH Castricum (Noord-Holland) T: 0251 661 095.
E: geversduin@kennemerduincampings.nl alanrogers.com/NL6862

The comfortable, family site of Gerversduin lies in an area of forests and sand dunes. The site offers 614 pitches of which 221 are for touring units and 24 for accommodation to rent. They have good shade and privacy, and all pitches have 4-16A electricity connections. The pitches without electricity have a unique location and cars must be parked elsewhere. In high season, many activities are organised for youngsters including the unusual opportunity to join a forestry worker for the day. The beach is only 4 km. away and is easily accessible by bike or on foot.

Facilities

Four sanitary blocks with WCs, open style washbasins, preset hot showers and family shower rooms including baby room. Facilities for disabled visitors. Laundry with washing machines and dryers. Supermarket. Snack bar and café for meals with large terrace (weekends only in low season). Recreation area. Sports pitch. Play area. Bicycle hire. WiFi (free). Only gas barbecues are permitted.

Open: 26 March - 25 October.

Directions

On A9 (Amsterdam-Alkmaar) take N203 exit and go north towards Castricum. In Castricum follow signs to station. From there go south towards Heemskerk via Beverwijkse straatweg (site signed).
GPS: 52.53038, 4.64839

Charges guide

Per unit incl. 4 persons and electricity	€ 22.00 - € 39.50

For latest campsite news, availability and prices visit
alanrogers.com

Castricum
Kennemer Duincamping Bakkum
Zeeweg 31, NL-1901 NZ Castricum aan Zee (Noord-Holland) T: 0251 661 091.
E: bakkum@kennemerduincampings.nl **alanrogers.com/NL6872**

Kennemer Duincamping Bakkum lies in a wooded area in the centre of a protected dune reserve. There are 1,800 pitches of which 400 are used for touring units. These pitches are spacious and 300 are equipped with electricity (10A Europlug). Mobile homes and seasonal units use the remaining pitches in separate areas of the site. For safety and tranquillity the majority of the site is kept free of cars. Family activities and special entertainment for children are arranged in high season. The dunes are accessible from the site and offer opportunities for walking and cycling, with the beach a walk of only 25 minutes.

Facilities

Three toilet blocks for tourers with toilets, washbasins in cabins, free, controllable showers and family shower rooms. Facilities for disabled visitors. Laundry area. Excellent supermarket, baker, pizza, fish and chicken takeaways. Snack bar and restaurant. Gas supplies. Play area. Sports pitch. Tennis. Bicycle hire. Activities for children and teens. WiFi over part of site (charged). Motorbikes and dogs are not accepted.

Open: 27 March - 25 October.

Directions

On the A9 between Alkmaar and Amsterdam take exit west onto the N203. Turn left onto the Zeeweg (N513) and after a few kilometres the site is on the right. GPS: 52.5614, 4.6331

Charges guide

Per unit incl. 4 persons	
and electricity	€ 22.00 - € 40.45
extra person (over 2 yrs)	€ 3.50

De Cocksdorp
Landal Sluftervallei
Krimweg 102, NL-1795 LS De Cocksdorp (Noord-Holland) T: 0222 316 214. E: sluftervallei@landal.nl
alanrogers.com/NL5515

Landal Sluftervallei is a good family site, part of a large, well run group (Landal GreenParks). Surrounded by grassland and dunes, 2 km. from the sea on the island of Texel, there are 60 pitches for touring units with electricity (10-16A) plus 16 mobile homes for hire, together with an adjoining chalet bungalow park. The site is sheltered by trees and shrubs, which also separate the various camping areas. There are excellent facilities for recreation at the bungalow park (ten minutes walk) including an indoor pool complex, as well as a shop, restaurant and bar. The island offers wide, sandy beaches and plenty of opportunities for walking and cycling in the dunes.

Facilities

Two updated toilet blocks each provide 8 WCs, 6 shower units and 8 washbasins. Microwave. Laundry. All other facilities are at the bungalow park: Shop, bar, restaurant, snack bar and takeaway, heated indoor pool, solarium, sauna (all open all season). Games room. Entertainment. Bowling. Miniclub. Minigolf. Boules. Tennis. Play area. Off site: Beach, sailing and fishing 2 km. Golf 2.5 km.

Open: 27 March - 2 November.

Directions

Take A9 from Amsterdam to Alkmaar, N9 to Den Helder and ferry signs to Texel. Follow signs to De Cocksdorp, then signs to site. GPS: 53.157775, 4.84385

Charges guide

Per unit incl. 2 persons	
and electricity	€ 26.00 - € 59.00
extra person	€ 4.95

De Cocksdorp
Camping De Krim Texel
Roggeslootweg 6, NL-1795 JV De Cocksdorp (Noord-Holland) T: 0222 390 111. E: info@krim.nl
alanrogers.com/NL6860

Camping De Krim Texel is an attractive, well maintained campsite which is open all year round and you are assured of a warm welcome. There are 857 pitches which include 470 for touring units and tents. All have electricity and 179 have electricity, water and drainage; there are 100 pitches with private sanitary facilities. There are separate areas for bungalows and mobile homes. The manager tells us that Texel records the lowest rainfall and the most hours of sunshine than any other part of the Netherlands. The site is 3 km. from the northern point of Texel.

Facilities

Five excellent toilet blocks, all heated, with baby rooms, washbasins in cabins, showers (free), family showers and facilities for disabled visitors. Free dishwasher. Microwave. Motorcaravan services. Gas. Laundry. Three restaurants and snack bar. Large supermarket. Outdoor (15/5-15/9) and indoor pools with slides. Sauna, massage and sunbeds. Riding. Minigolf. Bowling. Internet café. Indoor play paradise. Tennis. Multisports court. Bicycle hire. Skelter track. Entertainment. Max. 2 dogs. WiFi over site.

Open: All year.

Directions

From Amsterdam drive north towards Den Helder on the A9/N9 and take the ferry to Texel. From the boat take the N501 to the north of the island towards De Cocksdorp. Site is 500 m. from De Cocksdorp, signed on the left hand side. GPS: 53.15163, 4.85855

Charges guide

Per unit incl. 2 persons	
and electricity	€ 30.00 - € 44.00
incl. services	€ 42.00 - € 61.00
extra person	€ 3.50

FREE Alan Rogers Travel Card
Extra benefits and savings - see page 12

De Koog
Texelcamping Kogerstrand

Badweg 33, NL-1796 AA De Koog (Noord-Holland) T: 0222 317 208. E: info@texelcampings.nl
alanrogers.com/NL6850

A large, well managed site (divided into northern and southern areas), it is uniquely situated in the dunes and shrubs on the island of Texel. The unlevelled and numbered pitches are within five minutes walking distance of both the beach and the village. A total of 1,200 pitches includes 1,000 for tourers and 150 for seasonal caravans and tents. All caravan pitches have electricity and cable TV connections. Motorcaravans are only accepted outside July and August when they are placed in the parking area facing the dunes (with electricity). Cars are parked away from the pitches. The large, modern restaurant has an adjoining games and entertainment area, and prices are reasonable with families in mind.

Facilities

Seven clean, modern and heated buildings include washbasins in cabins, family bathrooms and showers on payment. Laundries with spin dryer and ironing board. Access to building by electronic card only. Restaurant/bar with takeaway, games and pool tables. Play area. Entertainment for children (May holiday and high season). WiFi (charged). Raised barbecues allowed except in very hot weather. Parking in Texel: annual € 15 vignette or € 2.50/hour. Off site: Supermarket, shops, bars, restaurants, disco in crowded but pleasant village.

Open: 30 March - 28 October.

Directions

Take A9 from Amsterdam to Alkmaar, N9 to Den Helder and ferry signs to Texel, follow signs to De Koog, then follow site signs.
GPS: 53.100934, 4.758464

Charges guide

Per unit incl. 2 persons and electricity	€ 10.00 - € 32.50
extra person (over 4 yrs)	€ 1.75 - € 3.10
dog	€ 4.00

Credit cards accepted up to € 50.

De Koog
Texelcamping De Shelter

Boodtlaan 43, NL-1796 BD De Koog (Noord-Holland) T: 0222 317 208. E: info@texelcampings.nl
alanrogers.com/NL6877

Camping de Shelter, on the island of Texel, is an all year site. There are just 70 pitches here, set out on small fields, surrounded by clusters of trees. Pitches are large (min. 100 sq.m) and equipped with electricity (16A), water and drainage, with little shade. The emphasis here is on peace and quiet, so there are no organised activities, except for children's entertainment in high season, shared with the sister site, Om de Noord, and relatively few amenities. Under 25s are not admitted unless accompanied by adults. The village of De Koog is within walking distance for shops and restaurants.

Facilities

One clean, modern toilet block has controllable, hot showers and some sinks in cubicles, two family shower rooms with baby bath, but no facilities for disabled visitors (these can be found at Om de Noord). Bread to order. Small playground. Boules. Football field. Children's entertainment (high season). High speed WiFi (charged). Cycling paths from site. Off site: Shops and restaurants in De Koog. Bicycle hire 500 m. Beach 800 m. Riding 2 km.

Open: All year.

Directions

Drive to Den Helder using A7 motorway. Directions to the ferry are clearly signed. On Texel, follow signs towards De Koog. Once in De Koog, continue until you see FC De Koog's football field with a road to the left, which leads to the site.
GPS: 53.104202, 4.769547

Charges guide

Per unit incl. 2 persons and electricity (plus meter)	€ 17.00 - € 39.00

De Koog
Texelcamping Om de Noord

Boodtlaan 80, NL-1796 BG De Koog (Noord-Holland) T: 0222 317 208. E: info@texelcampings.nl
alanrogers.com/NL6879

Camping Om de Noord is located on the island of Texel, 900 m. from a sandy dune beach and is a friendly, family site within walking distance of the lively village of De Koog. There are 147 level, grassy touring pitches (average 100 sq.m) all equipped with electricity, water and drainage. Thirty-six comfort plus pitches have their own private sanitation facilities. This is a lively site for children in peak season with many games and activities organised for them. Credit cards are not accepted.

Facilities

Modern and clean toilet block with family rooms. Facilities for disabled campers. Dishwasher. Launderette. Play area (up to 12 yrs). Activity and entertainment programme for children (high season). WiFi (charged). Texel parking scheme: annual vignette € 15 or € 2.50/h. Off site: Shops and restaurants in De Koog. Beach 900 m. Fishing and riding 2 km. Sailing 5 km. Golf 10 km. Boat trips for seal spotting and shrimping. Guided sand walks.

Open: 22 March - 27 October.

Directions

Drive to Den Helder on A7 motorway. Directions to ferry are clearly signed. On Texel, follow signs to De Koog. In De Koog, continue to FC De Koog's football field with a road to the left leading to site. Check in at sister site. GPS: 53.10317, 4.771076

Charges guide

Per unit incl. 2 persons and electricity (plus meter)	€ 17.00 - € 39.00
extra person	€ 0.35 - € 1.85

For latest campsite news, availability and prices visit
alanrogers.com

Groote Keeten
Camping Callassande

Voorweg 5A, NL-1759 NX Groote Keeten (Noord-Holland) T: 0224 581 663. E: info@callassande.nl
alanrogers.com/NL6876

Callassande is a popular family run site 900 metres from a sandy beach and welcomes families with teenagers. The 500 grassy pitches include 340 for tourers; half are 89 sq.m. with electricity (10A) and TV point, the other half are slightly larger and also have water and drainage. The indoor heated pool (charged) is fun for everyone with a large chute, a jacuzzi, a special paddling area and an opening roof for sunny days. There is a children's play area adjacent to the pool with a pirate ship, a new climbing dome and trampolines. Parents of young children should be aware of the canals that run around the edge of the site.

Facilities

Three, clean, modern toilet blocks have some washbasins in cubicles, family showers, baby rooms and facilities for disabled visitors. Launderette. Well stocked shop (mornings and weekends in low season). Bar/restaurant. Covered swimming pool with water slides. Play area. Internet café. Tennis. Bicycle hire. Sports field. Skateboard park. Activity and entertainment programme. WiFi over site (charged). Mobile homes and safari tents for rent. Off site: Sandy beach 900 m. Fishing 1 km. Riding 2 km. Golf 5 km. Walking and cycle routes.

Open: 1 April - 28 October.

Directions

Head north from Alkmaar on N9 (towards Den Helder) as far as Zand. Here, follow signs to Groote Keeten and the site. GPS: 52.856165, 4.71719

Charges guide

Per unit incl. 2 persons and electricity	€ 24.00 - € 39.50
extra person	€ 4.40
dog	€ 3.00

Julianadorp aan Zee
Camping 't Noorder Sandt

Noorder Sandt 2, NL-1787 CX Julianadorp aan Zee (Noord-Holland) T: 0223 641 266.
E: noordersandt@ardoer.com **alanrogers.com/NL6866**

Close to the marine city of Den Helder and about 600 m. from a wide, sandy beach is Camping 't Noorder Sandt. Adjacent to the site is the Duinvliet, a route for hikers, cyclists and horse riders – you can even do the route in a canoe! Some 223 open and shady touring pitches are available here. They are comfortable and are all equipped with 10A electricity; 60 also have water, drainage and cable connections. Also worth noting is the friendly atmosphere here and also the well maintained sanitary facilities. For many, the site's main attraction is its sub-tropical paradise pool complex. In the early mornings, it is only open for older people to start the day, and after 10am it is open to all. Clean air, space and relaxation are only a few of the site's advantages. You could walk on the Wad, try a spot of sea fishing, or take an excursion to one of the Dutch islands. The site is not far from the famous city of Alkmaar with its cheese market, and the Dutch capital of Amsterdam. A member of the Ardoer group.

Facilities

Two good toilet blocks with controllable hot showers and open style washbasins. Facilities for disabled campers. Laundry with washing machines and dryers. Well equipped campers' kitchen. Kiosk for basics. Restaurant. Indoor pool with fun pool and slide. Fishing. Riding. Bicycle hire. Canoes for hire. Entertainment team in high season. Free WiFi over site. Off site: Beach and sailing 600 m. Alkmaar and Amsterdam are nearby.

Open: 26 March - 26 October.

Directions

From the N9 take exit for Julianadorp and Julianadorp aan Zee. From Julianadorp follow the site signs. Site is to the north of Julianadorp aan Zee. GPS: 52.90667, 4.72499

Charges guide

Per unit incl. 2 persons and electricity	€ 22.00 - € 39.00
extra person (over 2 yrs)	€ 5.95
dog	€ 4.25

ADRESS Noordersandt 2
1787 CX Julianadorp aan Zee
The Netherlands
TEL +31 223 641 266
www.ardoer.com/noordersandt

't Noorder Sandt
CAMPING FUN FOR FAMILY AND PETS

FREE Alan Rogers Travel Card
Extra benefits and savings - see page 12

Hilversum
Camping De Zonnehoek

Noodweg 50, NL-1213 PZ Hilversum (Noord-Holland) T: 0355 771 926. E: info@campingzonnehoek.com

alanrogers.com/NL6835

Camping de Zonnehoek is situated in the beautiful wooded surroundings of Hilversum and the lakes of Loosdrechtse Plassen. It is a family run site which offers its guests a quiet holiday in a natural environment and lots of facilities for children. There are 120 spacious pitches with 60 for touring units. All pitches have 4A electricity and most have plenty of shade. A trip around the castles in the surroundings area takes you back to the 17th and 18th centuries. The Loosdrechtse Plassen are ideal for all kinds of watersports and fishing.

Facilities

One traditional and one modern toilet block are very clean. Washbasins in cubicles. Hot water for showers on payment (€ 0.50 coin). Facilities for disabled campers (key access). Laundry. Motorcaravan services. Bar and restaurant (all day in high season). Games area with games, books, electronic games and screen for films. Play area. Club for children and entertainment team. WiFi over site (charged). Off site: Watersports and fishing. Scenic trips by plane and parachute jumping. Golf 9 km.

Open: 15 March - 31 October.

Directions

Follow A1 from Amsterdam and take exit for Hilversum (N201). At roundabout turn right, right again at second roundabout and at next roundabout turn left. Continue on this road and site is on the left just after the airport. GPS: 52.19343, 5.15521

Charges guide

Per unit incl. 2 persons and electricity	€ 16.00
extra person	€ 3.00
child (6-12 yrs)	€ 1.50

Noord-Scharwoude
Droompark Molengroet

Molengroet 1, NL-1723 PX Noord-Scharwoude (Noord-Holland) T: 0226 393 444. E: info@molengroet.nl

alanrogers.com/NL5700

Molengroet is a pleasant, modern site close to a watersports complex and only 40 km. from Amsterdam. It is a good place to stop on the way to the Afsluitdijk (the 32 km. dyke across the top of the IJsselmeer) or as a holiday site for watersports enthusiasts. There are 295 pitches, 157 for tourers have electricity (10A) and TV point, and 100 of these also have water and waste water points. The standard pitches are on the small side. The remaining pitches have quality mobile homes. The café/restaurant was welcoming and the prices were reasonable. A member of the Holland Tulip Parcs Group.

Facilities

Modern, heated sanitary facilities. Motorcaravan services. Gas supplies. Shop. Restaurant/bar (evenings only). Café and takeaway snacks. Small outdoor swimming pool (heated in high season). Play area. Sports field. Boules. Fishing. Bicycle hire. WiFi over site (charged). Entertainment in high season. Off site: Watersports. Tennis, squash, sauna, and swimming nearby. Riding 250 m. Golf 5 km.

Open: 1 April - 31 October.

Directions

From Haarlem on A9 to Alkmaar take N245 towards Schagen. Site is southwest of Noord Sharwoude on the N245, signed to west on road to Geestermerambacht GPS: 52.69455, 4.77103

Charges guide

Per unit incl. 2 persons and electricity	€ 19.50 - € 30.00
extra person (over 2 yrs)	€ 3.00 - € 5.00
Camping Cheques accepted.	

Sint-Maartenszee
Duincamping De Lepelaar

Westerduinweg 15, NL-1753 BA Sint-Maartenszee (Noord-Holland) T: 0224 56 13 51. E: info@delepelaar.nl

alanrogers.com/NL6886

De Lepelaar is perfectly situated for experiencing wild camping among the dune roses, birch, and brier bushes, in a sheltered dune valley or on top of a dune. Some of the spacious pitches have electricity and no two are the same. De Kleine Stern snack bar has a terrace and offers reasonably priced dishes. Takeaway meals are also available. There is a bus stop adjacent to the site, and from late June to early September a bus service passes the various beaches, recreation areas and villages along the coast.

Facilities

Four heated toilet blocks with all necessary facilities. Hot showers (€ 0,60) or a bucket of hot water (€ 0,20) are available. Washing machine and dryer. Small shop stocking essentials and fresh bread. Good snack bar. Freezer. Bicycle hire. WiFi in reception area (charged). Off site: Beach 1.5 km. Riding 9 km. Golf 15 km.

Open: 23 March - 22 September.

Directions

From the N9 Alkmaar-Den Helder road take the exit for Sint-Maartenszee, towards the dunes. Continue straight on until you reach the dunes. At roundabout turn right and after 1.5 km. the site reception is on the left. GPS: 52.802603, 4.696484

Charges guide

Per unit incl. 2 persons and electricity	€ 20.00 - € 32.00
extra person	€ 3.00 - € 3.50
dog	€ 3.00 - € 3.50

For latest campsite news, availability and prices visit
alanrogers.com

Sint-Maartenszee
Camping Sint-Maartenszee

Westerduinweg 30, NL-1753 BA Sint-Maartenszee (Noord-Holland) T: 0224 561 401.
E: info@campingsintmaartenszee.nl **alanrogers.com/NL5740**

Within easy travelling distance of the attractive and interesting towns of North Holland, especially Alkmaar, this excellent family site is separated from the sea by 900 m. of grassy dunes. With the dune environment, the ground is basically sandy but grass has grown well and hedges are now established. Specialising in family holidays, unusually for the Netherlands only touring units are taken (with a bungalow park adjacent). The 325 pitches are arranged in lines backed by high hedging. All have 6A electricity and 123 are fully serviced with water, drainage and cable TV connections. There is a good restaurant/bar with an attractive terrace. Overlooking the minigolf, there is a sitting area with an open fire, board games and WiFi. This is a pretty and interesting area of the Netherlands and Sint Maartenszee is quite near the fascinating man-made barrier built to form the IJsselmeer, which allowed the reclamation of so much land.

Facilities

Two modern toilet blocks are in neat, low buildings. Hot water for showers is free (with a fascinating panel demonstrating how solar power helps to heat the water). Private washing cabins, family shower rooms, baby bathrooms and raised level showers for children. Three private bathrooms to rent. Kitchen with hot water on payment and microwave. Laundry room with washing machines and dryer on payment. Motorcaravan services. Gas. Shop. Restaurant/bar, takeaway (all season). Bicycle hire. Play areas. Minigolf. Recreation room. WiFi (charged). Off site: Fishing 1 km. Bus service from village to Alkmaar (cheese market Fridays April-Sept).

Open: 22 March - 29 September.

Directions

From Alkmaar, take N9 northwards towards Den Helder. Site is signed after 18 km. towards the sea at St Maartensvlotbrug. GPS: 52.79428, 4.68835

Charges guide

Per unit incl. 2 persons and electricity	€ 20.00 - € 36.00
extra person (over 2 yrs)	€ 4.00

No credit cards.

ADRESS Westerduinweg 30 | 1753 BA Sint Maartenszee | The Netherlands
TEL +31 224 561 401 | www.ardoer.com/sintmaartenszee
Sint Maartens Zee
ENJOY, NATURALLY
CAMPING

Tuitjenhorn
Campingpark De Bongerd

Bongerdlaan 3, NL-1747 CA Tuitjenhorn (Noord-Holland) T: 0226 391 481. E: info@bongerd.nl
alanrogers.com/NL5705

Campingpark De Bongerd is an attractive, child friendly site with 550 pitches. Of these, 159 are for touring units arranged separately from static units and seasonal pitches in a former orchard. The grass touring areas are immaculately kept with 10A electricity, drainage and cable TV connections. Some of the pitches are smaller than others. The main attraction at this site is a large indoor play hall, De Holle Bolle Boom, which is where the enthusiastic entertainment team is based. There are ponds for adventure play with floating games and small beaches, and an open-air pool (10x15 m) with paddling pool. In high season and school holidays the site organises an extensive activity programme. De Bongerd is a pretty site with friendly management and English is spoken.

Facilities

Modern toilet block with preset, hot showers (free), washbasins (open and in cabins) and toilets. Toilets and washbasins for children. Fully equipped baby room. Laundry with washing machines and dryers. Shop, bar and restaurants (April-Sept). Swimming and paddling pools. Indoor play hall and several outdoor play areas. Playing field. Tennis. Boules. Bicycle hire. Fishing. Entertainment programme. WiFi over site (charged). Off site: Beach, golf and riding 10 km.

Open: 28 March - 29 September.

Directions

Site is north of Tuitjenhorn, which is some 15 km. north of Alkmaar. It is well signed on the N245 road to Schagen. GPS: 52.735064, 4.774407

Charges guide

Per unit incl. 2-5 persons and all services	€ 28.90 - € 46.50
extra person	€ 3.50 - € 5.40
dog	€ 2.35

Camping Cheques accepted.

FREE Alan Rogers Travel Card
Extra benefits and savings - see page 12

CAPITAL: ZWOLLE

Overijssel sits on sandy soil dissected by rivers and streams, except in the northwest, where polders and lakes dominate. It has three regions: Kop van Overijssel, Twente and Salland.

The meandering IJssel river carves a route through the classic landscape of Holland; past beaches, ports and the unswerving lines of the Mastenbroek polder, one of the oldest in the Netherlands. The flood plains stand in sharp contrast to the Hanseatic towns of Kampen, Zwolle, Deventer and Hasselt; beautiful towns on shimmering water, where monuments from the past stand proudly in a contemporary setting. Salland, a lesser known part of eastern Holland, is a paradise for cyclists with romantic castles, tree-lined roads and traditional farms.

Weerribben-Wieden National Park is the principal low-lying marshland of Northwest Europe – an endless maze of narrow strips of water, mysterious forests and swampy reed beds. Twente is the country seat of the Netherlands, where historic towns and villages, and impressive estates such as Twickel and Weldam now stand alongside the newer wellness resorts. In the peaceful Vechtdal, with its Saxon farmhouses and ancient forests, nature imposes her own unique atmosphere of verdant tranquillity.

Places of interest

Giethoorn: 'Green Venice' where electric boats glide silently through the water and under the characteristic high bridges.

Kampen: city of monuments with no less than 500 examples including old and new town halls, the new tower and three city gates.

Zwolle: founded in the 9th century, with many historic buildings dating from the 15th century - the golden age of Zwolle.

Hattem: old town with historic buildings, the Anton Pieck Museum and the National Bakery Museum.

Industrial heritage in Twente: cycling and walking trails taking in buildings used in the textile and metal industries.

Delden: Salt Museum – all you need to know about salt, including that it is extracted at the nearby Twickel estate.

Attractions

Slagharen: discover and enjoy over 40 attractions including shows and parades in this family adventure park.

Estate Anningahof: sculpture park on the edge of Zwolle with new exhibitions annually.

Hellendoorn: adventure park with more than 30 attractions, including a new show based on the Excalibur legend.

De Holterberg: part of the Sallandse Ridge National Park with nature diorama, museum, Canadian war cemetery, minigolf and five restaurants.

De Scheg sports complex: superb swimming facility with adventure river, bubbles, 80 m. water slide, etc.

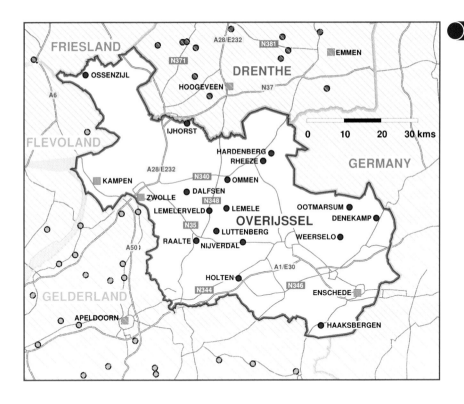

Dalfsen
Vechtdalcamping Het Tolhuis
Het Lageveld 8, NL-7722 HV Dalfsen (Overijssel) T: 0529 458 383. E: info@tolhuis.com

alanrogers.com/NL6000

Vechtdalcamping Het Tolhuis is a pleasant, well established site with 195 pitches. Of these, 70 are for tourers, arranged on well kept, grassy lawns off paved and gravel access roads. All touring pitches have 4-10A electricity, water, waste water, cable and WiFi. Some are shaded by mature trees and bushes. The touring pitches are located apart from static units. To the rear of the site is an open-air pool (25x8 m. and heated by solar power) with a small paddling pool for toddlers with new attractive terracing. The only disadvantage is a railway that runs along the back of the site, but this should not cause too many problems.

Facilities

Two heated toilet blocks, an immaculate new one to the front and an older one to the back, with toilets, washbasins (open style and in cabins) and controllable hot showers (key). Some rain and body showers. Special, attractive children's section. Family shower rooms. Baby room. Laundry. Small shop (bread daily). Restaurant/bar also serves snacks and drinks. Open-air pool with paddling pool. Playing field. Playground and trampoline. Entertainment team for children (high season). ATM point. WiFi over site (charged). Gas barbecues only. Dogs are not accepted in high season. Off site: Riding 3 km. Fishing 5 km. Golf 7 km.

Open: 1 April - 1 October.

Directions

From the A28 take exit 21 and continue east towards Dalfsen. Site is signed in Dalfsen.
GPS: 52.50228, 6.3224

Charges guide

Per unit incl. 2 persons and electricity	€ 25.00 - € 40.25
extra person	€ 3.50
dog (not high season)	€ 4.00
No credit cards.	

Denekamp

Camping De Papillon

Kanaalweg 30, NL-7591 NH Denekamp (Overijssel) T: 0541 351 670. E: info@depapillon.nl

alanrogers.com/NL6470

De Papillon is perhaps one of the best and most enjoyable campsites in the Netherlands. All 245 touring pitches are spacious (120-160 sq.m), all have electricity (4/10/16A), and 220 have water and drainage. An impressive, new sanitary block has state-of-the-art equipment and uses green technology. There is a new entertainment centre with outdoor auditorium for children, and the water play area by the adventure playground and covered, heated pool is among the most imaginative and exciting we have seen. The restored heathland area offers opportunities for nature lovers; there is also a large fishing lake and a swimming lake with beach area and activities. A member of Leading Campings group.

Facilities

Two large sanitary buildings with showers, toilets, washbasins in cabins, facilities for babies and for disabled visitors. Laundry room. Spacious reception area with supermarket, restaurant, bar and takeaway. Heated pool with children's pool and sliding roof. Lake swimming with sandy beach. New adventure play area and smaller play areas. Pétanque. Bicycle hire. Fishing pond. Tennis. Pets to stroke. Luxury bungalows to rent (good views). New water spray park for children up to 13 yrs. WiFi (free).

Open: 29 March - 1 October.

Directions

From the A1 take exit 32 (Oldenzaal-Denekamp) and continue to Denekamp. Pass Denekamp and turn right at village of Noord-Deurningen and follow signs to site. GPS: 52.39200, 7.04900

Charges guide

Per unit incl. 2 persons and 4A electricity	€ 27.00
incl. full services	€ 30.50
extra person	€ 4.25

Haaksbergen

Camping Scholtenhagen

Scholtenhagenweg 30, NL-7481 VP Haaksbergen (Overijssel) T: 053 572 2384.
E: campingscholtenhagen@planet.nl **alanrogers.com/NL6442**

In the province of Overijssel, with its green landscape of ancient forests, fens, moors and farmland, Scholtenhagen is a welcoming campsite near the village of Haaksbergen. The 100 touring pitches (up to 120 sq m.) are set amongst established trees and hedges, which offer some shade, together with many pitches for long term units. All touring pitches have access to electricity (10A Europlug) and 35 also have water and waste water. Next to the site (free tickets from reception) is a leisure pool complex with areas for relaxing and sun bathing together with a sauna and Turkish bath.

Facilities

Sanitary facilities with provision for families, babies and visitors with disabilities. Washing machines and dryers. Motorcaravan services. Bar, restaurant and takeaway (10/7-25/7). Multisports field. Play areas. Heated indoor swimming pool (2/1-31/12). Games room. Boules area. Television room. Entertainment programme for adults and children, and miniclub (high season). Bicycle hire. WiFi on part of site (free). Torches useful. No charcoal barbecues.

Open: All year.

Directions

Site is about 15 km. southwest of Enschede. Turn south from the N18 south of Haaksbergen and follow signs to site. GPS: 52.14805, 6.72479

Charges guide

Per unit incl. 2 persons and electricity	€ 27.60
extra person	€ 6.00
child (1-12 yrs)	€ 5.50
dog	€ 5.00

Hardenberg

Sprookjescamping De Vechtstreek

Grote Beltenweg 17, NL-7794 RA Rheeze-Hardenberg (Overijssel) T: 0523 261 369.
E: info@sprookjescamping.nl **alanrogers.com/NL5990**

It would be difficult for any child (or adult) to pass this site and not be curiously drawn to the oversized open story book which marks its entrance. From here young children turn the pages and enter the exciting world of Hannah and Bumpie, two of the nine characters around which this site's fairytale theme has been created. There are 270 touring pitches (all with 6-12A electricity) mostly laid out in small bays. Indoor and outdoor pools for children are excellent, and a new outdoor pool with terrace caters for adults and older children. There is a comprehensive daily recreation programme for children.

Facilities

Three modern, well equipped and heated toilet blocks with baby rooms, separate child sections and family showers. Two laundry rooms. Sauna, solarium and jacuzzi. Well stocked supermarket, restaurant, snack bar and takeaway (all season). Play areas. Fairytale water play park (heated). Daily activity club. Football field. Theatre. Swimming, fishing and boating area at rear of site (200 m). WiFi (free).

Open: Easter - 30 September and last two weeks of October.

Directions

From Ommen take N34 Hardenberg road for 9 km. Turn right on N36 and go south for 3.5 km. Turn left at first crossroads and after 200 m. left again on local road towards Rheeze. Follow signs for Sprookjescamping. GPS: 52.54614, 6.57103

Charges guide

Per unit incl. 2 persons and electricity	€ 26.25 - € 44.00
extra person	€ 3.30 - € 4.75

For latest campsite news, availability and prices visit

alanrogers.com

Hardenberg
Camping De Zandstuve

Grose Beltenweg 3, NL-7794 RA Rheeze-Hardenberg (Overijssel) T: 0523 262 027. E: info@zandstuve.nl
alanrogers.com/NL5995

De Zandstuve rightly promotes itself as a holiday village for children. Amenities include an attractively decorated indoor pool with two fun pools (one in forest style, the other as a shipwreck), an outdoor pool, little play areas on most fields and a giant indoor play castle. Large, grassy, circular meadows surrounded by mature trees (which provide some shade in summer) provide 400 pitches with 360 used for touring units. All have 6/16A electricity and a water tap, and 360 full service pitches include electricity, water, drain and TV aerial point. There is also a full entertainment programme in high season with theatre and musical nights. Single sex groups are not accepted.

Facilities

Three modern toilet blocks with toilets, washbasins (some in cabins) and controllable hot showers. Family bathrooms. Baby room. Facilities for disabled visitors. Washing machines and dryers. Motorcaravan services. Shop. Bar/restaurant and takeaway. Heated indoor and outdoor pools. Entertainment for children (high season). Play areas and indoor play castle (€ 5). Bicycle hire. WiFi (charged).
Open: 28 March - 23 October.

Directions

From Zwolle follow N340 road east towards Ommen and from there the N34 east towards Hardenberg. Site is signed 2 km. from Hardenberg. GPS: 52.55862, 6.58761

Charges guide

Per unit incl. 2 persons and electricity	€ 21.00 - € 43.00

Hardenberg
Vakantiepark Het Stoetenslagh

Elfde Wijk 42, NL-7797 HH Rheezerveen-Hardenberg (Overijssel) T: 0523 638 260. E: info@stoetenslagh.nl
alanrogers.com/NL6004

Arriving at Het Stoetenslagh and passing reception, you reach the pride of the campsite; a large natural lake with several little beaches. Many hours can be spent swimming, canoeing or sailing a dinghy here. There are 309 spacious grass touring pitches (120-140 sq.m) divided between several fields and arranged around clean sanitary buildings. Each field also has a small volleyball area and climbing frames. You may choose between nature pitches, standard pitches or serviced pitches with water, drainage, 10A electricity and cable connection. There are climbing frames for children, much space for playing, a children's club and, particularly popular with little ones, a small animal farm.

Facilities

Three toilet blocks include private cabins, baby facilities, family showers and facilities for disabled visitors. Beach shower. Washing machines and dryers. Motorcaravan services. Shop. Restaurant with bar. Snack bar with takeaway. Disco, bowling, curling and archery (all indoor). New indoor pool. Natural pool with sandy beaches. Canoeing. Play areas. Fishing. Bicycle hire. Activities for children and teenagers. Bouncy castle. WiFi (free).
Open: 1 April - 30 September.

Directions

From A28 exit at junction 22 onto N377 towards Slagharen. Before Slagharen take N343 towards Hardenberg. Continue past Lutten exit then first right. Site is in 3 km. GPS: 52.58694, 6.53049

Charges guide

Per serviced pitch incl. 2 persons, electricity, water and waste water	€ 22.50 - € 40.00
extra person	€ 4.50

Hardenberg
Recreatiecentrum 't Rheezerwold

Larixweg 7, NL-7796 HT Hardenberg (Overijssel) T: 0523 264 595. E: info@rheezerwold.nl
alanrogers.com/NL6005

Situated in the beautiful countryside around Hardenberg, this site offers a wide range of facilities. There are 90 large, comfortable pitches on grass, arranged in small fields. All are numbered, have 6-10A electricity, water and drainage, and access is easy. There are 55 pitches with full services. Seasonal units occupy 100 pitches but these are away from the touring area and do not infringe on the appearance of the site. Much emphasis is put on family entertainment and this is a site run with families in mind. The Palstring family will make you most welcome. Amenities include a large, glass-roofed centre, two swimming pools, one indoor, the other outdoor and both are heated.

Facilities

Clean, well maintained toilet blocks have showers in cubicles, hot water on payment. Facilities for disabled visitors. Laundry. Small, well stocked shop (July/Aug and holidays, then w/ends only). Restaurant/snack bar. Bar with large screen TV. Heated outdoor and indoor pools, separate pool for young children. Sauna. Solarium. Entertainment daily in season. Tennis. Playgrounds. Air trampoline. Boules. Bicycle hire. WiFi (charged).
Open: 1 April - 30 October.

Directions

From Zwolle take N34 north and look for the ANWB board at km. 29.0. Site is well signed. From Hardenberg take N34 south and look for the same board. GPS: 52.574459, 6.56604

Charges guide

Per unit incl. 2 persons and electricity	€ 18.50 - € 26.50
extra person (over 2 yrs)	€ 3.00 - € 3.50
dog (max. 2)	€ 2.00

FREE Alan Rogers Travel Card
Extra benefits and savings - see page 12

Hardenberg
Camping De Vechtvallei

Rheezerweg 76, NL-7795 DA Hardenberg (Overijssel) T: 0523 25 18 00. E: info@devechtvallei.nl

alanrogers.com/NL6443

Camping De Vechtvallei is in the River Vecht valley, surrounded by magnificent, varied scenery of forests, dunes and lakes. Of the 170 pitches, 45 are for touring, on grass and separated by hedges. All have 16A electricity and 14 are fully serviced. There are central play areas for young children. In addition, there are chalets, hiker cabins and bungalows to rent. The countryside can be appreciated from the restaurant and bar terrace and explored on foot and by bicycle on the many paths and tracks. Visitors can enjoy the sports and activities offered by the site that range from volleyball to flower arranging.

Facilities

Modern, heated sanitary facility with small toilets for children, baby bathroom. Restaurant and takeaway with terrace (all season). Swimming pool and jacuzzi (heated 1/5-1/9). Small children's outdoor pool (May-Aug). Football and volleyball fields. Trampolines. Basketball. Holiday activity programme for all ages. Flower arranging workshop (on request). Internet café. Bicycle hire. WiFi over site (charged). Off site: Hiking and cycle tracks nearby. River De Vecht for canoeing and fishing 500 m.

Open: 1 April - 31 October.

Directions

Site is 6 km. southwest of Hardenberg. From A35 take exit 31 onto N36 for 22.7 km. then east onto Beerzerweg. After 350 m. turn left onto Stuwdijk and continue onto Rheezerweg. After 2.4 km. turn right onto restricted usage road and campsite is on right. GPS: 52.535536, 6.569633

Charges guide

Per unit incl. 2 persons and electricity	€ 15.00 - € 20.00
extra person	€ 3.25

Holten
Camping De Holterberg

Reebokkenweg 8, NL-7451 HL Holten (Overijssel) T: 0548 361 524. E: info@campingdeholterberg.nl

alanrogers.com/NL6490

De Holterberg, family run for 62 years, is located in the Sallandse Heuvelrug nature reserve near the Holterberg hill. The wooded site is open all year with 250 level pitches, all with 6A electricity. A new, impressive reception with a separate bar/restaurant are in traditional, thatched buildings. Children will love the animal park and the new play area with its large equipment. The site has very large woods for walking and is very close to long-distance paths. Solar energy use and a new wood burning system promote its green image.

Facilities

Three solar heated toilet blocks (one older) with toilets, washbasins and controllable free hot showers (in cabins). Family shower rooms. Baby room. En-suite facilities for disabled visitors. Laundry. Free cooking facilities. Bar/restaurant and takeaway. Bread in season. Heated outdoor swimming pool (May-Sept). Multisports court. Bicycle hire. Cross-country skiing in winter. Minigolf. Several playgrounds. Animal farm. Boules. Internet. Recreation team in high season. Horse pasture for rent.

Open: All year.

Directions

Follow the A1 from Amsterdam-Enschede and take exit for Markelo-Holten Oost. Continue towards Holten and just before village take N350 towards Rijssen. At roundabout site is signed. GPS: 52.291584, 6.434064

Charges guide

Per unit incl. 2 persons and electricity	€ 20.80 - € 25.10
extra person (over 2 yrs)	€ 6.00 - € 6.90

IJhorst
Familiecamping De Vossenburcht

Bezoensweg 5, NL-7955 PT IJhorst (Overijssel) T: 052 244 1626. E: info@devossenburcht.nl

alanrogers.com/NL6502

A pleasant, wooded family campsite in a rural location in the north of the country, De Vossenburcht has 385 pitches of which 305 are seasonal and 80 are available for tourers. They are level, a few in the open but mainly among the trees, and with electrical connections available. This is one of the most beautiful parts of Overijssel where you can still enjoy the beautiful forests and farmland. Nearby are moors, fens and attractive old farmhouses. The village of IJhorst has a few shops whilst the neighbouring towns of Meppel, Hoogeveen and Zwolle offer a wider choice of shops, bars and restaurants.

Facilities

Heated sanitary block with provision for babies, children and disabled visitors. Washing machines and dryers. Motorcaravan service point. Shop. Bar with pool table and TV, snack bar with takeaway provision (1/4-1/11). Heated outdoor swimming and children's pools (1/5-15/9). Large children's playground. Children's entertainment in high season. Table tennis and table football. WiFi throughout (charged). Off site: IJhorst 850 m. Bicycle hire 2 km.

Open: All year.

Directions

From A28 (Zwolle/Groningen) leave at exit 24 (De Wijk). At roundabout under motorway, head northeast for 4.8 km. then bear right for 2 km. to IJhorst. Continue along Heerenweg for 800 m. where site is signed to right. GPS: 52.65664, 6.30191

Charges guide

Per unit incl. 2 persons and electricity	€ 19.50 - € 25.00
extra person	€ 3.50

Lemele
Natuurcamping De Lemeler Esch

Lemelerweg 16, NL-8148 PC Lemele (Overijssel) T: 0572 331 241. E: info@lemeleresch.nl
alanrogers.com/NL6460

This site is reminiscent of camping as it used to be, but with modern facilities including 190 spacious grass pitches for touring units, 114 with all comforts such as water, drainage, electricity, cable TV, WiFi and even a private bathroom if desired. The pitches are arranged on large grass meadows, some with shade from tall trees, others more in the open. The natural woodland setting gives this site a special atmosphere that allows children to explore and make friends. The good playground and a heated swimming pool are additional fun for children. This site will also appeal to adults as there are kilometres of cycling and walking tracks in the woods and across the moors.

Facilities

Good modern toilet block with controllable showers, open style washbasins and well decorated facilities for children. Baby room. Family shower rooms. Facilities for disabled visitors. Private sanitary facilities for rent. Laundry. Shop for basics. Bar/restaurant. Heated outdoor swimming pool with paddling pool. Playing field. Indoor play hall. Bicycle hire. WiFi over site (charged). Entertainment team. Accommodation to rent. Dogs are not accepted.

Open: 27 March - 26 October.

Directions

From the A1 take exit 28 and continue north on the N347 all the way to Lemele. Site is signed on the N347. GPS: 52.46711, 6.42478

Charges guide

Per unit incl. 2 persons and electricity	€ 19.85 - € 46.25
extra person	€ 4.40 - € 5.60

Lemelerveld
Camping Heidepark

Verbindingsweg 2A, NL-8151 PP Lemelerveld (Overijssel) T: 0572 371 525. E: info@campingheidepark.nl
alanrogers.com/NL6487

Camping Heidepark is centrally located in Overijssel, near the Salland Ridge, and convenient for excellent hiking and cycling routes. This southern tip of the Overijssels Vecht valley has a great deal to offer holidaymakers. Heidepark is a car-free site, set in spacious, landscaped parkland. There are 100 touring pitches (all with 6/10A electricity, water, drainage and TV connections) spread across eight camping fields. Pitches are arranged around the edge of the grassy fields and are bordered by thick woods. A large, indoor activity room will appeal to all children, including teenagers. There is plenty of space for children to play safely in the middle of each field.

Facilities

Two modern toilet blocks with baby room. Family shower room and facilities for children. Laundry. Shop. Terrace bar. Heated swimming and paddling pools with terrace. Natural swimming pool adjacent. Play areas. Play attic for children. Indoor playground. Tennis. Football. Library. Bicycle and go-kart hire. Separate fields for dog owners. WiFi throughout (charged).

Open: 1 April - 1 October.

Directions

From A28 motorway (Amersfoort-Zwolle), take exit 18 (Zwolle-Zuid), and then N35 (Almelo/Heino). At Raalte head towards Ommen, and then Lemelerveld, and follow signs to site. At Verbindingsweg, site is by Sportpark Heideberg. GPS: 52.439897, 6.346163

Charges guide

Per unit incl. 2 persons and electricity	€ 17.50 - € 37.00

Luttenberg
Recreatiepark De Luttenberg

Heuvelweg 9, NL-8105 SZ Luttenberg (Overijssel) T: 0572 301 405. E: receptie@luttenberg.nl
alanrogers.com/NL5810

A new indoor pool and wellness centre opened in 2012 at this very smart woodland site, which is well placed for either an active or peaceful holiday. It is a large park with 190 touring pitches (all with 10A electricity) in a central area off tarmac access roads. The large, individual pitches are numbered and separated, in rows divided by hedges and trees, with easy access. New larger 200m² pitches are also available. There is a large bar and eating area with terrace and a small, separate restaurant. There is a comprehensive activity programme for children in high season. A member of the Holland Tulip Parcs.

Facilities

Two heated sanitary blocks with controllable showers. The newer block has family showers, a baby room and good facilities for disabled visitors. Small laundry. Motorcaravan services. Gas. Shop, bar and restaurant (low season: Fri-Sun). Outdoor swimming pool (01/07-31/08). New indoor pool (01/04-30/09) and wellness centre (1/4-30/9). Library. TV room with area for children. Tennis. Football. Boules. Bicycle hire. Minigolf. WiFi over site (free).

Open: 31 March - 1 October.

Directions

From N35 Zwolle-Almelo turn on N348 Ommen road east of Raalte, then turn to Luttenberg and follow signs. From A1 (Amsterdam-Hengelo) take exit 23 at Deventer on N348, then as above. GPS: 52.42830, 6.46127

Charges guide

Per unit incl. 2 persons and electricity	€ 22.00 - € 32.00

Camping Cheques accepted.

FREE Alan Rogers Travel Card
Extra benefits and savings - see page 12

Nijverdal
Overijssel Vakantiepark Mölke

Molendijk 107, NL-7466 PD Zuna/Nijverdal (Overijssel) T: 0548 512 743. E: info@molke.nl
alanrogers.com/NL5815

You will receive a warm welcome at Vakantiepark Mölke, which is located on the banks of the lovely River Regge, around 5 km. south of Nijverdal. This river is ideal for canoeing and boat trips (hire available on site) and there are endless opportunities for cycling and walking in this region. This is a family site with much to do for children of all ages, with its excellent new indoor play area and ten-pin bowling alley. The 75 touring pitches (all with 4-16A electricity) are in three categories: standard, comfort (with water and drainage) and super comfort (with private sanitary unit). A range of quality rental accommodation is available. The shop, bar and large, friendly restaurant and the reception are closed on Sunday.

Facilities

Two toilet blocks are fairly modern and very clean. Free showers. Facilities for disabled visitors (key access). Small laundry. Shop. Bar. Child friendly restaurant. Café with terrace overlooking harbour. Snack bar. Indoor pool (12x8 m) and paddling pool. Indoor and outdoor play areas. Activity and entertainment programme (July/Aug). Canoe hire. Boat trips on the Regge. Tennis. Sports field. Archery. 10-pin bowling. WiFi over site (charged).

Open: Easter - 25 October.

Directions

Mölke is near the N347 between Rijssen (1 km) and Nijverdal (5 km) in the small village of Zuna. Site is well signed. GPS: 52.32633, 6.51873

Charges guide

Per unit incl. 2 persons and electricity	€ 28.00 - € 39.00
extra person	€ 4.50
dog	€ 2.50

Nijverdal
Camping De Noetselerberg

Holterweg 116, NL-7441 DK Nijverdal (Overijssel) T: 0548 612 665. E: noetselerberg@ardoer.com
alanrogers.com/NL6464

This is a true paradise for children – Camping De Noetselerberg has several play areas and fields for children and also a splendid covered play area for when weather is less than pleasant. There is a sub-tropical style swimming pool with a pirate ship and a 35 m. water slide. A recreation team provides hours of organised fun for children. The 200 grass touring pitches are spacious and are arranged on open fields which are surrounded by trees and shrubs. All have 10A electricity, water and drainage. Good quality facilities include a well equipped toilet block and a fine bistro, De Oale Sté. The forest of the national park begins at the site for those who enjoy nature.

Facilities

Three well located toilet blocks provide washbasins (open style and in cabins), toilets and controllable hot showers. Facilities for children. Family shower room. Facilities for disabled visitors. Laundry with washing machines, dryer and spin dryer. Shop. Bar/restaurant. Indoor and outdoor pools with slide and fun pool (1/5-1/9). Bicycle hire. Indoor playground. Full entertainment programme in high season. WiFi (charged). Off site: Riding 10 km. Golf 15 km.

Open: 23 March - 27 October.

Directions

From the A1 take exit 28 and continue on the N347 towards Nijverdal. Follow the site signs in Nijverdal. GPS: 52.34991, 6.45458

Charges guide

Per unit incl. 2 persons and electricity	€ 22.00 - € 37.00
extra person (over 2 yrs)	€ 4.00
dog (max. 1)	€ 3.00

Ommen
Camping De Kleine Wolf

Coevorderweg 25, Stegeren, NL-7737 PK Ommen (Overijssel) T: 0529 457 203. E: info@kleinewolf.nl
alanrogers.com/NL5975

Camp De Kleine Wolf is close to Vecht in a beautiful part of the eastern Netherlands making it an ideal base for walking or cycling through the woods or along the River Vecht. The site has 550 pitches, including 360 for touring units, all with electricity (8A), water, drainage and TV point. They are on large, grassy fields surrounded by mature trees that provide shade, and most have a little play area. This site actively encourages teenage visitors, having a special clubroom and plenty of sports provision. There is also a full activity programme in high season for younger children.

Facilities

Two modern blocks provide toilets, washbasins (some in cabins) and controllable hot showers. Child size toilets, showers and washbasins. Family bathroom. Baby room. Facilities for disabled visitors (key). Laundry facilities. Shop (daily in season). Bar/restaurant. Indoor (10x5 m) and outdoor (20x10 m) pool with paddling pools. Play areas and indoor play attic. Rowing lake. Fishing pond. Football field. Volleyball. Minigolf. Boules. WiFi over site (charged).

Open: 1 April - 23 September.

Directions

From Zwolle follow N340 east towards Ommen and from there the N34 towards Hardenberg. Site is on the left on the N34. GPS: 52.54462, 6.49545

Charges guide

Per unit incl. 2 persons, electricity and services	€ 21.00 - € 40.00
extra person	€ 4.00 - € 4.50
dog (max. 1)	€ 4.00

For latest campsite news, availability and prices visit
alanrogers.com

Ommen
Camping De Roos

Beerzerweg 10, NL-7736 PJ Beerze-Ommen (Overijssel) T: 0523 251 234. E: info@campingderoos.nl
alanrogers.com/NL5980

De Roos is a family run site in an Area of Outstanding Natural Beauty, truly a nature lovers' campsite, immersed in an atmosphere of tranquillity. It is situated in Overijssel's Vecht Valley, a unique region set in a river dune landscape on the River Vecht. The river and its tributary wind their way unhurriedly around and through this spacious campsite. It is a natural setting that the owners of De Roos have carefully preserved. The 275 pitches and necessary amenities have been blended into the landscape with great care. Pitches, most with electricity hook-up (6A Europlug), are naturally sited, some behind blackthorn thickets, in the shadow of an old oak, or in a clearing scattered with wild flowers. For some there are lovely views over the Vecht river. De Roos is a car-free campsite during peak periods – vehicles must be parked at the car park, except on arrival and departure. Motorcaravan owners can drive to their pitch then cycle or walk for the duration of their holiday. Vehicles are allowed on site in low season at extra cost. Swimming, fishing and boating are possible in the river, or from an inlet that runs up into the site where there is a small beach with a protected area for swimming and landing stages with steps. The enthusiastic owners have compiled walking and cycling routes written in English.

Facilities

Four well maintained sanitary blocks are kept fresh and clean. The two larger blocks are heated and include baby bath/shower and wash cabins. Launderette. Motorcaravan services. Gas supplies. Health food shop and tea room serving snacks (1/5-1/9). Bicycle hire. Playgrounds and field for kite flying. Sports field. Football. Volleyball. Boules. River swimming. Fishing. Internet (charged). Dogs are not accepted. Torch useful. Bungalows for rent.

Open: 11 April - 30 September.

Directions

Leave A28 at Ommen exit 21, join N340 for 19 km. to Ommen. Turn right at lights over bridge (River Vecht) and immediately left towards Beerze. Site on left after 7 km. GPS: 52.51075, 6.515059

Charges guide

Per unit incl. 2 persons and electricity	€ 19.70 - € 22.70
extra person	€ 3.20 - € 3.90

Ommen
Vrijetijdspark Beerze Bulten

Kampweg 1, NL-7736 PK Beerze-Ommen (Overijssel) T: 0523 251 398. E: info@beerzebulten.nl
alanrogers.com/NL5985

Beerze Bulten is a large leisure park with superb indoor and outdoor amenities, so you can enjoy yourself whatever the weather. A large, partly underground 'rabbit hole' provides a big indoor playground for children, a theatre for both indoor and outdoor shows, a buffet, a superb full wellness spa and a very large, specially designed indoor pool. Beerze Bulten has 550 pitches, mainly for touring units, but also accommodation for hire (all year). In the shade of mature woodland, all the pitches are level and numbered, and all have 10A Europlug electricity, water, drainage and TV connections. To the rear of the site is a large lake area with a sandy beach and new, exciting adventure play equipment.

Facilities

Several toilet blocks are well placed around the site, with washbasins in cabins and hot showers. Laundry. Shop. Bar and snack bar/restaurant with open-air terrace. Heated indoor and outdoor pool complex and spa centre. Multisports court. Bicycle hire. Indoor and outdoor play areas. Entertainment (July/Aug). WiFi over site (charged).

Open: April - November (accommodation all year).

Directions

From A28, take exit 21 (Ommen) and continue east towards Ommen. From Ommen, follow N34 northeast and turn south on N36 at crossing. Site is signed from there. GPS: 52.51139, 6.54618

Charges guide

Per unit incl. 2 persons and full service pitch	€ 23.00 - € 45.30
extra person	€ 4.00 - € 5.20

FREE Alan Rogers Travel Card
Extra benefits and savings - see page 12

Ommen
Camping De Koeksebelt

Zwolseweg 13, NL-7731 BC Ommen (Overijssel) T: 0529 451 378. E: info@koeksebelt.nl
alanrogers.com/NL6466

Camping De Koeksebelt is a well maintained, green site with 250 fully serviced, spacious touring pitches. All are equipped with 10A electricity, water, drainage and TV cable connections and are accessed off paved roads. Some hardstandings are available. Many of the pitches are on the banks of the river and are ideal for anglers as they can fish from their pitch. Good play areas will appeal to both children and their parents. The sanitary facilities are modern and very well maintained. The site borders a large wooded area and is within walking distance of the town of Ommen.

Facilities

Three modern toilet blocks with toilets, washbasins in cabins and controllable hot showers. Free bathroom. Baby room. Toilet for disabled visitors. Laundry with washing machines, dryers, spin dryer, iron and board. Small shop for basics. Bar/restaurant and takeaway (1/4-30/9). New outdoor heated swimming pool. Playing field. Tennis. Fishing. Watersports. Boules. Free boats for fishing. Bicycle hire. WiFi (charged). Max. 2 dogs.

Open: 27 March - 27 October.

Directions

From A28 take exit for Ommen and go east towards Ommen on N340. In Ommen, go right to cross River Vecht. After 300 m. turn right at exit r102 and site is on the right after 500 m. GPS: 52.51668, 6.41395

Charges guide

Per unit incl. 2 persons
and electricity   € 26.00 - € 37.50
No credit cards.

Ootmarsum
Camping de Haer

Rossummerstraat 22, NL-7636 PL Ootmarsum (Overijssel) T: 0541 291 847. E: info@dehaer.nl
alanrogers.com/NL6489

Camping de Haer is an attractive, family owned site in the municipality of Dinkelland, in the Dutch province of Overijssel. It is close to the picturesque town of Ootmarsum with its numerous art galleries, quaint streets and restaurants. The site has been in the Brun family for many years and is now run by brothers Bryan and Niels, who are slowly modernising the facilities. There are 120 level grass touring pitches (120-130 sq.m), some shaded, all with electricity (6A), water and drainage. There are three hardstandings for motorcaravans. It is an ideal location for couples looking for a peaceful site, and for families with young children who will enjoy the excellent play equipment. A sepkey (€ 15) is required for facilities using hot water.

Facilities

One large, modern sanitary block is spotlessly clean and has washbasins in cubicles, showers (on payment) and facilities for families and disabled visitors. Launderette. Bar, restaurant and takeaway (July/Aug). Outdoor swimming pool (1/5-30/9). Play area. Minigolf. Sports field. Free WiFi over site. Off site: Fishing 1 km. Shops 2 km. Riding and bicycle hire 2 km. Golf 15 km.

Open: 1 April - 1 November.

Directions

The site is on the N736 Ootmarsum-Oldenzaal road, 1.5 km. from Ootsmarsum and is well signed. GPS: 52.39006, 6.90168

Charges guide

Per unit incl. 2 persons and electricity   € 20.00
extra person (over 1 yr)   € 2.50
dog (max. 2)   € 1.50

Ossenzijl
Recreatiecentrum De Kluft

Hoogeweg 26, NL-8376 EM Ossenzijl (Overijssel) T: 0561 477 370. E: info@dekluft.nl
alanrogers.com/NL6230

De Kluft is located on the border of the two Dutch provinces of Friesland and Overijssel at the heart of the Weerribben-Wieden National Park. It is attractively situated with most of the pitches being along open waterways. The site has a very impressive range of amenities including a marina, hotel, restaurant and lodges. One area of the site is close to the marina and canoes, electric boats, rowing boats and bicycles can all be hired. Most of the 180 touring pitches have a view across the water (drainage variable) and all have electrical connections (6A). Children will be entertained by a very well designed play area, and at the small beach by a natural lake that is suitable for swimming.

Facilities

Five modern toilet blocks are spread over the site. They are clean and well maintained with showers (on payment) and good provision for children and disabled visitors. Motorcaravan services. Shop for basics (May-Aug). Restaurant and snack bar. Swimming in river and lake. Canoe school. Fishing. Bicycles, canoes, kayaks and sloops for hire. Hotel with eight rooms. Lodges to rent. Free WiFi over site. Group accommodation.

Open: 1 April - 30 October.

Directions

From A6 motorway take exit 15 (De Munt) and follow N331 and N352 towards Wolvega. Turn right in Kuinre and after 1.5 km. left to Ossenzijl (5 km). In Ossenzijl the site is clearly signed. GPS: 52.80785, 5.93188

Charges guide

Per unit incl. 2 persons and electricity   € 22.95
extra person   € 4.50
child (3-11 yrs)   € 2.50

For latest campsite news, availability and prices visit
alanrogers.com

Raalte
Familievakantiepark Krieghuusbelten

Krieghuusweg 19, NL-8102 SV Raalte (Overijssel) T: 0572 371 575. E: info@krieghuusbelten.nl

alanrogers.com/NL6509

Krieghuusbelten is a fabulous, 16-acre family fun park in the heart of Overijssel, between the villages of Raalte and Lemelerveld. The site is a great choice for families with children of all ages. Youngsters are kept busy by the animation team, with musicals, crafts and even a ghost walk! Older children can choose from a wide range of sporting activities, and the white-knuckle rides at Hellendoorn are only 11 km. away. The touring pitches are set over ten small fields, each with 20-30 pitches and a safe play area. All are fully serviced, have 10A electricity and shade from mature trees. The site's five-acre pond is well stocked, and dinghy sailing is permitted. Dogs are not accepted.

Facilities

Three heated sanitary blocks are well equipped and include family shower rooms, baby rooms, washbasins in cabins and facilities for disabled visitors. Hot water on payment (key). Laundry. Well stocked shop with fresh bread. Bar, restaurant with terrace and takeaway. Covered swimming pool. Multisports pitch. WiFi (charged).

Open: 1 April - 1 October.

Directions

Leave A1 at exit 26 and follow N332 north for 14 km. After Heeten turn right and follow signs for site. GPS: 52.42725, 6.31003

Charges guide

Per unit incl. 2 persons and electricity	€ 17.50 - € 30.70
extra person	€ 4.60

Rheeze
Camping 't Veld

Grote Beltenweg 15, NL-7794 RA Rheeze (Overijssel) T: 0523 26 22 86. E: info@campingtveld.nl

alanrogers.com/NL6498

Camping 't Veld is situated in the Vecht Valley and is surrounded by forest and lakes. Of the 250 pitches, 110 are available for touring, all with 6/10A electricity. Five pitches are fully serviced and four have private sanitary units. The site is well laid out and all of the grassy touring pitches are divided between eight small, hedged fields. There are also two safari tents for hire along with three mobile homes. On-site facilities include a shop, bar and restaurant, all of which are first class and open all season. The all-weather pool at the entrance is an added bonus to this beautifully located site that would particularly suit families with young children and pre-teens.

Facilities

One central, modern and heated sanitary block with hot showers, private cabins, a baby bathroom and facilities for disabled visitors. Laundry facilities. Motorcaravn service point. Shop, bar and restaurant. Swimming pool with retractable roof. Paddling pool. Play area on each touring field. Sports field. Fishing. Bicycle hire. WiFi throughout (charged). Off site: Hiking and cycle tracks nearby. The River De Vecht is nearby for canoeing, boating and fishing.

Open: 29 March - 27 September.

Directions

From A35 take exit 31 onto the N36 for 23 km. then east onto Beerzerweg. After 350 m. turn left onto Stuwdijk and continue to Rheezerweg. After 2.5 km. turn right and continue for 2 km. Campsite is on the left. GPS: 52.54685, 6.57155

Charges guide

Per unit incl. 2 persons and electricity	€ 17.00 - € 27.50
extra person	€ 2.50 - € 3.45

Weerselo
Camping De Molenhof

Kleijsenweg 7, NL-7667 RS Reutum/Weerselo (Overijssel) T: 0541 661 165. E: info@demolenhof.nl

alanrogers.com/NL6480

De Molenhof is a pleasant family site which generally caters for children under 12 rather than teenagers. It has 450 well laid out pitches of which 430 are for touring units, all with water, drainage, electricity (10A) and cable connections. Children will enjoy themselves in the covered, adventure playground or the two heated swimming pools (one outdoor, one covered) with a large slide on the outside. The entertainment team provides a full daily programme in high season, including theatre nights in De Hooischuur, a specially designed entertainment hall.

Facilities

Four toilet blocks, three fairytale themed for children, provide washbasins (open style and in cabins), control-lable showers, bathrooms and a baby room. Facilities for disabled visitors. Launderette. Motorcaravan service. Well stocked shop (3/4-27/9). Bar (3/4-27/9). Restaurant (3/4-1/9). Pancake restaurant. Swimming pools (outdoor, 2/5-1/9; indoor 3/4-27/9). Playgrounds (1 covered). Sports court. All-weather sports area. WiFi over site.

Open: 3 April - 27 September.

Directions

Follow A1 from Amsterdam east to Hengelo and take exit 31, Hengelo Noord. Go through Deurningen to Weerselo and from there the N343 towards Tubbergen and site signs. GPS: 52.36200, 6.81400

Charges guide

Per unit incl. 2 persons and electricity	€ 18.50 - € 39.00
Camping Cheques accepted.	

FREE Alan Rogers Travel Card
Extra benefits and savings - see page 12

CAPITAL: UTRECHT

Utrecht, the smallest province of the
Netherlands, has plenty to offer the visitor
in regions such as the Utrecht Hill Ridge,
its very own Lake District, the Vecht and the
rural Green Heart. Notable cities are Utrecht
and Amersfoort.

The suburbs of Utrecht merge with commuter
towns such as Nieuwegein and Houten in the
south and Maarssen in the north. Southwest
of this urban area is rural Lopikerwaard and
northwest, the peat-rich lands of Vinkeveen and
Mijdrecht. North of the city of Utrecht are the
River Vecht and the Loosdrecht Lakes, two of
the region's most popular recreational areas.

The eastern part of the province is bisected by
the Utrecht Hill Ridge. Along the southern flank of
the old glacial moraine are leafy oases like Zeist
and Doorn. Between the hills and the Rhine lies
the rural district of Kromme-Rijn, centre of fruit
cultivation with Wijk bij Duurstede at its heart.
On the other side of the hills lies the Gelderland
Valley with the town of Veenendaal. The northeast
corner of the province is occupied by the city of
Amersfoort and the Eemland polder. At the former
Zuiderzee you'll find the archetypal town of
Bunschoten-Spakenburg.

Places of interest

Utrecht: city with narrow streets, interesting
shops, lively squares and canals and the
imposing Dom Tower; Central Museum with
a wide variety of exhibitions.

Amersfoort: Museum Flehite, Armando
Museum, Mondriaan House, Eem harbour,
a brewery and a children's farm.

Langbroek: rural village and site of the first
'donjons' built in the 12th century; several
castles.

Oudewater: charming historic town featuring
witches' scales, a rope factory and museum.

Wijk bij Duurstede: located on the shores
of the River Lek with many attractions,
including Duurstede Castle, a church
with flat-roofed tower, and the world's
only drive-through windmill.

Attractions

Boat Cruises: shipping company
Schuttevaer provides year-round tourist
and party cruises, in and around the city
of Utrecht.

Makeblijde Gardens: landscape design park
featuring 16 modern gardens, including
a jungle and a Zen garden.

Dick Bruna House: displays of work by
Bruna, Dutch author, illustrator and creator
of the internationally famous Miffy, the little
rabbit.

Amersfoort Zoo: home to over 1,000 animals
and 130 species.

Kasteel Huis Doorn: late 18th-century
renovated castle, located in a beautiful
wooded park, best known as the home of
Germany's ex-emperor, William II.

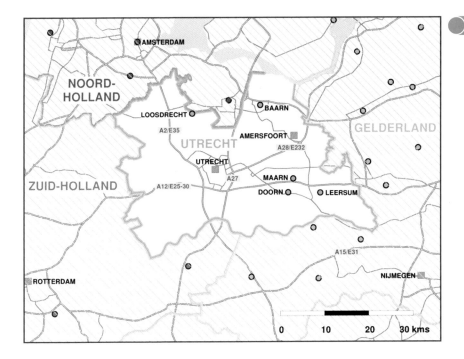

Baarn
Allurepark De Zeven Linden
Zevenlindenweg 4, NL-3744 BC Baarn (Utrecht) T: 0356 668 330. E: info@dezevenlinden.nl

alanrogers.com/NL6824

De Zeven Linden was created in 1938 and since then has been a popular site for those seeking a peaceful holiday in a natural setting. There are 261 spacious touring pitches (6-10A electricity), some shaded by trees, and spread over 13 separate fields. Unusually, the whole area is car free, which goes a long way to ensuring peace and quiet, as well as improving safety for children around the site. The site is located on the northern fringe of the Utrechtse Heuvelrug, a heavily forested area. Within walking distance you can visit Drakensteyn castle, Soestdijk palace and the beautiful village of Lage Vuursche. Pitches are large and grassy, mostly with electrical connections. A unique feature here is the Hut Forest, where you can build your own bivouac or hut.

Facilities

Modern, child friendly and spacious toilet blocks (two heated in low season). Two blocks have special family rooms with family showers and a separate children's area. Special facilities for disabled visitors. Washing machine and dryer. Small shop (bread daily). Snack bar/takeaway (weekends in low season). Small field with animals. Football pitch. WiFi over site (charged). Hut forest. Off site: Recently renovated swimming pool, Bosbad de Vuursche 600 m. Riding and bicycle hire 3 km. Fishing and golf 5 km.

Open: 31 March - 17 October.

Directions

Approaching from the west, site is well signed from the N415 Hilversum-Baarn road shortly before reaching the intersection with the N221.
GPS: 52.19652, 5.24747

Charges guide

Per unit incl. 2 persons,	
water and electricity	€ 24.15
extra person	€ 3.00
child (2-12 yrs)	€ 2.00

Doorn

RCN Het Grote Bos

Hydeparklaan 24, NL-3941 ZK Doorn (Utrecht) T: 0343 513 644. E: hetgrotebos@rcn.nl
alanrogers.com/NL6828

Het Grote Bos (the large forest) is ideally located for a tranquil woodland holiday, but is also an ideal base to explore the western part of the Netherlands, or for visits to Amsterdam, Utrecht and Amersfoort. The site is located in the grounds of a former estate called Hydepark, and the prevailing atmosphere still reflects this parkland setting. Touring fields with 270 pitches are surrounded by high trees and are marked out by shrubs and hedges. Leisure amenities include attractive play areas, a heated outdoor pool complex (with slides and a children's pool) and a multisports terrain. A survival course has been built in the trees around the site.

Facilities

Six toilet blocks around the site. Launderette. Motorcaravan services. Restaurant, café/bar, takeaway. Bakery and supermarket. Heated outdoor pool with lazy river, water slides, children's pool and sunbathing area. Sports hall. Picnic area. Various themed play areas (such as a butterfly garden). Fitness trail. Tennis courts. Minigolf. Basketball. Bicycle and go-kart hire. Mobile homes and chalets to rent. WiFi throughout (charged). Torches useful.

Open: April - October.

Directions

From A12 motorway take Driebergen/Rijsenburg exit, turn right on N225 towards Driebergen/Rijsenburg. Turn left after 200 m. (Loolaan) and then (600 m) take second exit on the roundabout. Turn left in 2.5 km. on Hydeparklaan to site.
GPS: 52.056117, 5.313716

Charges guide

Per unit incl. 2 persons and electricity	€ 22.80 - € 34.05

Leersum

Molecaten Park Landgoed Ginkelduin

Scherpenzeelseweg 53, NL-3956 KD Leersum (Utrecht) T: 0343 489 999.
E: landgoedginkelduin@molecaten.nl **alanrogers.com/NL6827**

The Ginkelduin estate is located within the woods of the Utrechtse Heuvelrug National Park. The park extends over 95 ha. and is an Area of Outstanding Natural Beauty consisting of woodland, moors and drifting sands. The car-free estate includes this high quality campsite, a member of the Molecaten group, with generously sized pitches (225 for touring with 10A electricity) fringed with mature trees. There is plenty here for children, including indoor and outdoor swimming pools, a large football pitch and a special ten-pin bowling area. There are fully equipped tents, apartments and bungalows for rent.

Facilities

Two large and centrally located toilet blocks have some washbasins in cabins. Controllable showers and family shower room. Baby bathroom. Good facilities for disabled visitors. Restaurant. Bamboo garden with brasserie, snack bar and supermarket. Indoor pool with whirlpool and Turkish bath, solarium. Heated outdoor pool (8/5-2/9) with slide, paddling pool and sunbathing area. Playgrounds. Minigolf. Bowling alleys. Tennis. Bicycle hire. Children's entertainment. WiFi (charged). Dogs are not accepted.

Open: 29 March - 1 November.

Directions

From A12 motorway exit 22 follow signs to Woudenberg, Leersum and Maarsbergen. Continue on N225 as far as Leersum. After 1 km. turn left on Bentincklaan. Site is well signed from here.
GPS: 52.028336, 5.457705

Charges guide

Per unit incl. 2 persons, water and electricity	€ 22.50 - € 42.00
No credit cards.	

Loosdrecht

Recreatiecentrum Mijnden

Bloklaan 22A, NL-1231 AZ Loosdrecht (Utrecht) T: 0294 233 165. E: info@mijnden.nl
alanrogers.com/NL6830

Mijnden is in a central position in the Vechtstreek, one of the most beautiful parts of the Netherlands. The Recreatiecentrum is located amidst typically Dutch countryside alongside the River Drecht and close to cities such as Amsterdam, Utrecht and Hilversum. The site has 120 level pitches for tourers, some on hardstanding, all with 10A electricity and 20 with water and drainage. The pitches are on grassy fields and almost all provide lovely views over the lake. There are also 80 seasonal pitches. The site has its own boat slipway so you could bring your own boat and navigate the Loosdrechtse Plassen. The waterfront is not fenced or gated.

Facilities

Three modern, heated sanitary blocks with showers on payment, washbasins, toilets and facilities for disabled visitors. Launderette. Motorcaravan services. Supermarket (1/4-15/9). Restaurant and snack bar (1/4-1/10). A natural spring water paddling pond with a beach area. New play area. Sports field. Boat slipway. Children's entertainment (July/Aug). Fishing. Bicycle hire. WiFi over site (charged).

Open: 7 April - 30 September.

Directions

Take A2 from Utrecht towards Amsterdam. Exit for Hilversum after bridge turn right. Drive through village of Loenen and turn left to site.
GPS: 52.20260, 5.03013

Charges guide

Per unit incl. 2 persons and electricity	€ 21.00 - € 26.00
extra person	€ 5.00

For latest campsite news, availability and prices visit
alanrogers.com

Maarn

Allurepark Laag Kanje

Laan van Laagkanje 1, NL-3951 KD Maarn (Utrecht) T: 0343 441 348. E: allurepark@laagkanje.nl

alanrogers.com/NL6832

This is a perfect region for a hospitable stay in a wooded and hilly environment, still dominated by peace and quiet, space and style. Originally part of a great estate, Allurecamping Laag Kanje has been developed into a top quality campsite over the last 40 years with the unusual, but attractive feature that cars are not allowed in the camping area. This is a spacious site with a relaxed and tranquil atmosphere. There are 800 pitches in total, mainly for privately owned mobile homes, 150 are available for touring with 5A electricity. The park is located at the heart of the forest, so sandy beaches may be the last thing you would expect here. However, there is a fine sandy beach 100 m. from the site, which surrounds a beautiful swimming lake.

Facilities

Modern toilet blocks with special facilities for children and disabled visitors. Four blocks are heated in the low season. Laundry facilities. Motorcaravan services. Small restaurant and snack bar. Well stocked shop with fresh products available daily. Entertainment and activity programme for adults and children. Bicycle hire. WiFi throughout (charged). Dogs are not accepted.
Off site: Riding 1 km. Golf 2 km. Fishing 3 km. Hiking and cycling. Utrecht, Amersfoort, Zeist, Wijk bij Duurstede museum. Dolfinarium at Hardewijk (dolphin aquarium). Lake swimming. Beach and woods adjacent.

Open: 1 April - 1 October.

Directions

Heading south from Amersfoort on the N227 towards Doorn, site is well signed shortly before arrival at the village of Maarn.
GPS: 52.07724, 5.37932

Charges guide

Per unit incl. 2 persons and electricity	€ 22.50
extra person	€ 2.50
child (2-12 yrs)	€ 1.50

No credit cards.

FREE Alan Rogers Travel Card
Extra benefits and savings - see page 12

CAPITAL: MIDDELBURG

The province of Zeeland comprises several peninsulas that were once separate islands, as the name of 'Sea Land' indicates. It includes Zeeuwsvlaanderen (Sea Land Flanders), a strip of land along the Belgian border.

Zeeland sits mainly on clay intersected with canals and former creeks, while the south of the region is sandy. Outside the dykes, the land is mainly salt marshes and mud flats, while along the coast there are dunes; the largest can be seen on Schouwen-Duiveland, the north coast of Walcheren, and in the south. Despite the impact of the war and the demolition of many old buildings in the 'fifties and 'sixties, the capital Middelburg still has over 1,200 communal and national monuments, most notably the gothic Town Hall, the abbey with its 'Long John' tower, and the Arsenal.

Zeeland has the cleanest beaches in the Netherlands as well as the most sunshine. The vast polders etch straight lines into the landscape, but also visible are the outlines of ancient, jagged polders nestling between small dykes. Reminders of Zeeland's fascinating history are everywhere: fossilised sharks' teeth on the beach, magnificent merchants' houses from the Golden Age, and echoes of the dramatic floods of 1953. It's a wonderful region for hiking, cycling, skating and riding along the dunes, beaches and flower-clad dykes, but also for exploring the mudflats and salt marshes.

Places of interest

Veere: one of Zeeland's most beautiful old cities with historic church, 15th-century town hall, Campveerse tower; cafés and restaurants.

Goeree-Overflakkee: the Grevelingen Dam and the Brouwersdam are wonderful for swimming, (kite) surfing, diving, fishing and sailing; Ouddorp and Middelharnis have a good selection of shops.

Colijnsplaat: a paradise for fish lovers; modern fishing port and fascinating fish auction every Thursday; fishermen's festivals in August are an absolute must!

Borssele: attractive, symmetrical village of tree-lined streets, lawns and beautiful old houses; the 'Mountain of Troy' mound – a remnant of the castle of the once powerful lords of Borssele (c.1243); early 18th-century working corn mill, open Saturdays.

Attractions

Delta Park Neeltje Jans: centre for nature, culture and technology with films and exhibitions showing the catastrophic floods of 1953 and the world famous Delta Works sea defences.

Vuurtorens: Breskens, Westkapelle and Haamstede have beautiful old lighthouses, some open to the public.

Shipping Company Verhoef: runs cruises on the Westerschelde, where you can see seals, and on the busy Gent to Terneuzen canal.

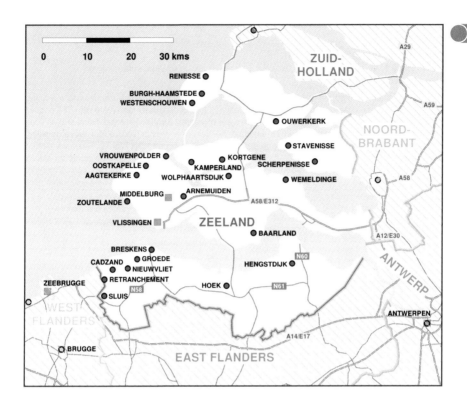

Aagtekerke
Camping Westhove
Zuiverseweg 2, NL-4363 RJ Aagtekerke (Zeeland) T: 0118 581 809. E: westhove@ardoer.com
alanrogers.com/NL6990

Camping Westhove is an ideal site for all ages and has some high quality play facilities for children. It is situated on the island Walcheren (the garden of Zeeland). There are 366 spacious pitches of which 275 are for touring with 6A electricity. The possibilities are endless – whether you wish to enjoy the beach, nature or the towns. There are marked tracks through the woods and dunes, and historical villages and towns with opportunities for cycling, walking and riding. The site's sanitary facilities are of a high standard, and there is an excellent new wellness and fitness centre.

Facilities
Three heated sanitary units with washbasins in cabins, showers and WCs and en-suite facilities. Baby room. Free hot water. Launderette with ironing facilities. Well stocked supermarket. Bar. Good restaurant. Snack bar. Fresh bread is available daily. Heated indoor swimming pool. Paddling pool. Excellent wellness and fitness centre. Indoor and outdoor play areas. Sports field. Boules. Bicycle and tricycle hire. Entertainment team in high season. Miniclub. Recreation area. TV. Electronic games. WiFi (charged). Dogs are not accepted in high season. Off site: Golf and beach 1.5 km. Shops, bars, restaurants and disco in Domburg 2 km.

Open: 30 March - 28 October.

Directions
From A58 take exit for Domburg and Oostkapelle (N57 and N287). Just before entering Domburg site is signed and is a left turn (Zuiverseweg) and on left after 900 m. GPS: 51.55578, 3.51516

Charges guide
Per unit incl. 2 persons and electricity	€ 20.00 - € 44.00
extra person	€ 5.00
dog	€ 2.50

Baarland

Comfortcamping Scheldeoord

Landingsweg 1, NL-4435 NR Baarland (Zeeland) T: 0113 639 900. E: scheldeoord@ardoer.com

alanrogers.com/NL5575

The site is situated behind the Westerschelde dyke, from where you can watch the passing sea-going ships and below the dyke one can fish from the beach. It is a good quality family site with 514 pitches including 214 for touring units. The touring pitches are pleasantly arranged in small fields and all have electricity (6/16A), water, drainage and TV aerial connection. One area is reserved for those travelling with disabilities and this is located near one of the very well equipped toilet blocks. There are heated indoor and outdoor pools with a slide (unsupervised), both with excellent separate areas for young children. A member of the Ardoer group.

Facilities

Three excellent, modern toilet blocks include washbasins (open style and in cabins) and en-suite shower rooms with controllable showers (card operated). Attractive children's section. Bathrooms for rent. Facilities for disabled visitors. Laundry. Motorcaravan services. Supermarket. Restaurant and bar. Snack bar with takeaway. Indoor and outdoor pools with paddling pools. Play areas. Tennis. Bicycle hire. Fishing. Entertainment (July/Aug). WiFi (charged).

Open: 1 April - 30 October.

Directions

From the A58 take exit 35 to 's Gravenpolder. Then follow signs to Hoedekenskerke and then south for Scheldeoord and the campsite. GPS: 51.39675, 3.89825

Charges guide

Per unit incl. 2 persons and electricity	€ 21.00 - € 49.00
extra person	€ 5.00

Breskens

Droompark Schoneveld

Schoneveld 1, NL-4511 HR Breskens (Zeeland) T: 0117 383 220. E: info@droomparkschoneveld.nl

alanrogers.com/NL6930

This site is well situated within walking distance of Breskens and it has direct access to sand dunes and the beach 500 m. beyond. It has 165 touring pitches and these are kept apart from the static caravans. All have electricity and cable TV, 27 also have water and waste connections. They are laid out in fields which are entered from long avenues that run through the site. One toilet block serves the touring area. The site entrance complex includes reception and information about children's entertainment. The ferry link to Breskens from Vlissingen takes pedestrians and cyclists only, a tunnel is now open for motor vehicles. You could also visit the ancient towns of Brugge and Gent which make comfortable day trips. The area is renowned for its excellent provision for cyclists, and excursions along the dunes and through the various nature reserves are safe and secure.

Facilities

One large sanitary block has showers, wash cubicles, child size toilets and washbasins, baby room, en-suite unit for disabled visitors, laundry, dishwashing and vegetable preparation areas. Motorcaravan services. Well stocked supermarket (5/4-31/10). Bar. Restaurant and takeaway. 10-pin bowling. Indoor pool with fun pool and mini-slide. Wellness area with sauna, hot tub and solarium. Tennis. Play area. Entertainment (July/Aug). Bicycle hire. WiFi.

Open: All year.

Directions

From the east and the Terneuzen end of the Westerschelde Tunnel, take N61 west towards Breskens. At Schoondijke continue north on N676 to Breskens. Site lies 1 km. west of Breskens (signed). GPS: 51.40107, 3.53475

Charges guide

Per unit incl. 2 persons and electricity	€ 14.00 - € 35.00

Camping Cheques accepted.

Got yours yet?

Extra benefits and savings - see page 12

Advantage all the way
alan rogers
Travel Card

For latest campsite news, availability and prices visit
alanrogers.com

Burgh-Haamstede
Camping Ginsterveld

Maireweg 10, NL-4328 GR Burgh-Haamstede (Zeeland) T: 0111 651 590. E: info@ginsterveld.nl
alanrogers.com/NL6936

This is a fantastic family site for both parents and children. Not only is the nearby wide sandy beach popular, but there is also a swimming paradise with different water levels, a lazy river, water slides (one 40 m. long), pools for toddlers and children, a whirlpool and a steam cabin. With other amenities including several play fields, bicycle hire and spacious play areas, this site is ideal for children. There are 590 pitches, 250 for touring, all with electricity (8/16A). Spacious and surrounded by trees and shrubs, every pitch has plenty of privacy. The surrounding woodland and dunes are home to many species of bird. A member of the Ardoer group.

Facilities

Two excellent heated toilet blocks. Washbasins in cabins and large controllable showers. Motorcaravan services. Shop. Restaurant. Bar. Takeaway. Good heated indoor pool. Tennis. Sports field. Good playgrounds. Pets are not accepted. WiFi throughout (free). Off site: Beach and fishing 2 km. Riding 4 km. Golf 10 km.

Open: 28 March - 26 October.

Directions

From the A15 take exit 17 towards Middelburg. Follow the N57 towards Burgh-Haamstede and site is well signed from the centre. GPS: 51.71617, 3.729

Charges guide

Per unit incl. 2 persons and electricity	€ 19.00 - € 36.00
extra person	€ 5.25

Cadzand
Camping Wulpen

Vierhonderdpolderdijk 1, NL-4506 HK Cadzand (Zeeland) T: 0117 391 226. E: info@campingwulpen.nl
alanrogers.com/NL5535

Camping Wulpen is located in the southernmost resort in the Netherlands, with a wide, clean beach nearby. This is a quiet, sheltered, well maintained site with excellent sanitary facilities. Most of the 100 spacious touring pitches (80-130 sq.m) have electricity (6/10A), water and drainage. There is a recreation room with table tennis, several playgrounds and a room dedicated to children's activities in high season. Other leisure activities include boules, football and volleyball. Throughout the site there is an emphasis on attention to detail and those interested in the environment will appreciate the diversity in plant life in specially created and tended gardens.

Facilities

Two heated toilet blocks are clean and well maintained, and two additional units are used in peak season. Laundry facilities. Shop with newspapers, fresh bread, ice-creams and gas. Games room. Playgrounds. Outdoor fitness equipment. Spacious sports area. WiFi over part of site (charged). Off site: The Zwin nature reserve. Cycling and walking. The historic villages of Retranchement, Aardenburg and IJzendijke.

Open: 1 April - 15 October.

Directions

From Breda/Eindhoven on A58 take Terneuzen exit to the Westerschelde Tunnel. After tunnel, turn right at roundabout towards Oostburg then Cadzand. At Cadzand go right at mill and then take first right. The site is on your left. GPS: 51.3699, 3.41670

Charges guide

Per unit incl. 2 persons and electricity	€ 18.70 - € 22.75
extra person	€ 4.45 - € 5.45

Cadzand
Molecaten Park Hoogduin

Zwartepolderweg 1, NL-4506 HT Cadzand (Zeeland) T: 0117 391 235. E: hoogduin@molecaten.nl
alanrogers.com/NL6937

Molecaten Park Hoogduin can be reached in less than two hours' drive from Calais. The location of this site is imposing, and, as its name Hoogduin suggests, it can be found within high dunes. Just over the dunes, there is a broad sandy beach with a panoramic view over the site and the surrounding area. This beach is well known as one of the cleanest in the Netherlands, and slopes gently into the sea. Pitches are large and grassy, and all have electricity (6/10A). They are divided by high trees and shrubs.

Facilities

Four clean, well maintained sanitary units housed in variety of buildings. Facilities for disabled campers (key access). Very well stocked supermarket. Restaurant with pub and terrace, takeaway. Sports pitches. Trampoline. Several play areas throughout the site. Volleyball. Games room. Activity and entertainment programme (4-10 yrs; high season). Bicycle hire. WiFi (charged). Chalets for rent. Off site: Sandy beach (adjacent). Cadzand-Bad 2 km. Sluis 6 km. Knokke 7 km. Bruges 20 km.

Open: All year.

Directions

From the south take the E40 motorway (in Belgium) to Oostkamp take E403 to Brugge (Bruges) and Knokke-Heist. Follow this road into the Netherlands following directions to Cadzand. Continue on N674. At the T-junction (at the coast) turn right and you will find the site after 1 km. GPS: 51.38453, 3.41397

Charges guide

Per unit incl. 2 persons, water and electricity	€ 14.00 - € 32.50
extra person	€ 3.90

FREE Alan Rogers Travel Card
Extra benefits and savings - see page 12

Groede

Strandcamping Groede

Zeeweg 1, NL-4503 PA Groede (Zeeland) T: 0117 371 384. E: info@strandcampinggroede.nl

alanrogers.com/NL5510

A warm welcome awaits you at Strandcamping Groede, which has all you need for the perfect family seaside holiday. Family run and located close to one of the cleanest sandy beaches in the Netherlands, it aims to cater for the individual needs of visitors with pitches available for all tastes. There are 870 pitches in total, 500 for tourers, the majority of these with electrical connections (4/10A). Sympathetic landscaping has taken the natural surroundings of the dunes and sand to create areas for larger groups, families, and for those who prefer peace and quiet. The seaside feel continues in the layout of the comprehensive sports and play areas and in the brasserie and other main buildings.

Facilities

Excellent toilet facilities are very clean and include some private cabins, baby baths, a family room and a dedicated unit for visitors with disabilities. Motorcaravan services. Gas. Shop, restaurant and snack bar (all w/ends only in low seasons). Recreation room. Trampoline. Bouncy castle. Sports area. Several play areas (bark base). Activities for children (July/Aug). Bicycle hire. Fishing. WiFi over site (free). Off site: Riding 1 km. Golf 11 km. Free bus service for campers from Breskens to Knokke.

Open: 27 March - 2 November.

Directions

From Breskens take the coast road for 5 km. to site. Alternatively, the site is signed from Groede village on the more inland Breskens-Sluis road.
GPS: 51.39582, 3.48772

Charges guide

Per unit incl. 2 persons and electricity	€ 19.70 - € 46.00
extra person	€ 4.00

No credit cards.

Hengstdijk

Recreatiecentrum De Vogel

Vogelweg 4, NL-4585 PL Hengstdijk (Zeeland) T: 0114 68 16 25. E: info@de-vogel.nl

alanrogers.com/NL7014

Recreatiecentrum De Vogel is a spacious, lively, family friendly campsite with excellent facilities. It lies in the De Vogel Park, north west of Antwerp, close to a lake with a sandy beach and is open all year. Its many facilities include indoor and outdoor swimming complexes with slides, indoor and outdoor playgrounds, sports areas and a high season entertainment programme for the whole family. There are 550 pitches with 125 good sized, grassy pitches for touring, all amongst natural vegetation and shrubs, all with 10A Europlug. After a busy day, you can unwind in the sauna and solarium or have a leisurely drink around the pools and play areas. On the lake there is windsurfing, sailing, kayaking, and pedaloes are for hire at the lakeside. The surrounding area is ideal to explore by bike (rental on site) or on foot; details of routes are available from reception.

Facilities

Two clean, modern toilet blocks, one heated. Showers on payment (by key). Facilities for children and disabled visitors. Laundry facilities. Motorcaravan services. Shop (1/4-1/10). Bars, restaurants and takeaway (all season). Indoor heated (1/4-30/10) and outdoor (1/6-31/8) swimming and paddling pools with slides. Indoor and outdoor play areas. Fishing. Tennis. Minigolf. Kayak and pedalo hire. Children's club (July/Aug). Children's farm. Bicycle hire. WiFi (free in restaurant). Off site: Bus stop at entrance. Golf 3 km. Historic town of Hulst.

Open: 6 January - 20 December.

Directions

Leave E34 between Ghent and Antwerp at exit 11 (Hulst). Take N403 then N290 north for 12 km. to Ter Hole. Turn west on N290 for 2.5 km. Take N688 (Vogelweg) for 3.5 km. to site.
GPS: 51.34207, 3.9902

Charges guide

Per unit incl. 2 persons and electricity	€ 16.00 - € 32.00
extra person (over 3 yrs)	€ 3.50
dog	€ 1.50

5 star campsite – accommodations for rent
group accommodations

animation team – indoor swimmingpool
indoor playground

Vogelweg 4, 4585 PL Hengstdijk   0114 68 16 25   info@de-vogel.nl   www.de-vogel.nl

For latest campsite news, availability and prices visit
alanrogers.com

Hoek
Oostappen Vakantiepark Marina Beach
Middenweg 1, NL-4542 PN Hoek (Zeeland) T: 0115 481 730. E: info@braakman.nl
alanrogers.com/NL5520

Situated on the shores of the Braakmanmeer (a slightly brackish lake) this holiday park provides fun for the whole family. The comprehensive recreation areas are also open to day visitors. The 210-hectare site is divided by tall trees into several touring areas of varied sizes, both open and shaded. A wide range of pitches are available, from the most simple without a power supply, to luxury camping beside the water with full services including 6A electricity, TV, water and sewerage connections. In addition, there is a range of luxury bungalows, mobile homes and seasonal caravan pitches.

Facilities

Six fully equipped toilet blocks include facilities for disabled visitors. Laundry facilities in almost every block. Supermarket. Bar. Restaurant. Lake swimming with slides, diving board, beach and water play equipment. Play area with pool for small children. Sports field. Tennis (tuition all year). Amusement hall (games). Minigolf. Basketball. Fitness trail. Activity and entertainment team. Watersports and sailing on the lake. Fishing (with disabled access). Petting farm and aviary. WiFi over part of site (charged).

Open: All year.

Directions

From A58 (Bergen op Zoom-Middelburg) take exit for Terneuzen to Westerscheldetunnel. At roundabout turn right to Hoek, Breskens and Oostburg. GPS: 51.314635, 3.725972

Charges guide

Per unit incl. 2 persons	
and electricity	€ 13.50 - € 33.00
extra person	€ 3.50

Kamperland
Camping De Molenhoek
Molenweg 69a, NL-4493 NC Kamperland (Zeeland) T: 0113 371 202. E: info@demolenhoek.com
alanrogers.com/NL5570

This rural, family run site makes a pleasant contrast to the livelier coastal sites in this popular holiday area. There is an emphasis on catering for the users of the 300 permanent or seasonal holiday caravans and 100 tourers. Eighty of these have 6A electricity, water and drainage. The site is neat and tidy with surrounding hedges and trees giving privacy and some shade, and electrical connections are available. A large outdoor pool area has ample space for swimming, children's play and sun loungers. Entertainment, including dance evenings and bingo, is organised in season.

Facilities

Two very clean and well appointed sanitary blocks include some washbasins in cabins and facilities for children. Toilet and shower facilities for disabled visitors and for babies. Laundry facilities. Motorcaravan services. Bar/restaurant with terrace and large TVs and LCD projection. Snack bar. Heated outdoor swimming pool (15/5-15/9). Playground. Bicycle hire. Pool tables. Sports field. Entertainment for children and teenagers. WiFi (free). Off site: Tennis and watersports nearby. Shop 800 m.

Open: 1 April - 27 October.

Directions

Site is west of the village of Kamperland on the island of Noord Beveland. From the N256 Goes-Zierikzee road, exit west onto the N255 Kamperland road. Site is signed south of this road. GPS: 51.57840, 3.69642

Charges guide

Per unit incl. 2 persons	
and electricity	€ 21.00 - € 36.00
extra person	€ 2.00 - € 5.00
dog	€ 4.00 - € 5.00

Kamperland
RCN de Schotsman
Schotsmanweg 1, NL-4493 ZG Kamperland (Zeeland) T: 0113 371 751. E: schotsman@rcn.nl
alanrogers.com/NL6924

De Schotsman is located on the island of Noord-Beveland, on the shores of Veerse Meer. It has its own marina with a slipway and a good selection of boats for hire for all abilities. In the high season, there is a full programme of windsurfing and sailing lessons. There is also a large, heated, outdoor pool with a separate children's pool, and an inviting restaurant with a terrace overlooking the lake. It is within reach of the ports of Hook of Holland, Zeebrugge, Dunkerque, and two and a half hours from Calais, so may also be ideal for a short break in the low season.

Facilities

Four spacious sanitary units are very clean and well equipped and have facilities for disabled visitors. Launderette. Bakery and well stocked supermarket. Bar, restaurant with lake view terrace, and takeaway, heated outdoor pool with separate children's pool, slides and water chute and paddling pool. Sports hall. Play area. Bicycle and go-kart hire. Fishing. Windsurf, pedalo and canoe hire. Lake beach. Marina. Slipway. WiFi (charged).

Open: 28 March - 27 October.

Directions

From autoroute A58 Bergen op Zoom-Vlissingen, take exit Zierikzee (N256). Then go left to join N255 to Kamperland. From here the site is clearly signed (to the left). GPS: 51.568527, 3.662787

Charges guide

Per unit incl. 2 persons	
and electricity	€ 22.00 - € 39.50
dog	€ 4.95 - € 7.50

FREE Alan Rogers Travel Card
Extra benefits and savings - see page 12

Kortgene
Camping en Villapark De Paardekreek

Havenweg 1, NL-4484 NT Kortgene (Zeeland) T: 0113 302 051. E: paardekreek@ardoer.com

alanrogers.com/NL5585

Located directly on the Veerse Meer, with access to the vast lake, this superb family site has additional but not sole, appeal for watersports enthusiasts. There are both seasonal pitches and 120 pitches for touring units, all fully serviced including 10A electricity, television and WiFi. The pitches are pleasant and some are directly by the water's edge and with boat launching facilities, water and a sailing school on site, many units have a boat of some sort. There is an exciting indoor water adventure play park with a long water chute and a small beach also allows swimming and zip wire fun over the water.

Facilities

Three very good toilet blocks and one smaller unit include en-suite shower rooms. Excellent facilities for children and disabled visitors. Motorcaravan services. Pleasant bar with terrace. Restaurant. Snack bar with takeaway. Indoor heated water adventure area and water chute. Adventure play areas. Indoor play area. Lake swimming. Mooring facilities. Bicycle hire. Pedal kart hire. Dune buggy hire. Entertainment for children in high season. WiFi (charged).

Open: 27 March - 1 November.

Directions

From the A256 take exit signed Goes, Zierikzee. Follow N256 through Oost Westweg and Oudedijk. In the village of Kortgene the site is well signed. GPS: 51.5511, 3.80834

Charges guide

Per serviced pitch incl. 2 persons	€ 25.00 - € 45.00
extra person	€ 5.00
dog	€ 5.00

Nieuwvliet
Camping International

Sint Bavodijk 2D, NL-4504 AA Nieuwvliet (Zeeland) T: 0117 371 233. E: international@ardoer.com

alanrogers.com/NL5525

This is a large, well managed site sheltered partly by trees and shrubbery, which also separate the various camping areas and the extensive activity area for children of all ages. It is ideal for family holidays, offering a wide range of entertainment opportunities on the site, whatever the weather, as well as access to the nearby beaches. Different types of touring pitch are available, all with electricity (6A) and most with water, drainage and cable TV. Thirty-three pitches have individual sanitary units. A modern, clean and well maintained sanitary block serves the remaining touring pitches. A member of the Ardoer Group.

Facilities

One major sanitary building has free showers, dishwashing sinks. Microwave. Bar and lounge with library, board games, LCD projector TV screen. Small shop for basics and bakery (high season and weekends). Snack bar/takeaway. Water play area with slides, water features and paddling pool for under 10s. Indoor and outdoor play/craft areas. Football. Tennis. Boules. Volleyball. Chess. Bicycle hire. WiFi over site (charged).

Open: 1 April - 31 October.

Directions

From Belgium: take N49 to Kaprijke/Breskens, enter the Netherlands at IJzendijke and follow signs to Breskens and Schoondijke. At roundabout in Breskens turn left to Groede and Cadzand, following site signs. GPS: 51.37468, 3.46944

Charges guide

Per unit incl. 2 persons and electricity	€ 17.00 - € 37.00
extra person	€ 4.50

Nieuwvliet
Camping Zonneweelde

Baanstpoldersedijk 1, NL-4504 PS Nieuwvliet (Zeeland) T: 0117 371 910. E: info@campingzonneweelde.nl

alanrogers.com/NL5530

This family run site, only 600 m. from kilometres of wide, sandy beaches, is ideal for family holidays. Children will enjoy a walkway and a large slide through the dunes to reach the beach. There are 70 touring pitches, a wide choice of luxury holiday cottages and log cabins, plus places for 50 seasonal caravans. Electricity (10A) is available throughout. The Natural Reserve of Het Zwin is nearby (ideal for birdwatching) and many interesting villages are in the area. The landscape is perfect for exploring on bicycles along the safe, well signed routes.

Facilities

Two modern, heated, well maintained sanitary buildings provide roomy adjustable showers and some washbasins in cabins. Family shower room. Children's bathroom. Laundry facilities. Supermarket. Restaurant, bar and terrace. Separate takeaway. Swimming pool (unheated) and separate pool for children with slides and water features. Play areas and sports field. Boules. Volleyball. Children's entertainment (in holiday periods). Excursions for adults (low season). Bicycle hire. WiFi over site.

Open: 1 April - 31 October.

Directions

From Westerscheldetunnel, turn right at roundabout to Breskens-Hoek-Oostburg. At Schoondijke roundabout follow Breskens/Groede, turn left at first lights to Groede/Nieuwvliet then right at first roundabout in Nieuwvliet. Site is signed. GPS: 51.382207, 3.458188

Charges guide

Per unit incl. 2 persons and electricity	€ 20.00 - € 41.00

For latest campsite news, availability and prices visit
alanrogers.com

Oostkapelle
Camping De Pekelinge

Landmetersweg 1, NL-4356 RE Oostkapelle (Zeeland) T: 0118 582 820. E: pekelinge@ardoer.com

alanrogers.com/NL6926

Camping De Pekelinge is a good quality, family site only 3 km. from the beach. There are 320 spacious touring pitches, all with electricity (10A). These include special pitches for motorcaravans and four pitches with private bathrooms and car parking, designed for visitors with disabilities. The site is of a high standard and its imaginative facilities are designed for both good and bad weather. Good sports facilities include an all-weather swimming pool with a slide (65 m), a children's pool and water play areas, plus an indoor play area. Food and drink can be enjoyed at the Grand Café complex.

Facilities

Sanitary facilities include family bathrooms and facilities for disabled visitors. Private sanitary units on many pitches. Launderette. Well stocked supermarket. Café. Snack bar. All-weather swimming pool with water chute and paddling pool. Water play areas. Indoor and outdoor play areas. Football pitch. Tennis. Volleyball. Beach volleyball. Basketball. Air trampolines. Climbing wall. 2 PlayStations. Small animal farm. Bicycle hire. Dogs are not accepted in July/Aug. Free WiFi over site. Off site: Beach 3 km.

Open: 22 March - 3 November.

Directions

From A58 take Domburg exit. Continue on N57 towards Domburg and Oostkapelle. Take the N287 towards Oostkapelle. Site is well signed from the town. GPS: 51.55715, 3.55161

Charges guide

Per unit incl. 2 persons	
and electricity	€ 20.00 - € 46.00
extra person	€ 4.50
dog (excl. July/Aug)	€ 2.50

Oostkapelle
Camping Park & Wellness Ons Buiten

Aagtekerkseweg 2a, NL-4356 RJ Oostkapelle (Zeeland) T: 0118 581 813. E: onsbuiten@ardoer.com

alanrogers.com/NL6928

Camping Ons Buiten is a high quality site set amongst the landscapes of the Zeeuws, just 2.5 km. from the sea. The pitches are a minimum of 100 sq.m. and are serviced with electricity, cable TV, water and drainage. The pitch areas are kept free of cars, with parking adjacent. Ons Buiten is a destination for the whole family, and many activities are organised in high season for all ages. Children can play in the imaginative pool area, and adults can spoil themselves at the site's excellent wellness centre. The three sanitary units have delightful themed facilities for children.

Facilities

Toilet block including special facilities for children and disabled visitors. Private sanitary units on comfort pitches. Launderette. Motorcaravan services. Shared kitchen with fridge, microwave and hob. Supermarket. Bakery. Café/restaurant. Takeaway. Heated covered swimming pool. Play area. Sports pitch. Minigolf. Tennis. Wellness centre with sauna, salt cave and infrared cabin. WiFi over site (charged). Pets are not accepted. Off site: Beach 2.5 km. Golf 4 km.

Open: 31 March - 3 November.

Directions

From the A15 take exit 12 towards Middleburg and then the N57 for 50 km. and join the N287 (Waterstraat) towards Oostkapelle. Site is well signed. GPS: 51.56253, 3.54627

Charges guide

Per unit incl. 2 persons	
and electricity	€ 24.00 - € 67.00
extra person	€ 5.50

Ouwerkerk
Kampeerterrein De Vier Bannen

Weg v.d. Buitenlandse Pers A, NL-4305 RJ Ouwerkerk (Zeeland) T: 0111 642 044.

E: informatie@vierbannen.nl **alanrogers.com/NL7030**

De Vier Bannen is located in a beautiful forested area, with extensive stretches of water created by the flood of 1953. There are 170 spacious pitches, including 100 comfort pitches equipped with WiFi, water, drainage and electricity (4/16A). They are spread over several fields, surrounded by trees and shrubs. On-site amenities for children include a bouncy castle and a range of play equipment, as well as a nature trail and park to develop their knowledge of the environment. There is a pub/restaurant adjacent to the site. Close by is a small sandy beach from where you can swim in the Oosterschelde. The area is perfect for fishing, diving, canoeing, kayaking, hiking and cycling along the Oosterschelde.

Facilities

Single toilet block includes showers and open style washbasins. Facilities for disabled visitors. Motorcaravan services. Laundry. Play equipment. Nature trail. WiFi over part of site (charged). Mobile homes for rent. Dogs are not accepted. Off site: Pub/restaurant. Small beach and swimming in the Oosterschelde. Fishing. Watersports.

Open: 15 March - 31 October.

Directions

Follow the N59 Rotterdam-Zierikzee and take exit Ouwerkerk (2 km. east of Zierikzee). From there follow the ANWB camping signs. GPS: 51.61783, 3.98668

Charges guide

Per unit incl. 2 persons and electricity	€ 18.90
extra person	€ 4.50

FREE Alan Rogers Travel Card
Extra benefits and savings - see page 12

Renesse
Camping de Oase

Roelandseweg 8, NL-4325 CS Renesse (Zeeland) T: 0111 461 358. E: info@campingdeoase.nl
alanrogers.com/NL5555

De Oase is situated on the outskirts of Renesse, a lively, North Sea holiday resort with long, sandy beaches. Campers will have free transport to the beach, around Schouwen-Duiveland, one of the islands in Zeeland, and further afield to Goes and Middelburg. It is ideal for those who enjoy an active holiday, being connected to the many cycle and walking tracks that are laid out in this typically flat Dutch landscape. There are 450 pitches, including 146 for touring units. They are grassy and spacious and all have electricity (6/10A), water, drainage and WiFi; 90 are also equipped with TV connections.

Facilities

Modern, clean and spacious sanitary facilities include rooms for babies, children and disabled visitors. Family showers. Launderette. Supermarket with fresh bread. Recreation areas. Sports fields. Entertainment for children in high season. Free local transport. Dogs are not accepted. Off site: Renesse centre 300 m. Beach 1.5 km. Dreischor (Europe's Greenest Village 2001) 12 km.

Open: 15 March - 1 November.

Directions

Site is just south of Renesse. Follow signs for Renesse Transferium and site is opposite. GPS: 51.72838, 3.77179

Charges guide

Per unit incl. 2 persons and electricity	€ 22.50 - € 32.50
extra person (over 3 yrs)	€ 5.00

Renesse
Camping De Wijde Blick

Lagezoom 23, NL-4325 CP Renesse (Zeeland) T: 0111 468 888. E: wijdeblick@ardoer.com
alanrogers.com/NL5560

The Van Oost family run this neat campsite in a pleasant and personal way. It is located on the outskirts of the village of Renesse in a quiet rural spot. From May to September a free bus runs to Renesse and the beach, just 2 km. away. De Wijde Blick has 328 pitches with 218 for touring units, all with electricity (6/10A) and TV connections, and 90-120 sq.m. in area. Of these, 16 have private sanitary facilities and 202 are fully serviced. There are 20 attractively arranged motorcaravan pitches with hardstanding, and ten special 'bike and hike' pitches for those touring without a car. Cars are parked away from pitches.

Facilities

Three first class, modern toilet blocks are heated, with clean facilities including washbasins in cabins, controllable showers and facilities for disabled campers. Microwave and fridge. Bath (on payment). Laundry (with pleasant waiting area). Gas supplies. Motorcaravan services. Shop. Restaurant/bar (15/3-31/10). Swimming pool (1/5-20/9; can be covered). Free WiFi over site. Good playgrounds. Air trampoline. Volleyball area. Open-air theatre. Bicycle hire. Activities for children. Breakfast service available.

Open: All year.

Directions

Renesse is on the island of Schouwen (connected to the mainland by a bridge and three dams). From the N57 from Middelburg take the Renesse exit. After 2 km. follow road 106 to the left and then site signs. Site is on the east side of the village. GPS: 51.71843, 3.76713

Charges guide

Per unit incl. 2 persons	€ 19.00 - € 35.00
extra person	€ 5.00

Renesse
Strandpark De Zeeuwse Kust

Helleweg 8, NL-4326 LJ Renesse/Noordwelle (Zeeland) T: 0111 468 282.
E: info@strandparkdezeeuwsekust.nl alanrogers.com/NL6948

Whether you want relaxation, something for the children, the seaside or activities, you will find all of these at De Zeeuwse Kust located just 250 m. from the sea with its beautiful sandy beach. The outstanding, hotel standard facilities contained within the centrally located building are in a class of their own, offering a haven whatever the weather. From the open plan kitchen, the oversized wooden stools, to the open fireplace, they are all first class. This site has 218 spacious and comfortable pitches, all with electricity (16A), water, waste water and TV connections. There are 32 pitches with private sanitary provision. The modern sanitary unit is heated and includes facilities for children and disabled visitors.

Facilities

Modern, first class sanitary building providing showers, washbasins, private cabins, family shower rooms and other facilities for children and disabled visitors. Launderette. Motorcaravan services. Shop/mini-market. Fresh bread (all year). Heated swimming pool. Play areas (indoors and outdoors). Sports field. Games room with Xbox stations. Small film theatre. Entertainment team (special holidays, weekends and July/Aug). Whirlpool. Sauna. First aid post. WiFi (free). Dogs welcome all year.

Open: All year (with most facilities).

Directions

From the A15 take exit 12 towards Middelburg. Follow the N57 through Ouddorp and then turn right on the N652. Immediately turn left for the N651 and follow to Noordwelle. Site is well signed. GPS: 51.739062, 3.802369

Charges guide

Per unit incl. 2 persons, electricity, water and waste water	€ 20.00 - € 46.00
No credit cards.	

For latest campsite news, availability and prices visit
alanrogers.com

Renesse
Camping International Renesse

Scharendijkseweg 8, NL-4325 LD Renesse (Zeeland) T: 0111 461 391. E: info@camping-international.net

alanrogers.com/NL6950

Situated 300 m. from the beach at Renesse in Zeeland, this is a friendly, family run site. Its owners have set a high standard, which is demonstrated by the immaculate and tastefully decorated sanitary facilities. There are 200 pitches, all for touring units and with electricity connections (16A). These are a generous size and laid out in bays and avenues surrounded by hedging. Around a courtyard area beyond reception is a supermarket and a bar which is attractively decorated with novel figures and the owner's personal memorabilia. Outside bench seating and umbrellas turns this corner of the site into a popular meeting place.

Facilities

Two luxury sanitary blocks provide showers, washbasins (some in cabins) and a baby room. Laundry room. Motorcaravan services. Supermarket. Bar. Games room. TV. Play area. Bicycle hire. Entertainment in high season for all. Max. 1 dog.

Open: 1 March - 31 October.

Directions

From Zierikzee follow N59 to Renesse for 15 km. and turn right at roundabout (before town) onto local road signed R101. Continue for 1 km. and turn left, then first right to site on right.
GPS: 51.73981, 3.78912

Charges guide

Per unit incl. 2 persons	€ 28.00 - € 46.00
extra person	€ 5.00
child (2-9 yrs)	€ 4.00
electricity (per kWh)	€ 0.40

Renesse
Camping Julianahoeve

Hoogenboomlaan 42, NL-4325 DM Renesse (Zeeland) T: 0111 461 414. E: julianahoeve@ardoer.com

alanrogers.com/NL6952

A very large site with 1,400 pitches, mainly for mobile homes and chalets, Camping Julianahoeve still retains a few pitches for touring units and tents. You cannot get much closer to the sea, and a path leads through the dunes to the beach. All the main touring pitches are large and fully serviced. Some have individual sanitary units, and others have hardstandings. Located in the sunniest area of the Netherlands, this is an ideal site for a family holiday by the beach. A member of the Ardoer group.

Facilities

Several well appointed toilet blocks serve the site with facilities for younger children, babies and disabled visitors. Individual sanitary units available. Launderette. Supermarket. Bar. Brasserie. Café with terrace. Snack bar. Indoor pool complex with 60 m. water slide. Play areas. Sports pitches. Theatre with entertainment for all ages. WiFi. Dogs are not accepted. Off site: Fishing 500 m. Golf and riding 1 km. Boat launching 5 km.

Open: 1 April - 6 November.

Directions

From the A5 take exit 12 and follow the N57 through Ouddorp, then follow signs to Renesse. Site is well signed from the town. GPS: 51.72738, 3.75897

Charges guide

Per unit incl. 2 persons and electricity	€ 20.00 - € 58.00
extra person (over 2 yrs)	€ 5.25
child (2-4 yrs)	€ 3.50

Retranchement
Camping Cassandria Bad

Strengweg 4, NL-4525 LW Retranchement (Zeeland) T: 0117 392 300. E: info@cassandriabad.nl

alanrogers.com/NL5502

Cassandria Bad was established in 1992, lying very close to the Belgian border and the resort of Cadzand Bad, just under 2 km. from the nearest North Sea beach. Pitches are grassy and spacious; some are privately let for the full season. All pitches are equipped with 10A electricity and free cable TV connections. Except for loading and unloading, cars are not allowed in the camping area, but a large parking area is provided. On-site amenities include a bar, snack bar, shop services and games room. During high season, lots of activities are organised, including karaoke, bingo and sports tournaments.

Facilities

Two clean and well maintained sanitary units with free showers, and two family bathrooms in the main block. Good laundry facilities. Small shop (fresh bread daily). Bar with LCD projector and screen. Snack bar. Sports fields with volleyball, and 2 football pitches. Games room with table football, air hockey and electronic games. Trampoline. Several well appointed and interesting play areas. Bicycle hire. WiFi over site (charged). Max. 1 dog.

Open: 23 March - 31 October.

Directions

Approaching from the west and Bruges, use the Belgian N31 and then N376 towards Knokke-Heist and then across the Dutch border to Sluis. Here take the road to Groede and turn left towards Cadzand Bad at the second crossroads. Site is well signed from here. GPS: 51.36613, 3.38583

Charges guide

Per unit incl. up to 4 persons and electricity	€ 25.50 - € 33.50
extra person	€ 4.50

FREE Alan Rogers Travel Card
Extra benefits and savings - see page 12

Retranchement
Camping De Zwinhoeve

Duinweg 1, NL-4225 LX Retranchement (Zeeland) T: 0117 392 120. E: zwinhoeve@ardoer.com

alanrogers.com/NL6944

Camping De Zwinhoeve is a family campsite that lies directly on the dunes and borders of Belgium and Holland. Within minutes you can either be on the beach of the North Sea or in the nature reserve, Het Zwin. The site has 411 spacious pitches, of which 120 are for touring and all with 10A electricity. The comfort pitches also have water, drainage and cable TV, while super comfort pitches have private sanitary units. Facilities include a supermarket, a restaurant and a bar where you can relax and enjoy a drink. The wellness area has a sauna, massage and a jacuzzi. In high season, an entertainment programme is arranged for children.

Facilities

Heated toilet block including a baby room and facilities for disabled visitors. Launderette. Well stocked shop. Bar. Restaurant. Snack bar with takeaway. Play area. Entertainment and miniclub (high season). Recreation and sports areas. TV. Sauna. Cycle routes. WiFi over part of site (charged). Off site: Golf 9 km. Fishing. Swimming in the sea. Various watersports.

Open: 14 March - 26 October.

Directions

The site is on the coastal border with Belgium, 10 km. from Knokke-Heist. From Sluis-Breskens N675, exit towards Retranchement N674 and follow site signs. GPS: 51.36621, 3.3739

Charges guide

Per unit incl. 2 persons, water and electricity	€ 20.00 - € 49.00
extra person (over 2 yrs)	€ 5.00

Scherpenisse
Vakantiepark De Pluimpot

Geertruidaweg 3, NL-4694 PH Scherpenisse (Zeeland) T: 0166 662 727. E: pluimpot@ardoer.com

alanrogers.com/NL7086

De Pluimpot is located on the island of Tholen, in the east of Zeeland, and lies adjacent to a beach and also to the Oosterschelde National Park. Around 300 pitches are occupied by mobile homes but there are a further 50 touring pitches. These are all equipped with cable TV connections and 6A electricity. Pitches are large (100 sq.m) and well shaded. On-site leisure amenities include bicycle and go-kart hire, an 18-hole minigolf course and two children's playgrounds; guests have free admission to a local swimming pool. There is good road access to a slipway for boat launching, with ample parking. A member of the Ardoer group.

Facilities

Three heated sanitary units, two for the touring pitches, have controllable showers, one with disability access. Private cabins available. Baby bath and changing facilities. Bath with jacuzzi (charged). Laundry. Bar/brasserie. Small shop. Play area. Minigolf. Sports competitions. Sports field. Fishing. Activity and entertainment programme. Boat launching 750 m. Free WiFi over part of site. Mobile homes and chalets for rent. Off site: Watersports. Cycle trips. Riding. Oosterschelde National Park.

Open: 1 April - 31 October.

Directions

Approaching from Bergen op Zoom, head west on N286, passing Tholen. Continue to Sint Maartensdijk and then follow signs to site. GPS: 51.533259, 4.074536

Charges guide

Per unit incl. 2 persons and electricity	€ 20.00 - € 28.00
extra person	€ 4.50
child (2-12 yrs)	€ 3.00

Sluis
Camping De Meidoorn

Hoogstraat 68, NL-4524 LA Sluis (Zeeland) T: 0117 461 662. E: info@camping-meidoorn.eu

alanrogers.com/NL5505

This is a friendly, family run site within 400 m. of the historic city of Sluis on the Belgian border, yet bounded by mature trees, open countryside and a small lake. Laid out in groups divided by hedges and small trees, there are 250 pitches including about 100 for touring units and six cabins. Public transport operates in July and August between Breskens, Sluis and Knokke, which is free to guests and can take you to the coast. The bus stop is 100 m. away and buses run every hour.

Facilities

One large sanitary building provides modern showers, washbasins with cold water, two private cabins, facilities for disabled visitors. All hot water is charged. Launderette (coins). Recreation room (with toys). Bar and restaurant with simple menu. Takeaway. Playground and sports field. Boules. Air hockey. Pool table. Fishing (licence from reception). Children's art and craft sessions (Mon, Wed, Fri). WiFi (charged). Off site: Tennis 500 m. (charged).

Open: 1 April - 1 November.

Directions

From Calais, Dunkerque, Ostend or Brugge take N374 to Sluis. GPS: 51.313372, 3.391305

Charges guide

Per unit incl. 2 persons and electricity	€ 19.00 - € 25.00
extra person	€ 2.50

For latest campsite news, availability and prices visit

alanrogers.com

Stavenisse
Camping 't Oude Dorp
Keetenweg 10, NL-4696 PD Stavenisse (Zeeland) T: 0166 692 421. E: campingtoudedorp@planet.nl
alanrogers.com/NL7085

Camping 't Oude Dorp is a family campsite in the southwest of the Netherlands, located on the island of Tholen in the province of Zeeland. The site is next to the Oosterschelde National Park, which is a wild and natural area of salt water and mud flats that is well known for watersports, cycling and birdwatching. The eight touring pitches are generously sized (140-150 sq.m), some have shade, and all have electricity (16A Europlug) and water. There are also 115 permanent pitches including cabins, chalets, mobile homes and caravans to rent. One chalet has been specially adapted for disabled visitors. The campsite is an excellent starting point for walking and cycling.

Facilities	Directions
Heated prefabricated toilet block has hot showers and facilities for children. Room for disabled visitors (key). Washing machines, dryers and iron. Bar. Restaurant. Snack bar. TV. Heated outdoor swimming pool. Two children's pools with water slides. Large sports field. Go-karts (free). Play area. Entertainment (high season). WiFi throughout (charged). Beach. Fishing.	The site is north of Antwerp. From Antwerp travel north on A12 leading to A4 and then A58. Exit at N259 for N286 towards Stavenisse. After Stavenisse follow signs for site. GPS: 51.60278, 4.03811

Open: 31 March - 31 October.

Charges guide

Per unit incl. 2 persons and electricity	€ 17.00
extra person	€ 5.00
child (2-11)	€ 4.00

Vrouwenpolder
Camping Oranjezon
Koningin Emmaweg 16a, NL-4354 KD Vrouwenpolder (Zeeland) T: 0118 591 549. E: info@oranjezon.nl
alanrogers.com/NL7066

Oranjezon (orange sun) is an environmentally conscious, family run site located close to the sand dunes of the Schouwen-Duiveland peninsula. It is a pleasant fifteen minute stroll to the beach following a path across a nature reserve and through the dunes to the sea. There are 400 pitches here varying in size and price but all have 6/10A electricity. On-site amenities include a swimming pool with separate shallow area for young children, two children's playgrounds and an area with chickens, ducks and goats. The shop stocks essentials, newspapers and some household items; fresh bread is available every morning.

Facilities	Directions
Two main sanitary units are modern and have free showers, colourful children's area, a family room and facilities for disabled visitors. There are four smaller units around the site. Private sanitary units on 18 pitches. Motorcaravan services. Shop. Café/restaurant. Snack bar. Swimming pool. Paddling pool. Wellness area with sauna, cold tub and solarium. Play areas. Small animal area for children. Activity team (high season; under 13s). WiFi over site (charged). Off site: Vrouwenpolder 3 km.	From A58 motorway, take exit for Domburg (N57) and follow signs for Oostkapelle. At Serooskerke go towards Oostkapelle/Domburg (N287). After 3 km. (after green/white hotel) turn right into Munnikweg. Continue for 2.5 km. turn left into campsite access road. GPS: 51.58402, 3.58479

Open: 31 March - 21 October.

Charges guide

Per unit incl. 4 persons and electricity	€ 23.50 - € 43.50
extra person	€ 4.00

Wemeldinge
Camping Linda
Oostelijke kanaalweg 4, NL-4424 NC Wemeldinge (Zeeland) T: 0113 621 259. E: info@campinglinda.nl
alanrogers.com/NL6915

Camping Linda is a welcoming, family run site, situated behind the dyke on the shores of the Oosterschelde, with direct access to a small beach. The area is ideal for watersports enthusiasts and particularly popular with divers. Pitches are a good size, level and grassy, with 70 out of 350 places reserved for touring. Most of these are situated in the quieter part of the site, across a narrow lane close to the beach access and fishing. Other pitches are closer to the reception area. All have electricity (6/10A), water and TV connection. In high season, a full entertainment programme is organised.

Facilities	Directions
Two modern, clean sanitary buildings with showers (coin operated) and washbasins (some in cabins). Well equipped children's shower and baby room. No facilities for disabled visitors. Motorcaravan services. Laundry. Small shop (w/ends only). Bar and large function room. Snack bar/takeaway. Play areas and playing field. Games room and indoor adventure play area. Bicycle hire. Max. 2 dogs. WiFi throughout (free).	From the south, take A58 towards Vlissingen. Leave at exit 35 and head north towards Kapelle. Continue on N670 to Wemeldinge. Site is next to Yacht Haven and is well signed. GPS: 51.516122, 4.007424

Open: 1 April - 1 November.

Charges guide

Per unit incl. 2 persons and electricity	€ 16.00 - € 23.00
extra person	€ 3.00

FREE Alan Rogers Travel Card
Extra benefits and savings - see page 12

Zeeland

Westenschouwen
Camping Duinoord
Steenweg 16, Duinoord aan Zee, NL-4328 RM Westenschouwen (Zeeland) T: 0111 658 888.
E: duinoord@ardoer.com **alanrogers.com/NL6942**

Camping Duinoord lies directly beside a wide sandy North Sea beach and a large forest. The site itself is divided between two locations: Duinoord aan Zee and Landgoed Duinoord. The main site and reception are beside the sea and forest. There are 100 serviced touring pitches with 4/6A electricity, water, drainage and cable TV. Camping Landgoed Duinoord is five minutes away and is set peacefully in the polders. The pitches here are larger and less enclosed. Both sites have a similar ambience of space and tranquillity and the proximity of the beach and the forest make them special.

Facilities

Good, clean sanitary provision on both sites, incorporating a full range of facilities. Laundry facilities. Bakery. Small paddling pool with water jets. Recreation room with weekly theatrical productions. Outdoor football table. Play areas for under 12s. Off site: Bars and restaurants close to beach access. Shop 300 m. Bicycle hire 500 m. Golf and riding 2 km.

Open: All year.

Directions

From Rotterdam follow the A15 to the west and take exit 12, signed Brielle and Middelburg onto the N57. Follow for 42 km. until Westenschouwen. From here site is 1.5 km. and signed. GPS: 51.67228, 3.70629

Charges guide

Per unit incl. 2 persons
and electricity   € 17.00 - € 41.00
extra person (over 2 yrs)   € 4.50 - € 5.00

Wolphaartsdijk
Camping De Veerhoeve
Veerweg 48, NL-4471 NC Wolphaartsdijk (Zeeland) T: 0113 581 155. E: info@deveerhoeve.nl
alanrogers.com/NL5580

This is a family run site near the shores of the Veerse Meer, which is ideal for family holidays. It is situated in a popular area for watersports and is well suited for sailing, windsurfing and fishing enthusiasts, with boat launching 100 m. away. A sandy beach and recreation area, ideal for children, is only a five minute walk. As with most sites in this area there are many mature static and seasonal pitches. However, part of the friendly, relaxed site is reserved for touring units with 90 marked pitches on grassy ground, all with electrical connections. A member of the Holland Tulip Parcs group.

Facilities

Sanitary facilities in three blocks have been well modernised with full tiling. Hot showers are on payment. Laundry facilities. Motorcaravan services. Supermarket (all season). Restaurant and snack bar. TV room. Tennis. Playground and playing field. Games room. Bicycle hire. Fishing. Accommodation for groups. Max. 1 dog. WiFi (charged). Off site: Slipway for launching boats 100 m. Riding 2 km. Golf 5 km.

Open: 1 April - 30 October.

Directions

From N256 Goes-Zierikzee road take Wolphaartsdijk exit. Follow through village and signs to site (one site sign is obscured by other road signs and could be missed). GPS: 51.54678, 3.81345

Charges guide

Per unit incl. up to 4 persons
and electricity   € 23.00 - € 25.00
Camping Cheques accepted.

Wolphaartsdijk
Camping 't Veerse Meer
Veerweg 71, NL-4471 NB Wolphaartsdijk (Zeeland) T: 0113 581 423. E: info@campingveersemeer.nl
alanrogers.com/NL6920

This well cared for, family run site is situated beside the Veerse Meer, on the island of Zuid-Beveland, in Zeeland. Emphasis at this site is on a neat and tidy appearance, quality facilities and a friendly reception. The site occupies both sides of Veerweg with one side providing seven touring pitches with individual sanitary facilities and fully serviced hardstanding pitches for motorcaravans. On the other side are the main buildings and 40 generous touring pitches, many fully serviced and separated by hedging, and a tent field. Further seasonal and static places are kept apart. A feature of this campsite is a narrow canal crossed by a bridge, leading to an area of seasonal units. Some attractive chalets are for rent.

Facilities

The single, modern toilet block is clean and has showers (token operated), open style wash areas, two wash cabins, facilities for children, and a baby bath. Laundry with book/magazine exchange. Motorcaravan services. Bar. Play area. Trampoline. Boules. Organised events for all in high season. Bicycle hire. Fishing. Free WiFi over site. Off site: Supermarket 500 m. Bars, restaurants and minigolf at the watersports marina complex 900 m. Riding 1.5 km. Golf 6 km.

Open: 1 April - 31 October.

Directions

From N256 Goes-Zierikzee road take Wolphaartsdijk exit heading west. Turn right after 1 km. and follow signs to Veerse Meer (the lake) along Kwistenburg, bearing left on to Aardebolle-weg, right turn onto Veerweg at mini roundabout and site reception is to left in 500 m. GPS: 51.54436, 3.81242

Charges guide

Per unit incl. 2 persons
and electricity   € 15.00 - € 22.50
No credit cards.

172

For latest campsite news, availability and prices visit
alanrogers.com

Zoutelande
Camping De Meerpaal

Werendijkseweg 14, NL-4374 NB Zoutelande (Zeeland) T: 0118 561 300. E: meerpaal@ardoer.com

alanrogers.com/NL7074

Camping Resort De Meerpaal is a high quality site located close to the beach and dunes, and within walking or cycling distance of the seaside town of Zoutelande. There are 75 large, grassy touring pitches here and all but three, which are set aside for motorcaravans, have sanitary units on the pitch. The resort offers hotel style accommodation in chalets, and there are a number of privately owned chalets. On-site amenities include a woodland area and a nature reserve of wetland, flowers and shrubs. The attractive reception area has a wellness centre, a restaurant and separate snack bar. Zoutelande is nearby with shops, cafeteria and restaurants; it holds regular markets with food and antiques stalls. A pleasant walk to the town passes through pine woods and sand dunes or along the beach to the seafront promenade. The area is known as the Zeeuwse Rivièra for its sunny climate and long, sandy beaches.

Facilities	Directions
Two good, clean sanitary units serve part of the site. Many pitches with own sanitary units (WC, shower, dishwashing sinks, electricity and water). Laundry with washing machines and dryer. Small shop with fresh bread, eggs and basics. Bar with terrace. Restaurant. Takeaway meals. Wellness with saunas and massage. Play area. Boules. Sports field. Mini club for under 12s. Woodland walks and nature area on site. Free WiFi.	Approaching from the east, take A58 (E312) to Middelburg and near Vlissingen, take N288 north to Zoutelande. At Groot Valkenisse turn left at lights (site signed) then right at first roundabout. Follow signs to the site. GPS: 51.49562, 3.50578

Open: 16 February - 3 January.

Charges guide

Per unit incl. 2 persons	
and electricity	€ 21.00 - € 43.00
with own sanitary unit	€ 28.00 - € 54.00

Zoutelande
Camping Janse

Westkapelseweg 59, NL-4374 ND Zoutelande (Zeeland) T: 0118 561 359. E: info@campingjanse.nl

alanrogers.com/NL7076

Camping Janse is in the far southwest of Zeeland. It is a family, seaside site on the edge of sand dunes with the beach directly behind. There are 136 touring pitches, all 95 sq.m. with 6A electricity and water nearby, plus bungalows and caravans to rent. Some motorcaravan pitches are partly paved, and a field area (without electricity) is set aside for young people with small tents. Daily fresh bread is available and for other provisions the supermarket is 50 m. away. A restaurant with a terrace and play area for children is directly opposite the campsite entrance. In addition to the attraction of the sea and beach, there are opportunities for sports and activities on the site, and during the holiday period an organised activity programme runs three times a week.

Facilities	Directions
Sanitary building with heating, washbasins in cubicles and baby bath. Facilities for disabled campers (key access). Washing machine. Microwave. Dishwasher. Motorcaravan services. Fresh bread. Animal corner. Sand pit. Boules. Books, magazines and toys to borrow. Activity programme during holiday period (3 times a week). Trampoline. Telephone. WiFi (free in games room). Dogs are not accepted. Off site: Restaurant opposite. Beach a few minutes walk over the dunes. Supermarket 50 m.	Take the E312/A58 around the south of Middelburg then onto the N288 through Vlissingen and Zoutelande, after which the site is just over 1 km. on left. GPS: 51.51046, 3.466318

Open: 28 March - 2 November.

Charges guide

Per unit incl. 2 persons	
and electricity	€ 19.95 - € 31.70

CAPITAL: DEN HAAG (THE HAGUE)

Zuid-Holland is an historically rich province with much to offer the tourist: lakes, rivers and the sea provide endless opportunities for watersports, while the flat landscape is ideal for cycling and walking.

Together with Nord-Holland, Zuid-Holland is one of the most prosperous areas of the lowlands. Most industry these days is confined to the middle sized Dutch towns and cities, but everywhere you will see evidence of the country's more extensive commercial past, particularly in the cities of Rotterdam and The Hague.

The modern port of Rotterdam is a vibrant city packed with art and cultural activities – galleries, concert halls, theatres and museums abound. In The Hague, the seat of government, royal palaces, stately embassies and town houses give the city a regal atmosphere; a stone's throw from the city are the resorts of Scheveningen and Kijkduin and the theme parks of Duinrell and Drievliet.

In the north of Zuid-Holland is the landscape of the Holland Lakes, an area dotted with lakes, rivers and drainage canals, all interspersed with wide, open polders. The Green Heart, hidden between the big cities of the Randstad, is a vast oasis of peace and tranquillity that lends itself to a variety of open-air activities. With its coastline and pleasant resorts, the bulb region also has much to offer visitors who want a summer beach holiday.

Places of interest

The Hague (Den Haag): important museums such as the Mauritshuis, The Hague Municipal Museum and Panorama Mesdag.

Rotterdam: Museum Boymans van Beuningen, contemporary architecture and culture, port area.

Leiden: large student population brings this historical city to life, with many bars, restaurants and good museums.

Gouda: famous for its cheese, 'stroopwafels' and beautiful 15th-century town hall.

Delft: medieval centre with canals, bridges, squares and historic façades - a charming backdrop whether shopping or just taking a relaxing stroll.

Attractions

Bulb Region: its extensive and colourful tulip fields make a truly unique sight in spring.

Duinrell: large theme park for the whole family.

Madurodam: famous miniature city where you can enjoy the highlights of the Netherlands on a scale of 1:25.

Animal parks: Avifauna, bird park in Alphen aan den Rijn, Blijdorp Zoo in Rotterdam

Vlaggetjesdag Scheveningen: famous festival in mid June celebrating the arrival of the first herring; Scheveningen resort with a casino, large hotels, discos and theatres.

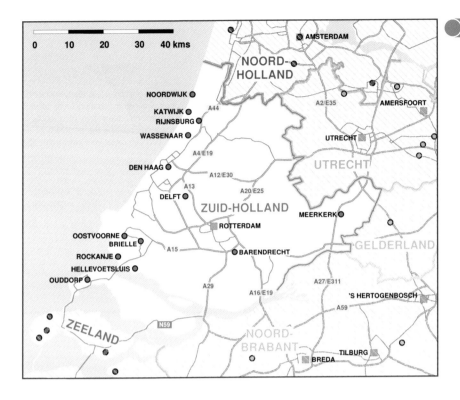

Barendrecht
Camping De Oude Maas

Achterzeedijk 1A, NL-2991 SB Barendrecht (Zuid-Holland) T: 0786 772 445.

E: info@recreatieparkdeoudemaas.nl **alanrogers.com/NL5610**

This site is easily accessed from the A15 southern Rotterdam ring road and is situated right by the river, so it is well worth considering if you are visiting Rotterdam or just want a peaceful stop. The 65 touring pitches are pleasantly sited away from the residential section, all are on grass and have 10A hook-up. There is a pleasant separate touring area for 11 motorcaravans with electricity, water and waste water connections in a hedged group near the marina and river. The Oude Maas (Old Meuse) carries barges that make up much of the passing river traffic. The site has a section for seasonal units and mobile homes in a woodland setting, well back from the river on level grass. The small town of Heerjansdam is within 1,500 m. and has shops, bars and restaurants.

Facilities

One toilet block provides all necessary facilities including a unit for disabled visitors and a baby room. Launderette. Motorcravan services. Fishing. Good play area with swings, slides and climbing frames for all ages. Bicycle hire. WiFi (charged). Max. 1 dog. Off site: Swimming pool nearby. Riding 8 km. Golf 10 km. Rotterdam city centre reached by bicycle or train from Barendecht Station 4 km.

Open: All year.

Directions

Best approached from Hook/Rotterdam then A29 Rotterdam-Bergen op Zoom motorway. Leave A29 at exit 20 (Barendrecht) and follow signs for Heerjansdam and site. GPS: 51.83361, 4.55236

Charges guide

Per unit incl. 2 persons and electricity	€ 20.00
extra person	€ 4.00
child (0-12 yrs)	€ 2.50
dog	€ 2.50

FREE Alan Rogers Travel Card
Extra benefits and savings - see page 12

Brielle

Camping De Krabbeplaat

Oude Veerdam 4, NL-3231 NC Brielle (Zuid-Holland) T: 0181 412 363. E: info@krabbeplaat.nl

alanrogers.com/NL6980

Camping De Krabbeplaat is a family run site situated near the ferry port in a wooded, recreation area next to the Brielse Meer lake. There are 448 spacious pitches, with 68 for touring units, all with 10A electricity, cable connections and a water supply nearby. A nature conservation plan exists to ensure the site fits into its natural environment. The lake and its beaches provide the perfect spot for watersports and relaxation and the site has its own harbour where you can moor your own boat. This excellent site is very convenient for the Europort ferry terminal.

Facilities

One large and two smaller heated toilet blocks in traditional style provide separate toilets, showers and washing cabins. High standards of cleanliness. Dedicated unit for disabled campers and provision for babies. Warm water is free of charge. Dishwasher (free). Launderette. Motorcaravan services. Supermarket, snack bar, restaurant and takeaway (all season). Recreation room. Youth centre. Tennis. Playground and play field. Animal farm. Bicycle and children's pedal hire. Canoe, surf, pedal boat and boat hire. Fishing. WiFi over site (charged).

Open: 28 March - 30 September.

Directions

From the Amsterdam direction take the A4 (Europoort), then the A15 (Europoort). Take exit for Brielle on N57 and, just before Brielle, site is signed. GPS: 51.9097, 4.18536

Charges guide

Per unit incl. 2 persons and electricity	€ 19.50 - € 28.00
extra person	€ 3.45
child (under 12 yrs)	€ 2.90

Delft

Vakantiepark Delftse Hout

Korftlaan 5, NL-2616 LJ Delft (Zuid-Holland) T: 0152 130 040. E: info@delftsehout.nl

alanrogers.com/NL5600

Pleasantly situated in Delft's park and forest area on the eastern edge of the city, is this well run, modern site. It has 160 touring pitches quite formally arranged in groups of four to six and surrounded by attractive trees and hedges. All have sufficient space and electrical connections (10A Europlug). Modern buildings near the entrance house the site amenities. A good sized first floor restaurant serves snacks and full meals and has an outdoor terrace overlooking the swimming pool and pitches. Walking and cycling tours are organised and there is a recreation programme in high season.

Facilities

Modern, heated toilet facilities include a spacious family room and children's section. Facilities for disabled visitors. Laundry. Motorcaravan services. Shop for basic food and camping items (all season). Restaurant, takeaway and bar (28/3-1/10). Small outdoor swimming pool (30/4-15/9). Adventure playground. Recreation room. Bicycle hire. Gas supplies. Max. 1 dog. WiFi (free). Off site: Fishing 1 km. Riding and golf 5 km. Regular bus service to Delft centre.

Open: 28 March - 1 November.

Directions

From Rotterdam take exit 9, turn right at traffic lights towards IKEA. At IKEA roundabout turn left and drive parallel to motorway. At end of street, turn right and site is on left in 300 m. Do not follow sat nav. GPS: 52.01767, 4.37908

Charges guide

Per unit incl. 2 persons and electricity	€ 26.50 - € 36.00
extra person (3 yrs and older)	€ 3.50

Den Haag

Vakantiecentrum Kijkduinpark

Machiel Vrijenhoeklaan 450, NL-2555 NW Den Haag (Zuid-Holland) T: 0704 482 100. E: info@kijkduinpark.nl

alanrogers.com/NL5640

This is an ultra modern, all-year-round centre and family park with many chalets, villas and bungalows for rent and a large indoor swimming pool complex. The wooded touring area is immediately to the left of the entrance, with 330 pitches in shady glades of bark-covered sand. All pitches have electricity (10A), water, waste water and cable TV connections. In a paved central area are a supermarket, a snack bar and a restaurant. The main attraction here is the Meeresstrand, 500 m. from the site entrance. This is a long, wide sandy beach with flags to denote suitability for swimming. Windsurfing is popular.

Facilities

Five modern sanitary blocks. Four private cabins for rent. Launderette. Snack bar. Shop. Restaurant. Supermarket. Indoor pool. Sun beds. Tennis. Bicycle hire. Special golfing breaks. Entertainment and activities organised in summer. WiFi over site (free in restaurant). Off site: Beach, golf and fishing 500 m. Riding 5 km.

Open: All year.

Directions

Site is southwest of Den Haag on the coast and Kijkduin is well signed as an area from all round Den Haag. GPS: 52.05968, 4.21118

Charges guide

Per unit incl. 5 persons and electricity	€ 38.00 - € 74.00
extra person	€ 5.00

For latest campsite news, availability and prices visit

alanrogers.com

Hellevoetsluis
Camping Caravaning 't Weergors

Zuiddijk 2, NL-3221 LJ Hellevoetsluis (Zuid-Holland) T: 0181 312 430. E: info@weergors.nl

alanrogers.com/NL6970

A rustic style site built around old farm buildings, 't Weergors has a comfortable mature feel. At the front of the site is a well presented farmhouse which houses reception and includes the main site services. The sanitary blocks have been renewed recently as has the farm accommodating an attractive à la carte restaurant and pancake outlet. The reception has also been renewed including a new minimarket from where you can order fresh bread. There are currently 100 touring pitches (plus seasonal and static places), with another field at the back of the site which was recently developed to provide a further 70 or 80 touring places. Some of the touring pitches are exceptionally large, divided by hedging with a 'drive in, drive out' system (cars charged if kept on pitch). Each pitch has a cable TV connection and the site now has WiFi Internet access. An appealing feature of this site is the lake which lies to the rear, offering a quiet corner where you might head for an evening stroll. The old centre of Hellevoetsluis is worthy of a visit and the bustling city of Rotterdam is not far.

Facilities

Three sanitary blocks have showers (by key), washbasins, some in cabins, children's showers and toilets plus baby baths. Laundry facilities. Motorcaravan services. Small shop (1/4-31/10). Restaurant and bar (snacks) and pancakes. Tennis. Internet access. Play area. Paddling pool. Organised entertainment in high season. Fishing pond. Bicycle hire. Rally field.

Open: 1 April - 31 October.

Directions

From Rotterdam join A15 west to Rozenburg exit 12 and join N57 south for 11 km. Turn left on N497 signed Hellevoetsluis and follow site signs for 4.5 km. to roundabout. Turn right at roundabout to site 1.5 km. on right. GPS: 51.82943, 4.11618

Charges guide

Per unit incl. 2 persons and electricity	€ 20.72
extra person	€ 3.50
child (3-12 yrs)	€ 2.50
dog	€ 1.75

Camping Cheques accepted.

Hellevoetsluis
Strandcamping De Quack

Parkweg 2, NL-3221 LC Hellevoetsluis (Zuid-Holland) T: 0181 312 646. E: info@dequack.nl

alanrogers.com/NL6965

Camping De Quack is situated on the former island of Voorne with direct access to the long sandy beaches along the Haringvliet and the North Sea. Two nature reserves on the other side offer a completely different landscape where you can see, for example, orchids, spoonbills and small deer. The spacious site provides 130 grass touring pitches (100 sq.m), all with electricity (10A). Visitors with dogs are restricted to a separate area of 35 pitches. You may choose where to park your car, either beside your pitch or in a separate parking area. The nearby sea, rivers and lake are ideal for those who like watersports.

Facilities

Modern, clean sanitary facilities with free showers. Facilities for disabled visitors. Laundry. Motorcaravan services. Supermarket. Snack bar. Games room. Sea canoe hire. Bicycle hire. Boat launching. Recreation and sporting field. Playgrounds. Pets' corner. Minigolf. Tennis. Recreation team for children in high season. Free WiFi over part of site. Hikers' cabins for rent. Off site: Restaurant at the adjacent bungalow park. The fortified village of Hellevoetsluis with a wide range of shops and an historic dry dock dating from 1802, 3 km. Tropical swimming pool in Stellendam 8 km. Brielle 10 km. Delta works (30 min). Rotterdam (30 min).

Open: 1 April - 31 October.

Directions

Camping De Quack is 3 km. west of Hellevoetsluis near the N57, the main link from the north to Zeeland and to the A15, which connects to the main motorways near Rotterdam. GPS: 51.83794, 4.09021

Charges guide

Per unit incl. 2 persons and electricity	€ 20.62 - € 23.12
extra person (over 3 yrs)	€ 3.75
dog	€ 1.75

FREE Alan Rogers Travel Card
Extra benefits and savings - see page 12

Katwijk
Recreatiecentrum De Noordduinen
Campingweg 1, NL-2221 EW Katwijk aan Zee (Zuid-Holland) T: 0714 025 295. E: info@noordduinen.nl
alanrogers.com/NL5680

This is a large, well managed site surrounded by dunes and sheltered partly by trees and shrubbery, which also separate the various camping areas. The 200 touring pitches are marked and numbered but not divided. All have electricity (10A) and 75 are fully serviced with electricity, water, drainage and TV connection. There are also seasonal pitches and mobile homes for rent. Entertainment is organised in high season for various age groups. A new complex with indoor and outdoor pools, restaurant, small theatre and recreation hall provides a good addition to the site's facilities. Seasonal pitches and mobile homes are placed mostly away from the touring areas and are unobtrusive.

Facilities

The three sanitary blocks are modern and clean, with washbasins in cabins, a baby room and provision for visitors with disabilities. Laundry. Motorcaravan services. Supermarket with fresh bread daily, bar, restaurant, takeaway (all 1/4-31/10). Recreation room. Swimming pool complex. Play area. Only gas barbecues are permitted. Dogs are not accepted. Off site: Riding 150 m. Beach and fishing 300 m. Golf 6 km. Katwijk within walking distance.

Open: All year.

Directions

Leave A44 at exit 8 (Leiden-Katwijk) to join N206 to Katwijk. Take Katwijk Noord exit and follow signs to site. GPS: 52.21103, 4.40978

Charges guide

Per unit incl. 2 persons and electricity	€ 23.00 - € 37.00
extra person	€ 4.50

Camping Cheques accepted.

Katwijk
Recreatiecentrum De Zuidduinen
Zuidduinseweg 1, NL-2225 JS Katwijk aan Zee (Zuid-Holland) T: 0714 014 750. E: info@zuidduinen.nl
alanrogers.com/NL6982

De Zuidduinen is a pleasant, family site of 5 ha. in a protected nature reserve beside the sea. The site is only 200 m. from the beach and the seaside town of Katwijk is within walking distance. There are around 200 touring pitches (70 sq.m) of which 15 are larger, serviced pitches (90 sq.m). All have 4A electricity and cable connections for TV and radio. Camping bungalows and dune houses are available for rent. A programme of entertainment and activities for all ages is provided by an enthusiastic team in high season. The dunes are an ideal setting for families with children and people looking for a relaxing holiday. There are several walking and cycling tracks in and around the dunes.

Facilities

The heated toilet block is clean and well equipped. Facilities for babies and disabled visitors. Laundry. Motorcaravan services. Shop, restaurant and takeaway (all 20/3-10/9). Playground. TV room. Boules. Free WiFi over site. Off site: Beach 200 m. Tennis 250 m. Bicycle hire 1 km. Riding 2 km. Golf 5 km.

Open: 1 April or 1 week before Easter - 30 September.

Directions

The site is just southwest of Katwijk. From A44 take exit 8 onto the N206 (Katwijk aan Zee) and then follow the signs to Zuid-Boulevard and the site. GPS: 52.19319, 4.38986

Charges guide

Per unit incl. 4 persons and electricity	€ 25.50 - € 40.00
extra person	€ 3.00

Meerkerk
Camping De Victorie
Broekseweg 75-77, NL-4231 VD Meerkerk (Zuid-Holland) T: 0183 352 741. E: info@campingdevictorie.nl
alanrogers.com/NL5690

Within an hour's drive of the port of Rotterdam you can be pitched on this delightful, spacious site in the green heart of the Netherlands. De Victorie, a working farm and a member of an organisation of farm sites, offers an alternative to the bustling seaside sites. A modern building houses reception, an open plan office and a space with tables and chairs, where the friendly owners may well invite you to have a cup of coffee. The 100 grass pitches (100-200 sq.m) are level and have 6A electricity supply. Everything about the site is surprising and contrary to any preconceived ideas.

Facilities

The main sanitary block is kept spotlessly clean, tastefully decorated and fully equipped. Showers are on payment. Laundry room. Additional sanitary facilities are around the site. Farm shop and small bar (once a week). Play area. Trampoline. Play field. Fishing. Riding. WiFi throughout (charged). Off site: Bicycle hire 2 km.

Open: 15 March - 31 October.

Directions

From Rotterdam follow A15 to junction with A27. Proceed 6 km. north on A27 to Noordeloos exit (no. 25) and join N214. Site is signed 200 m. after roundabout at Noordeloos. GPS: 51.93623, 4.95748

Charges guide

Per unit incl. 2 persons and electricity	€ 12.50
extra person	€ 3.00

No credit cards. Large units may be charged extra.

For latest campsite news, availability and prices visit
alanrogers.com

Noordwijk
Camping le Parage
Langevelderlaan 43, NL-2204 BC Noordwijk (Zuid-Holland) T: 0252 375 671. E: info@leparage.nl
alanrogers.com/NL6992

Camping le Parage is set in an area of woodland and dunes and its French name can be translated as 'the area behind the dunes'. The site borders a nature area where you can enjoy plenty of cycling and walking tracks. There are 150 pitches of which 34 are for touring units, all with 4A electricity. Arranged over several fields, they are surrounded by hedges. A riding school is next door (50 m) and you can even bring your own horse. The surrounding area offers plenty of things to do. There are opportunities for swimming and watersports either in the sea or the lake. In spring you can enjoy the lovely blossoming bulb fields.

Facilities

Two heated sanitary blocks for tourers are very clean and include free preset showers and open style washbasins. Baby room. Laundry facilities. Bar. Restaurant. Snack bar with takeaway. Well stocked shop. Play area. Sports area. Riding. Games room. TV. WiFi over part of site (charged). Off site: Beach 1.5 km. Shops. Restaurants. De Keukenhof. Pretpark Duinrell. Sealife Naturalis.

Open: 15 March - 1 October.

Directions

From the N206 take exit for, and turn towards, Langevelderslag. Take second turn to the left and at the end turn right. The site is well signed. GPS: 52.282454, 4.486778

Charges guide

Per unit incl. 4 persons, water and electricity	€ 23.00
extra person (over 2 yrs)	€ 2.50

Oostvoorne
Molecaten Park Kruininger Gors
Gorsplein 2, NL-3233 XC Oostvoorne (Zuid-Holland) T: 0181 482 711. E: kruiningergors@molecaten.nl
alanrogers.com/NL6978

Kruininger Gors can be found just 30 minutes from the busy port of the Hook of Holland. This is a very green campsite located close to the banks of Lake Brielle (Brielse Meer). The site is made up of pitches (80 for tourers, most with electricity, 6A Europlug) on fields which are divided by high trees and shrubs. This is a spacious site with plenty of space for children to safely play. The site is within walking distance of a sandy lake beach (good for younger children). For older children and all those who love the outdoors, it is an ideal place to go surfing, sailing and water-skiing. The lake and neighbouring Lake Oostvoorne are also very popular with anglers.

Facilities

One main toilet block has some washbasins in cabins, baby room and facilities for disabled visitors. Restaurant with pub and terrace. Various shops including supermarket and baker. Takeaway. Sandy lake beach. Play area. Small deer park. Tennis. Bicycle hire. Activity and entertainment programme. Dogs are not accepted. WiFi over site (charged). Off site: Lake beach. Oostvoorne 2 km. Sea beach 5 km. Rotterdam 30 km.

Open: 31 March - 1 October.

Directions

From Hook of Holland, follow signs to Rotterdam on A20. At exit 13 follow signs to Rotterdam-Zuid, Hoogvliet. After 7 km. take A15 towards Hellevoetsluis, Europoort. Follow A15 (becomes N15) for 25 km. to exit 8 (Oostvoorne). Follow road for 1.5 km. and turn left. GPS: 51.922583, 4.105344

Charges guide

Per unit incl. 2 persons and electricity	€ 15.00 - € 18.00

Ouddorp
Recreatiepark De Klepperstee
Vrijheidsweg 1, NL-3253 ZG Ouddorp (Zuid-Holland) T: 0187 681 511. E: info@klepperstee.com
alanrogers.com/NL6960

De Klepperstee is a good quality, family site. The site itself is peacefully located in tranquil countryside amid renowned nature reserves and just outside the village of Ouddorp in Zuid-Holland. It offers excellent recreation areas that are spread over the centre of the site giving it an attractive open parkland appearance which is enhanced by many shrubs, trees and grass areas. The 338 spacious touring pitches are in named avenues, mostly separated by hedging and spread around the perimeter, together with the seasonal and static caravans. There is a new 24-hour, drive-in motorcaravan park with 16A electricity, sanitary facilities and a service point.

Facilities

One main sanitary block and a number of WC/shower units around the touring area provide free hot showers, washbasins, some in cabins (hot water only), baby bath and shower and child size toilets. Unit for disabled visitors. Laundry. Motorcaravan services. Supermarket. Restaurant, bar and takeaway. Play areas. Tennis. TV, pool and electronic games. Entertainment. No single sex groups.

Open: Easter - 31 October.

Directions

From Rotterdam follow A15 west to Rozenburg exit 12 and join N57 south for 22 km. Take exit for Ouddorp and follow signs for Stranden. Site is on the left after 3 km. GPS: 51.8161, 3.89958

Charges guide

Per unit incl. up to 4 persons	€ 14.50 - € 18.00
incl. 16A electricity	€ 18.50 - € 22.50
extra person	€ 2.50

FREE Alan Rogers Travel Card
Extra benefits and savings - see page 12

Ouddorp
RCN Toppershoedje

Strandweg 2-4, NL-3253 LR Ouddorp (Zuid-Holland) T: 0187 682 600. E: toppershoedje@rcn.nl
alanrogers.com/NL6988

Toppershoedje is a great choice for a seaside holiday. A large, sandy beach is easily reachable on the other side of the dunes (five minutes on foot). This beautiful beach is probably the main appeal of this site, particularly as it gently slopes into the sea and is therefore ideal for children. Even in high season the beach is never crowded. Toppershoedje has spacious, grassy pitches with 10A electricity, but shade is limited. It is located at the western end of the island of Goerre-Overvalkkee, and close to Lake Grevelingen. This lake is very popular with watersports enthusiasts.

Facilities

Three heated sanitary blocks with showers, washbasins in cubicles and facilities for babies and disabled campers. Launderette. Restaurant, bar, takeaway, bakery. Sports hall. Play area. Multisports terrain. Bicycle and go-kart hire. WiFi over site (charged). Mobile homes and chalets to rent. Off site: Supermarket 300 m. Sandy beach 5 minutes' walk. Ouddorp 3 km.

Open: 20 March - 27 October.

Directions

Head towards the centre of Ouddorp on N57 signed Oosterweg. Follow this road for 1.5 km. and turn left at the last T-junction onto Vrijheidsweg. Turn left at the next roundabout 600 m. and then turn right after 200 m. GPS: 51.823484, 3.916803

Charges guide

Per unit incl. 2 persons	
and electricity	€ 19.50 - € 35.00
dog	€ 4.95 - € 7.50

Rijnsburg
Recreatiecentrum Koningshof

Elsgeesterweg 8, NL-2231 NW Rijnsburg (Zuid-Holland) T: 0714 026 051. E: info@koningshofholland.nl
alanrogers.com/NL5630

This popular site is run in a personal and friendly way. The 200 pitches for touring units (some with hardstandings for larger units) are laid out in small groups, divided by hedges and trees and all with 10A electrical connections. Cars are mostly parked in areas around the perimeter and 100 static caravans, confined to one section of the site, are entirely unobtrusive. Reception, a pleasant, good quality restaurant, bar and a snack bar are grouped around a courtyard-style entrance which is decorated with seasonal flowers. The site has a small outdoor, heated pool (13.5x7 m) with a separate paddling pool and imaginative children's play equipment. A member of the Holland Tulip Parcs Group.

Facilities

Three good toilet blocks, two with underfloor heating, with washbasins in cabins and provision for disabled visitors. Laundry facilities. Motorcaravan services. Gas supplies. Shop (1/4-15/10). Bar (1/4-1/11). Restaurant (1/4-10/9). Snacks and takeaway (1/4-1/11). Small outdoor pool (unsupervised; 15/5-15/9). Indoor pool (1/4-1/11). Adventure playground and sports area. Tennis. Fishing pond (free). Bicycle hire. Entertainment in high season. Max. 1 dog, accepted in a limited area of the site. WiFi.

Open: 16 March - 16 November.

Directions

From N44/A44 Den Haag-Amsterdam motorway, take exit 7 for Oegstgeest and Rijnsburg. Turn towards Rijnsburg and follow site signs. GPS: 52.20012, 4.45623

Charges guide

Per unit incl. 2 persons	
and electricity	€ 25.00 - € 30.00
extra person	€ 3.75
Camping Cheques accepted.	

Rockanje
Molecaten Park Rondeweibos

Schapengorsedijk 19, NL-3235 LA Rockanje (Zuid-Holland) T: 0181 401 944. E: info@molecaten.nl
alanrogers.com/NL5590

Rondeweibos is a pleasant family site within walking distance of a sandy North Sea beach. The flora and fauna in this beautiful dune area is unusual, and, adjacent to the site, there is a pretty lake, Het Quakjeswater, home to various birds including spoonbills and silver herons. The sea here is calm and excellent for younger children to swim, play or paddle. All pitches at Rondeweibos are comfort pitches, and there is also the option of renting a private sanitary unit (with shower, toilet and wash basin). A number of mobile homes (beach home caravans) are available for rent.

Facilities

Sanitary facilities in two blocks (one new) provide neat, clean, acceptable facilities with hot showers on payment. One block can be heated. Supermarket. Restaurant and bar with terrace, takeaway. Heated outdoor pool with children's pool and slides. Tennis. Sports field. Play areas. Bicycle hire. Activity programme. WiFi over site (charged). Off site: Bus service 100 m. Beach is a 10-minute walk.

Open: 1 April - late October.

Directions

Approaching on A15 follow directions towards Hellevoetsluis and N57. Join N57 and drive towards Brielle/Hellevoetsluis/Middelburg. After 7 km, at the roundabout, head towards Rockanje. The site is well signed. GPS: 51.856222, 4.082483

Charges guide

Per unit incl. 2 persons	
and electricity	€ 20.00 - € 38.50

For latest campsite news, availability and prices visit
alanrogers.com

Rockanje
Molecaten Park Waterbos

Duinrand 11, NL-3235 CC Rockanje (Zuid-Holland) T: 0181 401 900. E: waterbos@molecaten.nl
alanrogers.com/NL6975

Molecaten Park Waterbos is a small, friendly campsite located behind sand dunes on the island of Voorne. The site is within easy walking distance of the broad sandy beach at Rockanje. This beach slopes gradually and is ideal for young children. There are 340 pitches here, of which 140 are for touring units, shaded by large trees and located on a number of grassy fields, often with play areas at the centre. There is a choice of basic, comfort and comfort-plus pitches, all with electricity (6/10A). The latter group are deluxe pitches, each equipped with an individual shower, toilet and washbasin. There are also mobile homes, luxury accommodation and fully equipped tents for hire.

Facilities

Restaurant with bar and terrace, takeaway. Small shop for bread and basics. Heated outdoor swimming pool (29/4-1/9). Fishing pond. Play area. Bicycle and go-kart hire. Entertainment and activity programme. WiFi over site (charged). Dogs are not accepted. Off site: Beach adjacent. Rockanje, Brielle, Hellevoetsluis, Voornes Duin and Rotterdam port. Sub-tropical swimming pool 10 km.

Open: 1 April - 28 October.

Directions

From Hook of Holland head towards Rotterdam on A20. At exit 13 follow Rotterdam-Zuid. After 7 km. join A15 towards Hellevoetsluis. Continue to Rozenburg (now N15) then N57 to Hellevoetsluis. After 8 km. take 3rd junction to right (Rockanje), in town centre follow signs. GPS: 51.879991, 4.053982

Charges guide

Per unit incl. 2 persons and electricity	€ 19.25 - € 33.50

Wassenaar
Holiday & Amusement Park Duinrell

Duinrell 1, NL-2242 JP Wassenaar (Zuid-Holland) T: 0705 155 255. E: info@duinrell.nl
alanrogers.com/NL5620

A very large site, Duinrell's name means 'well in the dunes' and the water theme is continued in the adjoining amusement park and in the extensive indoor pool complex. The campsite itself is very large with 750 touring places on several flat, grassy areas (60-140 sq.m) and it can become very busy in high season. As part of a continuing improvement programme, the marked pitches have electricity, water and drainage connections and some have cable TV. Amenities shared with the park include restaurants, takeaways, pancake house, supermarket and theatre. Entry to the popular pleasure park is free for campers – indeed the camping areas surround and open out from the park.

Facilities

Six heated toilet blocks serve the touring areas. Laundry facilities. Amusement park and Tiki tropical pool complex. Restaurant, cafés, pizzeria and takeaways (weekends only in winter). Supermarket. Entertainment and theatre with shows in high season. Rope Challenge trail and training circuit. Bicycle hire. Mini-bowling. All activities have extra charges. WiFi over site (charged). Off site: Beach 4 km.

Open: All year.

Directions

Site is signed from N44/A44 (Den Haag-Amsterdam), but from the south the turning is 5 km. after passing sign for start of Wassenaar town – then follow site signs. GPS: 52.14642, 4.38737

Charges guide

Per unit incl. 2 persons and electricity	€ 30.50 - € 38.50
extra person	€ 10.50

Wassenaar
Camping Duinhorst

Buurtweg 135, NL-2244 BH Wassenaar (Zuid-Holland) T: 0703 242 270. E: info@duinhorst.nl
alanrogers.com/NL5625

Camping Duinhorst is set in the centre of a richly wooded area just north of The Hague (Den Haag). The site is close to the rolling dunes that run between the lively sea resort of Scheveningen and the quieter beaches of the Wassenaarse Slag. There are around 420 pitches, including 160 for touring units. All are equipped with electricity (6/10A), cable TV, waste water hook-ups and mains water points. A variety of small and large, open and shaded pitches are available for tents with a limited number of electricity hook-ups. The Paviljoen Duinhorst restaurant is located above the sanitary building near the tennis court and swimming pool.

Facilities

Heated toilet blocks have facilities for babies and disabled visitors. Launderette with dishwasher, washing machines, dryers and ironing facilities. Shop. Cafeteria with takeaway. Restaurant. Snack bar. Bar. Outdoor wading and swimming pools. Recreation team (July/Aug and holidays). Recreation hall. TV. Amusement arcade. Tennis. Bicycle hire. WiFi over site (free). Dogs are not accepted.

Open: 1 April - 30 September.

Directions

From north take A44, later N44, to Den Haag. After viaduct turn right at 2nd lights (van Alkemadelaan) towards Scheveningen. Turn right at 3rd lights (Wassenaar). Immediately left and right again. At roundabout first exit. Take first exit (Duindigt) and small sign Duinhorst. GPS: 52.11149, 4.34364

Charges guide

Per unit incl. 2 persons and electricity	€ 20.80 - € 29.50

FREE Alan Rogers Travel Card
Extra benefits and savings - see page 12

Accommodation

Over recent years many of the campsites featured in this guide have added large numbers of high quality mobile homes and chalets. Many site owners believe that some former caravanners and motorcaravanners have been enticed by the extra comfort they can now provide, and that maybe this is the ideal solution to combine the freedom of camping with all the comforts of home.

Quality is consistently high and, although the exact size and inventory may vary from site to site, if you choose any of the sites detailed here, you can be sure that you're staying in some of the best quality and best value mobile homes available.

Home comforts are provided and typically these include a fridge with freezer compartment, gas hob, proper shower – often a microwave and radio/cassette hi-fi too, but do check for details. All mobile homes and chalets come fully equipped with a good range of kitchen utensils, pots and pans, crockery, cutlery and outdoor furniture. Some even have an attractive wooden sundeck or paved terrace – a perfect spot for outdoors eating or relaxing with a book and watching the world go by.

Regardless of model, colourful soft furnishings are the norm and a generally breezy décor helps to provide a real holiday feel.

Although some sites may have a large number of different accommodation types, we have restricted our choice to one or two of the most popular accommodation units (either mobile homes or chalets) for each of the sites listed.

The mobile homes here will be of modern design, and recent innovations, for example, often include pitched roofs which substantially improve their appearance.

Design will invariably include clever use of space and fittings/furniture to provide for comfortable holidays – usually light and airy, with big windows and patio-style doors, fully equipped kitchen areas, a shower room with shower, washbasin and WC, cleverly designed bedrooms and a comfortable lounge/dining area (often incorporating a sofa bed).

In general, modern campsite chalets incorporate all the best features of mobile homes in a more traditional structure, sometimes with the advantage of an upper mezzanine floor for an additional bedroom.

Our selected campsites offer a massive range of different types of mobile home and chalet, and it would be impractical to inspect every single accommodation unit. Our selection criteria, therefore, primarily takes account of the quality standards of the campsite itself.

However, there are a couple of important ground rules:

* Featured mobile homes must be no more than 5 years old

* Chalets no more than 10 years old

* All listed accommodation must, of course, fully conform with all applicable local, national and European safety legislation.

For each campsite we have given details of the type, or types, of accommodation available to rent, but these details are necessarily quite brief. Sometimes internal layouts can differ quite substantially, particularly with regard to sleeping arrangements, where these include the flexible provision for 'extra persons' on sofa beds located in the living area. These arrangements may vary from accommodation to accommodation, and if you're planning a holiday which includes more people than are catered for by the main bedrooms you should check exactly how the extra sleeping arrangements are to be provided!

Charges

An indication of the tariff for each type of accommodation featured is also included, indicating the variance between the low and high season tariffs. However, given that many campsites have a large and often complex range of pricing options, incorporating special deals and various discounts, the charges we mention should be taken to be just an indication. We strongly recommend therefore that you confirm the actual cost when making a booking.

We also strongly recommend that you check with the campsite, when booking, what (if anything) will be provided by way of bed linen, blankets, pillows etc. Again, in our experience, this can vary widely from site to site.

On every campsite a fully refundable deposit (usually between 150 and 300 euros) is payable on arrival. There may also be an optional cleaning service for which a further charge is made. Other options may include sheet hire (typically 30 euros per unit) or baby pack hire (cot and high chair).

BE0732 Camping Floreal La Roche

see report page 44

Route de Houffalize 18, B-6980 La Roche-en-Ardenne, Belgium

AR1 – LUXE CARAVAN – Mobile Home

Sleeping: 2 bedrooms, sleeps 4: 1 double, 2 singles, sofa bed, pillows and blankets provided

Living: heating, TV, shower, separate WC

Eating: fitted kitchen with hobs, microwave, coffee maker, fridge, freezer

Outside: table & chairs, parasol, barbecue

Pets: not accepted

AR2 – SAFARITENT – Lodge Tent

Sleeping: 2 bedrooms, sleeps 4: 2 doubles, pillows and blankets provided

Living: heating

Eating: fitted kitchen with hobs, coffee maker, fridge, freezer

Outside: table & chairs, parasol

Pets: not accepted

Other (AR1 and AR2): bed linen, cot, highchair to hire

Open: All year		
Weekly Charge	AR1	AR2
Low Season (from)	€ 154	€ 245
High Season (from)	€ 490	€ 490

Travelling in Europe

When taking your car (and caravan, tent or trailer tent) or motorcaravan to the continent you do need to plan in advance and to find out as much as possible about driving in the countries you plan to visit. Whilst European harmonisation has eliminated many of the differences between one country and another, it is well worth reading the short notes we provide in the introduction to each country in this guide in addition to this more general summary.

Of course, the main difference from driving in the UK is that in mainland Europe you will need to drive on the right. Without taking extra time and care, especially at busy junctions and conversely when roads are empty, it is easy to forget to drive on the right. Remember that traffic approaching from the right usually has priority unless otherwise indicated by road markings and signs. Harmonisation also means that most (but not all) common road signs are the same in all countries.

Your vehicle

Book your vehicle in for a good service well before your intended departure date. This will lessen the chance of an expensive breakdown. Make sure your brakes are working efficiently and that your tyres have plenty of tread (3 mm. is recommended, particularly if you are undertaking a long journey).

Also make sure that your caravan or trailer is roadworthy and that its tyres are in good order and correctly inflated. Plan your packing and be careful not to overload your vehicle, caravan or trailer – this is unsafe and may well invalidate your insurance cover (it must not be more fully loaded than the kerb weight of the insured vehicle).

There are a number of countries that have introduced low emission zones in towns and cities, including Germany, Czech Republic, Denmark, Italy and Sweden. For up-to-date-details on low emission zones and requirements please see: www.lowemissionzones.eu

CHECK ALL THE FOLLOWING:

- GB sticker. If you do not display a sticker, you may risk an on-the-spot fine as this identifier is compulsory in all countries. Euro-plates are an acceptable alternative within the EU (but not outside). Remember to attach another sticker (or Euro-plate) to caravans and trailers. Only GB stickers (not England, Scotland, Wales or N. Ireland) stickers are valid in the EU.

- Headlights. As you will be driving on the right you must adjust your headlights so that the dipped beam does not dazzle oncoming drivers. Converter kits are readily available for most vehicles, although if your car is fitted with high intensity headlights, you should check with your motor dealer. Check that any planned extra loading does not affect the beam height.

- Seatbelts. Rules for the fitting and wearing of seatbelts throughout Europe are similar to those in the UK, but it is worth checking before you go. Rules for carrying children in the front of vehicles vary from country to country. It is best to plan not to do this if possible.

- Door/wing mirrors. To help with driving on the right, if your vehicle is not fitted with a mirror on the left hand side, we recommend you have one fitted.

- Fuel. Leaded and Lead Replacement petrol is increasingly difficult to find in Northern Europe.

Compulsory additional equipment

The driving laws of the countries of Europe still vary in what you are required to carry in your vehicle, although the consequences of not carrying a required piece of equipment are almost always an on-the-spot fine.

To meet these requirements you should make sure that you carry the following:

- FIRE EXTINGUISHER

- BASIC TOOL KIT

- FIRST AID KIT

- SPARE BULBS

- TWO WARNING TRIANGLES – two are required in some countries at all times, and are compulsory in most countries when towing.

- HIGH VISIBILITY VEST – now compulsory in France, Spain, Italy and Austria (and likely to become compulsory throughout the EU) in case you need to walk on a motorway.

- BREATHALYSERS – now compulsory in France. Only breathalysers that are NF-approved will meet the legal requirement. French law states that one breathalyser must be produced, but it is recommended you carry two in case you use or break one.

Insurance and Motoring Documents

Vehicle insurance

Contact your insurer well before you depart to check that your car insurance policy covers driving outside the UK. Most do, but many policies only provide minimum cover (so if you have an accident your insurance may only cover the cost of damage to the other person's property, with no cover for fire and theft).

To maintain the same level of cover abroad as you enjoy at home you need to tell your vehicle insurer. Some will automatically cover you abroad with no extra cost and no extra paperwork. Some will say you need a Green Card (which is neither green nor on card) but won't charge for it. Some will charge extra for the Green Card. Ideally you should contact your vehicle insurer 3-4 weeks before you set off, and confirm your conversation with them in writing.

Breakdown insurance

Arrange breakdown cover for your trip in good time so that if your vehicle breaks down or is involved in an accident it (and your caravan or trailer) can be repaired or returned to this country. This cover can usually be arranged as part of your travel insurance policy (see below).

Documents you must take with you

You may be asked to show your documents at any time so make sure that they are in order, up-to-date and easily accessible while you travel.

These are what you need to take:

- Passports (you may also need a visa in some countries if you hold either a UK passport not issued in the UK or a passport that was issued outside the EU).

- Motor Insurance Certificate, including Green Card (or Continental Cover clause)

- DVLA Vehicle Registration Document plus, if not your own vehicle, the owner's written authority to drive.

- A full valid Driving Licence (not provisional). The new photo style licence is now mandatory in most European countries.

Personal Holiday insurance

Even though you are just travelling within Europe you must take out travel insurance. Few EU countries pay the full cost of medical treatment even under reciprocal health service arrangements. The first part of a holiday insurance policy covers people. It will include the cost of doctor, ambulance and hospital treatment if needed. If needed the better companies will even pay for English language speaking doctors and nurses and will bring a sick or injured holidaymaker home by air ambulance.

Personal Holiday insurance (continued)

An important part of the insurance, often ignored, is cancellation (and curtailment) cover. Few things are as heartbreaking as having to cancel a holiday because a member of the family falls ill. Cancellation insurance can't take away the disappointment, but it makes sure you don't suffer financially as well. For this reason you should arrange your holiday insurance at least eight weeks before you set off.

Whichever insurance you choose we would advise reading very carefully the policies sold by the High Street travel trade. Whilst they may be good, they may not cover the specific needs of campers, caravanners and motorcaravanners.

Telephone 01580 214000 for a quote for our Camping Travel Insurance with cover arranged through leading leisure insurance providers.
Alternatively visit our website at: alanrogers.com/insurance

European Health Insurance Card (EHIC)

Make sure you apply for your EHIC before travelling in Europe. Eligible travellers from the UK are entitled to receive free or reduced-cost medical care in many European countries on production of an EHIC. This free card is available by completing a form in the booklet 'Health Advice for Travellers' from local Post Offices. One should be completed for each family member. Alternatively visit www.ehic.org.uk and apply on-line. Please allow time to send your application off and have the EHIC returned to you.

The EHIC is valid in all European Community countries plus Iceland, Liechtenstein, Switzerland and Norway. If you or any of your dependants are suddenly taken ill or have an accident during a visit to any of these countries, free or reduced-cost emergency treatment is available – in most cases on production of a valid EHIC.

Only state-provided emergency treatment is covered, and you will receive treatment on the same terms as nationals of the country you are visiting. Private treatment is generally not covered, and state-provided treatment may not cover all of the things that you would expect to receive free of charge from the NHS.

Remember an EHIC does not cover you for all the medical costs that you can incur or for repatriation - it is not an alternative to travel insurance. You will still need appropriate insurance to ensure you are fully covered for all eventualities.

Travelling with children

Most countries in Europe are enforcing strict guidelines when you are travelling with children who are not your own. A minor (under the age of 18) must be accompanied by a parent or legal guardian or must carry a letter of authorisation from a parent or guardian. The letter should name the adult responsible for the minor during his or her stay. Similarly, a minor travelling with just one of his/her parents, must have a letter of authority to leave their home country from the parent staying behind. Full information is available at www.fco.gov.uk

Travelling with dogs

Many British campers and caravanners prefer to take their pets with them on holiday. However, pet travel rules changed on 1 January 2012 when the UK brought its procedures into line with the European Union. From this date all pets can enter or re-enter the UK from any country in the world without quarantine provided they meet the rules of the scheme, which will be different depending on the country or territory the pet is coming from. Please refer to the following website for full details: www.gov.uk/take-pet-abroad

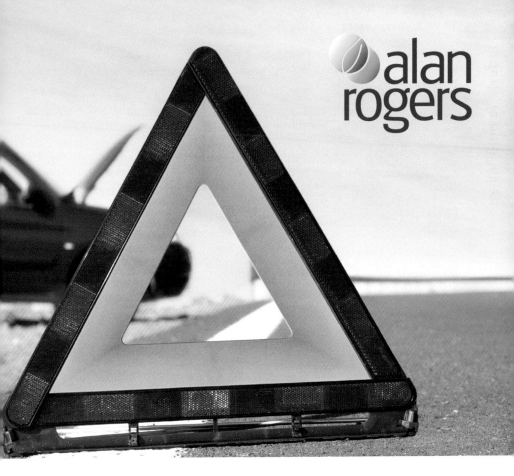

Looking for competitively priced insurance for your camping or caravanning holiday?

We have been entrusted with readers' campsite holidays since 1968. Choosing the right campsite is one thing; having proper, suitable travel insurance is another.

Personal Travel Insurance

Ideal for self-drive holidays in Europe, and including cover for camping equipment. Family policies are available.

- 24 hour travel advice line and multi lingual medical assistance

- Repatriation and evacuation cover

- Repatriation due to serious illness of relatives at home

Vehicle Assistance Insurance

The vehicle assistance service is provided by Allianz Global Assistance and a network of over 7,500 garages and agents. Serving 3 million people a year, they are well used to looking after the needs of campsite-based holidaymakers.

- Roadside assistance

- Vehicle repatriation (and alternative driver)

- Cover prior to departure

Get a quote and and start looking forward to your holiday with confidence!

01580 214000
alanrogers.com/insurance

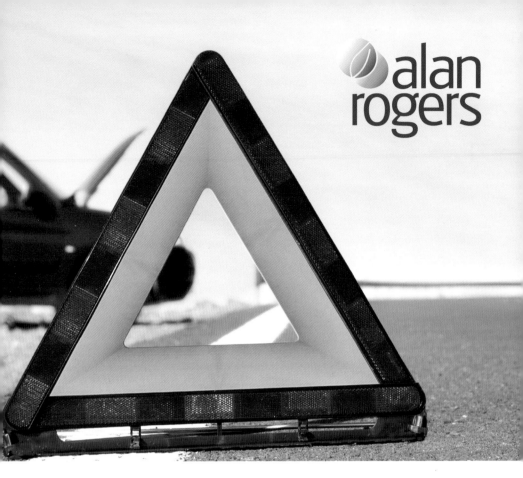

Looking for competitively priced insurance for your camping or caravanning holiday?

We have been entrusted with readers' campsite holidays since 1968. Choosing the right campsite is one thing; having proper, suitable travel insurance is another.

Personal Travel Insurance

Ideal for self-drive holidays in Europe, and including cover for camping equipment. Family policies are available.

- 24 hour travel advice line and multi lingual medical assistance

- Repatriation and evacuation cover

- Repatriation due to serious illness of relatives at home

Vehicle Assistance Insurance

The vehicle assistance service is provided by Allianz Global Assistance and a network of over 7,500 garages and agents. Serving 3 million people a year, they are well used to looking after the needs of campsite-based holidaymakers.

- Roadside assistance

- Vehicle repatriation (and alternative driver)

- Cover prior to departure

Get a quote and and start looking forward to your holiday with confidence!

01580 214000
alanrogers.com/insurance